The Trump years have been examined from almost every possible angle, usually focusing on and criticizing the man and his policies of the moment. This book combines ethnographic research (for instance, of Latinx, Jewish, and transgender communities) with historical context to illustrate how Trump is a product of an older and deeper political culture in the United States and how that political culture contains other elements that contrast and compete with the Trumpian narrative. Fascism may be a stream of American political culture, pre-dating Trump, but it is not the only stream, which is cause for hope.

— *Jack David Eller is Associate Professor (Emeritus) of Anthropology at the Community College of Denver, USA.*

RACE, GENDER, AND POLITICAL CULTURE IN THE TRUMP ERA

This book demonstrates the fragility of democratic norms and institutions, and the allure of fascist politics within the Trump era.

The chapters consider the antagonistic cultural practices through which divergent political machinations, including white (patriarchal) nationalism, are staged, and examine the corresponding policies and governing practices that threaten the civil rights, security, and wellbeing of racialized minorities, immigrants, women, and gender nonconforming people. The book contributes to social theory on nation-building by delineating processes of exclusion, intimidation, and violence, with a focus on rhetoric, performance, semiotics, music, affectivity, and the power of media. Various chapters also analyze creative, restorative, and at times unruly practices of community building, which reknit the social fabric with expansive visions of the polity.

This anthropology-led volume incorporates contributions from a number of disciplines including sociology, American studies, communication, and Spanish, and will be of interest to scholars across the social sciences and humanities.

Christine A. Kray is Professor of Anthropology at Rochester Institute of Technology, USA.

Uli Linke is Professor of Anthropology at Rochester Institute of Technology, USA.

RACE, GENDER, AND POLITICAL CULTURE IN THE TRUMP ERA

The Fascist Allure

Edited by Christine A. Kray and Uli Linke

LONDON AND NEW YORK

First published 2022
by Routledge
2 Park Square, Milton Park, Abingdon, Oxon OX14 4RN

and by Routledge
605 Third Avenue, New York, NY 10158

Routledge is an imprint of the Taylor & Francis Group, an informa business

© 2022 selection and editorial matter, Christine A. Kray and Uli Linke; individual chapters, the contributors

The right of Christine A. Kray and Uli Linke to be identified as the authors of the editorial material, and of the authors for their individual chapters, has been asserted in accordance with sections 77 and 78 of the Copyright, Designs and Patents Act 1988.

All rights reserved. No part of this book may be reprinted or reproduced or utilised in any form or by any electronic, mechanical, or other means, now known or hereafter invented, including photocopying and recording, or in any information storage or retrieval system, without permission in writing from the publishers.

Trademark notice: Product or corporate names may be trademarks or registered trademarks, and are used only for identification and explanation without intent to infringe.

British Library Cataloguing-in-Publication Data
A catalogue record for this book is available from the British Library

Library of Congress Cataloging-in-Publication Data
Names: Kray, Christine A., editor. | Linke, Uli, editor.
Title: Race, gender, and political culture in the Trump era : the fascist allure / edited by Christine A. Kray and Uli Linke.
Description: New York : Routledge, 2022. | Includes bibliographical references and index.
Subjects: LCSH: Trump, Donald, 1946– —Political and social views. | United States—Politics and government—2017– | Sex role—Political aspects—United States. | Minorities—United States—Social conditions—21st century. | Hispanic Americans—United States—Social conditions—21st century. | Racism—Political aspects—United States—History—21st century. | United States—Race relations—Political aspects—History 21st century. | Political culture—United States—21st century. | Fascism—United States.
Classification: LCC E913 .R33 2022 | DDC 305.80097309/05—dc23
LC record available at https://lccn.loc.gov/2021010451

ISBN: 978-0-367-47317-4 (hbk)
ISBN: 978-0-367-47315-0 (pbk)
ISBN: 978-1-003-03481-0 (ebk)

DOI: 10.4324/9781003034810

Typeset in Bembo
by codeMantra

To Annalea Kray and in memory of Karl Linke

CONTENTS

List of illustrations   xi
Acknowledgments   xiii
List of contributors   xv

Introduction: the fascist allure   1
Christine A. Kray and Uli Linke

PART I
Love and patria   **23**

1 Love politics: the nation form and the affective life of the state   25
Uli Linke

2 The glamour of Ivanka: white supremacy and the question of women's equality in the Trump administration   47
Aidan Smith

3 The sticky imagery of white feminism   68
Christine A. Kray

PART II
The cultural policing of borders   99

4 "Your racist ass did too much": hypermasculinity, Donald Trump, and rap music   101
Matthew Oware

5 Commonplace terror: everyday harassment of Latinx immigrants in Central Florida   118
Mary Vickers and Nolan Kline

6 Snakes on the baseball field: unmasking political images of Latinx criminality   135
Corinne Kentor

PART III
Re/visions: crafting social justice   153

7 Engendering white nationalism   155
Jeff Maskovsky

8 Craft activism, violence, and memory-making: Jewish Hearts for Pittsburgh   174
Hinda Mandell

9 Reframing the US–Mexico border crisis: prosecutorial and parental rhetoric in the Kamala Harris presidential campaign   194
Joshua D. Martin

10 This is how we win: on unruly hope, autocracy, and transgender children   213
Sally Campbell Galman

Index   *231*

ILLUSTRATIONS

Figures

I.1	Members of the DC National Guard stand on the steps of the Lincoln Memorial as demonstrators protest against police brutality and the death of George Floyd, June 2, 2020	2
I.2	President Trump at St. John's Episcopal Church, Washington, DC, June 1, 2020	3
1.1	President Trump at Mount Rushmore, July 3, 2020	28
1.2	Fox News interview with President Trump in the otherwise off-limits Lincoln Memorial, May 3, 2020	37
2.1	Seated next to her father, Advisor to the President Ivanka Trump delivers remarks at the American Workforce policy advisory board meeting, June 26, 2020	48
3.1	An estimated 8–12,000 people visited Susan B. Anthony's grave in Rochester, NY on Election Day, 2016	69
3.2	President Trump signs the Women's Suffrage Centennial Commemorative Coin Act, November 25, 2019	70
3.3	Maria Lila Meza Castro and her children run from tear gas fired by US Border Patrol, Tijuana, Mexico, November 25, 2018	71
3.4	Ted Aub's "When Anthony Met Stanton" statue, located in Seneca Falls, was commissioned by New York State in 1998 to mark the 150th anniversary of the 1848 convention	77
3.5	Frances Ellen Watkins Harper (1825–1911)	86
8.1	A crochet Jewish Heart that author Hinda Mandell made in 2018 for the Jewish Hearts for Pittsburgh craft campaign	175

Tables

9.1	Prosecutorial Language in @KamalaHarris Border Tweets, 2017–2019	205
9.2	Parental Language in @KamalaHarris Border Tweets, 2017–2019	206

ACKNOWLEDGMENTS

The editors express gratitude to Rochester Institute of Technology and College of Liberal Arts Interim Dean LaVerne McQuiller-Williams for financial support for this volume in the form of a Faculty Research Fund grant.

We are grateful for the careful attention and critical insights of our editors, Katherine Ong and Alexandra McGregor, as well as three anonymous reviewers. Our conceptual work for this volume benefited from conversations with and feedback along the way from Tamar Carroll, Quetzil Castañeda, Jacqueline Fewkes, Peggy Sanday, and Penelope Kelsey.

Throughout our work on this book, our families listened patiently; raised questions; and gave us purpose, motivation, and the courage to take risks. We thank them for their continued support.

CONTRIBUTORS

Sally Campbell Galman is Professor of Child and Family Studies at the University of Massachusetts-Amherst College of Education. Her arts-based research focuses on childhood and gender. An award-winning cartoonist, she is the author of the *Shane* series of qualitative methods comics. Keep up with her at sallycampbellgalman.com.

Corinne Kentor is a PhD candidate in Anthropology & Education at Teachers College at Columbia University and a Research Fellow at the City University of New York (CUNY). Her research focuses on immigration and higher education policy. Her dissertation investigates the postsecondary trajectories of mixed-status siblings in New York and southern California.

Nolan Kline (PhD, MPH) is Assistant Professor at Rollins College. His book, *Pathogenic Policing: Immigration Enforcement and Health in the U.S. South* (Rutgers), describes the health-related consequences of immigration policies and police practices in Atlanta, Georgia. As an applied, medical anthropologist, his work overlaps with public health, law, and activism.

Christine A. Kray (PhD, University of Pennsylvania) is Professor of Anthropology at Rochester Institute of Technology. She co-edited *Nasty Women and Bad Hombres: Gender and Race in the 2016 US Presidential Election* (with Tamar W. Carroll and Hinda Mandell, University of Rochester Press, 2018). Her coauthored book on Yucatan's Social War and British Honduras is under advance contract.

Uli Linke (PhD, UC Berkeley) is Professor of Anthropology at Rochester Institute of Technology. Her principal areas of interest include the political anthropology of the body, critical race theory, visual culture, violence and genocide, and the politics of memory and suffering.

Hinda Mandell is Associate Professor in the School of Communication at Rochester Institute of Technology, and is editor of *Crafting Dissent: Handicraft as Protest from the American Revolution to the Pussyhats* (Rowman & Littlefield, 2019), co-curator of the 2019–2020 exhibit *Crafting Democracy: Fiber Arts and Activism*, and co-editor of the eponymous book. She's on Instagram: @crochetactivism.

Joshua D. Martin is Assistant Professor of Spanish at the University of North Georgia. He holds a PhD in Hispanic Studies from the University of Kentucky, and his research interests include the representation of masculinity and space (particularly borders) in literature and political discourse.

Jeff Maskovsky is Professor of Anthropology at the Graduate Center, and Professor of Urban Studies at Queens College, City University of New York (CUNY). His research and writing focus on poverty, welfare, health, security, and governance in the urban United States. His most recent publication is the co-edited anthology, *Beyond Populism: Angry Politics and the Twilight of Neoliberalism* (West Virginia University Press, 2020).

Matthew Oware is the Irving May Professor of Human Relations in Sociology at the University of Richmond. He has numerous scholarly publications, including *I Got Something to Say* (Palgrave Macmillan, 2018) on the intersections of rap music, masculinity, race, and gender. He teaches courses on race and ethnicity, masculinity, Africana studies, and hip hop.

Aidan Smith directs Tulane University's Newcomb Scholars, a cohort of feminist undergraduate researchers. Her book, *Gender, Heteronormativity, and the American Presidency* (Routledge 2017), provides a discourse analysis of campaign communications from the arrival of television to the present. Her latest project explores maternal politics across a spectrum of social media influencers.

Mary Vickers holds a BA in International Relations and Spanish from Rollins College. She is serving as a Jesuit Volunteer in New Mexico before pursuing a PhD in sociocultural anthropology. Her research interests include Latinx immigrants in US society, political and legal anthropology, and activist methodologies.

INTRODUCTION

The fascist allure

Christine A. Kray and Uli Linke

> They do not believe in anything visible, in the reality of their own experience; they do not trust their eyes and ears but only their imaginations.
> —*Hannah Arendt,* The Origins of Totalitarianism

> The most self-consciously visual of all political forms, fascism presents itself to us in vivid primary images.
> —*Robert O. Paxton,* The Anatomy of Fascism

Smackdown

"I can't breathe," George Floyd said more than 20 times while police officer Derek Chauvin kneeled on his neck for 9 minutes and 29 seconds, and two other officers pinned him down. "They'll kill me, they'll kill me" were his final words on May 25, 2020, in Minneapolis, Minnesota, while being arrested on suspicion of using a counterfeit $20 bill (Oppel and Barker 2020).

News of Mr. Floyd's murder ignited weeks of nightly Black Lives Matter protests in thousands of cities and towns across the United States, and some internationally. Floyd's death occurred just as most of the country was beginning to reemerge from the COVID-19 pandemic-related quarantine. Already, 100,000 Americans had died. Millions of people had been furloughed or laid off, and with unemployment sharply on the rise and businesses failing, the country entered the worst economic crisis since the Depression. Many blamed President Trump for inaction on the pandemic and for inciting racist violence. Most public opposition took the form of peaceful protest, but instances of rioting, looting, graffiti writing, and attempts to topple statues of Confederate generals and other historical figures associated with slavery, colonialism, and genocide triggered forcible police crackdowns against demonstrators (Eligon 2020).

DOI: 10.4324/9781003034810

FIGURE I.1 Members of the DC National Guard stand on the steps of the Lincoln Memorial as demonstrators protest against police brutality and the death of George Floyd, June 2, 2020.
Credit: Win McNamee/Getty Images.

In Washington, DC, thousands of protestors assembled at the National Mall and in Lafayette Square, across from the White House, which was defended by a protective barrier. The president tweeted that if demonstrators should enter the White House yard, they would be met with "the most vicious dogs, and most ominous weapons" (@realdonaldtrump, May 29, 2020). On May 31, DC National Guard soldiers were sent out to quell demonstrations and protect property. The next day, the president wanted to invoke the Insurrection Act of 1807 and deploy active-duty military troops; yet his daughter, Ivanka Trump, provided him with another idea for a "way of demonstrating toughness. He would march across Lafayette Square to St. John's Episcopal Church, damaged by fire the night before" (Baker et al. 2020). On camera, before a row of US flags in the White House Rose Garden, he announced that he was "dispatching thousands and thousands of heavily armed soldiers, military personnel, and law enforcement officers" and declared himself "your president of law and order" (Trump 2020b). In Lafayette Square, officers and agents of the Military Police, Secret Service, National Guard, Park Police, and members of other agencies then forcibly dispersed the crowd with horses, batons, shields, a chemical irritant (possibly tear gas), and flash-bang grenades to make way for the president's entourage, which included the Attorney General, the White House Chief of Staff, the Defense Secretary, the National Security Advisor, the chairman of the Joint Chiefs of Staff, the press secretary, and the president's daughter and son-in-law. Eyes turned to Ivanka, standing in her stiletto heels, carrying a

FIGURE I.2 President Trump at St. John's Episcopal Church, Washington, DC, June 1, 2020.
Credit: Brendan Smialowski/Getty Images.

$1500 white Max Mara designer handbag, out of which she pulled a Bible. The president stood before the church, held the Bible aloft, and declared: "We have the greatest country in the world. We're going to make it even greater." That night he tweeted: "Many arrests. Great job done by all. Overwhelming force. Domination" (Baker et al. 2020).

This incident—a staged spectacle, a show of overwhelming force, which marshaled the symbolic power of nationalism, male domination, feminine beauty, and Christian faith—is used here as an example of the fascist cultural style of politics frequently seen in the Trump era. Trump administration actions related to the George Floyd protests led several mainstream political commentators (Gessen 2020a; Goldberg 2020; Green and Nader 2020; Hasan 2020; Szalai 2020; Tharoor 2020) to finally apply what many of them called the "F word," fascism, to Donald Trump's governing style. The United States does not have a fascist government (yet), nor was Donald Trump an unrestrained fascist president. Nevertheless, as philosopher Jason Stanley (2018) proposed, in the absence of a fascist system, actors can still exercise "fascist politics." While there is no scholarly consensus on a definition of fascism, for our purposes here, we take its central (interrelated) elements to be: authoritarianism (undergirded by patriarchy), racist nationalism, militancy, and a narrative of victimhood and stolen glory. At the heart of fascism is a story: *The people were once whole and strong, but have been besieged by enemies, both foreign and domestic. Along comes a leader who promises to fight their enemies, by whatever means necessary, and return them to their state of glory, should they cede control to him.*

Fascism is spectacular: to consolidate autocratic power, a political leader must persuade people that he commands the force and the ruthlessness to subdue and humiliate their foes. Our book analyzes the formation of political culture in the Trump era—a process in which we are witnesses, observers, and participants. Our book centrally focuses on the fascist allure. We inquire how fascist-style politics can be made seductive and alluring, and we show that the cultural seeds of fascism have been dispersed across American life, from rap music to fashion, schools, sports, online communities, museums, monuments, and commemorative events. A political leader with authoritarian fantasies can leverage those cultural elements to gain broad support for autocratic rule. While certain aspects of Donald Trump's leadership style—showmanship and a willingness to lie—have been particularly well-honed, in most other respects, his presidency was quintessentially American, borne of a national culture that contains a dispositive potential for fascist politics.

Spectacle

The presidency of a former reality television show host presents a unique opportunity to study the role of cultural performance in the political process. The contributors to this volume utilize the methods of cultural studies, visual anthropology, ethnography, digital ethnography, rhetorical analysis, media studies, and autoethnography to tease out tactics or strategies of persuasion through signs, symbols, symbolic actions, and material culture. Our focus on the cultural production of politics is guided by the recognition that a national political system is always in a state of becoming. Never fixed, it exists as much in the imagination of the citizens as it is encoded in government institutions. In (finally) acknowledging this dynamic complexity of nation-building, political anthropologists, according to Rasanayagam, Beyer, and Reeves (2014, 11), have begun to "displace the state as an external, encompassing object," and instead aim to "'unmask' … its imagined and constructed nature and emphasize … the process, practices, and performances that produce the mask or effect." Building on this approach, our book attempts to analytically dissect and theorize the formative process of fascist political culture.

Following anthropologists Michael Lempert and Michael Silverstein (2012), several authors in this volume employ multimodal analyses of a politician's public persona. In Lempert and Silverstein's view, the array of political personae constitutes a "bestiary" of "political animals." Each politician communicates a message about themselves not only through the referential meaning of their words, but also dramaturgically through "clothing and staging to gesture and speech" (26). The various chapters in this book examine the theatric/dramatic spectacles of political culture through ways of speaking, gesture, props, settings, aesthetics, and performances in the Trump era (see also Dick 2019; Goldstein and Hall 2017; Hall, Goldstein, and Ingram 2016). Historian Robert Paxton (2004, 9) suggested that "[t]he most self-consciously visual of all political forms, fascism presents itself to us in vivid primary images." This book illuminates and scrutinizes that vivid imagery.

Donald Trump is a performer, but what is he performing, and why? Since Donald Trump announced his presidential candidacy in June 2015, scholars and political commentators have struggled to make sense of his political persona. Iconoclastic, bombastic, uncouth, studiously blunt, lacking prior experience in public service, and emerging out of a career as a celebrity reality television host and real estate mogul—some wondered whether his campaign was serious or merely an extended television infomercial for the Trump Organization. While many in the media treated him initially as an entertainer, and well into his presidency most journalists, perhaps hamstrung by their professional standards, were unwilling to characterize his behavior as "racist," "sexist," and "lying" (cf. Gessen 2020b); nevertheless, his Janus-faced nature was soon clear to us and other critics. He had two audiences and a different script for each. When surrounded by supporters, he was jovial and jocular, but against his political detractors and others whom he opposed—Muslims, undocumented immigrants, Democratic leaders, members of the mainstream news media, Black Lives Matter protestors, "blue states," the FBI, Antifa (anti-fascist activists [Bogel-Burroughs and Garcia 2020]), and those whom he called the "deep state"—he directed a dark, thunderous hostility. Moreover, he demonstrated a willingness to skirt, bend, and even break the law to inflict harm.

Donald Trump's decades of experience in sales and his turn as host of ABC's *The Apprentice* and *The Celebrity Apprentice*, in which he, with flourish, fired a contestant in each episode, lent him the dramaturgical skills to stage and perform tyranny. In front of cameras, Donald Trump embraced and relished all manner of violence, legal and extralegal, directed at foes (Wright 2018). During the 2016 presidential election, he proposed to "bring back torture!" (Gordon 2017) and hesitated to condemn the World War II-era internment camps for Japanese-Americans and Japanese immigrants (Scherer 2015). He encouraged violence against protestors at his rallies (Tiefenthäler 2016) and told an assembled crowd of police officers not to worry about physically roughing up those under arrest (Rhodan 2017). His first official pardon was of an Arizona sheriff with a conviction related to alleged abusive tactics and racial profiling used against suspected undocumented immigrants (Davis and Haberman 2017), signaling that he approved of illegal use of force against those whom he opposed; his subsequent clearing of the records of three soldiers convicted or accused of war crimes (Philipps 2019) sent the same signal. For his proposed wall stretching along the United States-Mexico border he envisioned a medieval design—painted black so that it would burn the skin of those trying to scale it, with spikes at the top—to cause anticipated injuries that the president "describe[d] in graphic terms" (Miroff and Dawsey 2019). In addition, with aides,

> the president had often talked about fortifying [it] with a water-filled trench, stocked with snakes or alligators, prompting aides to seek a cost

estimate. He wanted the wall electrified, [and again] with spikes on top that could pierce human flesh. After publicly suggesting that soldiers shoot migrants if they threw rocks, the president backed off when his staff told him that was illegal. But later in a meeting ... he suggested that they shoot migrants in the legs to slow them down.

(Shear and Davis 2019)

Violent reveries and murderous fantasies extended to Twitter, where Trump retweeted a meme of himself striking Hillary Clinton with a golf ball (@realdonaldtrump, September 17, 2017) and retweeted a doctored video showing him beating up a man whose face was replaced with the CNN logo (July 2, 2017), as he frequently called journalists "the enemy of the people." At a campaign rally, he laughed at how police hit MSNBC reporter Ali Velshi "in the knee with a canister of tear gas" while covering a Black Lives Matter protest (although it was a rubber bullet), and called it "the most beautiful thing"; at another rally two days later, he again laughed at that incident, then described how police picked up another reporter and "They threw him aside like a bag of popcorn. But honestly, when you watch the crap we've all had to take....It's actually a beautiful sight" (Oh 2020). All staged for public consumption, these statements constituted promises to his supporters that he would use any means necessary to crush common enemies.

In addition to the way Trump embraced violence referentially, he also performed tyranny by piping anger into US households through all available media. Unmatched in his power to gain and maintain media attention, he used a variety of media to saturation bomb the US public with vitriol from sunup to sundown. By 6:00 am, he would typically launch tweet storms of SCREAMING CAPITAL LETTERS and multiple exclamation points (!!!) to complain about and threaten adversaries (see also Colley 2018), and the first stories of the day in the news and social media would be the morning's abusive tweets. The days would be marked with televised interviews and press conferences, in which he fumed, bellowed, and lashed out at one enemy after another. He frequently took questions from reporters on the White House lawn as he boarded or exited a helicopter, so that he would have to shout over the sounds of the propeller; while the words were not always clear, the screaming was. In the evenings, campaign rallies (always televised, at least in part) took on the atmosphere of wrestling matches in which he would summon up the full energy of his body to punctuate his speech with menacing grimaces, angry gestures, and lurching might. The audience would match his intensity with intimidatory chants of "Build the Wall!," "Lock Her [Hillary Clinton] Up!," and "Lock Him [Barack Obama] Up!." Connolly (2017, 27) also described the rallies:

> He confides to his audience that he would like to beat up protestors, and he urges the crowd to turn and scream at the media 'scavengers' and 'scum' assembled immediately behind them. His personal guards tolerate no protest

and are rough on peaceful protesters. And he joins the speeches to the shock politics of rapid fire executive orders to keep the world roiling.

Journalists churned out news stories of all of this to such an extent that it sometimes felt as if a dark cloud of rage had descended and enveloped the country. That is to say, the mediated spectacles of punishment often felt tyrannical.

Donald Trump's spectacularization of violence and of punishment, coordinated with executive orders to inflict the punishment as promised, brings to mind philosopher Michel Foucault's (1977) "spectacle of the scaffold." In medieval Europe, according to Foucault, the body of the citizen was the slate upon which the sovereign inscribed his power. Public torture and execution of the criminal's body served as punishment, deterrence, and, most importantly, the means by which the sovereign both demonstrated and exercised power. Since crime was an offense against the king, the public execution was "a ceremonial by which a momentarily injured sovereignty is reconstituted. It restores that sovereignty by manifesting it as its most spectacular" (48). The punishment was excessive because it was "a policy of terror: to make everyone aware, through the body of the criminal, of the unrestrained presence of the sovereign. The public execution did not re-establish justice; it reactivated power" (49). It was a "theatre of terror" (49) because of its dual functions of punishment and domination through violence and intimidation.

Surveying the scholarship on Trumpian politics, we initiated this book project out of a sense that two (interrelated) things were missing: a sustained analysis of cultural performance and the infliction of pain. In our first planning session in 2018, Uli Linke said, "Can we call it fascism?" Christine Kray hesitated, wondering if the use of that term would make us seem unserious within academic circles. Indeed, most of those aforementioned summer of 2020 essays called it the "F word," acknowledging that term is highly charged, incendiary, and steadily avoided in journalism and academia, as a bogeyman—as if fascism were a thing of the past, associated only with long-since deceased, murderous dictators. We forged ahead with the book project, using euphemisms to describe the performances of antipathy and domination characteristic of Trump's style. We ultimately acknowledged, however, that while avoiding the word "fascist" in print would be safer, doing so would obscure a critical element of the political culture of the Trump era.

The prince

Why does Donald Trump perform cruelty? What are the anticipated gains? Donald Trump's punitive political style is particularly confounding within the context of recent social theory. Since the English translation of sociologist Max Weber's *Economy and Society* (1978), social theorists have tended to agree that domination secured by force (or the threat of force) is brittle, as it stirs up resentment and exposes itself to challenge. Social science scholarship, therefore, has emphasized affirmative processes for the accumulation of power. In other words, scholars have focused on how consent is manufactured, or the means by which subjects are persuaded to being governed. These gentler means of persuasion include: the imagination of a political community (Anderson 1991); the rational rule of law (Weber 1978); the invention of tradition (Adams 2000; Hobsbawm and Ranger 1983); the neoliberal promise of equality, rights, citizenship, and justice (Giddens 1998); and the cultivation of both patriotism (Althusser 2001) and habits of self-discipline (Foucault 1977) within citizen-subjects by state institutions (Althusser 2001; Foucault 1977) and hegemonically, through aligned and "interlocking...social, and cultural forces" (Williams 1977, 108; see also Gramsci 1971). Gone in the modern state, said Foucault, were the punitive practices—such as the spectacle of the scaffold—of the sovereign. Instead, within modernity, the "rational-legal system" (Weber 1978) of the modern nation-state—through its anonymous bureaucracy and standardized mechanisms of punishment—was what ensured compliance with the law.

Within modernity, liberated by the anonymous bureaucracy from the burden of being the face of punishment, the leader is freed to secure legitimacy by way of establishing bonds of love with the populace. Linke's chapter in this volume explores the problematics of "love" in the Trump presidency. Weber (1978) perceived that within the plebiscitary democracy ("the most important type of *Führerdemokratie*") of the United States, "[t]he leader (demagogue) rules by virtue of the devotion and trust which his political followers have in him personally" (268). We have wanted to love our leaders. Moreover,

> [i]t is characteristic of the *Führerdemokratie* that there should in general be a highly emotional type of devotion to and trust in the leader. This accounts for a tendency to favor the type of individual who is most spectacular, who promises the most, or who employs the most effective propaganda measures in the competition for leadership.
>
> *(269)*

Given all of this, we would conclude that in a representative democracy, a punitive, hostile relationship between the political candidate and the citizenry is therefore neither necessary (because the bureaucratic state institutions enforce the law) nor advisable (because it would compromise their popularity). Donald Trump's hostile, antagonistic leadership style therefore represents a conundrum. Is there a place for antagonistic leadership within a democracy? Why was Trump's antagonism a winning political strategy?

In this regard, Donald Trump followed in the footsteps of other authoritarian leaders who have positioned themselves as the stern patriarch of the nation, protecting their children, while using punitive measures to contain and suppress those considered threats to the nation, its people, and its values. The spectacle of the scaffold remains. Throughout the twentieth century, authoritarian leaders violated civil rights, employed state terror to intimidate dissidents, and committed atrocities in the name of national interest and security. With its avowed commitment to human rights and liberties on the global stage, the United States was seen as impervious to authoritarianism. However, Finchelstein, Piccato, and Stanley (2020)—historians and a philosopher—warned against the assumption of American exceptionalism, stating that:

> to blanch at the dropping of an 'f'-bomb—to reserve 'fascism' as a museum label for long-extinct foreign curiosities and dismiss the Trump government as too American or too dumb to be fascistic—is to abdicate our responsibilities as thinking citizens.

Donald Trump has projected cruelty, yes, but strategically so. Again, he addressed two audiences: one, his people, from whom he desired love and toward whom he was affable, and two, those whom he opposed, toward whom he directed outrage, hostility, violence, and threats of violence and loss of liberties. As philosopher Hannah Arendt (1958, 341) wrote: "In totalitarian countries propaganda and terror present two sides of the same coin." Trump's supporters may have been willing to forgive his rudeness and hostility because they have not been directed at them. *Washington Post* columnist Richard Cohen (2018) surmised that, in their view, "He hates the right people." Trump promised to inflict suffering on the people they hate. Consequently, even though Trump violated norms of "presidential behavior," he may have been following a different playbook. Although his first wife claimed that he kept a copy of Hitler's speeches on his nightstand (Brenner 1990), next to it might also have been Niccolò Machiavelli's (1998) *The Prince*, which reads:

> a prince, and especially a new prince, cannot observe all those things for which men are held good, since he is often under a necessity, to maintain his state, of acting against faith, against charity, against humanity, against religion. And so he needs to have a spirit disposed to change as the winds of fortune and variations of things command him, and … not depart from good, when possible, but know how to enter into evil, when forced by necessity.
>
> *(70)*

> …So let a prince win and maintain his state: the means will always be judged honorable, and will be praised by everyone. For the vulgar are taken in by the appearance and the outcome of a thing, and in the world there is no one but the vulgar.
>
> *(71)*

The F word

What do we mean by "fascist"? A few scholars have labeled Donald Trump as fascist or fascistic (Cole 2019; Connolly 2017; Snyder 2018), while using the word with trepidation, knowing that it has been misused in popular parlance, and even reduced to a facile smear. Scholars disagree on whether to consider it as a political form, an ideology, or an historical development, and what should be its defining elements (Mann 2004). Semiotician Umberto Eco, who was a child in Mussolini's Italy, described fascism as a "*fuzzy* totalitarianism, a collage of different philosophical and political ideas, a beehive of contradictions," but that nevertheless "emotionally it was firmly fastened to some archetypal foundations" (1995).

As a political form, Paxton (2004, 218) defined fascism as

> a form of political behavior marked by obsessive preoccupation with community decline, humiliation or victimhood and by compensatory cults of unity, energy and purity, in which a mass-based party of committed nationalist militants, working in uneasy but effective collaboration with traditional elites, abandons democratic liberties and pursues with redemptive violence and without ethical or legal restraints goals of internal cleansing and external expansion.

This definition usefully entails identity (in-group and out-group), a historical narrative (victimhood), and what he called "mobilizing passions"—political aims that emerge out of that sense of victimhood (219). However, Paxton's definition imagines a later stage of fascist development—fascism as a fully developed political form, in which a party has been organized, alliances have been made, paramilitary groups have been assembled, and large-scale initiatives have been undertaken. For our purposes, we want to consider fascist sentiments, a fascist style, and the fascist allure, which can percolate in the imagination and behavior of a single individual. We follow Stanley's (2018) lead, as he referred to "fascist politics," a term that does not presuppose the existence of a fascist state, nor even a fascist movement or ideology. We trace fascist politics in action, as a political style.

We see the core (interrelated) features of fascist politics as: (1) racist nationalism, (2) victimhood, (3) authoritarianism, and (4) militancy. A nationalist is a person with a well-developed sense of the nation ("the people") as a bounded entity and who believes that the state's primary duty should be to advance the interests of the nation—the "imagined political community" (Anderson 1991). Racist nationalism binds members of the nation form by biopolitical imaginaries of inclusion and exclusion, and morphs into the next attribute by a machination of harm and sense of victimization committed by enemy-others. Victimhood refers to a belief that the people have been harmed and lowered from a more honored state by enemies, from within and without. An authoritarian or an autocrat is a leader who aims to centralize power and exercises it unilaterally. Militancy refers to a readiness (an eagerness?) to use force to protect the group. Consequently, the narrative (mentioned above) that connects these elements is: *The people were once whole and strong, but have been besieged by enemies, both foreign and domestic. Along comes a political leader who promises to fight their enemies, by whatever means necessary, and return them to their state of glory, should they cede control to him.* Furthermore, as Eco (1995) wrote: "The first appeal of a fascist or prematurely fascist movement is an appeal against the intruders. Thus Ur-Fascism is racist by definition."

The fascist allure

What is the allure of fascism? Spectacle in politics offers redemption, deliverance, a promise, a chance to be lifted up and transported out of the daily, dreary humdrum to become heroes in a story of mythical destiny. Nation-states with grand ambitions have even grander spectacles (Adams 2000; Geertz 1980; Kertzer 1985; Skidmore 2004), in which an honored, traditional past, and a present repainted in technicolor lead to a resplendent (utopian) future. Legal scholar Thurman Arnold (1935, iii) observed that: "Every individual…constructs for himself a succession of little dramas in which he is the principal character. No one escapes the constant necessity of dressing himself in a series of different uniforms or silk hats, and watching himself go by." The spectacle of the state provides a script into which we can insert ourselves in the role of leading character. We believe because the masses "do not believe in anything visible, in the reality of their own experience; they do not trust their eyes and ears but only their imaginations" (Arendt 1985, 351). If not our life, it *could* be our life, and that is all that matters.

As a political style, fascism is glossy, enhanced by the mass reproduction of images through camera technology (Benjamin 2002). Just as race is implicated in the logic of fascism, so is gender, which adds color, style, and passion to fascist aesthetics. Indeed, other works on authoritarian and fascist politics have discussed gender and race as secondary elements, but this book brings those elements to the foreground by showing how they are part of the central narrative about the nation. The authoritarian (masculine) leader is cast as the steely patriarch of the family and the nation. The relations within the family (heterosexual, patriarchal) become the iconography by which the nation form is interpreted (Mosse 1985). As Stanley (2018, 6) wrote:

> The leader is the father of the nation, and his strength and power are the source of his legal authority, just as the strength and power of the father of the family in patriarchy are supposed to be the source of his ultimate moral authority over his children and wife.

The women in the patriarch's family decoratively represent different aspects of his power. As anthropologist Lauren Derby (2009) wrote of President Rafael Trujillo of the Dominican Republic, the wife represents legitimacy; the daughter, ranked below the father in both gender and age, "presents a more tender and lovable face for the state than the patriarch" (133); and the mistress represents virility and conquest.

The patriarch also introduces dynamics of narcissism and domination. In Sigmund Freud's theory of the fascist Superman, "the members of a group stand in need of the illusion that they are equally and justly loved by their leader" (quoted in Adorno 1982, 126). Philosopher and sociologist Theodor Adorno wrote that as the people identify with the champion-father, who embodies antipathy toward the out-group, they get "narcissistic gain," adding that fascist propaganda "suggests continuously…that the follower, simply through belonging to the in-group, is better, higher and purer than those who are excluded" (130). Adorno added that, within this propaganda:

> The superman must still resemble the follower and appear as his 'enlargement.' Accordingly, one of the basic devices of personalized fascist propaganda is the concept of the 'great little man,' a person who suggests both omnipotence and the idea that he is just one of the folks, a plain, red-blooded American.… The leader's image gratifies the follower's twofold wish to submit to authority and to be the authority himself.
>
> *(127)*

Within fascist politics, violence is aestheticized. Because of the fascist pathos of the people's stolen valor, *"life is permanent warfare,"* according to Eco (1995), and *"everybody is educated to become a hero."* The ideal death is the heroic death, the reward for which is "a supernatural happiness." One of the "mobilizing passions" of fascism, according to Paxton (2004, 220), is "the beauty of violence and the efficacy of the will, when they are devoted to the group's success." The allure of fascism, sadomasochistic at its core, is the thrill of the masculinist takedown, or a smackdown in wrestling terminology, entailing both domination and humiliation of the foe—the flourish of which heralds a glorious future.

Political culture in the Trump era

Donald Trump has performed the role of a fascist leader, as the champion of the American people, eager to fight and restore the people's stolen valor. He is a nationalist; however, as chapters in this volume illustrate, President Trump primarily envisions the *real* Americans as white, Christian, and conservative-leaning, the ones he calls "the silent majority," borrowing Richard Nixon's term. During his 2016 presidential campaign and his first two years in office, the constituent Other—the racialized outsider against which he defined "America"—were Latin American immigrants and Muslims. As his term in office stretched on, more antipathy was directed at Puerto Ricans, and even more so, at Blacks, especially those associated with the Black Lives Matter movement. Disgust directed at "cities" became a stand-in for a critique of Blacks and all Democratic leadership. Toward the end of his first term, repeated warnings to "suburban housewives" that Democratic presidential candidate Joe Biden would, if elected, "destroy your suburbs," with the help of (Black) New Jersey Senator Cory Booker (who was most famous for his broad smile and gentle manner) (Scott 2020) became just one more example of how, in Trump-era political culture, the intersections of race and gender formed the frontiers of difference and desire.

President Trump has acted in authoritarian or autocratic fashion, as several scholars have discussed (Dent 2019; Gessen 2020b; Lachman 2019; Levitsky and Ziblatt 2018; Smith 2019). Anthropologist-journalist Sarah Kendzior (2020, 4) wrote that Trump, even in his 2016 campaign, ran it "like an autocrat-in-waiting: scapegoating immigrants and minorities, threatening journalists who refused to coddle him, vowing to repeal rights and protections, and expressing a preference for dictators over democratic allies." Yet beyond authoritarianism and nationalism, there remains the punitive aspect of Trump's persona. As president, Donald Trump positioned himself as the gritty, steadfast leader of his "silent majority" and he promised (and carried out those promises) to punish those to whom they were opposed. He was a street fighter, one who used whatever methods necessary to defeat his foe. For him, violence was a "beautiful thing." Evangelical leader, Jerry Falwell, Jr.—whose endorsement helped Trump clinch the Republican nomination in 2016—tweeted that

> Conservatives & Christians need to stop electing 'nice guys'. They might make great Christian leaders but the US needs street fighters like @realDonaldTrump at every level of government b/c the liberal fascists Dems are playing for keeps & many Repub leaders are a bunch of wimps!
> (@JerryFallwellJr, September 28, 2018)

The street fighter quality was a central factor in Trump's appeal in the 2016 election. The 2016 American National Election survey asked respondents whether they agreed that "What our country really needs is a strong, determined leader who will crush evil and take us back to our true path" and "Our country will be great if we honor the ways of our forefathers, do what the authorities tell us to do, and get rid of the 'rotten apples' who are ruining everything" (Smith 2019, 212). Positive responses to those questions comprised a "Domineering Leader" (DL) preference. Sociologist David Norman Smith and his colleagues discovered that "most of the … voters who supported Trump in 2016 concurred that evil and rotten apples should be crushed," and these DL preferences were more predictive of a vote for Trump than were "Republican identification, populism, gender, education, income, and sentiments towards minorities" (213). In other words, Donald Trump's menacing, punitive style, rather than intimidating or repelling voters, was the source of his broad appeal.

While some scholars have called Trump a populist (e.g., Gusterson 2017), historian Timothy Snyder aptly coined the term "sadopopulism." He elaborated that, a populist

> is someone who proposes policies to increase opportunities for the masses, as opposed to the financial elites. [However,] Trump was something else: a sadopopulist, whose policies were designed to hurt the most vulnerable

> part of his own electorate. Encouraged by presidential racism, such people could understand their own pain as a sign of still greater pain inflicted upon others.
>
> *(2018, 274)*

In other words, many Trump supporters appeared to prefer policies that might incidentally hurt themselves and their own families, so long as others, whom they viewed as undeserving, suffered as well or more.

Fascistic politics need not include symbols associated with European fascism, such as brown-shirted thugs, military parades with tanks in the streets, and youth education camps. Fascism takes different surface forms. As literary scholar Sarah Churchwell (2020) noted: "Fascism's ultra-nationalism means that it works by normalizing itself, drawing on familiar national customs to insist it is merely conducting political business as usual." If fascist politics are a political style, then the seeds of fascism can be found within any political system. What this book contributes to the conversation on fascism is *culture*. As a political style, fascist politics has to draw from an existing cultural repertoire of signs, aesthetics, meanings, emotions, and meaningful practices, and is often exercised through the cultural realms of beauty, fashion, commemoration, rallies, and other demonstrations of might. Our book shows how a leader with authoritarian ambitions can draw from the cultural well in the pursuit of power. Our contributors' chapters show that within the United States prior to Trump's ascendance, there were cultural elements that might make a leader with authoritarian ambitions seem plausible, even desirable: the *seeds of fascism*.

In fact, it may not be that the spectacle of the scaffold (or the seductive pageantry of punishment) is "back," but more that it has been there all the while, and has moved from the recesses into the foreground of politics and the national imagination, even into the White House. In their chapter in this book, Mary Vickers and Nolan Kline note that Donald Trump's railings about an invasion of criminal Latin American immigrants resulted in white central Floridians deputizing themselves to police internal borders and harass Latinx immigrants in public spaces. In her chapter, Hinda Mandell uses the concept of "stochastic terrorism," which refers to a terrorist attack that, while not directly ordered by a leader, is nevertheless predictable based upon the antagonism directed at a group by that leader. That label applies to both the 2018 massacre at the Pittsburgh Tree of Life (discussed by Mandell) and the 2019 massacre at an El Paso Walmart (discussed by Corinne Kentor as well as Vickers and Kline), both carried out by white gunmen who feared a "Hispanic invasion" of the United States. Subsequently, on August 25, 2020, at a Black Lives Matter protest in Kenosha, Wisconsin, a 17-year-old (white boy) from Illinois (Kyle Rittenhouse) crossed state lines with his semi-automatic rifle and shot and killed two protestors and injured a third. This attack followed upon his attendance a Trump campaign rally, and after a "Kenosha Guard" Facebook group asked whether there were "Any patriots willing to take up arms and defend [our] City tonight from the evil thugs?"

(NBC Chicago 2020). Apparently unconcerned about the optics, Matt Gaetz, a Republican congressman from Florida, tweeted, "The mob wants to destroy America. We need PATRIOTS who will defend her" (@mattgaetz, August 26, 2020); other prominent Republicans, including the president and the president's eldest son, rushed to defend the shooter (Korecki and Cadelago 2020). In scores of instances in mid-2020, automobile drivers barreled into crowds of protestors (Hauck 2020), and armed militias and Proud Boys worked alongside the police to forcibly disperse protest actions (Hvistendahl and Brown 2020). Stated differently, while in mid-2020 there might not have been large, organized paramilitary forces aligned with and working alongside the military and police to quell civil unrest, volunteers were at the ready.

Overview of the book

Our book is organized as follows. Several of the chapters demonstrate how pre-existing cultural beliefs, practices, aesthetics, and styles are part of a cultural repertoire of signs and meanings that can be wielded in fascist politics. As such, they demonstrate the fascist potential latent within US culture. Part I: Love and Patria concerns how cultural beliefs, practices, and aesthetics related to femininity and masculinity present a glorified image of patriarchy and whiteness and were leveraged by President Trump in his consolidation of white nationalist power. Uli Linke, in Chapter 1, takes up the problematics of the affective state and "love" in the Trump presidency, as the president, casting himself in the role of the charismatic strongman, aimed to bind voters to him through the bonds of love, even as he governed through (terrorizing) demonstrations of might. Mount Rushmore emerged as a useful staging ground for the exercise of (white male) authoritarian terror against racialized minorities. In Chapter 2, Aidan Smith uses Gramsci's notion of the "war of position" to analyze how Ivanka Trump's image (her feminine glamour and her daughterly love and adoration) provided the cosmetic gloss to soften the rough edges of her father's persona, and became part of the cultural manufacture of consent to Trump's ascendance as a patriarchal strongman and head of a dynastic family. In Chapter 3, Christine Kray discusses the role of commemoration in the accumulation of white nationalist power. She shows how women's suffrage commemorative activities in 2020, including by President Trump, constituted a "white feminist" historical narrative of what was in fact a "white feminist" suffrage movement, thereby serving to make racial inequality in the present seem logical and erasing the ongoing struggle for voting rights.

While Part I considered practices of exaltation, Part II: The Cultural Policing of Borders looks at masculinist patterns of denigration, harassment, and humiliation in the United States that shore up white supremacy and that all too readily erupt in racist violence. In Chapter 4, Matthew Oware reviews how Donald Trump's combative, domineering style of masculinity was lauded in and otherwise mirrored by similar styles in rap music for decades. However, when Trump used that same combative, domineering style in the denigration and exclusion of immigrants as part of his political campaign, his popularity waned in the rap world. As mentioned above, in their chapter, Vickers and Kline trace Trump's racializing and alienating (*sensu* Coutin) campaign to cast immigrants as criminal and show how it was met by an army of self-appointed citizen-deputies in central Florida who policed internal borders through everyday harassment in quotidian spaces. Corinne Kentor, in Chapter 6, situates Trump's criminalization of immigrants within settler-colonial dynamics which "iteratively recreated historically situated specters of organized subversion." Trump's phrase, "bad *hombres*," echoed a long-standing border tradition of linguistic and phenotyping stereotyping, which was similarly manifested in an incident in which boys speaking Spanish at a school baseball game were inexplicably a cause of terror, and the 2019 massacre of Latinx people in El Paso.

Part III of the book, Re/Visions: Crafting Social Justice, describes cultural tactics of resistance to the racist, misogynist, and transphobic strikes launched by the Trump administration and its political allies. Asserting more equitable visions of the polity, citizens crafted and staged expressions and practices of empathy, love, and joy. In Chapter 7, Jeff Maskovsky makes the case for scholarship in service of human rights. If the community one studies is intent upon the denigration of others—as was the case for alt-right online communities which required feminine submission to create and sustain the white supremacist society they aimed to build—scholarship should expose such machinations rather than protect them under the ethically vacuous stance of cultural relativism. In Chapter 8, Hinda Mandell describes the 2018 massacre at the Pittsburgh Tree of Life synagogue that was inspired by a Trump-promoted conspiracy theory that Jews were providing financing for a Hispanic "invasion" of the United States. Women used "womanly" yarn crafts as an "art of gentle protest" in the Jewish Hearts for Pittsburgh project, seeking to induce healing through demonstrations of love and shared grief. Joshua Martin, in Chapter 9, unpacks the "crisis narratives" of Trump's anti-immigration strategies, and he reveals how, in her presidential campaign, California Senator Kamala Harris reversed the script, asserting that because of her background as a prosecutor, she would be "smart" (rather than "tough") on crime, and moreover, she reframed those men as members of families—in particular, as fathers who care for their families. In the final chapter, Sally Campbell Galman shows how, in consideration of evangelical Christian voters, the Trump White House steadily chipped away at the rights of transgender people through administrative actions and in the courts. In coordinated fashion, family members of transgender children disrupted this work with "unruly politics," or tactics of joyful mischief.

Coda

As we put the finishing touches on this introduction, the 2020 election was a month away. To counter anti-racism efforts, on Constitution Day, President

Trump had delivered a speech, using original copies of the Declaration of Independence and the Constitution at the National Archives as a backdrop. He announced a "1776 Commission" to "promote patriotic education," blaming "left-wing indoctrination" that drew attention to slavery and its legacies as the source of civil unrest (Trump 2020a). Thereupon followed the Executive Order on Combating Race and Sex Stereotyping (Exec. Order No. 139500, 85 Fed. Reg. 60683 (2020)) which forbade government agencies, the military, government contractors, and grantees from using any materials in diversity sensitivity workshops that would teach that "men and members of certain races, as well as our most venerable institutions, are inherently sexist and racist." In essence, he rolled out the government-propaganda element of classical fascist politics. He had been broadcasting that Democrats would steal the election, but that he would use the Supreme Court—to which he added another justice just in time—to secure a victory (Crowley 2020).

Now, as this book heads into production, Trump has lost his bid for a second term in office. However, he received the second highest number of votes ever cast for a US presidential candidate (74.2 million), second only to his opponent, Joseph Biden (81.2 million) (Lewis 2020). Moreover, as regards the Electoral College, Biden's margin of victory was razor-thin. Had just 42,844 votes in Wisconsin, Georgia, and Arizona gone the other way, Trump would have won the electoral vote and a second term (Chinni 2020). When 60 court challenges and attempts to have officials in swing states decertify the votes all failed, he incited supporters (including Proud Boys, Oath Keepers, and members of other white power groups and militias) to launch an insurrectionist attack on the Capitol Building to intercept the counting of the electoral college votes on January 6, 2021. He encouraged the rioters on Twitter, and as the attack on the Capitol raged throughout the afternoon, according to one close advisor, Trump watched the violence unfold on television, pleased by the evident dedication of his supporters. Pressured by advisors, hours later, he released a video telling the rioters, "We have to have peace. So go home. We love you. You're very special" (Parker, Dawsey, and Rucker 2021). While he was impeached for a second time by the Democratic-led House of Representatives (Fandos 2021), he was acquitted in the Senate as 43 Republican Senators declared him not guilty (the yes votes falling below the 2/3 of the members of the chamber requirement for conviction). His popularity among Republican voters immediately rebounded to pre-January 6 levels, and he remained their top choice by far for the 2024 Republican presidential candidacy (Yokley 2021).

Ultimately, however, this book is not about Donald Trump (or not just about him), but about a broader political culture of white, patriarchal, nationalist authoritarianism and cruelty, of which his political ascendance is a key indicator. As we show in this book, there is a substratum of American culture with all of the ingredients for fascist politics: racism, hegemonic masculinity, misogyny, heterosexism, transphobia, authoritarianism, militancy, and the aestheticization of domination. The elements are primed for a would-be autocrat to undermine the well-being, rights, and liberties of people of ethnic and religious minorities, women, LGBTQ people, and, in fact, all citizens. In a similar vein, anthropologist Alexander Dent (2019, 195) perceived that "authoritarian discourse resides in a variety of places in our quotidian affairs… [and] we need to ethnographically investigate the kinds of places where monologic discourse resides." Democracy is not a state of being, but a state of doing, and we all have a role to play. We take inspiration from the creative artists and mischief makers who spin out new visions and stitch principles of equality and compassion into the social fabric.

References

Adams, Laura. 2000. *The Spectacular State: Culture and National Identity in Uzbekistan.* Durham, NC: Duke University Press.

Adorno, Theodor W. 1982. "Freudian Theory and the Pattern of Fascist Propaganda." In *The Essential Frankfurt School Reader*, edited by Andrew Arato and Eike Gebhart, 118–137. New York: Continuum. First published in 1951.

Althusser, Louis. 2001. "Ideology and Ideological State Apparatuses." In *Lenin and Philosophy and other Essays*, translated by Ben Brewster, 85–126. Reprint edition. New York: Monthly Review Press. First published in 1970.

Anderson, Benedict. 1991. *Imagined Communities: Reflections on the Origin and Spread of Nationalism.* Revised edition. London: Verso.

Arendt, Hannah. 1958. *The Origins of Totalitarianism.* Second, enlarged edition. Cleveland, OH: World Publishing.

Arnold, Thurman W. 1935. *The Symbols of Government.* New Haven, CT: Yale University Press.

Baker, Peter, Maggie Haberman, Katie Rogers, Zolan Kanno-Youngs, and Katie Benner. 2020. "How Trump's Idea for a Photo Op Led to Havoc in a Park." *New York Times*, June 2, 2020. https://www.nytimes.com/2020/06/02/us/politics/trump-walk-lafayette-square.html.

Benjamin, Walter. 2002. "The Work of Art in the Age of Its Technological Reproducibility." In *1935–1938*, edited by Howard Eiland and Michael W. Jennings, translated by Edmund Jephcott, Howard Eiland, and others, 101–133. Vol. 3 of *Walter Benjamin: Selected Writings*. Cambridge, MA: Belknap Press of Harvard University Press.

Bogel-Burroughs, Nicholas, and Sandra E. Garcia. 2020. "What Is Antifa, the Movement That Trump Wants to Declare a Terror Group?" *New York Times*, June 2, 2020. https://www.nytimes.com/article/what-antifa-trump.html?action=click&module=RelatedLinks&pgtype=Article.

Brenner, Marie. 1990. "After the Gold Rush." *Vanity Fair*, September 1990. https://archive.vanityfair.com/article/share/e515a2cd-a51b-4f83-8d61-6ebb9a104e0a.

Chinni, Dante. 2020. "Did Biden Win by a Little or a Lot? The Answer Is…Yes." *NBC News*, December 20, 2020. https://www.nbcnews.com/politics/meet-the-press/did-biden-win-little-or-lot-answer-yes-n1251845.

Churchwell, Sarah. 2020. "American Fascism: It Has Happened Here." *New York Review of Books*, June 20, 2020. https://www.nybooks.com/daily/2020/06/22/american-fascism-it-has-happened-here/.

Cohen, Richard. 2018. "Why People Like Trump." *Washington Post*, July 23, 2018. https://www.washingtonpost.com/opinions/why-people-like-trump/2018/07/23/36514540-8ea2-11e8-bcd5-9d911c784c38_story.html.

Cole, Mike, 2019. *Trump, the Alt-Right and Public Pedagogies of Hate and for Fascism: What Is to Be Done?* New York: Routledge.

Colley, Dawn F. 2018. "Trump, Illusory Truths of Patriotism, and the Language of the Twittersphere." In *President Donald Trump and His Political Discourse: Ramifications of Rhetoric via Twitter*, edited by Michele Lockhart, 33–51. New York: Routledge.

Connolly, William E. 2017. "Trump, the Working Class, and Fascist Rhetoric." *Theory & Event* 20 (1): S23–37. https://muse.jhu.edu/article/650860.

Crowley, Michael. 2020. "Trump Won't Commit to 'Peaceful' Post-Election Transfer of Power." *New York Times*, September 23, 2020. https://www.nytimes.com/2020/09/23/us/politics/trump-power-transfer-2020-election.html.

Davis, Julie Hirschfeld, and Maggie Haberman. 2017. "Trump Pardons Joe Arpaio, Who Became Face of Crackdown on Illegal Immigration." *New York Times*, August 25, 2017. https://www.nytimes.com/2017/08/25/us/politics/joe-arpaio-trump-pardon-sheriff-arizona.html.

Derby, Lauren H. 2009. *The Dictator's Seduction: Politics and the Popular Imagination in the Era of Trujillo*. Durham, NC: Duke University Press.

Dick, Hilary Parsons. 2019. "'Build the Wall!': Post-Truth on the US-Mexico Border." *American Anthropologist* 121 (1): 179–185. https://doi.org/10.1111/aman.13189.

Eco, Umberto. 1995. "Ur-Fascism." *New York Review of Books*, June 22, 1995. https://www.nybooks.com/articles/1995/06/22/ur-fascism/.

Eligon, John. 2020. "Black Lives Matter Grows as Movement While Facing New Challenges." *New York Times*, August 28, 2020. https://www.nytimes.com/2020/08/28/us/black-lives-matter-protest.html.

Fandos, Nicholas. 2021. "House Lays Out Case Against Trump, Branding Him the 'Inciter in Chief.'" *New York Times*, February 10, 2021. https://www.nytimes.com/2021/02/10/us/politics/trump-senate-impeachment-trial.html.

Finchelstein, Federico, Pablo Piccato, and Jason Stanley. 2020. "Alexandria Ocasio-Cortez Is Right to Warn of 'Fascism in the United States.'" *New Republic*, August 20, 2020. https://newrepublic.com/article/158999/alexandria-ocasio-cortez-right-warn-fascism-united-states.

Foucault, Michel. 1977. *Discipline and Punish: The Birth of the Prison*. Translated by Alan Sheridan. New York: Pantheon Books. First published in 1975.

Geertz, Clifford. 1980. *Negara: The Theatre State in Nineteenth-Century Bali*. Princeton, NJ: Princeton University Press.

Gessen, Masha. 2020a. "Donald Trump's Fascist Performance." *New Yorker*, June 3, 2020. https://www.newyorker.com/news/our-columnists/donald-trumps-fascist-performance?utm_source=onsite-share&utm_medium=email&utm_campaign=onsite-share&utm_brand=the-new-yorker.

———. 2020b. *Surviving Autocracy*. New York: Riverhead Books.

Giddens, Anthony. 1998. *The Third Way: The Renewal of Social Democracy*. Cambridge, UK: Polity Press.

Goldberg, Michelle. 2020. "Trump's Occupation of American Cities Has Begun." *New York Times*, July 20, 2020. https://www.nytimes.com/2020/07/20/opinion/portland-protests-trump.html.

Goldstein, Donna M., and Kira Hall. 2017. "Postelection Surrealism and Nostalgic Racism in the Hands of Donald Trump." *HAU: Journal of Ethnographic Theory* 7 (1): 397–406. http://dx.doi.org/10.14318/hau7.1.026.

Gordon, Rebecca. 2017. "Donald Trump Has a Passionate Desire to Bring Back Torture." *The Nation*, April 6, 2017. https://www.thenation.com/article/archive/donald-trump-has-a-passionate-desire-to-bring-back-torture/.

Gramsci, Antonio. 1971. *Selections from the Prison Notebooks of Antonio Gramsci*. Edited and translated by Quintin Hoare and Geoffrey Nowell Smith. New York: International Publishers.

Green, Mark, and Ralph Nader. 2020. "The F-Word: No Other Way to Describe Trump's Fascism 2.0." *The Nation*, August 28, 2020. https://www.thenation.com/article/politics/trump-fascism-republican-convention/.

Gusterson, Hugh. 2017. "From Brexit to Trump: Anthropology and the Rise of Nationalist Populism." *American Ethnologist* 44 (2): 209–214. https://doi.org/10.1111/amet.12469.

Hall, Kira, Donna M. Goldstein, and Matthew Bruce Ingram. 2016. "The Hands of Donald Trump: Entertainment, Gesture, Spectacle." *HAU: Journal of Ethnographic Theory* 6 (2): 71–100. https://doi.org/10.14318/hau6.2.009.

Hasan, Medhi. 2020. "Medhi Hasan: It's Time We Use the F-Word: Fascism." *MSNBC.com*, July 24, 2020. https://www.msnbc.com/all-in/watch/mehdi-hasan-it-s-time-we-use-the-f-word-fascism-88251973935.

Hauck, Grace. 2020. "'I Would Be Very Careful in the Middle of the Street': Drivers Have Hit Protestors 66 Times Since May 27." *USA Today*, July 9, 2020. https://www.usatoday.com/story/news/nation/2020/07/08/vehicle-ramming-attacks-66-us-since-may-27/5397700002/.

Hobsbaum, Eric, and Terence Ranger, eds. 1983. *The Invention of Tradition*. Cambridge: Cambridge University Press.

Hvistendahl, Mara, and Alleen Brown. 2020. "Armed Vigilantes Antagonizing Protestors Have Received a Warm Reception from Police." *The Intercept*, June 19, 2020. https://theintercept.com/2020/06/19/militia-vigilantes-police-brutality-protests/.

Kendzior, Sarah. 2020. *Hiding in Plain Sight: The Invention of Donald Trump and the Erosion of America*. New York: Flatiron Books.

Kertzer, David I. 1985. *Ritual, Politics, and Power*. New Haven, CT: Yale University Press.

Korecki, Natasha, and Christopher Cadelago. 2020. "With a Hand from Trump, the Right Makes Rittenhouse a Cause Célèbre." *Politico*, September 1, 2020. https://www.politico.com/news/2020/09/01/trump-rittenhouse-kenosha-support-407106.

Lachman, Richard. 2019. "Trump: Authoritarian, Just Another Neoliberal Republican, or Both?" *Sociologia, Problemas e Práticas* 89: 9–31. https://doi.org/10.7458/SPP20198915753.

Lempert, Michael, and Michael Silverstein. 2012. *Creatures of Politics: Media, Message, and the American Presidency*. Bloomington: Indiana University Press.

Levitsky, Steven, and Daniel Ziblatt. 2018. *How Democracies Die*. New York: Broadway Books.

Lewis, Sophie. 2020. "Joe Biden Breaks Obama's Record for Most Votes Ever Cast for a U.S. Presidential Candidate." *CBS News*, December 7, 2020. https://www.cbsnews.com/news/joe-biden-popular-vote-record-barack-obama-us-presidential-election-donald-trump/.

Machiavelli, Niccolò. 1998. *The Prince*. Edited and translated by Harvey C. Mansfield. Second edition, Chicago: University of Chicago Press.

Mann, Michael. 2004. *Fascists*. Cambridge: Cambridge University Press.

Miroff, Nick and Josh Dawsey. 2019. "Trump Wants His Border Barrier to be Painted Black with Spikes. He Has Other Ideas, Too." *Washington Post*, May 16, 2019. https://www.washingtonpost.com/national/trump-wants-his-border-barrier-to-be-painted-black-with-spikes-he-has-other-ideas-too/2019/05/16/b088c07e-7676-11e9-b3f5-5673edf2d127_story.html.

Mosse, George L. 1985. *Nationalism and Sexuality: Respectability and Abnormal Sexuality in Modern Europe*. New York: Howard Fertig.

NBC Chicago. 2020. "Who Is Kyle Rittenhouse? What We Know about the 17-Year-Old Arrested in Kenosha Shooting." August 27, 2020. https://www.nbcchicago.com/

news/local/who-is-kyle-rittenhouse-what-we-know-about-the-17-year-old-arrested-in-kenosha-shooting/2329610/.

Oh, Inae. 2020. "Trump Gleefully Praises Violence against Journalists as a 'Beautiful Sight.'" *Mother Jones*, September 23, 2020. https://www.motherjones.com/politics/2020/09/trump-ali-velshi/.

Oppel, Richard A., Jr., and Kim Barker. 2020. "New Transcripts Detail Last Moments for George Floyd." *New York Times*, August 11, 2020. https://www.nytimes.com/2020/07/08/us/george-floyd-body-camera-transcripts.html.

Parker, Ashley, Josh Dawsey, and Philip Rucker. 2021. "Six Hours of Paralysis: Inside Trump's Failure to Act After a Mob Stormed the Capitol." *Washington Post*, January 11, 2021. https://www.washingtonpost.com/politics/trump-mob-failure/2021/01/11/36a46e2e-542e-11eb-a817-e5e7f8a406d6_story.html.

Paxton, Robert O. 2004. *The Anatomy of Fascism*. New York: Vintage Books.

Philipps, Dave. 2019. "Trump Clears Three Service Members in War Crimes Cases." *New York Times*, November 22, 2019. https://www.nytimes.com/2019/11/15/us/trump-pardons.html.

Rasanayagam, Johan, Judith Beyer, and Madeleine Reeves. 2014. "Introduction: Performances, Possibilities, and Practices of the Political in Central Asia." In *Ethnographies of the State in Central Asia: Performing Politics*, edited by Madeleine Reeves, Johan Rasanayagam, and Judith Beyer, 1–28. Bloomington: Indiana University Press.

Rhodan, Maya. 2017. "President Trump Tells Police Officers Not to Be 'Too Nice' with Suspects." *Time*, July 28, 2017. https://time.com/4878838/president-donald-trump-police-officers/.

Scherer, Michael. 2015. "Exclusive: Donald Trump Says He Might Have Supported Japanese Internment." *Time*, December 8, 2015. https://time.com/4140050/donald-trump-muslims-japanese-internment/.

Scott, Eugene. 2020. "Cory Booker, a Product of the Suburbs, Is Coming to Ruin the Suburbs, According to Trump." *Washington Post*, September 4, 2020. https://www.washingtonpost.com/politics/2020/09/04/cory-booker-product-suburbs-is-coming-ruin-suburbs-according-trump/.

Shear, Michael D., and Julie Hirschfeld Davis. 2019. "Shoot Migrants' Legs, Build Alligator Moat: Behind Trump's Ideas for Border." *New York Times*, October 2, 2019. https://www.nytimes.com/2019/10/01/us/politics/trump-border-wars.html.

Skidmore, Monique. 2004. *Karaoke Fascism: Burma and the Politics of Fear*. Philadelphia: University of Pennsylvania Press.

Smith, David Norman. 2019. "Authoritarianism Reimagined: The Riddle of Trump's Base." *Sociological Quarterly* 60 (2): 210–223. https://doi.org/10.1080/00380253.2019.1593061.

Snyder, Timothy. 2018. *The Road to Unfreedom: Russia, Europe, America*. New York: Tim Duggan Books.

Stanley, Jason. 2018. *How Fascism Works: The Politics of Us and Them*. New York: Random House.

Szalai, Jennifer. 2020. "The Debate Over the Word 'Fascism' Takes a New Turn." *New York Times*, June 10, 2020. https://www.nytimes.com/2020/06/10/books/fascism-debate-donald-trump.html.

Tharoor, Ishaan. 2020. "Is It Time to Call Trump the F-Word?" *Washington Post*, June 3, 2020. https://www.washingtonpost.com/world/2020/06/03/trump-protests-fascism/.

Tiefenthäler, Ainara. 2016. "Trump's History of Encouraging Violence." *New York Times*, March 14, 2016. https://www.nytimes.com/video/us/100000004269364/trump-and-violence.html.

Trump, Donald J. 2020a. "Remarks by President Trump at White House Conference on American History." *Whitehouse.gov*, September 17, 2020. https://www.whitehouse.gov/briefings-statements/remarks-president-trump-white-house-conference-american-history/.

———. 2020b. "Statement by the President." *Whitehouse.gov*, June 1, 2020. https://www.whitehouse.gov/briefings-statements/statement-by-the-president-39/.

Weber, Max. 1978. *Economy and Society: An Outline of Interpretive Sociology*. Edited and translated by Guenther Roth and Claus Wittich. Berkeley: University of California Press.

Williams, Raymond. 1977. *Marxism and Literature*. Oxford: Oxford University Press.

Wright, Jennifer. 2018. "All the Times Trump Has Incited Violence against People He Dislikes." *Harper's Bazaar*, October 30, 2018. https://www.harpersbazaar.com/culture/politics/a24431408/how-trump-encourages-violence/.

Yokley, Eli. 2021. "Trump Emerges from Impeachment Trial with Sturdy Backing from GOP Voters." *Morning Consult*, February 16, 2021. https://morningconsult.com/2021/02/16/trump-gop-support-impeachment-poll/.

PART I
Love and patria

1
LOVE POLITICS

The nation form and the affective life of the state

Uli Linke

> Donald Trump is a lost soul. [He] has the most limited vocabulary than anyone in the history of the presidency. And so, there are many words Donald Trump does not understand, words of all sizes. But the single most important word Donald Trump does not understand is one we all understand. [A]nd, very sadly for him, it's possible that he has never felt this in his entire life: Love! Love is the single most important word that Donald Trump does not understand. It seems [he] was never taught anything about love. Donald Trump is a man who does not know what it is to love or be loved. He has no comprehension of the concept of Christian love or romantic love or marital love. He does not now, never has, and never will understand the word love, and so he feels nothing when he separates children from their parents at the southern border.... The most dangerous thing about the most dangerous president that this country has ever had is that Donald Trump feels nothing.
>
> Lawrence O'Donnell, *The Last Word*
> (MSNBC Live) February 6, 2020

> The country is crying out for leadership. Leadership that can unite us [and] bring us together. Leadership that can recognize the pain and deep grief of communities that have had a knee on their neck for too long.... We are all called to love one another as we love ourselves. That's hard work. But it's the work of America—[to] make possible this nation's path to a more perfect union.... This is the United States of America.
>
> Vice President Joe Biden
> (CNN) Philadelphia, June 2, 2020

Described as incompetent, unfeeling, and empathically impotent, the former celebrity mogul Donald Trump has habitually ghosted the halls of the White House while indulging in plush life at one of his golf resorts. After the 2016

DOI: 10.4324/9781003034810-1

electoral win, the office of the US presidency came to be occupied by a "reactionary fantasist" (Sullivan 2017), whose boundless self-obsessions with power have energized public debates and grassroots movements on racial justice, women's rights, and gender inequalities (Bonilla-Silva 2019; Carruthers 2019; Kray, Carroll, and Mandell 2018; Lebron 2017; Mandell 2019; Maxwell 2020; Smith 2018). The public spectacles of "transgression, excessive opulence, and civil lawlessness" that Donald Trump, the 45th US president and commander-in-chief, instigated by his norm-breaking attitudes and actions must be understood "as part of a long history of white privilege and hypocrisy" (Goldstein and Hall 2017, 402–403). With a focus on this legacy of whiteness and race, this chapter explores the paradoxical entanglement of tropes of nationhood, love, terror, and masculinity.

In the second decade of the twenty-first century, the sources and emblems of political power have once again been locked in corporeal practices: blood-right, white supremacy, racial violence, male dominance. The aggrandizement of the president's body continually fed on the denigration of the racialized body as it was criminalized, medicalized, dehumanized, and rendered disposable (Alexander 2020; Bobo 2017; Butler 2018; Maskovsky and Bjork-James 2020). Donald Trump, an autocratic leader, an aspirant king, imagined a lineage of his blood-heirs to the seats of political power, while caging and stealing migrant children at the southern border (Soboroff 2020). In Trump's fortified America, racialized human beings—Black, Indigenous, Latinx, and Asian—inspired an intense apprehension, generating both fear and resentment, making them targets of street violence and state terror: dispossessed of rights, they have been brutalized, silenced, and murdered (Hannah-Jones 2018; Peeples 2020; Washington Post Database 2020). Drawing on anti-racist, postcolonial, feminist analysis (Butler 2020; Feldman 2018; Ransby 2018), this chapter examines how, in this era of the fleshly/carnal president, tropes of fascist masculinity and, as such, the fascist allure of power have been retrieved from the historical archives to perform and enact white privilege—in a democratic nation-state.

Attempts to theorize the tactics of political power under late capitalism require us to rethink the state apparatus as a site of meaning production, emotional investment, and fantasy (Buck-Morss 2000; Comaroff and Comaroff 2016; Taussig 1992; Wolf 2001; Žižek 1989). Moreover, as I argue here, modern nation-states are not just imagined or discursive regimes but also embodied forms. Political worlds have a sensual and emotive dimension: the life of the state has a corporal grounding. Modern governmentalities act on and inhabit the body. This hypothesis is corroborated by the pervasive presence of state culture and political terror in the everyday life of communities of color in North America. As such, there is an urgency to systematize and synthesize the theoretical tools for engaging the operations of contemporary state systems. An examination of nations as imagined political communities (Anderson 1991) must be expanded to include research on how conceptions of peoplehood are forged under the impact of global capitalism, media technologies, scientific ideology, and medical paradigms or health systems

(Fassin 2012; Feldman 2015; Gilroy 2004; Hardin 2019; Mbembe 2001; Nairn and James 2005; Ticktin 2011). Our analytic preoccupations, whereby we see the state either as an institution, a discourse, as culturally imagined or socially constructed, tend to coexist with little interpretative integration. Anthropological understandings of the state's capacity for mass violence and political terror (Bauman 1989; Hinton and Hinton 2015; Robben 2018; Scott 1998) are frequently staged against the magico-mythical qualities of the nation and the performative practices through which its terrifying history is remembered (Cassirer 1946; Hinton 2018; Linke 1999; Stoller 1995; Taussig 1997). Building on these insights, and through a critical reading of the fascist allure of whiteness and male power in the Trump era, my aim is to offer alternative possibilities for thinking about justice, equality, and human rights by interrogating the affective dimensions of the state. This approach is important for several reasons.

Rethinking the state of whiteness: national politics from a global perspective

The pivotal conditions for domination and exploitation that Michael Omi and Howard Winant (1994) so eloquently termed *racialization* are no longer produced solely from within the ideological territory of nation-states. The assignation of racial meanings to concrete practices, peoples, and places has been globalized. In other words, the expansive capitalist system is at once also a "global racial formation" (Winant 2001, 3, 6). Although the codex of race has not entirely lost its local or culturally specific imprints, racial formations are evident on a planetary scale, as a worldwide phenomenon that is propelled by the phantasms of racial neoliberalism (Goldberg 2009), which propagate ever new imaginaries of spaces, origins, and the relative value of human life. The racializing projects forged by Euro-American nation-states continue to be tethered to the remnants of a worldwide regime of colonial domination to conjoin the logic of white supremacy in its multiple iterations (Mbembe 2018). The president's attempt to negotiate a "bill of love" for US immigration policies provides a pertinent example (Merica 2018; Naylor 2018). When tasking a bipartisan committee of Democratic and Republican lawmakers to negotiate "a deal" that was to include both a future policy for the 800,000 DACA recipients (or DREAMers), the Americanized children of undocumented immigrants, and additional measures for tightening the nation's border security, Donald Trump proceeded to reveal his underlying commitments. The "bill of love" emerged as a rhetorical flourish, a circumlocution, for the ethnoracial whitening of the US population, which was to be accomplished by linking the fate of migrants and their offspring to the termination of the diversity visa lottery program and to ending family-based "chain migration," but above all else to categorical immigration restrictions and the funding for a southern (US-Mexico) border wall (Camera 2018; Davis, Stolberg, and Kaplan 2018; Korte and Shesgreen 2018). As such, Trump's "bill of love" served as a blueprint for metamorphosing the United States into a premodern

28 Uli Linke

fortress-castle. When further publicizing his intent to dismantle the existing protections for migrant families from Haiti and several African countries, Trump demanded "to know why he should accept immigrants from 'shithole countries' rather than places like Norway" (Dawsey 2018), a Scandinavian nation presumed to be inhabited by white people. As globalization "repudiates fixed territories, sacred spaces, and hard boundaries in favor of unstable flows" (Luke 2004, 121–122), the expansive reach of neoliberal capitalism has transformed the ways in which racial hegemonies are sustained and perpetuated by a nation's closed "biometric borders" (Mbembe 2018). In the United States, a country marked by an intensified desire to build fortified enclosures and to control bodies in motion, what *Washington Post* White House Bureau Chief Philip Rucker tweeted about as "Donald Trump's push to amplify racism" and to "weaponize white grievance" (@PhilipRucker, July 4, 2020) can be unmasked. Traces of such recalibrations are evident in other political realms.

Imagine this scene (see Figure 1.1). At a campaign rally in South Dakota, on the evening prior to America's Independence Day, 2020, Trump made his way to the main stage, walking down a ramp, then briefly stopped, turning to the cameras: raising his clenched fist up to his fleshy profile, weathered skin sagging, with lackluster make-up, crowned by thinning, yellow strands of hair, he stood in visual proximity to national history—behind him, carved into the rock of Mount Rushmore, the towering stone sculptures of the country's iconic presidents (Finchelstein 2020), a naturalizing metaphor of political power. According

FIGURE 1.1 President Trump at Mount Rushmore, July 3, 2020.
Credit: Andrea Hanks/The White House.

to news reports, it had been "Trump's dream" to become immortalized as part of the monument, and a White House aide had previously contacted Governor Kristi Noem of South Dakota to inquire about "the process for adding presidents to Mount Rushmore" (Cathey 2020). After initially rejecting the revelation as "fake news," Trump confirmed his desire for achieving representational immortality as "a good idea" (@realDonaldTrump tweet, August 9, 2020; Ehrlich 2020). Motivated by his hunger for uncontestable symbols of political legitimation, the US president surrounded himself with images, tropes, and people that would bolster his assertions of leadership and strength. Supported by White House staff, plus a general and Defense Secretary Mark Esper, he rallied federal military troops to his side to, as Esper said, "dominate the battlespace" of Black Lives Matter protesters in Washington DC (Ryan and Lamothe 2020). The deployment of paramilitary units, "masked federal agents in camouflage and fatigues," recurred in Portland (OR) to repress protests against racist police violence (Prose 2020). Trump threatened to use such federal forces as a measure of crowd-control in other US cities with diverse populations and Democratic mayors, including New York, Baltimore, Chicago, and Atlanta (Baker, Kanno-Youngs, and Davey 2020). The call to "white power," as publicized and reified by Trump's social media ventriloquism (Wootson, Jr. 2020), was at once a call to dark-love—not an enduring affection for the nation, but rather a summons to mobilize state violence against non-white citizens. Among the dehumanizing practices authorized by such rallying calls for a White America are acts of atrocity, including the execution of Black men in public view, in the street, captured on camera—killings committed by police officers in uniform (Glaude 2020). What are the implications of this turn to whiteness for the American body politic? And how does such an allegiance to white supremacy fit into the political fabric of a global context?

American democracy, like global capitalism, holds an often-invoked promise for a better world, a way of life in which the violent barriers of racial consciousness have been pushed aside, even obliterated, by a universal quest for justice, human rights, and prosperity. National histories of genocide and racial terror, seen as symptoms of a failed modernity, are located in the past, a temporal order that is opposed to an emergent future, a world of possibilities, a terrain without frontiers (Linke 2014). But such a turn to desired or projected states of being, as I argue here, tends to divert critical attention from the deeply entrenched and persistent project of mapping global disparities by race. Globalization has not produced a singular or unified world-order. Neoliberal capitalism does not operate "as a non-contradictory, uncontested space" (Hall 2000, 32). In the new millennium, in the twenty-first century, the national order of things, including "the relationship among residence, race, and rights" (Appadurai 2003, 346), has been destabilized. Nation forms, cultural imaginaries, and social lives engage economic possibilities along different and sometimes contradictory trajectories. Under such volatile conditions, global processes "open up the possibility for the (re)articulation of racial, sexual, and national identities" (Thomas and Clarke 2006, 27). As "long-established colonial and Orientalist tropes" are "revivified"

(Graham 2006, 256), patterns of racial ordering likewise persist in the endeavors of international organizations, worldwide policy-making, globalized culture industries, and the transborder transactions among nation-states. The modes of racial dehumanization are likewise evident in the "the vast gaps between North and South" and the corresponding "planetary correlation of darkness and poverty" (Winant 2001, 305). Yet racialization also persists in the ways in which Euro-Americans continue to imagine themselves against "other bodies" across national borders and continental divides. Such entrenched systems of racial signification have real-world consequences for the reallocation of power and privilege on a global scale. This is especially true, as Paul Gilroy observed, when a corresponding representational schema "assigns differential value to lives lost according to their locations and supposed racial origins or considers that some human bodies are more easily and appropriately humiliated, imprisoned, shackled, starved and destroyed than others" (2003, 263). The impetus for these tensive and sometimes violent realities of racial inequality has been rendered opaque by an emphasis on the "redistributive, democratizing, and empowering effects" (Winant 2001, 301). The dangerous underbelly of national politics can thereby be (mis)perceived as a beneficent, liberatory force.

With the disposition for unity, and utopian "redemptive promise of wholeness" (Eley and Suny 1996, 26), nation-states take hold of society's interior spaces, reaching into the somatosensory recesses of daily life. In the domestic interior, political passions are concentrated through techniques and memories of the body (Connerton 1989). In the United States, as in other countries, such bodily modalities and signifying practices are however not affectively neutral. Rather, they are entwined with the state's "nervous system" (Taussig 1992), a system of moral codes, emotions, and experiences agitated by the governing apparatus. With an eye toward the "structure of feelings" (Williams 1977) with which the state apparatus tends to flow through everyday life-worlds, this chapter engages those instances where the political field asserts its presence through bodily experience, and engrafts itself in and through the senses. In offering a critique of political culture in the Trump era, this chapter moves from the theatrics of love to an analysis of the somatosensory state, central to which are the former president's aberrant racial politics and the prosthetics of national passion.

Love of country: nation, passion, and sensation

The sensual or emotional register of modern states, perhaps because of a preoccupation with the masculine-rational edifice of government, received relatively little attention in the anthropological literature of the twentieth century. Previous works, as Benita Parry observed, sought to uncover how political regimes "entered the social fabric, the intellectual discourse, and the life of the imagination" (1993, 24). The world of emotions (fear, terror, pain, love) escaped notice, subtly excluded, as if somehow left untouched by the intimacies of state power. In the twenty-first century, after slavery, empire, colonial atrocities, two world wars, fascism, genocide, and Nazi death camps, such analytic "oversights" seem absurd.

Analytic blind zones such as these only make sense if understood as anthropological complicities with political power, an interpretation confirmed when we look back to tenacious claims about the tangible unreality of states. Theorized as a disembodied abstraction, "the state," as Radcliffe-Brown proclaimed in *African Political Systems*, "does not exist in the phenomenal world; it is a fiction" (1940, xxiii). Although postcolonial critics have uncovered "precisely the existence and reality of the political power of this fiction, its powerful insubstantiality" (Taussig 1992, 113), earlier scholars, while reifying the state-thing as an abstract entity, began to explain the discernible manifestations of statehood in terms of a cultural symbiosis. "The state," Michael Walzer asserted, "has no palpable shape or substance. The state is invisible: it must be personified before it can be seen, symbolized before it can be loved, imagined before it can be conceived" (1967, 194). From this perspective, the formations of political affect and, correspondingly, the sensual apprehension of political fields, were construed as mere reverberations or echoes of the order of signs. Here, the state was envisioned solely as a cognitive construct. Political sentiments presumably came into being as side-effects or byproducts of a semiotic conceptual operation. Such notions belong to those "pernicious postulates" (Tilly 1984) that I wish to contest. Political sentiments, I argue, are more than symptomatic surfaces. Political emotions possess a formative power, an embodied agency, which is, at least in part, constituted by the existential ground of being: our lived experience, and our engagements with state officials—government agents, civil servants, bureaucrats, law enforcement, police officers, and military.

Without a doubt, personification, symbolization, and imagination *are* discursive forms whereby the state-making thing, as Foucault observed, "is rooted deep in the social nexus" and, as it were, is brought "into being" to "live in society" (1983, 222). But such socio-corporal animations also continuously feed on a "sensualization of power" (Rabinow and Dreyfus 1983, 173). This very link between power and sense experience, although widely acknowledged by the late twentieth century, had been largely confined to discussions of national sentiments: the entanglements of nation, emotion, and devotion. As Craig Calhoun observed: "The discourse of nations is couched especially in terms of passion and identification" (1997, 3). Likewise, in their introductory remarks to *Becoming National*, Geoff Eley and Ronald Grigor Suny pointed to "'pleasure' and 'desire' as categories of political understanding" that must be considered when studying "the power of national loyalty," "the meanings and effects of a sense of national identity," and the formation of the "intimate connections between personhood and belonging to a nation" (1996, 19, 24, 25). Yet despite such a consistent invocation of nation and sensation, the subsequent dissection of the political matrix of emotional labor has tended to fall short. The modalities of national fervor such as loyalty, solidarity, and love or the sense of belonging and "feeling at home" have been glossed over, repeatedly mentioned, yet prone to reification in categorical terms, given ontological status, and narrated as commonplace clichés. Indeed, by privileging the discursive machinations of postcolonial state-making, even with the analytic turn toward performance, agency, and the subject, the politics of affect have all but been ignored.

This is surprising because feelings or affectivities are clearly not "outside the matrix of power" (Rabinow and Dreyfus 1983, 182). The logic of emotions is firmly rooted in the social, and, under late capitalism, the entire "system of feelings," as Baudrillard observed, has become an "organized extension" of individuals constituted as "a productive force" (1995, 202). Yet our understanding of the modernist coupling of affect and power requires further deliberation. Although political gestures, symbols, and language or national discourse can generate "emotions of loyalty" (Walzer 1967, 194), and even fasten "affect to political life" (Berlant 1991, 5), we need to inquire how a national ethos is enunciated or grounded in "the interiority of a meaning-giving subject" (Rabinow and Dreyfus 1983, 57). We might wonder whether there actually exists any congruence between nationalist discourse and a citizen's everyday sense-making. The anchorage of political passions in people's common sense-experience is one of the "difficulties involved in the 'work of nationalization'" (Brubaker 1998, 305, n29). The everyday formation of political sentiments "cannot properly be taken as given or axiomatic" (298), even when framed by state power. It is precisely this nexus between feeling subjects and political discourse that I want to explore further.

In his most enduring works on politics, *The Prince* (1513–1515) and *Discourses* (1513–1517), Niccolò Machiavelli explored the powerful "emotion of love of country," and the power of affection: "*Love* is a word he use[d] to refer to sentiment for country, an ancient usage," according to Sebastian De Grazia (1989), "transferring the term from concrete persons and things to the abstraction of country. The catalogue of objects of love and affection, ranging through spouse, offspring, kin, friends," and "although not existing anywhere in the same kind or degree," "take recourse in figures of speech, in analogy and metaphor," and in the "allegory of love of country" (142, 143, 144). Thinking along similar trajectories, from a politics of love to a speculative theory of state, Dipesh Chakrabarty (2000) asked why should a nation be "loved," what makes it "lovable," and then proceeded to inquire how these "feelings of devotion or adoration" take form (149). By juxtaposing distinct Bengali literary histories and "existing life practices," Chakrabarty engaged "the plurality of the category imagination," yet also brought to light those "radically contradictory modes of vision" with which the "nationalist eye" *sees* the nation (20, 178–179). Such a potential range in the syntax of national optics, which attests to "heterogeneous practices of seeing" and "perceiving" nationhood (149), has moved Chakrabarty to argue against the possibility of a single, totalizing register for the political field. For there are, he concluded, diverse "ways of being-in-the-world," wherein we "live within our different senses of ontic belonging" (254, 255). The formation of political subjectivities is thus not simply an effect or symptom of the ideo-symbolic machinations of national discourse. Rather, following this argument, political emotions are tied to divergent perceptual practices and lived experience, and, as I propose in this chapter, are engendered by the everyday modes of contact between embodied subjects and the political state apparatus. National passions are not a unitary surface or skin which envelopes the imagined totality of the state. Rather, such emotive figurations are linked to diverse possibilities of perception and experience.

Yet an anthropological analysis of modern nationhood has tended to treat political subjectivities as unmediated (sometimes organic) extensions of a hegemonic, dead logic—external to the subject. According to Michael Taussig:

> When the human body, a nation's flag, money, or a public statue is defaced, a strange surplus of negative energy is likely to be aroused from within the defaced thing itself. Something so strange emanates from the wound of sacrilege wrought by desecration: It is the cut of de/facement that releases this surplus, the cut into wholeness as holiness.
>
> (1999, 1, 3)

In this meaning-making universe of transference and dissociation, which brings forth an uncanny emotional discharge that magically erupts from the sacred body of signs, the feeling subject is absent: a non-presence. The emotional labor is, according to Taussig, mimetically performed by the defaced object, as a signifying fetish. Such an enigmatic erasure of subjectivities from the relations of signs and power necessarily incarcerates the analytic gaze in the hermeneutic space of discourse. This is a problematic closure of interpretation.

By similarly locating the affective trace within a semiotic system, Benedict Anderson asserted, "political love can be deciphered from the ways in which languages describe its object: either in the vocabulary of kinship (motherland, *Vaterland*, patria) or that of home" (1991, 143). Certainly, within nationalist discourse, terms of endearment like "*father* state" are used as metaphors to transport sentiments of domesticity and kinship to the level of the sovereign community, which like "the family," as Anderson claimed, has been traditionally conceived as the "domain of disinterested love and solidarity" (144). Yet these so commonly accepted metaphors of normative discourse require analytic disentanglement from political practice. The postulation of a unified field of discourse and affect is, I argue, an untenable conceptual fiction. Nevertheless, and in a similar vein, Eley and Suny proclaimed: "the nation has invariably been imagined via metaphors of family, and has accordingly replicated the patriarchy of conventional familial forms" (1996, 26). Such assertions are highly problematic. I certainly do not contest that the political economy of the nation has been infused with a moral economy that promotes marriage and the family as a state agenda. In the twentieth century, the figure of the traditional family form emerged as a governing agenda in Europe and the United States, which at the level of state politics was imbricated by moral discourses of heteronormativity, paternalistic masculinity, and, I would suggest, the promotion of a white public sphere. But our analytic grasp of the operation of these biopolitical regimes, when confined solely to the hermeneutic stratigraphy of the national imaginary, seems blatantly deficient.

Such procedures of semiotic decipherment, while bringing to light a political discourse of sacrality and/or legitimation, reveal in my assessment little about the complex ways in which the imaginaries of the nation-state take on a social life through the subjects' capacity to perceive, feel, and interpret. People's feelings about the nation cannot simply be inferred or asserted from the hegemonic/dominant order of discourse—a discourse conjured by governing elites. Anthropological musings about the production of political realities, as I have argued here, have to include the formative possibility of anti-state and anti-nationalist sentiments. We cannot ignore the existence of relative or oppositional subjectivities.

In a critical turn against the "problematic unity of the nation," Homi Bhabha (1990) effectively contested the alleged homogeneity of political fields. Yet, in this endeavor, he sidestepped the matter of political affect almost entirely. Given his analytic focus on the "constitutive contradictions of the national text," political sentiments come into view only through strategies of textual inquiry, as Bhabha put it, in "narratives and discourses that signify a sense of nationness" (1994, 308, 307). Here, the social life of political passions is deposited *into* the performative textuality of signs. But the political universe of contemporary nations is more than a mere system of cultural signification. Nations are discursive phantoms *with political bodies*. National imaginaries are never "superorganic" entities, to borrow Alfred L. Kroeber's (1917, 212) phrasing, that is, disembodied and bodiless or "unsubstantial" cultural figures. Rather, political fields and national spaces are corporal, somatosensuous formations: not just "sociohistorical ciphers" (Buck-Morss 1977, 102, 109), but fundamentally *bodied* productions. Such a perspective, I contend, posits a radically different perspective on the grammar of political affect and feeling.

Love—politically speaking

As the US president dreamed of an instantiation of political life in spectacle, with mass rallies, fireworks, roaring crowds, signs of love, and gestures of popular affection for *him*, millions of Americans were suffering, with tens, and later hundreds, of thousands dead or dying. When the world came under siege by an infectious virus (COVID-19), the ensuing health crisis laid bare and rendered visible the intensification of existing global, national, and regional inequalities. Amid widespread economic devastation, rising unemployment, food shortages, dangerous work conditions, restrictions on healthcare, institutional inhumanities (prisons, detention centers, care facilities), the abrogation of immigration and minority rights, and the persistent assault on vulnerable communities and spaces, the US president declared in April 2020: "A lot of people love Trump, right? A lot of people love me" (O'Donnell 2020b). Embattled by the ubiquity of racial violence, the evident failure in managing the US health pandemic, and the ongoing cruelties of language, action, and policy, the president's camera appearances lacked any signs of compassion. As MSNBC host, Lawrence O'Donnell (2020b) commented: "He never spoke one word of sympathy." Whenever encountering the televised façade of the head of state, we might conclude that the heart of the nation had grown stone-cold. White House leadership seemed less committed to staging the president as an empathic figure, as a caring father of the nation, and as a compassionate representative of the American body-politic than as a self-interested public figure longing to be loved—by all and everyone.

How is such an appetite for love, the neediness for affection by others, embedded in or woven through US political culture? On social media, including Twitter, at political rallies, at press conferences, and in interviews, the former president frequently invoked the term *love*, although in unconventional, sometimes perplexing, and even shocking ways. With an eye on the theater of international diplomacy, Trump conjured a politics of love for his platform of national leadership and media attention. By using a global network of governance, he began to forge personal friendships with aberrant heads of state and world leaders to remake himself in the image of a much-beloved, revered figure of authority: a man of wealth, respect, and power. When assuming the office of the president in 2017, faced with global political issues, including climate change, war, militarization, nuclear proliferation, and general matters of collective human survival, Donald Trump thought it best to trade personal insults with North Korean leader Kim Jung Un (Rucker and Dawsey 2019). Instead of relying on an established diplomatic taskforce, repeated weapons tests by North Korea spurred the US president to engage in mockery slights, such as "Little Rocket Man," comic-book-like epithets that increased his television ratings and media attention (Simon 2018). After having staged the interpersonal rift between himself and Kim Jung Un, the US president then, as self-proclaimed deal-maker, turned to love letters to mend the North Korean-American conflict:

> Trump gloats about the half-dozen or so letters Kim has written him as if he were a smitten teenager in possession of valentines from a crush. White House officials refer to the diplomatic correspondence jokingly as 'love letters.' Kim addresses Trump as 'Your Excellency' and employs flowery language to describe the president's energy and political smarts, according to people who have read them. Trump has shown the documents to dozens of Oval Office visitors and bragged about them in public. 'He wrote me beautiful letters, and they're great letters,' Trump said at a September rally in West Virginia. 'We fell in love'.
>
> *(Rucker and Dawsey 2019)*

Such an erotomania between two political leaders, both married men, might have been perceived as shocking or offensive to some, as a transgression of heteronormative masculinity, although the president's supporters cheered and laughed when Trump made the announcement of his love affair with the North Korean dictator at one of his rallies (Feffer 2019; Woodward 2020). A consummation of their relationship took the form of a summit meeting, and when it failed, the lovers' spat became a political spectacle on the world stage. Such instances of reality television reveal the president's longing for validation conferred upon him by others: the adoration by foreign heads-of-state and his fantasies of proximity to power.

Contiguity to blood-power or direct contact with the genealogical trace of royal legitimacy (kings, queens, emperors, or members of the nobility), that is, sovereign privilege inherited and not achieved, seems to grant a metonymic acclaim to presidential greatness. Trump's state visit to the United Kingdom in early June 2019 was thus not merely marked by a day of pomp in London, but "lunch with Queen Elizabeth II and tea with Prince Charles," and concluded with a "grand state dinner at Buckingham Palace" (Katz, Superville, and Riechmann 2019). Photo opportunities of Trump and his children together with the royal family were central to this occasion, marking political ascent. Ignoring the public protests, the US president commented: "There were thousands of people cheering, waving the American flag. It was tremendous spirit and love. There was great love" (in Braverman 2019). Although the visible crowds, according to various news reports (Samuels 2019), were actually protests against Trump's UK visit, the American president noted: "London part of trip is going really well. The Queen and the entire Royal family have been fantastic. The relationship with the United Kingdom is very strong. Tremendous crowds of well-wishers and people that love our Country" (in Cabrera 2019). When abroad, in London, standing at the center of public attention, Trump tweeted that he saw "Great love all around" (@realDonaldTrump, June 3, 2019). Immersed in love, touched by royalty, empowered by fortune, wealth, and privilege, the grandeur of presidential authority was bolstered by yet another sign of power: evidence of a loyal following to carry out his political commands. The former New York City mayor Rudy Giuliani took on this role: as the president's personal attorney, he became a "key player" in the "'hoax' of impeachment" (Watson 2019). In fact, Giuliani "traveled to Ukraine in pursuit of political dirt on former Vice President Joe Biden and his son, Hunter. Trump then suggested Giuliani 'does this out of love'" (Neale 2019). Such an act of love-devotion, performed across international borders, was later deemed a transgression of presidential authority.

Theatrics, spectacle, and showmanship became the dramaturgic tools of a political illusionist, who enacted his vision of the American presidency on the global stage. Trump's cultivation of interpersonal relations with political strongmen (including China's Xi Jinping, Saudi Arabia's Crown Prince Mohammed bin Salman, Russia's Vladimir Putin, and North Korea's Kim Jong Un), the pursuit of financial self-interest, the demand for personal loyalty by devotees, and the ability to thereby command them to take clandestine actions on his behalf, and his repeated invocation of love as a public trope of "charismatic authority" (Weber 1978, 215) provided screen memories for Trump's exercise of raw/naked political power. In ordinary life, expressions of love serve to consolidate social relationships by a reciprocity of emotions, whether in a partnership or a family, a community, and nation. This notion was most recently articulated by Jill Biden, speaking at the Democratic National Convention in August 2020: "We found that love holds a family together. How do you make a broken family whole? The same way you make a nation whole. With love and understanding–and with small acts of kindness" (in Groppe 2020). Yet when such sentiments of love are invoked between heads of state to pledge reciprocal support for international human rights abuses, such as the ethnocide of Turkic Muslims in China or the murder of a Saudi journalist in Turkey or the execution of former Russian officials in London (Bolton 2020; Washington Post Editorial Board 2020a, 2020b), and when used as a platitude in US politics to conceal systemic racism, inequality, and the normalization of police violence, such speech-acts expose what Hannah Arendt (1964) called the "banality of evil." By a reliance on select symbolic props and settings (Figure 1.2; see also Rogers 2020), rhetoric, gendered body politics, violent racism, the policing of protests, the criminalization of political opposition, and the authoritarian wielding of power, the former president's occupancy of the White House was, following Masha Gessen (2020), a performance of fascism:

> A power grab is always a performance of sorts. It begins with a claim to power, and if the claim is accepted—if the performance is believed—it takes hold. Much as he played a real-estate tycoon in the most crude and reductive way, Trump is now performing his idea of power as he imagines it. In his intuition, power is autocratic; it affirms the superiority of one nation and one race; it asserts total domination; and it mercilessly suppresses all opposition. Whether or not he is capable of grasping the concept, Trump is performing fascism.

FIGURE 1.2 Fox News interview with President Trump in the otherwise off-limits Lincoln Memorial, May 3, 2020.
Credit: Anna Moneymaker/New York Times/Redux.

The affective life of the state

My focus on the sensual life of the state, national sentiments, and spectacles of love provides alternative venues for thinking about political fields. Situated at the nexus of late modernity and global capitalism, the making of docile bodies also produces disorders and voids: a muting of affect, of memory, and of time. The conditions of modern life, as Walter Benjamin observed, ushered in an "increasing atrophy of experience" (1983, 113). But in this age of the copy, the simulacrum, the artifact, and what I call the dead zones of affect and sensual crisis, the state-making apparatus begins to propagate counter-experiences of intense sensual realism by flowing through the pleasure zones of sex, leisure, and consumption. In this chapter, I have briefly examined several of these complex sites, where discourse, representation, and practice collide or interlock, and where the traces of the political field not only materialize through a system of signs but become a felt presence through "a curious linking of power and pleasure" (Rabinow and Dreyfus 1983, 173). At this nexus, the semio-prosthetic contours of the state apparatus are fastened or moored to the sensual fabric of everyday experience.

During his 2016 election campaign, and in the early years of his presidency, Donald Trump had adopted a political style that flaunted transgressive behavior as entertainment in a "heavily mediatized public sphere" (Hall, Goldstein, and Ingram 2016, 75). His performative stagecraft epitomized excess, exaggeration, and hyperbole in language and action. Trump retained this form of showmanship through the end of his presidency. Central to the initial success of this public media president were his "derisive uses of humor, vulgarity, and body gesture" (Goldstein and Hall 2017, 398). The grotesque theatrics of blood, sex, and genitalia emerged as ingredients of political satire, public comedy, and as such carnivalesque entertainment, as Bakhtin (1984) might have concluded. Posing as a "man of the people," defying political correctness by cyberbullying, menstrual shaming, and sexually predatory behavior, Trump's disruptive obsessions directed popular attention to the nether-regions of the body. The focus on corporality emerged as a comic interlude in politics, infused by intensifying popular excitement about the president's unending carnal desires. Trump's physicality (hands, hair, buttocks, penis, sexuality, obesity, orange skin) garnered notice as a cipher of spectacle, dramatizing a masculine "wilding" or unruly manliness. American political culture had become saturated by body talk. However, as I have suggested throughout this chapter, the focus of political discourse took a radical turn during the final years of the president's term in office. Although the theatrics of the body persisted, we observed a shift in the cultural discourse of US politics: from sex with women to love-bonds with other strongmen (bromance), and from male desires of the flesh to a national politics of race (Black Lives Matter), violence, and border enclosure.

Political power, I have suggested, operates through the senses. The microphysics of statehood enter into a visual, acoustic, spatial, and even tactile or tangible presence, magnifying "the citizens' pleasure" by a multitude of interventions in public life, including the spectacular productions of ritual, media, and violence (Trommler 1998, 27). In these arenas of power, in turn, political ideation "presses close to its object," to borrow the words of Adorno, "as if through touching, smelling, tasting, it wanted to transform itself" (1970, 11). Thus, even when the state circulates in the political imagination of its subjects as discourse or "ideological fantasy" (Žižek 1989), it incites apprehension through sensuous practices. Since, as Adorno asserted, "the act of cognition itself has a somatic character" (Buck-Morss 1977, 83, 248 n14), we need to rethink the work of nationalization in terms of a dialogic social praxis, which treats the subjects' reflective capacity as firmly embodied in lived experience. In his work on *Phantom Communities*, Scott Durham (1998), however, warned us that "the coherence of this experience" may be intrinsically problematic:

> [Sensual realism] emerges from heterogeneous domains of social practice that, in their stubbornly serial and fragmentary character, may lead us to doubt our capacity as individual or collective subjects to articulate, in a coherent narrative or representational schema, our shifting relations to these ubiquitous images [and sensory fields] as we pass from one sphere or cultural subsystem to the next.
>
> *(3)*

Yet this very incoherence of sensual fields is precisely matched to the operations of state power. As Navaro-Yashin observed, the state is not a fixed or static entity; rather, like a phantom, it haunts a multitude of sites, it "appears in many guises and constantly transfigures itself" (2002, 2). This figure of the *flexible* state, taken together with the uneven adhesion or union of sensual and emotive fields, suggests that the totalization of national culture and, likewise, the production of normative subjectivities are never unproblematic—and in fact can never be completely achieved. For the spaces of everyday experience also contain a nation's "interruptive interiority," as Homi Bhabha (1994, 310) phrased it, a disjunctive or incongruous plurality of political experiences from which alternatives of sense-making and interpretation may emerge. This fissure in the social fabric of the nation's interior—this paradox of non-integration—opens a potentially antagonistic space that is only in part sutured by state ideology (Žižek 1989). Or, stated differently, the work of nationalization reveals an ongoing "constitutive incompletion," as Ernesto Laclau (1989, xiv) phrased it, which introduces into the very architecture of political space certain conditions of possibility; these may, as I have argued, engender alternative constructions of political identity or discursive hegemonic rearticulations, and a range of national passions.

The "nation," as Max Weber stated long ago, "is a community of sentiment manifest in a state" (1994, 25). But the formation of national sentiments or the love of a country is neither inevitable, self-apparent, nor natural. Political passions are tied to a cultural history of the senses, to specific forms of governing, to technologies of communication, and to the making of subjectivities under neoliberal capitalism. An analysis of contemporary statehood must turn its eye toward "the nervous system" (Taussig 1992), that is, the sensuous realism of *feeling the nation*, as I have argued, which brings into play the entire sensorium of the body, including the micro-politics of sense experience as well as the polymorphous incitements to affectivity that are evident in the making of political subjects. In other words, my focus on the sensual life of the state advocates further scrutiny of the somaticity—the somatosensuous *gestalt*—of nation-states and the formative moments of political experience. In Trump's America, with the notable intensification of state violence, assaults on democracy, and exclusionary governing practices, we witnessed ironically the unprecedented formation of a politics of love and national belonging. A persistently "violent fantasist," infused by a misogynist, racializing, and "toxic masculinity" (Zirin 2017), the US president emerged as a head of state who had succumbed to the fascist allure. Yet even after George Floyd's killing, in the face of a violent death, and from the voices of political protest, the late Representative John Lewis (MSNBC 2020) taught us that there is an alternative vision of "family" and belonging, whether within the affective nation-state or the world community, whereby we are unified, in our diversity, by sentiments and principles of humanitarian love:

> It is a sad time. It is a very dark hour for all Americans. We must continue to teach the way of peace, the way of love, the philosophy and the discipline of non-violence. And never, ever give up on our brothers and sisters. We are one people. We are one family. We all live in the same House. Not just the American House. But the World House. This is the only House that we have. If we cannot save this House for our children, and their children, there would not be any place for any of us to live and to survive.

Acknowledgments

A short text excerpt on racialization in section "Rethinking the state of whiteness: national politics from a global perspective" draws on my earlier publication: Linke (2014) "Racializing Cities, Naturalizing Space," published by Antipode, vol. 46, issue 5, pp. 1222–1239 (www.blackwell-synergy.com). Copyright @ Uli Linke. I gratefully acknowledge the journal, its editorial board, and Blackwell Publishing. My attempts to analyze the "fascist allure" of the Trump presidency rework some of the material from my journal article: Linke (2006) "Contact Zones: Rethinking the Sensual Life of the State," published in Anthropological Theory, vol. 6, issue 2, pp. 205–225. Copyright @ Sage Publication. The permission to use this material is gratefully acknowledged.

References

Adorno, Theodor W. 1970. *Über Walter Benjamin*. Frankfurt: Suhrkamp Verlag.
Alexander, Michelle. 2020. *The New Jim Crow: Mass Incarceration in the Age of Color Blindness*. New York: New Press.
Anderson, Benedict. 1991. *Imagined Communities*, 2nd ed. London: Verso.
AP News. 2018. "Trump on Kim: Tough Talk... 'And Then We Fell in Love'." *Associated Press*, September 30, 2018. https://www.apnews.com/4d56f6e8f99d4eefb2f22b7a6dd072d0.
Appadurai, Arjun. 2003. "Sovereignty without Territoriality." In *The Anthropology of Place and Space*, edited by Setha M. Low and D. Lawrence-Zúñiga, 337–349. Oxford: Blackwell.
Arendt, Hannah. 1964. *Eichmann in Jerusalem: A Report on the Banality of Evil*, rev. and enlarged edition. New York: Viking Press.
Baker, Peter, Zolan Kanno-Youngs, and Monica Davey. 2020. "Trump Threatens to Send Federal Law Enforcement Forces to More Cities." *New York Times*, July 21, 2020. https://www.nytimes.com/2020/07/20/us/politics/trump-chicago-portland-federal-agents.html.
Baudrillard, Jean. 1995. "On Consumer Society." In *Rethinking the Subject*, edited by James D. Faubion, 193–203. Boulder: Westview Press.
Bauman, Zygmunt. 1989. *Modernity and the Holocaust*. Cambridge: Polity Press.
Benjamin, Walter. 1983. *Charles Baudelaire*. Translated by Harry Zohn. London: Verso.
Berlant, Lauren. 1991. *The Anatomy of National Fantasy*. Chicago: University of Chicago Press.
Bhabha, Homi K., ed. 1990. *The Nation and Narration*. London: Routledge.
Bhabha, Homi. 1994. "Narrating the Nation." In *Nationalism*, edited by John Hutchinson and Anthony D. Smith, 306–312. Oxford: Oxford University Press.
Bobo, Lawrence D. 2017. "Racism in Trump's America: Reflections on Culture, Sociology, and the 2016 US Presidential Election." *British Journal of Sociology* 68: 85–104. https://doi.org/10.1111/1468-4446.12324.
Bolton, John. 2020. *The Room Where It Happened: A White House Memoir*. New York: Simon & Schuster.
Bonilla-Silva, Eduardo. 2019. "Racists, 'Class Anxieties,' Hegemonic Racism, and Democracy in Trump's America." *Social Currents* 6 (1): 14–31. https://doi.org/10.1177/2329496518804558.
Braverman, David. 2019. "Our Man in London, Part 2." *The Daily Parker*, June 4, 2019. https://www.thedailyparker.com/post/2019/06/04/our-man-in-london-part-2.
Brubaker, Rogers. 1998. "Myths and Misconceptions in the Study of Nationalism." In *The State of the Nation*, edited by John A. Hall, 272–306. Cambridge: Cambridge University Press.
Buck-Morss, Susan. 1977. *The Origin of Negative Dialectics*. New York: The Free Press.
———. 2000. *Dreamworlds and Catastrophe*. Cambridge: MIT Press.
Butler, Paul. 2018. *Chokehold: Policing Black Men*. New York: New Press.
Butler, Judith. 2020. *The Force of Nonviolence: An Ethico-Political Bind*. London: Verso.
Cabrera, Cristina. 2019. "Beyond Blimps: How Trump's 'Crowds of Well Wishers' Are Trolling POTUS in London." *TPM Media*, June 3, 2019. https://talkingpointsmemo.com/news/trump-london-troll-protests-projections-blimp.
Calhoun, Craig. 1997. *Nationalism*. Minneapolis: University of Minnesota Press.
Camera, Lauren. 2018. "Trump Floats 'Bill of Love' to Fix DACA." *US News*, January 9, 2018. https://www.usnews.com/news/politics/articles/2018-01-09/trump-floats-bill-of-love-to-fix-daca.

Carruthers, Charlene. 2019. *Unapologetic: A Black, Queer, and Feminist Mandate for Radical Movements.* Boston: Beacon Press.

Cassirer, Ernst. 1946. *The Myth of the State.* New Haven, CT: Yale University Press.

Cathey, Libby. 2020. "Trump Denies WH Asked about Adding Him to Mount Rushmore, Then Calls It a 'Good Idea'." *ABC News*, August 10, 2020. https://abcnews.go.com/Politics/trump-denies-wh-asked-adding-mount-rushmore-calls/story?id=72281768.

Chakrabarty, Dipesh. 2000. *Provincializing Europe: Postcolonial Thought and Historical Difference.* Princeton: Princeton University Press.

Comaroff, Jean, and John L. Comaroff. 2016. *Theory from the South.* New York: Routledge.

Connerton, Paul. 1989. *How Societies Remember.* Cambridge: Cambridge University Press.

Davis, Julie Hirschfeld, Sheryl Gay Stolberg, and Thomas Kaplan. 2018. "Trump Alarms Lawmakers with Disparaging Words for Haiti and Africa." *New York Times*, January 11, 2018. https://www.nytimes.com/2018/01/11/us/politics/trump-shithole-countries.html.

Dawsey, Josh. 2018. "Trump Derides Protections for Immigrants from 'Shithole' Countries." *Washington Post*, January 12, 2018. https://www.washingtonpost.com/politics/trump-attacks-protections-for-immigrants-from-shithole-countries-in-oval-office-meeting/2018/01/11/bfc0725c-f711-11e7-91af-31ac729add94_story.html.

De Grazia, Sebastian. 1989. *Machiavelli in Hell.* Princeton: Princeton University Press.

Durham, Scott. 1998. *Phantom Communities: The Simulacrum and the Limits of Postmodernism.* Stanford: Stanford University Press.

Ehrlich, Jamie. 2020. "New York Times: White House Reached Out to South Dakota Governor About Adding Trump to Mount Rushmore." *CNN*, August 9, 2020. https://www.cnn.com/2020/08/09/politics/mount-rushmore-trump-southdakota/index.html.

Eley, Geoff, and Ronald Grigor Suny. 1996. "Introduction." In *Becoming National*, edited by Geoff Eley and Ronald Grigor Suny, 3–38. New York: Oxford University Press.

Fassin, Didier. 2012. *Humanitarian Reason: A Moral History of the Present.* Berkeley: University of California Press.

Feffer, John. 2019. "Trump's Bromance with Kim Is Gross, but Let the Love Letters Continue." *Foreign Policy in Focus*, March 5, 2019. https://fpif.org/trumps-bromance-with-kim-is-gross-but-let-the-love-letters-continue/.

Feldman, Allen. 2015. *Archives of the Insensible: Of War, Photopolitics, and Dead Memory.* Chicago: University of Chicago Press.

Feldman, Ilana. 2018. *Life Lived in Relief: Humanitarian Predicaments and Palestinian Refugee Politics.* Berkeley: University of California Press.

Finchelstein, Federico. 2020. "Trump's Mount Rushmore Speech Is the Closest He's Come to Fascism." *Foreign Policy*, July 8, 2020. https://foreignpolicy.com/2020/07/08/trumps-mount-rushmore-speech-fascist-politics-zeev-sternhell/.

Foucault, Michel. 1983. "Afterword: The Subject and Power." In *Michel Foucault: Beyond Structuralism and Hermeneutics*, edited by Paul Rabinow and Hubert L. Dreyfus, 2nd ed., 208–226. Chicago: University of Chicago Press.

Gessen, Masha. 2020. "Donald Trump's Fascist Performance." *New Yorker*, June 3, 2020. https://www.newyorker.com/news/our-columnists/donald-trumps-fascist-performance?utm_source=onsite-share&utm_medium=email&utm_campaign=onsite-share&utm_brand=the-new-yorker.

Gilroy, Paul. 2003. "'Where Ignorant Armies Clash by Night': Homogeneous Community and the Planetary Aspect." *International Journal of Cultural Studies* 6 (3): 261–276. https://doi.org/10.1177/13678779030063002.

———. 2004. *Between Camps: Nations, Cultures, and the Allure of Race*. London: Routledge.
Glaude, Eddie S., Jr. 2020. *Begin Again: James Baldwin's America and Its Urgent Lessons for Our Own*. New York: Random House.
Goldberg, David T. 2009. *The Threat of Race*. Oxford: Blackwell.
Goldstein, Donna M., and Kira Hall. 2017. "Postelection Surrealism and Nostalgic Racism in the Hands of Donald Trump." *HAU: Journal of Ethnographic Theory* 7 (1): 397–406. https://doi.org/10.14318/hau7.1.026.
Graham, Stephen. 2006. "Cities and the 'War on Terror.'" *International Journal of Urban and Regional Research* 30 (2): 255–276. https://doi.org/10.1111/j.1468-2427.2006.00665.x.
Groppe, Maureen. "'He Does It for You': Jill Biden Gives Personal Speech as Her Husband Receives DNC Nomination." *USA Today*, August 18, 2020. https://www.usatoday.com/story/news/politics/elections/2020/08/18/jill-biden-speech-dnc-convention-joe-biden-nomination/3396871001/.
Hall, Kira, Donna M. Goldstein, and Matthew Bruce Ingram. 2016. "The Hands of Donald Trump: Entertainment, Gesture, Spectacle." *HAU: Journal of Ethnographic Theory* 6 (2): 71–100. https://doi.org/10.14318/hau6.2.009.
Hall, Stuart. 2000. "The Local and the Global." In *Culture, Globalization, and the World-System*, edited by Anthony D. King, 19–39. Minneapolis: University of Minnesota Press.
Hannah-Jones, Nikole. 2018. "Taking Freedom: Yes, Black America Fears the Police. Here's Why." *Pacific Standard*, May 8, 2018. https://psmag.com/social-justice/why-black-america-fears-the-police.
Hannon, Elliot. 2018. "Trump Praises North Korean Dictator Kim Jong-Un: 'He Wrote Me Beautiful Letters…We Fell in Love'." *Slate*, September 30, 2018. https://slate.com/news-and-politics/2018/09/trump-praises-kim-jong-un-north-korea-we-fell-in-love-video.html.
Hardin, Jessica A. 2019. *Faith and the Pursuit of Health*. New Brunswick, NJ: Rutgers University Press.
Hinton, Alexander Laban. 2018. *The Justice Façade: Trials of Transition in Cambodia*. Oxford: Oxford University Press.
Hinton, Devon E., and Alexander L. Hinton. 2015. *Genocide and Mass Violence: Memory, Symptom, and Recovery*. Cambridge: Cambridge University Press.
Katz, Gregory, Darlene Superville, and Deb Riechmann. 2019. "Trump Says He Would Have 'Sued and Settled' If He Were Negotiating Brexit." *PBS News Hour*, June 4, 2019. https://www.pbs.org/newshour/world/watch-live-trump-and-may-holdnews-conference-in-london.
Korte, Gregory, and Deirdre Shesgreen. 2018. "In Extraordinary Public Negotiation with Congress, Trump Promises to Sign DACA Bill." *USA Today*, January 9, 2018. https://www.usatoday.com/story/news/politics/2018/01/09/trump-meets-congressional-leaders-immigration/1016369001/.
Kray, Christine A., Tamar W. Carroll, and Hinda Mandell, eds. 2018. *Nasty Women and Bad Hombres: Gender and Race in the 2016 US Presidential Election*. Rochester, NY: University of Rochester Press.
Kroeber, Alfred L. 1917. "The Superorganic." *American Anthropologist* 19 (2): 163–213. https://www.jstor.org/stable/660754.
Laclau, Ernesto. 1989. "Preface." In *The Sublime Object of Ideology*, edited by Slavoj Žižek, ix–xv. London: Verso.
Lebron, Christopher J. 2017. *The Making of Black Lives Matter: A Brief History of an Idea*. New York: Oxford University Press.

Linke, Uli. 1999. *German Bodies: Race and Representation after Hitler.* New York: Routledge.
———. 2006. "Contact Zones: Rethinking the Sensual Life of the State." *Anthropological Theory* 6 (2): 205–225. https://doi.org/10.1177/1463499606065037.
———. 2014. "Racializing Cities, Naturalizing Space: The Seductive Appeal of Iconicities of Dispossession." *Antipode* 46 (5): 1222–1239. https://doi.org/10.1111/anti.12012.
Luke, Timothy W. 2004. "Everyday Technics as Extraordinary Threats: Urban Technostructures and Non-Places in Terrorist Actions." In *Cities, War, and Terrorism*, edited by Stephen Graham, 120–136. Oxford: Blackwell. https://doi.org/10.1002/9780470753033.ch7.
Manchester, Julia. 2018. "Trump's Comments on Falling in Love with Kim Jong Un 'Shocking and Appalling,' Says Conservative Writer." *The Hill*, September 30, 2018. https://thehill.com/hilltv/rising/409245-trumps-comments-on-falling-in-love-with-kim-jong-un-are-shocking-and-appalling.
Mandell, Hinda, ed. 2019. *Crafting Dissent: Handicraft as Protest from the American Revolution to the Pussyhats.* London: Rowman & Littlefield.
Maskovsky, Jeff, and Sophie Bjork-James, eds. 2020. *Beyond Populism: Angry Politics and the Twilight of Neoliberalism.* Morgantown, WV: West Virginia University Press.
Maxwell, Zerlina. 2020. *The End of White Politics: How to Heal Our Liberal Divide.* New York: Hachette Books.
Mbembe, Achille. 2001. *On the Postcolony.* Berkeley: University of California Press.
———. 2018. "The Idea of a Borderless World." *Africa Is a Country*, November 11, 2018. https://africasacountry.com/2018/11/the-idea-of-a-borderless-world.
Merica, Dan. 2018. "Trump: Immigration Bill Should Be a 'Bill of Love'." *CNN*, January 9, 2018. https://www.cnn.com/2018/01/09/politics/donald-trump-bill-of-love-immigration/index.html.
MSNBC. 2020. "Civil Rights Icon Rep. John Lewis Calls for Love, Peace, and Nonviolence." Youtube.com, May 30, 2020. https://www.youtube.com/watch?v=BQlDXo0oEaI.
Nairn, Tom, and Paul James. 2005. *Global Matrix: Nationalism, Globalism, and State-Terrorism.* Ann Arbor, MI: Pluto Press.
Navaro-Yashin, Yael. 2002. *Faces of the State.* Princeton: Princeton University Press.
Naylor, Brian. 2018. "Trump Calls for 'Bill of Love' Allowing DACA Recipients to Remain." *NPR*, January 9, 2018. https://www.npr.org/2018/01/09/576824141/trump-calls-for-bill-of-love-allowing-daca-recipients-to-remain.
Neale, Spencer. 2019. "Out of Love: Trump Defends Giuliani Ukraine Trip in Search of Biden Dirt." *Washington Examiner*, December 17, 2019. https://www.washingtonexaminer.com/news/out-of-love-trump-defends-giuliani-ukraine-trip-in-search-of-biden-dirt.
O'Donnell, Lawrence. 2020a. "The Last Word: Prayer Breakfast Rant Shows Trump Doesn't Understand What Love Is." *MSNBC*, February 6, 2020. http://www.msnbc.com/transcripts/the-last-word/2020-02-06.
———. 2020b. "The Last Word." *MSNBC*, April 20, 2020. https://youtu.be/qWKjXXs3tJo.
Omi, Michael, and Howard Winant. 1994. *Racial Formation in the United States*, 2nd ed. New York: Routledge.
Parry, Benita. 1993. "Overlapping Territories and Intertwined Histories." In *Edward Said: A Critical Reader*, edited by Michael Sprinker, 19–47. Oxford: Blackwell.
Peeples, Lynne. 2020. "What the Data Say About Police Brutality and Racial Bias—and Which Reforms Might Work." *Nature*, June 19, 2020. https://www.nature.com/articles/d41586-020-01846-z.

Prose, Francine. 2020. "Watching Trump's Paramilitary Squads Descend on Portland, It's Hard Not to Feel Doom." *The Guardian*, July 20, 2020. https://www.theguardian.com/commentisfree/2020/jul/20/trump-shock-troops-portland-doomed.

Rabinow, Paul, and Hubert L. Dreyfus. 1983. *Michel Foucault: Beyond Structuralism and Hermeneutics*, 2nd ed. Chicago: University of Chicago Press.

Radcliffe-Brown, Alfred Reginald. 1940. "Preface." In *African Political Systems*, edited by Meyer Fortes, xi–xxiii. London: Oxford University Press.

Ransby, Barbara. 2018. *Making All Black Lives Matter: Reimagining Freedom in the Twenty-First Century*. Berkeley: University of California Press.

Robben, Antonius C. G. M. 2018. *Argentina Betrayed: Memory, Mourning, and Accountability*. Philadelphia: University of Pennsylvania Press.

Rogers, Katie. 2020. "Most Events in the Lincoln Memorial Are Banned. Trump Got an Exception." *New York Times*, May 4, 2020. https://www.nytimes.com/2020/05/04/us/politics/trump-lincoln-memorial.html.

Rucker, Philip, and Josh Dawsey. 2019. "'We Fell in Love': Trump and Kim Shower Praise, Stroke Egos on Path to Nuclear Negotiations." *Washington Post*, February 25, 2019. https://www.washingtonpost.com/politics/we-fell-in-love-trump-and-kim-shower-praise-stroke-egos-on-path-to-nuclear-negotiations/2019/02/24/46875188-3777-11e9-854a-7a14d7fec96a_story.html.

Ryan, Missy, and Dan Lamothe. 2020. "Trump Administration to Significantly Expand Military Response in Washington Amid Unrest." *Washington Post*, June 1, 2020. https://www.washingtonpost.com/national-security/defense-secretary-pledges-pentagon-support-to-help-dominate-the-battlespace-amid-unrest/2020/06/01/7c5b4630-a449-11ea-8681-7d471bf20207_story.html.

Samuels, Brett. 2019. "Trump Dismisses UK Protests as 'Fake News', Turns Down Meeting With Corbyn." *The Hill*, June 4, 2019. https://thehill.com/homenews/administration/446813-trump-dismisses-uk-protests-as-fake-news.

Scott, James C. 1998. *Seeing Like a State*. New Haven, CT: Yale University Press.

Simon, Scott. 2018. "Donald Trump 'Fell in Love' with Kim Jong Un." *NPR*, October 6, 2018. https://www.npr.org/2018/10/06/654857533/opinion-donald-trump-fell-in-love-with-kim-jong-un.

Smith, Aidan. 2018. *Gender, Heteronormativity, and the American Presidency*. New York: Routledge.

Soboroff, Jacob. 2020. *Separated: Inside an American Tragedy*. New York: HarperCollins.

Stoller, Paul. 1995. *Embodying Colonial Memories*. New York: Routledge.

Sullivan, Andrew. 2017. "Trump's Mindless Nihilism." *New York Magazine: Intelligencer*, October 13, 2017. https://nymag.com/intelligencer/2017/10/andrew-sullivan-trump-mindless-nihilism.html.

Taussig, Michael. 1992. *The Nervous System*. New York: Routledge.

———. 1997. *The Magic of the State*. New York: Routledge.

———. 1999. *Defacement*. Stanford: Stanford University Press.

Thomas, Deborah A., and Kamari Maxine Clarke. 2006. "Introduction." In *Globalization and Race*, edited by Kamari Maxine Clarke and Deborah A. Thomas, 1–34. Durham: Duke University Press.

Ticktin, Miriam I. 2011. *Casualties of Care: Immigration and the Politics of Humanitarianism in France*. Berkeley: University of California Press.

Tilly, Charles. 1984. *Big Structures, Large Processes, Huge Comparisons*. New York: Russell Sage Foundation.

Trommler, Frank. 1998. "The Historical Invention and Modern Reinvention of Two National Identities." In *Identity and Intolerance*, edited by Norbert Finzsch and Dietmar Schirmer, 21–42. Cambridge: Cambridge University Press.

Walzer, Michael. 1967. "On the Role of Symbolism in Political Thought." *Political Science Quarterly* 82 (2): 191–204. https://doi.org/10.2307/2147214.

Washington Post Database. 2020. "Police Shootings Database." *Washington Post*. Accessed June 26, 2020. https://www.washingtonpost.com/graphics/investigations/police-shootings-database/.

Washington Post Editorial Board. 2020a. "China Calls Them 'Kindness Students'. They're Actually Victims of Cultural Genocide." *Washington Post*, January 10, 2020. https://www.washingtonpost.com/opinions/global-opinions/china-calls-them-kindness-students-theyre-actually-victims-of-cultural-genocide/2020/01/10/17182d88-3243-11ea-91fd-82d4e04a3fac_story.html.

———. 2020b. "We Knew Trump Didn't Care for Human Rights in China. But This Is a New Low." *Washington Post*, June 20, 2020. https://www.washingtonpost.com/opinions/global-opinions/we-knew-trump-didnt-care-for-human-rights-in-china-but-this-is-a-new-low/2020/06/20/3987731c-b243-11ea-8758-bfd1d045525a_story.html.

Watson, Kathryn. 2019. "Trump Says Giuliani's Work in Ukraine Done 'Out of Love'." *CBS News*, December 16, 2019. https://www.cbsnews.com/news/trump-says-giulianis-work-in-ukraine-done-out-of-love-today-2019-12-16/.

Weber, Max. 1978. *Economy and Society: An Outline of Interpretive Sociology*, translated by Guenther Ross and Claus Wittich. Berkeley: University of California Press.

———. 1994. "The Nation." In *Nationalism*, edited by John Hutchinson and Anthony D. Smith, 21–25. Oxford: Oxford University Press.

Williams, Raymond. 1977. *Marxism and Literature*. Oxford: Oxford University Press.

Winant, Michael. 2001. *The World Is a Ghetto*. New York: Basic Books.

Wolf, Eric R. 2001. *Pathways of Power*. Berkeley: University of California Press.

Woodward, Bob. 2020. *Rage*. New York: Simon and Schuster.

Wootson, Cleve R., Jr. 2020. "'White Power' Video Was a Glimpse into Trump-Era Political Discourse in 'America's Friendliest' Retirement Community." *Washington Post*, July 4, 2020. https://www.washingtonpost.com/politics/white-power-video-was-a-glimpse-into-trump-era-political-discourse-in-americas-friendliest-retirement-community/2020/07/04/0ca405dc-bbc0-11ea-8cf5-9c1b8d7f84c6_story.html.

Zirin, Dave. 2017. "The Fragile, Toxic Masculinity of Donald Trump." *The Nation*, September 24, 2017. https://www.thenation.com/article/archive/the-fragile-toxic-masculinity-of-donald-trump/.

Žižek, Slavoj. 1989. *The Sublime Object of Ideology*. London: Verso.

2
THE GLAMOUR OF IVANKA

White supremacy and the question of women's equality in the Trump administration

Aidan Smith

> Perception is more important than reality. If someone perceives something to be true, it is more important than if it is in fact true. This doesn't mean you should be duplicitous or deceitful, but don't go out of your way to correct a false assumption if it plays to your advantage.
>
> Ivanka Trump, The Trump Card: Playing to Win in Work and Life, 166

Holding the title of "advisor to the president," Ivanka Trump occupied an unfamiliar space in the White House and the popular imagination during her father's time in office. From Alice Roosevelt to Lynda Bird Johnson to Patti Davis, other adult first daughters have gained notoriety for their fashion choices, pursuit of higher education, or critiques of their father's presidency, but no other daughter has taken on a role as a policy-maker or spokesperson for the administration. Coupled with the inclusion of her husband, Jared Kushner, among the president's senior staff, the pair raised questions about the role of the first family in the development of public policy at home and abroad. Ivanka Trump's role in her father's administration was simultaneously complicated and simple. As with all first children, she stood as a marker of the candidate's appropriate performance of reproductive heteronormativity, a normalized identity that privileges straightness and marginalizes queerness (Smith 2018). Her presence on the campaign trail signaled to would-be voters that this twice-divorced, thrice-married billionaire New Yorker was still a typical dad who had earned the love and support of his oldest daughter. Ivanka, along with her siblings, even earned recognition from her father's general election opponent, Hillary Clinton, as evidence of his humanity in spite of his brutal rhetoric. When asked during the final debate in 2016 what she admired about Donald Trump, Clinton stated that one of Trump's

DOI: 10.4324/9781003034810-2

few saving graces was his parenting skills. "I respect his children," she said. "His children are incredibly able and devoted, and I think that says a lot about Donald" (Allen 2016).

Yet what do we make of the glamorous Ivanka Trump herself, the former model raised in a penthouse apartment as the favorite daughter of a real estate mogul? "Glamour" offers a useful frame to consider Ms. Trump's role in her father's campaign as well as his administration (Figure 2.1). The etymology of the word offers a more nuanced understanding than the contemporary usage implying beauty, femininity, and fashion-sense. Instead, "glamour's" original meaning comes from an old Scots usage, meaning an illusion or magic spell (Merriam-Webster 2020). A "glamour" was a false representation of reality, generally cast by a sorcerer or magician to make something more appealing or attractive to the unwitting dupe. Stephen Gundle, author of *Glamour: A History*, wrote of the power and utility of glamour: "Glamour is a weapon and a protective coating, a screen on which an exterior personality can be built to deceive, delight, and bewitch" (2008, 4). I argue that it is this deception and bewitchment that has been intrinsic to Ivanka Trump's engagement in politics. Her alleged investment in women's empowerment provided cover to an administration involved in thwarting feminist policies for reproductive justice and transgender rights; her calls for expanded parental leave diverted attention from abusive child detention practices on the border; her brand of entrepreneurial "lean in" feminism ignored the exploitative labor practices in the Chinese factories that produced the clothes and shoes that bore her name.

FIGURE 2.1 Seated next to her father, Advisor to the President Ivanka Trump delivers remarks at the American Workforce policy advisory board meeting, June 26, 2020.

Credit: Tia Dufour/The White House.

The glamour spell that Ivanka Trump cast in her fashionably feminine attire, public motherhood presented via social media, and childlike deference to her father made it easy to forget the vast profits she made through shady real estate endeavors, among other profit streams that have yet to be made public.

Ivanka Trump is not a vacant vessel or a bobblehead devoid of her own strategy. She pivoted strategically to avoid confrontation and deflect responsibility from the cruelty perpetrated by her father and his administration like a chameleon that shifts to fill the need of the moment. A summer 2019 opinion poll revealed the appeal of a pretty young woman with apparently no real opinions: she had higher net favorability ratings than her father in Pennsylvania, Michigan, and Wisconsin, three crucial battleground states in 2020 (Kwong 2019). In her father's counterhegemonic assault on civil society, Ivanka Trump was a simulacrum, as individuals make whatever meaning of her words and deeds they like. The president's pseudo-wife or his daughter? Feminist or orthodox traditionalist? Jew or Gentile? Maternal figure or member of an authoritarian regime that divides families? A woman of many names and many identities, born Ivana Marie Trump in 1981, she took the name Yael Esther Kushner upon her conversion to Judaism in 2008. She is now known simply as Ivanka, one singular moniker for a woman who has become many things to many people. The deception inherent in the glamour spell is what makes it most dangerous, particularly for those implicated in the policies Ivanka Trump made her signature causes.

This chapter describes Ivanka Trump's engagement in the Trump administration as not only a beautiful feminine tool to further her father's initiatives but also as a cunning manipulator of her public image in pursuit of her own goals. Her glamorous personal style is marked by designer clothes and stilettos, perfect blonde hair, and immaculate makeup. To this, she added the affectation of a maternal identity performed on social media through photography of her young children and wealthy, attractive husband. What is real and what is illusion? Ms. Trump has weaponized her femininity to assuage accusations of racism and misogyny against her father's administration while simultaneously supporting policies intrinsically entwined with white supremacy and women's social and political marginalization. I argue that these efforts are more sinister than simply the cultivation of a pleasant public persona, but instead serve as the foundation for a larger effort to build a Trumpian political dynasty with Ivanka Trump and her husband, Jared Kushner, at the forefront.

This chapter is a discourse analysis of Ivanka Trump's engagement with both the 2016 campaign and the Trump administration. An analysis of her speeches, her media interviews, and her social media posts reveals a rhetoric that actively works to conceal the horrors of her father's public policies under a gauzy swath of platitudes and glitzy femininity. From her word choices to her strategic use of visual semiotics, she worked to use her normative femininity to maintain a personal brand that concealed her active engagement in graft and authoritarianism while simultaneously providing the Trump administration with a female surrogate whose silence and deflection defended policies of exclusion and cruelty.

Donald the revolutionary, Ivanka the conventional

Donald Trump's rise to political power is an ideal example of resistance against what his supporters viewed as a cultural hegemony of progressive politics that included space for women, gender minorities, and people of color. His 2016 campaign waged a war of counterhegemony against civil society via every modern method of communication available, offering a modern example of political theorist Antonio Gramsci's understanding of cultural politics. "In politics," he wrote, "the siege is a reciprocal one, despite all appearances, and the mere fact that the ruler has to muster all his resources, demonstrates how seriously he takes his adversary" (Gramsci 2014, 230). Ivanka's participation in her father's revolution provides evidence of an understanding of his administration's precarity as she nimbly tried to be all things to all people, traditionalist and feminist, Jew and Gentile, daughter and advisor to the commander-in-chief.

Instead of Gramsci's "war of maneuver," an outright physical conflict between classes featuring revolution, coercion, and coup, Trump positioned the mythical working, white middle-class as the subordinate group suffering from oppression, thereby strategically waging a "war of position." The 2016 electoral race became a struggle to gain influence and power through means of persuasion and rhetoric against what Donald Trump and his voters perceived as an oppressive regime by attacking its credibility ("fake news") and authority (with his refusal to submit tax returns, abide by the emoluments clause of the Constitution, and divest himself from his businesses). The theme of his outsider run was a push against what the president would call "political correctness," which he would counter by speaking openly and using insulting nicknames. Trump was nothing if not a disruptor, subverting norms among his own party as well as that of his Democratic challenger. Running on a claim to "drain the swamp," Trump defeated 16 primary contenders as well as his Democratic opponent (a woman), and his victory in each of these contests signaled what Gramsci would call evidence of desire for revolution among the constituents of the body-politic.

Ivanka Trump's outsized role in her father's campaign and administration was but another weapon in the Trump campaign's war of position, one that worked against a feminism that vigorously demanded humanity and equality for women. Ivanka's perpetually pleasant demeanor and seeming naiveté made her a perfect weapon in the push against the perceived hegemony of progressive politics. A culture war has different battlefields than a revolution, using "extremely complex mediums, diverse institutions, and constantly changing processes" (Buttigieg 1995, 7). I argue that Ivanka Trump has been but one of these complex mediums through which the political right worked to subvert what they perceived as the cultural hegemony of an America that increasingly acknowledged the claims for status of women and people of color. Her performed identity as a woman who claimed to be a feminist (when convenient) was but another glamour deployed to provide cover for brutality and cruelty in the guise of woman's empowerment.

Further, for those not entirely comfortable with the revolution anchored in cruelty, Ivanka Trump's familiar, feminine face worked to assuage claims of her father's misogyny and white supremacy in a number of ways, simultaneously strengthening her possible pursuit of elected office with the Republican base and negating any possibility of redemption with the left's resistance movement. Ivanka has attempted to function rhetorically as a normalizing force, simultaneously professing to advocate for equal pay, childcare, and gender equality while undermining real women and children subject to the implementation of the administration's punitive policies. When her father's first political move, Executive Order 13769, titled "Protecting the Nation from Foreign Terrorist Entry into the United States" (otherwise known as the "Muslim ban" because it limited travel for those coming from Muslim-majority countries), Ivanka said nothing. When a "zero tolerance" policy on immigration was implemented in 2018 at the southern border that resulted in the separation of children from their families, Ivanka posted images of herself in a warm embrace with her young son (McCarthy 2018). On December 22, 2019, in the same month that the Food and Drug Administration announced it was cutting nutrition benefits in the SNAP program to over 700,000 Americans living in poverty (USDA 2019), she tweeted, "Today marks 2 years since @POTUS signed the Tax Cuts and Jobs Act. Our pro-family, anti-poverty reforms are lifting all Americans!" with a link to a stylized video with quick cuts of news outlets reporting on the growing stock market and industrial opportunities, backed by a swelling orchestral score (@IvankaTrump). Apparently "all Americans" did not include those who needed food assistance. As these examples demonstrate, Ivanka actively ignored the punitive policies of the Trump administration or worked to conceal them under marketing tactics and a purported investment in women and children.

In the Trump presidency, his daughter served as one pillar of his administration's efforts to construct a nation that rewarded whiteness and feminine submissiveness. She reminded his conservative base of an investment in those womanly traits that allegedly "make American great again": a beautiful, compliant young mother who posted images of her children and pets on Instagram, uninvolved with the ugliness of policy-making. Yet for those in search of a liberated feminist entrepreneur, perhaps those white women voters that won Trump the presidency in 2016, Ivanka was the author of *Women Who Work: Rewriting the Rules for Success* (2017), a guidebook for those who aspired to have it all, wielding her high heels and highlighted blonde hair to affect an aura of idealized white femininity that entitled her to a place among the leaders of the world.

Daughter and diplomat

Ivanka Trump has had no professional experience beyond involvement in her family's corporate or entertainment enterprises. She has an undergraduate degree in business administration, but no studies in public policy, political science, or international affairs. Her foray into politics as her father's representative embodied what Andi Zeisler (2016) has dubbed "marketplace feminism": "While feminist movements seek to change systems, marketplace feminism prioritizes individuals. The wingwoman of neoliberalism, marketplace feminism's focus is on casting systemic issues as personal ones and cheerily dispensing commercial fixes for them" (255). Bluntly put, the solution to gender oppression can be found through consumption, a tactic that aligned perfectly with what Ivanka Trump had to offer the nation's women. She was an entrepreneur that leveraged name recognition gained on her father's reality television program to sell moderately priced women's work wear, shoes, and jewelry. Her brand communicated that hoary trope of the effortless perfection possible for those who wanted to have it all through the sensible purchase of affordable sheath dresses and pumps. In July 2018, Ivanka folded her namesake brand, not citing lagging sales or ethical concerns about her having a role in both this corporate entity and the executive branch, but instead affirming her transition into politics. She said:

> After 17 months in Washington, I do not know when or if I will ever return to the business but I do know that my focus for the foreseeable future will be the work I am doing here in Washington, so making this decision now is the only fair outcome for my team and partners.
>
> *(Abrams 2018)*

Though perhaps the marketplace was saturated with Ivanka's type of feminism, the shuttering of her personal business gestured toward a traditionalist, self-sacrificing femininity that placed the needs of her father, and by extension, the nation's first family, above personal fulfillment and gain.

Beyond providing an anchoring normative gender performance, Ivanka's presence in the West Wing mimicked the role she played on the television program *The Apprentice*, normalizing her role in decision-making and evoking nostalgia for a time when Trump was seen as a harmless huckster instead of a political player. Ivanka began appearing on the program in 2006, sitting in as a judge of the contestants as a member of the "board" that chose a winner each week. Frequently appearing with her brothers, Don Jr. and Eric, as representatives of the Trump Organization, the siblings stood at the side of their father as business leaders and decision-makers, signaling a tight family unit with patriarchal leadership at the center. The program, while successful, was itself an illusion. While Donald Trump presented himself as a real estate titan on the show, he had barely emerged from multiple bankruptcies and failed business endeavors like a modeling agency and a commercial airline. Her presence as an unpaid "advisor" to the president evoked this Hollywood posturing, normalizing the appointed position as a natural progression for the daughter of the then commander-in-chief. Situating the Oval Office as just another branch of the family business also offered cover to Ivanka's real estate developer and former newspaper publisher husband, Jared Kushner. Kushner's position carried more weight than his wife's as he held the title of senior advisor, placing the masculine head of household above his wife in the hierarchy of staff leadership.

Ivanka's unpaid internship: the office of the first family

To serve her father's administration as a woman providing a normative gender performance, Ivanka only needed to be present, and to affirm her father's policy choices by silent consent. Unlike her brothers, who were allegedly removed from policy discussions due to their leadership in the family's business, the Trump Organization, Ivanka functioned both as a marker of her father's parental success and as a pivotal advisor in his administration bent on disrupting the status quo. Her official biography on the White House's website provided a brief job description: "In her role, she focuses on the education and economic empowerment of women and their families as well as job creation and economic growth through workforce development, skills training and entrepreneurship" ("Ivanka Trump" n.d.). Marketplace feminism at its finest, perhaps: "empowerment" could be found through self-improvement, not structural change.

At the 2016 Republican National Convention (RNC), Ivanka's speech declared that her father would be an advocate for working women, particularly mothers:

> As President, my father will change the labor laws that were put into place at a time when women were not a significant portion of the workforce. And he will focus on making quality childcare affordable and accessible for all.
>
> As a mother myself, of three young children, I know how hard it is to work while raising a family. And I also know that I'm far more fortunate than most. American families need relief. Policies that allow women with children to thrive should not be novelties, they should be the norm.
>
> *(Drabold 2016)*

For all of the posturing, Ivanka Trump did not bring about, nor as an "advisor" persuade her father to implement, policies that would have brought these promises to fruition. Instead, there were decisions that jeopardized the health and welfare of women, those with children and without. She remained publicly silent as her father's administration enacted policies that separated women from their children at the border, denied trans people the right to serve their country in the armed forces, reduced the Office of Civil Rights' pursuit of sexual assault cases under Title IX, supported the defunding of Planned Parenthood, and appointed the most conservative judiciary in recent times.

As for those policies she explicitly claimed her father would support, there was little evidence to indicate that he or she had any intention to effect meaningful change for working women. In 2018, Ivanka united with Florida Senator Marco Rubio to develop a paid family leave policy that would draw from an individual's Social Security benefits at the time of retirement. Critics argued the plan would penalize those who could least afford an extended work life. Alan Barber, director of Domestic Policy at The Center for Economic and Policy Research, wrote in *Fortune magazine*,

> The irony is that people with these types of jobs often retire at 62 due to the physical nature of these jobs. As much as we need truly supportive family leave policies, the last thing we need is to have them come at the expense of future well-being in retirement.
>
> *(2018)*

Researchers at the Urban Institute noted that the plan as proposed was also not financially sustainable, putting pressure on an already ailing system. Senior Fellows at the Institute, Melissa M. Favreault and Richard W. Johnson, found: "This increase would permanently reduce participants' monthly Social Security retirement benefits about 3 percent. The proposed program would raise Social Security's annual costs, net of benefit offsets, about 1 percent, worsening the program's financing shortfall" (2018). Further, this model perpetuated a gendered problem implicit within a social safety net interwoven with lifetime earnings. Women typically earn less than men because of the wage gap, and have reduced lifetime earnings because they are more likely to perform unpaid labor as caregivers for family members (Gilbert 2006). Ivanka Trump's solution to parental leave would have compounded these inequities for women.

In 2017, the Trump administration, with the vocal support of Ivanka, eliminated a policy that required employers to report salary data to the Equal Employment Opportunity Commission (EEOC). Proposed in the Obama era, the plan would have required employers with over 100 staff to document how much they paid their workers by their gender, race, and ethnicity. The Trump administration dismantled the policy under the argument that it created an undue burden for businesses; "Ultimately, while I believe the intention was good and agree that pay transparency is important, the proposed policy would not yield the intended results," Ivanka said in a statement. "We look forward to continuing to work with EEOC [the Office of Management and Budget], Congress, and all relevant stakeholders on robust policies aimed at eliminating the gender wage gap," she claimed (Patton 2017). However, without quantitative evidentiary data to support claims of pay disparity, women and other workers faced challenges in bringing forth claims of discrimination.

Beyond data collection policies, Ivanka Trump said nothing about the inequity among her own colleagues. According to an analysis by economist Mark Perry of the American Enterprise Institute, a conservative think tank, the difference between men's and women's salaries almost tripled in the first year of the Trump presidency. A *Washington Post* assessment of the pay gap reported that the 37 percent discrepancy among men and women White House staffers is twice that of the national average of approximately 17 percent, and is wider than the average salary gap in 1980 (Ingraham 2017). As an unpaid advisor, with a reported net worth of over $300 million, Ivanka might need not have personally worried about the working women in the offices next door to her West Wing suite, but as the senior official in charge of such matters, her silence was deafening.

From a *Saturday Night Live* sketch to a *Washington Post* headline mocking Ivanka as "complicit" in the policies of her father's administration, backlash to her role as a surrogate for her father was swift and unrelenting (Rubin 2017). Yet Ivanka Trump was more than complicit with the actions of her father's administration. Instead, her role had been intentionally crafted to enhance her public profile at the expense of explicitly feminist endeavors. Her choices were not naïve or benign, but instead strategically deployed gendered tropes of dutiful daughterhood when pressed on her father's shortcomings. Ivanka dramatically bristled at the claims of complicity, telling CBS's Gayle King in an April 2017 interview that she simply did not understand the basis of such accusations.

> If being complicit is wanting to, is wanting to be a force for good and to make a positive impact then I'm complicit. I don't know that the critics who may say that of me, if they found themselves in this very unique and unprecedented situation that I am now in, would do any differently than I am doing,

she said. She continued:

> So I hope to make a positive impact. I don't know what it means to be complicit, but you know, I hope time will prove that I have done a good job and much more importantly that my father's administration is the success that I know it will be.
>
> *(King 2017)*

Ownership of personal responsibility for abandoning her purported mission for equality was absent, only loyalty to her father was of concern. By not condemning her father, she played her part as a foot soldier in the current war of position, demonstrating what a woman should do in an era that demands retrenchment from a feminism that requires equality and voice. Instead, Ivanka continued to stand by her man, a turn toward the past in a movement that sought to Make America Great Again.

Journalists appeared to understand her role as a daughter was primary over that of senior advisor. *Face the Nation* host Margaret Brennan interviewed Ivanka in December 2019 following the president's first impeachment in the House of Representatives. She posed softball questions like: "What is your dad's mood right now? I mean, he's talking about hurt to your family. Is that the way you feel it? Do you feel it in a personal way?" (CBS News 2019). Instead of engaging her subject with questions about the president's strategy to avoid his removal, Ms. Brennan sought Ms. Trump's insights on emotions as a daughter. Importantly, Ivanka was asked to share not only her father's feelings, but also her own. As she occupied this role of interlocutor, Ivanka Trump took the opportunity to dismiss the impeachment proceedings altogether, reifying sentiment over fact. "He said it didn't even feel like he was being impeached," she responded. What was perceived to be true was more important than what had really happened. Her title might have been "advisor," but by referring to President Trump as "your dad," Brennan acknowledged that this was Ms. Trump's real value as a subject.

As Ivanka occupied two roles at once, she wielded her privilege as not only a daughter but as a mother, two roles easily intelligible to a Republican base looking for traditional femininity in their women leaders. During her RNC speech in 2016, and throughout her time as her father's advisor, Ivanka claimed a maternal privilege common in political discourse. As a mother, her insights were naturalized as always already maternal, anchored in care and compassion for children. As the key advisor on matters concerning women and children, Ivanka was notoriously silent at the height of the controversial policy that forcibly separated nursing infants and disabled children from their mothers until *after* her father signed an executive order effectively ending the practice on June 20, 2018. Just minutes after the order was signed, Ivanka tweeted,

> Thank you @POTUS for taking critical action ending family separation at our border. Congress must now act + find a lasting solution that is consistent with our shared values; the same values that so many come here seeking as they endeavor to create a better life for their families.
>
> *(@Ivanka Trump)*

Ivanka's framing of the issue as a result of Congress's inaction erased the reality that the situation was the result of her father's directives in the first place.

In another era, this familial status of mother and daughter might have made her exempt from the condemnation lobbed at anti-family policies like the separation crisis at the border. However, criticism was harsh and constant, particularly as the first daughter posted images of her own children on her Instagram account, seemingly oblivious to the pain of those impacted by the administration's policies. Comedian Samantha Bee evoked anger when she showed an image of Ivanka holding her youngest child in a warm embrace at the height of the border crisis, vulgarly exhorting Ivanka to do something: "You know, Ivanka, that's a beautiful photo of you and your child, but let me just say, one mother to another: Do something about your dad's immigration practices, you feckless cunt! He listens to you!" Bee later apologized for using the profanity, but not for the sentiment. "I should have known that a potty-mouthed insult would be inherently more interesting to them than juvenile immigration policy," she said (de Moraes 2018).

But Ivanka Trump's seemingly tone-deaf post depicting an intimate moment with her child could be viewed more intentionally as part of a long history of white women's entrenchment in white supremacy. From slavery to lynching to Jim Crow policies, the protection of white women has played a pivotal role in the logic of white supremacy in the United States (Feimster 2009; Ferber 1998; Gilmore 1996). Ivanka's status as a mother was just as crucial to her glamour spell as her clothes, hair, and makeup, which was why she centered her social media accounts on photos of her children and their domestic play. This is significant when considering Ivanka's rhetorical role in the administration, which she herself identified on her social media platforms as "Wife, mother, sister, daughter." She should first be understood in relation to those men in power. Ivanka Trump has been but another white woman furthering white supremacist policies to her own benefit. From her role in the White House to her brand of clothing to her Instagram platform, she reminded the nation that she embodies what historian Hazel Carby would call "the prized objects of the western world" (1996, 110): blonde, thin beauty, enrobed in wealth and privilege, her children virtuous and innocent. Kathleen Blee has written extensively about motherhood and engagement in race-hate movements. Detailing white women's involvement in the Ku Klux Klan, she noted that an individual's investment in the safety of her own children functions as a tool to vilify non-whites. Thusly, it is not all children that benefit from the safety and succor of a maternal figure, only those who fit the white supremacist paradigm. Blee writes,

> 'Good' motherhood can provoke reactionary politics when, as for many in the twentieth century United States, it is defined fairly narrowly, as protecting and providing for one's own children, rather than as having a responsibility toward all children. Thus, although mothering can sensitize women to common experiences, promoting empathy and cooperation, the experience of being a mother can also generate fear and competition, even animosity and antagonism toward others.
>
> *(1997, 250)*

I argue that images of Ivanka Trump and her children, born into intergenerational wealth and whiteness on both sides of the family tree, reminded Trump's supporters of exactly why they believed those immigrant children should be excluded. As Anne Bonds wrote in her essay on the possessive geographies of white supremacy:

> Examining the reproduction of whiteness and white supremacist thinking therefore requires attention to the home and the spaces of everyday life, to care and community work and to the role of white women in nurturing and producing the white nation.
>
> *(2019, 5)*

An America that is "great again" reproduces an investment in heteronormative, conservative, nuclear family structures with white children that must be protected from those who would pose a threat to white supremacy and privilege. As Judith Butler (2009) argued, the consideration of a valuable life is intrinsically entwined with an individual's identity and their perceived value to the nation. Migrants suffering at the border did not merit the president's daughter's curtailing of her online performance of motherhood via Instagram. Ivanka Trump's silence in the face of the cruel policies enforced by her father's administration did not erase responsibility, and placed her squarely in the long legacy of white women who have benefitted from a status quo that marginalizes non-whites.

Ivanka's real "trump card" has been an implicit understanding of her privilege and its canny deployment in times of duress. Her status as the president's daughter served as a shield for her as well as her father. When criticism would arise about Donald Trump's racism and xenophobia, she demurred on the side of family love, declaring him a warm and generous man. This status also served as a reason to deny distasteful realities about her father, asserting that journalists inquiring about several women who have charged him with sexual assault are breaking an age-old taboo. She told NBC's Peter Alexander that "I think it's a pretty inappropriate question to ask a daughter if she believes the accusers of her father when he's affirmatively stated there's no truth to it." She continued, "I believe my father, I know my father, so I think I have that right as a daughter to believe my father" (McCausland 2018). Exercising this right of denial was a privilege denied to other women who worked in the West Wing, as well as anyone in the nation concerned about the character of the president. This easily pulled escape-hatch lever served both Trumps, allowing him to have a high-profile woman supporter in a cultural moment when the sexual misbehavior of high-profile men was central on the world stage.

Daughter/diplomat, Gentile/Jew

During her father's term in office, Ivanka did not just take a role in domestic affairs. She had access to the most exclusive halls of power on the world stage. In 2018 and 2019, she attended the G20, seated with heads of state like Angela Merkel, Xi Jinping, and Theresa May. She traveled to India to co-host a Global Entrepreneurship Summit with Prime Minister Narendra Modi. In 2020, she and her husband attended the World Economic Forum in Davos, Switzerland. Yet Ivanka Trump had little to no experience in matters of international relations, diplomacy, or economic policy when she represented the nation in these venues. Her status as the president's daughter conferred a respectability that others with her background could claim not for themselves. By virtue of familial ties, her presence in these halls of power was supposed to be unquestioned. The administration had been invested in the disruption of some norms, but not all. Traditional insistence upon qualifications or experience became unnecessary, yet gender norms, those so pivotal to Trump's war of position, stayed salient. Ivanka's demure femininity and inherited class status were enough to earn her a seat at the table, communicating with her father's political base that privilege based on unearned status, be it whiteness, wealth, or beauty, was more than enough.

Ivanka emerged as a pillar of her father's war of position particularly when her intersecting identities were deployed as evidence that her father was not a misogynist or an anti-Semite, pushing back against claims of his demonstrable white supremacy. Her flexible, ever-shifting identity allowed Trump to deploy his daughter's conversion to Orthodox Judaism strategically in the campaign, telling the American Israel Public Affairs Committee (AIPAC) in 2016, "I love Israel … I've been with Israel so long," he said. "My daughter Ivanka is about to have a beautiful Jewish baby!" (Haberman 2016). For evangelical Christians, who formed the core of Trump's voting bloc, Ivanka's Judaism was evidence that the Trump administration pushed against a secular state that would marginalize the religious. Much as he claimed that Americans could finally "say Merry Christmas again," Ivanka's piety stood counter to those women who would scorn obedience and familial service in worship of a feminism that eschews male superiority and calls for systemic change.

Ivanka's glamorous persona allowed her to be perceived as a liberated business woman as well as a conservative mother, much as it allowed her to be viewed as simultaneously Jewish and not Jewish, a shifting, liminal figure to be interpreted by her viewer. Her Instagram account (@ivankatrump) featured photos of her young children lighting a menorah in December 2017, while in 2018 it depicted images of the Kushner children standing in front of a Christmas tree or with their small fingers grasping for candy cane cookies. No caption contextualized the images of her Jewish children amid the trappings of a Christian celebration.

This was far from the only time Ivanka's Judaism was at the center of public discourse, often as the result of her father's desire to gain fidelity with that community and the American evangelicals who supported the state of Israel. Throughout the campaign and Trump's time in office, his daughter continued to surface as a frequent referent in her father's rhetorical struggle to assert that he believed in racial and ethnic equality. Ivanka and Jared Kushner were present at the opening of the American embassy in Jerusalem on May 14, 2018, after her father's decision to move the embassy from Tel Aviv to Jerusalem sparked riots that left almost 60 people dead in the Gaza region. Photographs of her posing with Israeli Prime Minister Benjamin Netanyahu and his wife Sara, smiling and seemingly oblivious to the bloodshed, set off condemnation (Mackey 2018). The Trumps' hometown newspaper, the *New York Daily News*, featured a photo of Ivanka on the front page the next day, with the screaming headline: "DADDY'S LITTLE GHOUL" and a subhead which read: "55 slaughtered in Gaza, but Ivanka all smiles at Jerusalem embassy unveil." Her glamorous appearance was not enough this time to divert attention away from the violence inherent in the Trump administration's policy choices, both at home and abroad.

Ivanka Trump became the administration's symbol of solidarity with Jewish Americans. Though the administration denied that it endorsed white supremacy or anti-Semitism, the 2018 Pittsburgh synagogue shooting forced a crisis of credibility on the matter (see Mandell's chapter in this volume) as many posed the same question asked by *The Washington Post*: "How much responsibility does

Trump bear for the synagogue shooting in Pittsburgh?" (Ioffe 2018). Ivanka and her family had already provided cover for a president who excused the neo-Nazis and other white supremacists who marched on Charlottesville, Virginia, in August 2017 chanting "Jews will not replace us," saying that there were "very fine people on both sides." Her father defended the white supremacists, even though some of them called her husband a "Jew bastard" (Solomon 2017). But the administration understood the utility of the Trump in-laws, eagerly engaging in identity politics when pressed for a defense. "He adores Jewish Americans as part of his own family," Sarah Huckabee Sanders, the White House press secretary, told reporters. "The president is the grandfather of several Jewish grandchildren. His daughter is a Jewish American, and his son-in-law is a descendant of Holocaust survivors" (Rogers and Haberman 2018). Donald Trump's daughter and her children were understood as living evidence of his lack of bigotry, just enough to keep him within the confines of civil society, while he still signaled to his base his intentions of countering the hegemony of political correctness.

Reflecting on the anniversary of the Charlottesville murders, *Newsweek* succinctly summarized Ivanka Trump's rhetorical role in the controversy with its headline, "Ivanka Says What Her Dad Couldn't Manage on Charlottesville, One Year On" (Sinclair 2018). Ivanka tweeted, "While Americans are blessed to live in a nation that protects liberty, freedom of speech and diversity of opinion, there is no place for white supremacy, racism and neo-Nazism in our great country" (August 12, 2018, @IvankaTrump). President Trump could not have used this kind of declarative language in the condemnation of the racist violence displayed that day without also condemning his base voters, a choice that he would never make and that would contradict the racist rhetoric he has used over the course of his public life. Reports claim that when Ivanka was challenged to explain her father's support of the rioters, she simply denied her father's remarks, in spite of the video evidence: "My dad didn't mean any of that." And even more directly, "That's not what he said" (Ward 2019, 191). True to the administration's tendency to declare an unflattering reality "fake news," Ivanka Trump simply claimed that it had not happened. Perception was, yet again, more important than reality.

The limits of the illusion

The glamour of Ivanka Trump may have been enough to create the perception that she was a powerful executive, a doting mother, and an international diplomat, but it has not been enough to shield her from criminal investigations for fraud. Perception is not reality in the eyes of the court, and her legal troubles predated her father's presidency. Beginning in 2011, she and her brothers had been investigated for felony fraud for false claims surrounding inflated sales reports for Trump SoHo, a luxury condo building in New York City. Though never charged, the Manhattan District Attorney's office investigated for years, only dropping the case after a hefty donation to the campaign of then-DA Cyrus

Vance (Eisinger et al. 2017). In 2016, Italian shoe design firm Aquazurra sued Ivanka Trump's clothing brand for trademark infringement, claiming that her company produced identical shoes to theirs. The corporations settled the suit out of court in late 2017 after a judge found that Ivanka would have to testify in court if the case were to proceed. Terms of the settlement were not released (Berthelsen 2017).

Donald Trump's presidency did not protect his daughter from all legal scrutiny. Ivanka and her brothers were named parties in a suit brought by the New York State attorney general against the Trump Foundation, the family's charitable organization. The Trump children were directly implicated as sitting members on the board of that foundation. A *New York Times* article provided insight into what prompted the suit: "As our investigation reveals, the Trump Foundation was little more than a checkbook for payments from Mr. Trump or his businesses to nonprofits, regardless of their purpose or legality," said Barbara D. Underwood, New York's attorney general, "[t]his is not how private foundations should function and my office intends to hold the foundation accountable for its misuse of charitable assets" (Hakim, Drucker, and Vogel 2018). The foundation was subsequently dissolved. In late 2019, the Trump Foundation settled the case with the State of New York, paying $2 million to eight nonprofit groups in acknowledgment of their bad practices, with the president admitting in court documents that the foundation had used funds for campaign functions and other self-dealing. Ivanka, Don Jr., and Eric were required by the court to undergo mandatory training to learn how to not defraud charities in the future (Ferré-Sadurní 2019).

"I try to stay out of politics," Ivanka said in a Fox News interview in 2017 (Nelson 2017). Yet for a person who claimed to want to stay out of politics, Ivanka Trump laid the groundwork for someone with political aspirations. Unusual, and frowned upon, but not unheard of, Ivanka's path to leadership mirrored that of her father's nemesis, Hillary Clinton, who took a high-profile position in her husband President Clinton's White House. Ivanka and Jared Kushner needed legal intervention to allow them to serve in West Wing operations at all. To push back against accusations of nepotism, the Justice Department issued a memo in January 2017 declaring the executive branch was exempt from the laws preventing the hiring of family members:

> Section 105(a) of title 3, U.S. Code, which authorizes the President to appoint employees in the White House Office 'without regard to any other provision of law regulating the employment or compensation of persons in the Government service,' exempts positions in the White House Office from the prohibition on nepotism in 5 U.S.C. § 3110.
>
> *(Office of Legal Counsel 2017, 1)*

Ivanka and Jared Kushner were then ushered into the West Wing with the full authority of the highest office in the land.

Given the fact that the presidency as an office is securely situated as the reproduction of a heteronormative nuclear family with a patriarchal leader at its head, the ascension of the first daughter might be construed as both a logical and natural next step for a young woman who wants to hold the office herself someday. Ivanka taking the Office of the Presidency would be groundbreaking in terms of her gender, but would be the third time that the child of a president followed in their father's footsteps. Though the veracity of the book has been called into question, Michael Wolff's incendiary tell-all *Fire and Fury: Inside the Trump White House* (2018) claimed a greater political dynasty might have been part of the plan:

> Balancing risk against reward, both Jared and Ivanka decided to accept roles in the West Wing over the advice of almost everyone they knew. It was a joint decision by the couple, and, in some sense, a joint job. Between themselves, the two had made an earnest deal: If sometime in the future the opportunity arose, she'd be the one to run for president. The first woman president, Ivanka entertained, would not be Hillary Clinton; it would be Ivanka Trump.
>
> *(2018, 272)*

Perhaps Ivanka's claim that she was not interested in politics was but another element of the deception she had woven throughout her time in the public eye. As Vicky Ward noted in her exposé on the couple she dubbed "Javanka": "That's the tell, the line that proves she intends to stay in politics" (2019, 237).

Ivanka has had plenty of supporters in her would-be pursuit of the presidency. Multiple memes featuring her face imposed upon an American flag mimic a campaign poster, calling for "Ivanka 2024." Gender figured prominently into one self-published book that called for her election, titled *Ivanka Trump 2024: Reasons Why Ivanka Will Be the First Lady President*. Authors Roopendra Bhargaw and Rachel Neubauer argued:

> With the current nasty climate in Washington, DC and in between power struggles, America will be fed up with the games of Machoism [sic] by 2024 and would prefer a caring attitude of a woman to handle the day-to-day business of American politics. Ivanka would be a great fit for the Presidency of the USA.
>
> *(2017, n.p.)*

Note the use of the term "lady" instead of "woman" or "female" in the title. Ivanka's glamour took center stage again. Her fashion style, her maternal persona, and her rise to power through a dominant, masculine father figure position her as a solution to the turmoil of the past, ironically a turmoil that she created and contributed to through her role in senior administration. Though this text is only 17 pages, it merits consideration because its popularity speaks to a grassroots investment in Ivanka as an idealized woman leader. Published by Amazon Digital Services, it was ranked highly among short reads in the Politics & Social Sciences section of their digital books, higher than many of the thousands available in that genre.

As a Republican woman, Ivanka would need to grapple with the gender dynamics facing others that have sought that office. Her flexible identity would serve her well in this dynamic. She would have to face the same challenges as her predecessors Carly Fiorina or Elizabeth Dole, navigating a party that resists feminism and women's leadership, no matter how watered down for easy consumption. As Kelly Dittmar notes in her essay on the 2016 election in *The Right Women: Republican Party Activists, Candidates, and Legislators*:

> The gendered context of the presidential election presented another challenge to Republican candidates, especially women. In nominating Donald Trump, a man with a documented history of making sexist remarks and a campaign strategy that embraced hypermasculinity, Republicans upheld an electoral environment in which power was defined in masculine terms and allocated along gender lines. Female candidates, particularly those running for federal office, were confronted with questions about balancing their party allegiance with their principles of gender equality and respect for women.
>
> *(2018, 133)*

Recent research demonstrates that gender differences in policy attitudes are more pronounced in the Republican Party than in the Democratic Party, with Republican women reporting significantly more moderate views than their male counterparts (Barnes and Cassese 2017). Ivanka, with all of the advantages at her disposal, would need to navigate the gender bias intrinsic to her would-be base.

Perhaps in an acknowledgment that it might not be strategic to position oneself as even slightly feminist, on January 20, 2018, the one-year anniversary of her father's inauguration, Ivanka changed her biography on Twitter to remove the claim that she was "a passionate advocate for the education and empowerment of women and girls." It then read, simply: "Wife, mother, sister, daughter. Advisor to POTUS on job creation + economic empowerment, workforce development & entrepreneurship" (@IvankaTrump). In March 2020, the main image of the advisor to the president on her Twitter account featured her holding her youngest son as she sat at her desk, pen in hand. Her maternal, conservative identity was fully on display in the photo, without the pesky taint of women's empowerment present in the text.

Ivanka made the most of her opportunity to raise her profile as a woman in charge in a Republican White House. Time will tell whether or not she is able to convert that to an autonomous power position without the auspices of her father's masculine authority. If she does choose to pursue her own political office, will her glamour spell be enough to be all things to all people? Will she be able to wage a war of position in a world of her own making, where women are subordinate, Jews are suspect, and feminism, even that anchored in the gospel of consumption, is abject? In her own words, Ivanka Trump acknowledged, "If someone perceives something to be true, it is more important than if it is in fact true" (2009, n.p.). She would be what we want her to be, when we want her to be it. Her public persona will be intrinsically linked to her father's administration and its policies anchored in authoritarian nationalist rhetoric and rooted in white supremacy. Her role in this revolution may prove so valuable as to make her political aspirations a victim of their own success.

References

Abrams, Rachel. 2018. "Ivanka Trump Is Shutting Down Her Fashion Brand." *New York Times*, July 24, 2018. https://www.nytimes.com/2018/07/24/business/ivanka-trump-brand-clothing.html.

Allen, Cooper. 2016. "Trump, Clinton End Debate with Compliments." *USA Today*, October 9, 2016. https://www.usatoday.com/story/news/politics/onpolitics/2016/10/09/hillary-clinton-donald-trump-debate/91831066/.

Barber, Alan. 2018. "Ivanka Trump's Paid Leave Policy Would Be Disastrous. Here Are Some Better Options." *Fortune.com*, June 15, 2018. https://fortune.com/2018/06/15/ivanka-trump-marco-rubio-paid-leave-family-act/.

Barnes, Tiffany D., and Erin C. Cassese. 2017. "American Party Women: A Look at the Gender Gap within Parties." *Political Research Quarterly* 70 (1): 127–141. https://doi.org/10.1177/1065912916675738.

Beasley, Maurine Hoffman. 2005. *First Ladies and the Press: The Unfinished Partnership of the Media Age*. Evanston, IL: Northwestern University Press.

Berthelsen, Christian. 2017. "Italian Company Drops Ivanka Trump Shoe Lawsuit." *Bloomberg News*, November 17, 2017. https://www.bloomberg.com/news/articles/2017-11-17/ivanka-trump-high-heeled-shoe-lawsuit-dropped-by-italian-company.

Bhargaw, Roopendra, and Rachel Neubauer. 2017. *Ivanka Trump 2024: Reasons Why Ivanka Will Be the First Lady President*. n.p.: Amazon Digital Services.

Blee, Kathleen. 1997. "Mothers in Race-Hate Movements." In *The Politics of Motherhood: Activist Voices from Left to Right*, edited by Alexis Jetter, Annelise Orleck, and Diana Taylor, 247–256. Hanover, NH: University Press of New England.

Bonds, Anne. 2019. "Race and Ethnicity II: White Women and the Possessive Geographies of White Supremacy." *Progress in Human Geography* (July): 1–11. https://doi.org/10.1177/0309132519863479.

Brodkin, Karen. 1998. *How Jews Became White Folks and What That Says about Race in America*. New Brunswick, NJ: Rutgers University Press.

Brownworth, Victoria A. 2017. "The Rise of Right-Wing Women." *Curve* 27 (4): 16–17.

Burns, Lisa M. 2008. *First Ladies and the Fourth Estate: Press Framing of Presidential Wives*. DeKalb, IL: Northern Illinois University Press.

Butler, Judith. 2009. *Frames of War: When Is Life Grievable?* New York: Verso Books.

Buttigieg, Joseph A. 1995. "Gramsci on Civil Society." *Boundary 2* 22 (3): 1–32. https://doi.org/10.2307/303721.

Carby, Hazel V. 1997. "White Woman Listen! Black Feminism and the Boundaries of Sisterhood." In *Black British Feminism: A Reader*, edited by Heidi Safia Mirza, 45–53. London: Routledge.

CBS News. 2019. "Transcript: Ivanka Trump Talks Impeachment on 'Face the Nation'." *CBS Interactive Inc.*, December 20, 2019. https://www.cbsnews.com/news/impeachment-ivanka-trump-transcript-ivanka-trumps-comments-on-impeachment-on-face-the-nation/.

Combs, Sandra L. 2013. "FLOTUS: Media Darling or Monster?" *Race, Gender & Class* 20 (1/2): 266–280. https://www.jstor.org/stable/43496918.

Conroy, Meredith. 2018. "Strength, Stamina, and Sexism in the 2016 Presidential Race." *Politics & Gender* 14 (1): 116–121. https://doi.org/10.1017/S1743923X17000642.

Correal, Annie, and Emily Cochrane. 2018. "Melania Trump's Parents Become U.S. Citizens, Using 'Chain Migration' Trump Hates." *New York Times*, August 9, 2018. https://www.nytimes.com/2018/08/09/nyregion/melania-trumps-parents-become-us-citizens.html.

Creedon, Pam. 2018. "Media Narratives of Gender in the Contentious Conservative Age of Trump." In *The Trump Presidency, Journalism, and Democracy*, edited by Robert E. Gutsche, Jr., 156–177. New York: Routledge.

de Moraes, Lisa. 2018. "Samantha Bee Apologizes Defiantly for Last Week's First-Daughter Slur on 'Full Frontal'." *Deadline.com*, June 6, 2018. https://deadline.com/2018/06/samantha-bee-ivanka-trump-apology-feckless-donald-trump-immigration-full-frontal-tbs-video-1202404885/.

Dittmar, Kelly. 2018. "Republican Women in the 2016 Election: Progress or Same Old Patterns?" In *The Right Women: Women as Republican Party Activists, Candidates, and Legislators*, edited by Malliga Och and Shauna L. Shames, 131–154. Santa Barbara, CA: Praeger.

Drabold, Will. 2016. "Read Ivanka Trump's Speech at the Republican Convention." *Time*, July 22, 2016. https://time.com/4417579/republican-convention-ivanka-trump-transcript/.

Eisinger, Jesse, Justin Elliot, Andrea Bernstein, and Ilya Marritz. 2017. "Ivanka and Donald Trump Jr. Were Close to Being Charged with Felony Fraud." *ProPublica*, October 4, 2017. https://www.propublica.org/article/ivanka-donald-trump-jr-close-to-being-charged-felony-fraud.

Favreault, Melissa M., and Richard W. Johnson. 2018. "Research Report: Paying for Parental Leave with Future Social Security Benefits." *Urban Institute*, April 19, 2018. https://www.urban.org/research/publication/paying-parental-leave-future-social-security-benefits.

Feimster, Crystal Nicole. 2009. *Southern Horrors: Women and the Politics of Rape and Lynching*. Cambridge, MA: Harvard University Press.

Ferber, Abby L. 1998. "Constructing Whiteness: The Intersections of Race and Gender in US White Supremacist Discourse." *Ethnic and Racial Studies* 21 (1): 48–63. https://doi.org/10.1080/014198798330098.

Ferré-Sadurní, Luis. 2019. "Trump Pays $2 Million to 8 Charities for Misuse of Foundation." *New York Times*, December 10, 2019. https://www.nytimes.com/2019/12/10/nyregion/trump-foundation-lawsuit-attorney-general.html.

Fox, Emily Jane. 2018. *Born Trump: Inside America's First Family*. New York: HarperCollins Publishers.

Gilbert, Neil, ed. 2006. *Gender and Social Security Reform: What's Fair for Women?* New York: Routledge.

Gilmore, Glenda Elizabeth. 1996. *Gender and Jim Crow: Women and the Politics of White Supremacy in North Carolina, 1896–1920*. Chapel Hill, NC: University of North Carolina Press.

Gramsci, Antonio. 2014. *The Antonio Gramsci Reader: Selected Writings 1916–1935*. Edited by David Forgacs. New York: New York University Press.

Gundle, Stephen. 2008. *Glamour: A History.* New York, NY: Oxford University Press.

Haberman, Maggie. 2016. "'An Easter Baby': For Ivanka Trump, It's a Boy, and Donald's Eighth Grandchild." *New York Times*, March 29, 2016: A14.

Hakim, Danny, Jesse Drucker, and Kenneth P. Vogel. 2018. "State Sues Trump Charity, Alleging Vast Misconduct." *New York Times*, June 15, 2018: A1.

Ingraham, Christopher. 2017. "White House Gender Pay Gap More Than Triples under Trump." *Washington Post*, July 5, 2017. https://www.washingtonpost.com/news/wonk/wp/2017/07/05/white-house-gender-pay-gap-more-than-triples-under-trump/.

Ioffe, Julia. 2018. "How Much Responsibility Does Trump Bear for the Synagogue Shooting in Pittsburgh?" *Washington Post*, October 28, 2018. https://www.washingtonpost.com/outlook/2018/10/28/how-much-responsibility-does-trump-bear-synagogue-shooting-pittsburgh/.

"Ivanka Trump." n.d. *The White House.* Accessed January 14, 2020. https://www.whitehouse.gov/people/ivanka-trump/.

King, Gayle. 2017. "Interview with Ivanka Trump on What It Means to Be 'Complicit'." *CBS This Morning*, April 4, 2017. https://www.youtube.com/watch?v=Cw0xln927lc.

Kwong, Jessica. 2019. "Will Ivanka Trump Win Her Father Re-Election? First Daughter More Popular than President in 2020 Swing States." *Newsweek*, June 18, 2019. https://www.newsweek.com/ivanka-trump-reelection-campaign-poll-swing-state-2020-1444595.

Mackey, Robert. 2018. "Ivanka Trump Opens U.S. Embassy in Jerusalem during Israeli Massacre of Palestinians in Gaza." *The Intercept*, May 14, 2018. https://theintercept.com/2018/05/14/ivanka-trump-opens-u-s-embassy-jerusalem-israeli-massacre-palestinians/.

McCarthy, Tom. 2018. "Ivanka Trump Photo with Son Sparks Backlash over Border Separations." *Guardian*, May 28, 2018. https://www.theguardian.com/us-news/2018/may/27/ivanka-trump-tweets-photo-backlash-border-separation-policy.

McCausland, Phil. 2018. "Ivanka Trump Says She Believes Father's Denials of Sex Misconduct." *NBC News*, February 25, 2018. https://www.nbcnews.com/politics/white-house/ivanka-trump-arming-teachers-option-needs-be-discussed-n850801.

Merriam-Webster. 2020. "The History of 'Glamour'." *Merriam-Webster Dictionary 2020.* https://www.merriam-webster.com/words-at-play/the-history-of-glamour.

Nelson, Louis. 2017. "Ivanka Trump: 'I try to stay out of politics'." *Politico*, June 26, 2017. https://www.politico.com/story/2017/06/26/ivanka-trump-politics-fox-interview-239945.

Office of the Legal Counsel. 2017. "Memorandum Opinion for the Counsel to the President, Application of the Anti-Nepotism Statute to a Presidential Appointment in the White House Office." In *Opinions of the Office of Legal Counsel 41*, January 20, 2017. https://www.Justice.Gov/Sites/Default/Files/Olc/Opinions/Attachments/2017/01/20/2017-01-20-Anti-Nepo-Stat-Who_0.Pdf.

Patton, Callum. 2017. "Ivanka Backs Trump Administration's Plan to Scrap Obama Rules Preventing Pay Discrimination." *Newsweek*, August 30, 2017. https://www.newsweek.com/ivanka-backs-trump-administrations-plan-scrap-obama-rules-preventing-pay-656751.

Phillips, Kristine. 2018. "Melania Trump's Immigration Lawyer Calls President's Attacks on 'Chain Migration' 'Unconscionable'." *Washington Post*, August 11, 2018. https://www.washingtonpost.com/news/politics/wp/2018/08/11/melania-trumps-immigration-lawyer-calls-presidents-attacks-on-chain-migration-unconscionable/.

Rogers, Katie, and Maggie Haberman. 2018. "Ivanka Trump and Jared Kushner Shape Trump's Pittsburgh Response." *New York Times*, November 1, 2018. https://www.nytimes.com/2018/10/30/us/politics/ivanka-kushner-pittsburgh-synagogue-shooting.html.

Rubin, Jennifer. 2017. "Ivanka Trump: Complicit and Ineffective." *Washington Post*, December 12, 2017. https://www.washingtonpost.com/blogs/right-turn/wp/2017/12/12/ivanka-trump-complicit-and-ineffective/.

Sinclair, Harriet. 2018. "Ivanka Trump Says What Her Father Couldn't on Charlottesville, One Year On." *Newsweek*, August 12, 2018. https://www.newsweek.com/ivanka-says-what-her-dad-couldnt-manage-charlottesville-one-year-1069834.

Smith, Aidan. 2018. *Gender, Heteronormativity, and the American Presidency*. New York: Routledge.

Solomon, Daniel J. 2017. "White Supremacist Hates That Trump 'Gave His Daughter to a Jew'." *Fast-Forward*, August 16, 2017. https://forward.com/fast-forward/380119/watch-white-supremacist-hates-that-trump-gave-his-daughter-to-a-jew/.

Trump, Ivanka. 2009. *The Trump Card: Playing to Win in Work and Life*. New York: Simon & Schuster.

———. 2017. *Women Who Work: Rewriting the Rules for Success*. New York: Portfolio.

USDA [United States Department of Agriculture]. 2019. "Final Rule: SNAP Requirements for Able-Bodied Adults without Dependents | USDA-FNS." December 5, 2019. https://www.fns.usda.gov/snap/fr-120419.

Ward, Vicky. 2019. *Kushner, Inc.: Greed, Ambition, Corruption: The Extraordinary Story of Jared Kushner and Ivanka Trump*. New York: St. Martin's Press.

Wolff, Michael. 2018. *Fire and Fury: Inside the Trump White House*. New York: Henry Holt and Company.

Zeisler, Andi. 2016. *We Were Feminists Once: From Riot Grrrl to CoverGirl®: The Buying and Selling of a Political Movement*. New York: Public Affairs/Perseus Books.

3
THE STICKY IMAGERY OF WHITE FEMINISM

Christine A. Kray

> "Memory work" is, like any other kind of physical or mental labor, embedded in complex class, gender and power relations that determine what is remembered (or forgotten), by whom, and for what end.
> —John Gillis, "Memory and Identity"

> To build a monument is to ratify our shared national project.
> —President Donald Trump's Executive Order No. 13934

Sticky images

On Election Day, 2016, at Mount Hope Cemetery in Rochester, NY, between 8 and 12,000 people stood in line for an hour and a half to two hours, not to vote—they had already done that—but to place their "I Voted" sticker on the gravestone of suffragist Susan B. Anthony (1820–1906). As Hillary Clinton appeared destined to become the first female president in US history, just four years shy of the centennial of the Nineteenth Amendment to the Constitution, which recognized women's right to vote, Anthony's grave became a center of commemorative activity (Figure 3.1). In my interviews with cemetery visitors, they expressed excitement about what appeared to be the imminent election of the country's first female president, but also dread about the public surge of racism, nativism, religious bigotry, and misogyny, for which they blamed Donald Trump. As if reciting the Litany, when describing him, they offered a series of epithets—"he is racist, sexist, etc."—always placing "racist" first in their lists. However, even while they were seriously concerned about racism, the cemetery visitors seemed unaware of Anthony's behaviors that have been identified as racist (Kray 2018). This sticky fact—that (mainly white) women could celebrate

DOI: 10.4324/9781003034810-3

FIGURE 3.1 An estimated 8–12,000 people visited Susan B. Anthony's grave in Rochester, NY on Election Day, 2016.
Credit: Christine Kray.

advances for women and decry racism, while taking part in a ceremony commemorating a suffragist tarnished by racism—set in motion the research for this chapter. Part of privilege, I discovered, is not having to learn other people's histories. And yet, the stories that are told about the past, including about the women's suffrage movement, are folded into a cultural machinery of exclusion and disenfranchisement in the present.

Fast-forward three years to November 25, 2019, when President Donald Trump signed H.R. 2423, The Women's Suffrage Centennial Commemorative Coin Act (Figure 3.2). This act, spearheaded by Republican congresswomen, called for a commemorative coin to be minted in honor of the Nineteenth Amendment's centennial. In the Oval Office ceremony, the president was surrounded by a cheering and smiling group of members of the Women's Suffrage Centennial Commission, all Trump appointees, mostly white, mostly Republican. One wore a white dress and a "Votes for Women" white, purple, and gold sash, reminiscent of the early twentieth century suffragists. The president invoked the memory of "many of the brave heroes who fought for the right to vote," and he named first Susan B. Anthony and her long-time collaborator, Elizabeth Cady Stanton (1815–1902). The assembled women thanked the president for his leadership, and he took credit, saying, "now I'm President, and we get things done" (White House 2019).

FIGURE 3.2 President Trump signs the Women's Suffrage Centennial Commemorative Coin Act, November 25, 2019.
Credit: Tia Dufour/The White House.

This ceremony celebrating the advances of women, featuring Anthony and Stanton, contrasted starkly with some other images from the second half of Trump's presidency. These sticky images—contradictory, unexpected, disquieting, or distressing—disrupt, bother, and force a response. For one, there is the photograph of Maria Lila Meza Castro, the asylum-seeking Honduran woman wearing a Disney's *Frozen* T-shirt, gripping the hands of her two children, both barefoot and wearing diapers, as they run from the tear gas lobbed at them by US Border Patrol (Figure 3.3) (Kyung-Hoon 2018). The innocence and vulnerability of the *Frozen* shirt and the children's bottom halves, protected only by disposable diapers, contrast with the militarized blast of tear gas, a chemical weapon banned in warfare by the 1925 Geneva Convention.

Then there is the video clip of Gianna Floyd, the six-year-old daughter of George Floyd, who was killed on May 25, 2020, by a police officer who kneeled on his neck for 9 minutes and 29 seconds. Floyd's murder was one of a few that set off months of Black Lives Matter (BLM) protests across the United States and in cities worldwide. In the video, Gianna sits atop the shoulders of a family friend, overlooking one such rally, and says, "Daddy changed the world" (Hohman 2020). Another photo was taken in a nail salon in Georgia in mid-May 2020, as, against the recommendation of federal health experts, the first governor lifted COVID-19 quarantine restrictions and reopened the state's businesses, with salons and gyms among the first. In the photo, an unidentified dark-skinned woman bends over, nearly completely enveloped in a plastic protective garment, as she buffs the nails of a white woman (Newcomb 2020).

FIGURE 3.3 Maria Lila Meza Castro and her children run from tear gas fired by US Border Patrol, Tijuana, Mexico, November 25, 2018.
Credit: Kim Kyung-Hoon/Reuters.

Collectively, these images expose the stark contrasts in women's lives in the United States. Women and girls of color fleeing violence in their home countries can be denied asylum and teargassed, can lose fathers to police violence, and can be put at risk of contracting a lethal virus in service to a white woman's beauty. At the same time, the president, whose policies undermined women's rights (see Smith's chapter in this volume), was applauded for his leadership by white women, while holding up as heroes Anthony and Stanton, both of whom demonstrated racism (discussed below). How is it that white women can celebrate "women's" advances while women of color shoulder such risks to their lives? In fact, inequalities among women on the basis of racial and ethnic identities are pervasive and deep in the United States. For example, while in 2018, white women on average earned 81.5 cents for every $1 earned by a non-Hispanic white man, Black women earned only 65.3 cents, and Hispanic women only 61.6 cents (Hegewish and Hartman 2019). This disparity holds even when narrowing the comparison to college-educated workers; in 2016, "white college-educated women made 31 percent less than white college-educated men, while black college-educated women made 38 percent less than white college-educated men" (New York Times Editorial Board 2017). Health disparities are also grim: for example, Black women were 2.5 times as likely to die during childbirth as white women in 2018 (CDC 2019). The Trump administration implemented several policies that further eroded the standing of and posed risks to the health, safety, and well-being of women of color, including: cuts to affordable housing initiatives (Weiss 2019); repeated attempts to scuttle the Affordable Care Act (Stolberg 2020); scaling back of Medicaid (Goodnough 2020), plus other proposed deep cuts to Medicare and Social Security (NBC News 2020); and blocking federal financial support for healthcare and family-planning agencies nationally (Belluck 2019) and internationally (Human Rights Watch 2018) if they include abortion services or referrals among their healthcare services.

In this chapter, I explore the cultural undercurrents that hold up a racist system that reproduces the inequalities borne by women of color in the United States. Inequalities can insinuate themselves into any society, but they can only be perpetuated year after year if abetted by a system of habituated thought and action that makes those inequalities seem natural and right. Many of our cultural conceptual frameworks and habits shore up inequalities by race and gender in the United States, but here I focus on one: what might be called the official history of women's suffrage, that is, a story about how women in the United States claimed voting rights, as this narrative is enshrined in national museums and commemorative activities. In this analysis, I draw upon the concept of "white feminism" and show how this particular narrative of women's suffrage is, in fact, a white feminist history. As such, it reinforces the structural violence of white supremacy and privilege.

White feminism and representational intersectionality

"White feminism" is a term used not to refer to the feminism of white women, but rather a perspective that women's experiences are similar, and therefore that feminism can be articulated irrespective of race (or national origin, class, religion, [dis]ability, sexuality, or any other crosscutting identity). It is called "white feminism," because it was the feminist perspective developed within the nascent "women's movement" of the 1970s, which was dominated by middle-class white women. Because these women developed the definition of feminism in accordance with what they thought women in general needed, the expressed "feminist" agenda in fact aligned with their own goals (hooks 1981, 1984; Hull and Smith 1982; Lorde 1984). In the 1970s in the United States, those goals prioritized parity with men in the workplace, educational achievement, and access to birth control. The term "white feminism" as an epithet to describe this universalist perspective was in use in Black feminist circles by the 1990s (Collins 2000).

However, women's experiences are not universal, but vary substantially in accordance with various crosscutting identities (race, class, sexuality, etc.). Simply put, women do not experience womanhood in the same way and consequently their aims for improving their lives as women differ markedly, and may include any number of other priorities, from police reform, to immigration reform, affordable healthcare, voting rights guarantees, access to affordable housing, and protection from white women's racism. Whether 1970s leaders who equated their goals with "women's goals" intended to exclude the diverse experiences and needs of other groups of women or were simply ignorant of them is irrelevant. As long as "women's needs" are defined in relationship to white women's goals (white feminism), this universalist feminism will reinforce existing inequalities. White feminism is ignorant, of course. It is also oppressive, as the agendas of subgroups are taken as irrelevant, or worse, "merely" problems of race or class and unrelated to gender. When "advances" are perceived in accordance with the goals of the (white) movement, these are declared to be advances for all women, and the specific needs of other women are not taken up. White feminism silences the voices of women of color, even while declaring victory in the name of "sisterhood." As Audre Lorde wrote:

> If white american [sic] feminist theory need not deal with the differences between us, and the resulting difference in our oppressions, then how do you deal with the fact that the women who clean your houses and tend your children while you attend conferences on feminist theory are, for the most part, poor women and women of Color? What is the theory behind racist feminism?
>
> *(1984, 112)*

Kimberlé Crenshaw (1989) developed the concept of "intersectionality" to capture the multiplicity of experiences generated out of people's intersecting identities. Most importantly, Crenshaw perceived that people who are marginalized along more than one axis, such as Black women, may experience multiple forms of oppression that cannot be predicted from the experiences of people disadvantaged only by one axis (such as Black men or white women), and that the overlapping nature of these oppressions creates intractable problems. She demonstrated, for example, how preferential hiring practices for women resulted in greater employment for white women, and preferential hiring practices for people of racialized minority groups resulted in greater employment for Black men, all the while Black women saw little change in their employment rate because they bore dual burdens of gender and race. Crenshaw's analysis followed upon the insight of the Combahee River Collective that "systems of oppression are interlocking. The synthesis of these oppressions creates the conditions of our lives" ([1977] 1982, 13).

Particularly relevant for this chapter is Crenshaw's (1991) theorization of "representational intersectionality." Many researchers have examined what Crenshaw called "structural intersectionality," or how people who are disadvantaged along two axes (such as Black women) have different experiences rooted in their structural position. However, less attention has been paid to what Crenshaw called "representational intersectionality, by which I mean the cultural construction" (245) of people in different positions related to these axes of distinction. Her legal analysis revealed, for example, how cultural ideas about Black women undermined their ability to attain justice in cases of rape at the levels of both adjudication and legislative reform. In a similar vein, Patricia Hill Collins (2000, 18) added to the concept of intersectionality the idea of the "matrix of domination [which] refers to how these intersecting oppressions are actually organized." She analyzed how prevailing images of Black women—the mammy, the matriarch, the welfare mother, and the Jezebel or hoochie—are "controlling images" (images designed to control) which wield sexism and racism simultaneously to define Black women as distinct from white women. Collins perceived that these images emerged out of the condition of slavery in the United States, configuring Black and white women in different, opposing ways in relationship to a single standard, the so-called "cult of true womanhood," characterized by the qualities of "piety, purity, submissiveness, and domesticity" (72). Collins argued that "These controlling images are designed to make racism, sexism, poverty, and other forms of social injustice appear to be natural, normal, and inevitable parts of life ... [and] are key in maintaining intersection oppressions" (69). In other words, women do not just have diverse experiences because of their diverse positions within a social field, but because they are interpellated or configured differently in the first place. In other words, gender and race are coconstructed; gender and race are not categories that exist in isolation, but male and female are conceptualized in relationship to race, just as race is engendered. (In this volume, Maskovsky uses the term "coconstitution" to refer to the same process.)

In this chapter, I consider how narratives about the past are one set of cultural representations through which gender and race are coconstructed. For any given set of events in the past, there are endless ways of telling the tale, all of which carry weighty implications for how we view one another in the present. Stories about the past are told from different perspectives, center upon certain individuals, establish teams, crown heroes, vilify villains, and are silent about other people altogether. These stories of belonging, exclusion, heroism, or irrelevance set the parameters by which we in the present evaluate the contours of the nation: who belongs, who is deserving, who are the givers, and who are the takers. As Gillis (1994, 3) phrased it: "'Memory work' is, like any other kind of physical or mental labor, embedded in complex class, gender and power relations that determine what is remembered (or forgotten), by whom, and for what end."

Museums and commemorative events are part of the infrastructure of public memory. With a footprint in the physical landscape, they bring people together to consume certain narratives about the past. In addition, "national" museums and commemorative events delineate the character of the nation: its people, its heroes, its values and priorities, and its destiny, borne somehow out of a mythic path and leading toward an almost predestined future. With the "national" title, their narratives bear the official stamp of approval, and their delineations of the nation are thus endorsed.

In what follows, I discuss how the predominant strand of suffragist commemoration in the twenty-first century entails a type of representational intersectionality. It is a white feminist history that defines women's advances in relationship to a universal (and therefore racist) definition. It reinforces white privilege in the United States because it casts white women as the heroes, whitewashes their racism, and erases the experiences of other women, in particular the fact that the Nineteenth Amendment was, for those other women, just one step in a much longer fight for voting rights. In prevailing public narratives about the women's suffrage movement in the United States, white women take the central, heroic role, winning the vote, supposedly, for all women, while women of color are relegated to the sidelines. Such narratives obscure racism and unequal access to the vote, in both past and present.

Suffragist commemoration and the 2016 election

Historical figures are putty in the hands of a skillful rhetorician. As candidates for federal office seek to represent "the people" in "the nation," they must position themselves as representative of the nation thus configured. Politicians frequently set themselves alongside historical heroes, to suggest, not so subtly, they are the right person to carry on the good work, to carry the torch toward the nation's predestined goal. In 2016, candidate Trump borrowed slogans from the campaigns of past presidents ("Make America Great Again" and "America First") to wax nostalgic about an era characterized by white male supremacy.

For her part, candidate Hillary Clinton, self-consciously aiming to be the country's first female president, aligned herself with early women's voting rights activists. The commemorative activity at Anthony's grave in 2016 can be attributed in part to Clinton's repeated invocation of those historical figures. On June 7, 2016, when Clinton became the presumptive Democratic nominee, to her victory speech, she wore a cream-colored jacket, white being the signature color of the early suffragists. Beginning her prepared remarks, she invoked the western New York suffragists, saying:

> Tonight's victory is not about one person. It belongs to generations of women and men who struggled and sacrificed and made this moment possible. In our country, it started right here in New York, a place called Seneca Falls, in 1848. When a small but determined group of women, and men, came together with the idea that women deserved equal rights, and they set it forth in something called the Declaration of Sentiments.
>
> *(Reilly 2016)*

Clinton was referring to the 1848 women's rights convention in Seneca Falls, whose primary convener, Elizabeth Cady Stanton, drafted the Declaration of Sentiments. Echoing the cadences of the Declaration of Independence, Stanton claimed various rights for women, including the vote. Seneca Falls is now the location of the Women's Rights National Historical Park—a complex of buildings, including Stanton's former home. Further aligning herself with the historic suffragists, in that same speech, Hillary Clinton noted that her mother was born on the day in which Congress passed the Nineteenth Amendment, and at other pivotal moments in her campaign, she wore white (Kray, Carroll, and Mandell 2018, 6).

On Election Day, the gates of Mount Hope Cemetery closed at 9:00 pm, and overnight, the news media announced Donald Trump as the surprise victor. As the exit poll results rolled out, one of the sharpest contrasts in voting patterns was the difference among women by racial identity. CNN exit polls showed that 52 percent of white women voted for Trump, while 94 percent of Black women, and 69 percent of Latinx women voted for Clinton (CNN 2016). In the digital world of the blogosphere and social media, the backlash by women of color against white women was swift and severe. Trump's victory was cast as yet another betrayal by white women of women of color. White women were lambasted not just for on average having preferred Donald Trump, but also for having celebrated early white suffragists, particularly Susan B. Anthony, in connection with the Clinton campaign. Anger at white women for Trump's victory was often channeled through critiques of historic white suffragist leaders (Dionne 2017; Ford 2017; Lampen 2016; Lange 2017; Ray 2017; Shabazz n.d.; Viera 2016). These critics were, in essence, fighting with history, or leveraging examples from the past to establish a pattern of injustices and assign blame in the present. Bené Viera (2016), for example, blogged:

> Now that the apocalypse has arrived, I want white feminists to lean in.... See, yesterday I peeped you all celebrating your white suffragette faves. Stanning for Susan B. Anthony and whatnot. Leaving flowers on her grave, being all cute trying to bow down to your sisters who paved the way for you.... While a handful of you were enthusiastically wearing white to the polls in honor of the white suffragists who fought for (white) women's right to vote in the 1900s, Trump was being elected president.

In addition, "white feminism" was invoked. On the day of the Women's March in January 2017, UC-Berkeley professor Raka Ray's (2017) Facebook post went viral:

> To my white friends demonstrating today:
>
> — Do not forget that y'all are the ones that got us here.
> — Do not forget that white feminism is white supremacy.
> — Do not forget that Susan B Anthony was a racist who argued for suffrage on the grounds that white women are more valuable than any black person.

From January 2017 through August 2020, I engaged in a methodology I have called an ethnography of a national conversation to study how commemoration of historic women's rights activists figured into national political debates. In this multi-method project, I collected data by: observing ritual activities and conducting interviews at Anthony's gravestone; engaging in digital ethnography, following how opinion writers, politicians, and activists were talking about the early suffragists and race; and attending suffrage commemorative activities and Women's Marches in Seneca Falls and Rochester. Finally, I analyzed how national museums and the Trump White House represented (or glossed over) race and racism in the early suffrage movement, as they crafted an official history of women's voting rights activism.

The official history

During Women's History Month, in March 2020, my fourth-grade daughter brought home her class's lesson about the women's suffrage movement. It featured Susan B. Anthony and Elizabeth Cady Stanton (Figure 3.4), and them only. Lisa Tetrault (2014) has documented the "myth of Seneca Falls," or a condensed version of the women's voting rights movement that has become enshrined in the national imagination. Tetrault traced how this narrative—which begins with the 1848 Seneca Falls convention and situates Anthony and Stanton as the movement's leaders—came to be laid down. Despite the myriad women's rights activists before and since Seneca Falls, and the sometimes sharp disagreements in

FIGURE 3.4 Ted Aub's "When Anthony Met Stanton" statue, located in Seneca Falls, was commissioned by New York State in 1998 to mark the 150th anniversary of the 1848 convention.
Credit: Christine Kray.

philosophy and tactics, Anthony and Stanton take center stage in the condensed version of suffrage history. The solidification of this particular telling of the story, according to Tetrault, can be traced in part to the fact that the two women, along with Matilda Joslyn Gage, put themselves at the center of that history in their six-volume *History of Woman Suffrage* (the final two volumes of which were completed by Ida Husted Harper following Stanton's and Anthony's deaths).

This popular narrative is sustained by national museums and statues that, quite literally, place Anthony and Stanton on a pedestal, and promote their vision of the country's political priorities. First, the Women's Rights National Historical Park, which is part of the National Park Service, was established in 1980, and includes the Wesleyan Methodist Church, where the 1848 convention was held, the main visitor's center, and the former homes of Stanton and two other activists. Susan B. Anthony's former home in Rochester, NY, is now the National Susan B. Anthony Museum & House, and was designated a National Historic Landmark in 1966. A third museum, the National Women's History Museum, while elevated by the term "national," is not in fact recognized as such by the federal government but is a private endeavor. It has no physical footprint but exists as a website with online exhibits, with a mission of educating the public, and it offers educational resources for teachers.

Taken together, these "national" museums, through their standing exhibits, brochures, and websites, put forward a specific narrative of the women's suffrage movement, which is lent the imprint of authority by their "national" title. It is critical to understand the story told by these institutions, because for many Americans, it will be the only story they learn about suffrage. It will be the story learned by generations of children on field trips, and by their teachers who compose classroom lessons on women's history. What follows is a summary of the story about women's suffrage communicated through the materials of the Women's Rights National Historical Park (WRNHP) and the National Susan B. Anthony Museum & House (NSBAMH):

> The women's suffrage movement, and Stanton and Anthony's personal activism, emerged out of the antislavery movement prior to the Civil War. Stanton's husband was a "popular abolitionist speaker" and the two honeymooned in 1840 at the World Anti-Slavery Convention in London, where the women were made to sit silently in the back of the room. There, Elizabeth Cady Stanton met Quaker reformer Lucretia Mott and they "vowed to hold a convention … to discuss the injustices against women" (WRNHP n.d.a). In 1848, Stanton and Mott invited other abolitionists and social reformers to the "First Women's Rights Convention" in which women "demand[ed] full and equal rights with men," including the vote (WRNHP 2018). Social reformers developed a philosophy of human rights intending to lift up enslaved people and women alike (visitor's center panels on "The Underground Railroad and the Women's Rights Convention," "Elizabeth Cady Stanton and the Underground Railroad," and "'In defense of Woman and the Slave'").

Susan B. Anthony was "a 19th century crusader. She worked for freedom and equality for all people, especially women and African Americans" (NSBAMH opening panel). She was a Quaker and as such "was brought up in a tradition of spiritual egalitarianism, the belief that all people are created equal. The Anthony family actively participated in the anti-slavery movement" (NSBAMH n.d.b) and their "farmhouse became a meeting place for abolitionists, including Frederick Douglass and William Lloyd Garrison" (NSBAMH n.d.a; see also Brown 2018).

Anthony and Stanton emerged as the core of the women's rights movement. After meeting in 1851, "[t]hey form an activist team and use temperance and abolition gatherings to address women's issues. Stanton writes speeches and devises strategy, while Anthony lectures and circulates petitions" (WRNHP 2018), They also remained committed to abolitionist work, as "[i]n 1856, Susan B. Anthony served as an American Anti-Slavery agent, arranging meetings, making speeches, putting up posters and distributing leaflets," and through the Woman's Loyal League during the war, the women collected "thousands of petitions to outlaw slavery" (NSBAMH n.d.a).

After the war and the abolition of slavery, the two women "narrowed their political focus to one goal: woman suffrage" (panel at WRNHP). However, a disagreement arose among social reformers about suffrage priorities in the late 1860s. The Fourteenth Amendment specified that only men could vote, and "[s]uffragists split over strategy" (WRNHP 2018). Anthony and Stanton "demanded new laws protect everyone's right to vote; black or white, man or woman. They were disappointed and disillusioned when women were excluded from voting rights under the newly adopted 14th and 15th Amendments" (NSBAMH n.d.a). A draft Fifteenth Amendment was to grant Black men the right to vote, but not women. Some social reformers considered it strategically unwise to push simultaneously for Black [male] suffrage and women's suffrage, whereas "Susan B. Anthony and Elizabeth Cady Stanton supported voting rights for African-American males but refused to postpone the work for woman's rights" (NSBAMH panel).

Consequently, the two groups parted ways, and "Stanton and Anthony form National Woman Suffrage Association (NWSA), which pushes for a women's suffrage amendment.... [O]thers organize American Woman Suffrage Association (AWSA) to support voting rights first for black males, then women" (WRNHP 2018). The disagreement turned ugly: "The Republicans, long-time allies, attacked women's rights organizers in New York and in Kansas. Stanton and Anthony turned to anyone who would support suffrage for white women, regardless of their stand on other issues, including African-American civil rights" (visitor's center panel on "The Battle for the Ballot").

Ultimately the strands of the movement were reunited, with Stanton and Anthony again at the helm. In 1892, the NWSA and AWSA merged to form the National American Woman Suffrage Association (NAWSA), first chaired by Stanton, then Anthony. A bill for an amendment was advanced, and in 1920, the "19th Amendment, nicknamed the 'Susan B. Anthony Amendment,' was ratified, extending voting rights to women throughout the United States" (WRNHP 2018).

The websites, brochures, and permanent exhibits of these two museums conclude the story of the struggle for women's voting rights with the passage of the Nineteenth in 1920. Taken as a whole, these museum materials establish Anthony and Stanton as staunch supporters of the rights of African Americans, point to a disagreement over voting rights priorities, but since we learn that the two strands of the movement were reunited under Stanton and Anthony's leadership, we gain the impression that the disagreement was inconsequential, and even though Anthony had died by the time the Nineteenth was adopted, since it bears her moniker, it should be read as "her" victory. The timeline of woman suffrage of the (online) National Women's History Museum (2018) does not depart from this basic narrative.

A white feminist history

This official narrative is problematic and racist in several respects. It reduces the story of women's suffrage to a story primarily of two white women, who are cast as both the backbone and the bookends of the movement, as they mark the beginning (the 1848 convention, of which Stanton was the main organizer) and the end (the adoption of the "Susan B. Anthony Amendment"). People of color who contributed to this movement of great national significance are largely missing from this telling. A critical issue that has been exposed by several historians is that the framing of Anthony and Stanton as anti-racist activists obscures the racist sentiments they expressed and the racist actions they took (discussed below). In addition—and most crucial for this chapter—is the fact that Stanton and Anthony's feminism was a white feminism (in the sense of being defined in relationship to white women's goals), and was therefore racist. Consequently, the narrative in which they are heroes reproduces the violence of that white (universal) feminism. I will discuss each of these points in turn.

While these two museums establish Stanton and Anthony as the backbone and the bookends of the women's suffrage movement, largely missing from the more permanent features of those museums (standing exhibits, brochures, and websites) are the people of color who labored in support of votes for women. In the Women's Rights National Historical Park visitor's center, Harriet Tubman is mentioned, but only with reference to her work on the Underground Railroad, not women's rights. The museum includes a full-size statue of Sojourner Truth, but in a section on the "cult of true womanhood" (or cultural ideas about femininity), and she is described as "one of the most powerful antislavery and women's rights speakers," and yet her contributions to the suffrage movement are not detailed beyond that. Frederick Douglass occupies a prominent position next to Stanton in the "First Wave" sculpture group in the visitors' center lobby, but in the panel texts, he is mentioned almost exclusively in reference to his abolitionist work, not that on behalf of women's rights. The Anthony museum gives much greater attention to Frederick Douglass, as a three-part panel is dedicated to Anthony and Douglass' friendship and their collaboration on antislavery and women's rights work, and Douglass' portrait is featured in the dining room, an important tour stop on the first floor. However, as Brown (2018) noted, the rift in their relationship caused by disagreement over the Fifteenth Amendment (discussed below) is not mentioned in the three-part panel. No other people of color who were activists on behalf of women's suffrage are featured in the museum's fixed materials. Overall, in these museums, people of color have been made invisible or forced to play roles as supporting characters.

This invisibility is a serious oversight as in recent decades, historians and cultural critics have done important scholarship to uncover the many contributions of people of color to the campaign for women's suffrage, including Douglass, Truth, Ida B. Wells-Barnett, Mabel Ping-Hua Lee, Gertrude Simmons Bonnin (Zitkála-Šá), Mary Church Terrell, Adelina Luna Otero-Warren, Harriet Purvis, Jr., Frances Ellen Watkins Harper, and innumerable others (Cahill 2020; Dionne 2020; Dudden 2011; Foner 1992; Fought 2017; Jones 2020; Parker 2020; Terborg-Penn 1998). In the standard imagining of the women's suffrage movement, it is a white movement, led by white heroines, while these other women and men are rendered invisible. Inclusivity in representation is important not just out of a spirit of fairness to their memory, but because the struggle for voting rights is one of the most important social movements in US history. If only white women get credit for this work, then all others appear as indebted takers in the span of history. Historical narratives focused (nearly exclusively) on white heroes enable white supremacists to mistakenly rest assured in their beliefs about outsized contributions of whites to the country's achievements.

Furthermore, the problems of the standard narrative go beyond a gap in reporting. Despite their framing by the national museums as social reformers, Stanton and Anthony said and did things of racist intent and racist effect that in fact made it more difficult for people of color (men and women) to vote. These racist actions have been exposed and examined in detail by historians and other scholars (Dionne 2020; DuBois 1999; Dudden 2011; Free 2015; hooks 1981; Lange 2020; Newman 1999; Terborg-Penn 1998; Tetrault 2014), so I will not belabor them here. Of primary concern are events surrounding the 1860s split over enfranchisement priorities.

As mentioned above, in the 1850s, various northern abolitionists and women's rights activists collaborated and began to articulate a common philosophy, conceptualizing both slavery and the inequalities borne by women as violations of human rights (Free 2012; Stevenson 2017). After the Civil War, as Reconstruction-era politicians debated voting rights for the freed people and former Confederates, Anthony and Stanton saw an opportunity to push for woman's suffrage simultaneously. Leading social reformers—men and women—disagreed, and in

May 1865, Wendell Phillips, the president of the American Anti-Slavery Society, said that while he supported women's suffrage, each issue should be pursued separately and "This hour belongs to the negro" (quoted in Free 2015, 53). Draft versions of a Fourteenth Amendment—which would extend citizenship to freedmen—began circulating, but various drafts indicated that the amendment would establish the vote as a male preserve. Consequently, in December 1865, Stanton and Anthony organized a petition campaign for women's suffrage, and they did so through a strategy of arguing for woman suffrage on the basis of citizenship, borrowing from the strategy developed before the war by abolitionists (109). Laura Free described how in May 1866, Anthony convened:

> the first National Women's Rights Convention since 1860. At this meeting, Anthony proposed a new political strategy: women's rights advocates should consolidate their efforts with those of supporters of black men's enfranchisement. This collaboration, she argued, would "concentrate all our forces for the practical application of our one grand, distinctive, national idea—Universal Suffrage." The convention agreed and formed the American Equal Rights Association (AERA). The AERA's primary goal, Elizabeth Cady Stanton declared, would be to "bury the black man and the woman in the citizen."
>
> *(133)*

While many of their Republican collaborators agreed in theory, they disagreed over strategy. The Fourteenth Amendment was passed by Congress in June 1866, and did specify voting as a male preserve, but was silent as to the enfranchisement of Black men. For northern Republican men, extending the vote to Black men in a Fifteenth Amendment seemed the logical next step, as it would be an expression of their developing philosophy of common "brotherhood" and human rights. There was also a sense of political urgency, since southern men were about to regain voting rights and, the Republicans believed, enfranchisement of Black men would increase the number of Republican voters as a counterweight to those white southerners (voter nullification). Given the urgent timing, many Radical Republicans were unwilling to weigh down the fight for Black male voting rights with the woman's issue (DuBois 1999; Dudden 2011; Free 2015; Terborg-Penn 1998).

At a meeting of the American Equal Rights Association in May 1867, the tension between "Negro [male] suffrage" and "woman suffrage" was growing. Elizabeth Cady Stanton argued that if Black men were enfranchised, "degraded, oppressed himself, he would be more despotic with the governing power than even our Saxon rulers are" (quoted in Dudden 2011, 98). She added,

> If all men are to vote, black and white, lettered and unlettered, washed and unwashed, the safety of the nation as well as the interests of woman demand that we outweigh this incoming tide of ignorance, poverty and vice, with the virtue, wealth, and education of the women of the country.
>
> *(98–99)*

Kansas became the battleground in which women and Black men were pitted against one another. In the fall of 1867, referenda for both "Negro [male] suffrage" and "woman suffrage" were on the ballot. Many Democrats argued that it was necessary to give white women the vote to protect those in their families from the supposed dangers of men of racialized minorities, and also so that white men's votes would not be overpowered by those of Black men. Stanton and Anthony, eager to gain support for woman's suffrage from Democrats, all too readily cast aside their earlier arguments about "universal suffrage" regardless of race or gender, and adopted the Democrats' explicitly racist arguments. They began to argue not just in favor of women voting, but against Black men. Anthony began traveling with and delivering pro-woman-suffrage speeches alongside George Francis Train, a Democratic-leaning racist. In January 1868, they continued their collaboration, as Train provided the funding for Stanton and Anthony's new women's rights newspaper, *The Revolution*. Through their newspaper and other channels, over the next year, the two women campaigned against the Fifteenth Amendment and argued for female enfranchisement before that of Black men, or argued for educational requirements for the vote, which would, they thought, achieve the same ends (Free 2015, 156–160). In October 1868, Stanton went so far as to back the Democratic vice-presidential candidate, Frank Blair, who argued that woman suffrage was necessary to protect white women from Black men (Free 2015, 159–160), even intimating that Black men would use their power to sexually overpower white women (Dudden 2011, 155). Stanton echoed Blair when, in February 1869, she used the case of a young woman accused of infanticide of a child conceived out of rape by a (rumored) Black man to argue that such men should not have the right to serve as jurors in cases involving "Saxon girls" (168). Similarly, in December 1868, Stanton wrote, "Think of Patrick and Sambo and Hans and Yung Tung" making laws for educated and refined women (166), a line that she later repeated (169).

Other members of the American Equal Rights Association were horrified by Stanton and Anthony's racist campaigning and their association with Train. In February of 1869, Congress passed the Fifteenth, which then needed ratification at the state level. At a fateful meeting of the AERA in May 1869, the group split over the amendment. Douglass argued that Black male suffrage was a matter of life or death in the Reconstruction-era South, and Anthony and Stanton disagreed vehemently. While Stanton's rhetoric was more often explicitly racist than was Anthony's, Anthony stood firm, arguing:

> The old anti-slavery school say women must stand back and wait until the negroes shall be recognized. But we say, if you will not give the whole loaf of suffrage to the entire people, give it to the most intelligent first…. If intelligence, justice, and morality are to have precedence in the Government, let the question of woman be brought up first and that of the negro last.
>
> *(quoted in Brown 2018, 127)*

As mentioned above, Anthony and Stanton broke away to form the National Woman Suffrage Association, which would push for woman suffrage, opposing the Fifteenth Amendment as written. The incrementalists of the American Equal Rights Association formed the American Woman Suffrage Association in Boston, intending to back the Fifteenth and subsequently press for woman suffrage. Even following ratification in 1870, Anthony continued to argue that woman suffrage was more important than Black male suffrage. For example, in a speech she delivered in 1873, following her arrest for illegal voting, she said:

> An oligarchy of wealth, where the rich govern the poor; an oligarchy of learning, where the educated govern the ignorant; or even an oligarchy of race, where the Saxon rules the African, might be endured; but this oligarchy of sex, which makes father, brothers, husband, sons, the oligarchs over the mother and sisters, the wife and daughters of every household; which ordains all men sovereigns, all women subjects, carries dissension, discord and rebellion into every home of the nation.
>
> *(quoted in Gordon 2000, 612)*

Stanton's and Anthony's actions throughout this period were racist in several respects. The arguments that they used were not just about women's worthiness, but about how men of color were unworthy. When faced with the possibility that Black men might vote before they did, they did not complain in private, but actively campaigned against those men, publicly denigrating them in speeches and writings, obstructing their chances to improve their lives through the electoral process. Even after Black men gained the vote on paper, Anthony's and Stanton's words on the printed page would have given fuel to others already inclined to suppress Black voting through other means or otherwise discriminate. While Stanton's rhetoric was often harsher than Anthony's, Anthony cannot be exonerated because they were co-editors of the newspaper and worked side-by-side for decades. If Anthony were offended by Stanton's writings, she could have prevented their circulation. Ultimately, their work in this time period was racist in rhetoric, purpose, and effect.

Even after the competition between Black men and (white) women over suffrage was ended by the ratification of the Fifteenth Amendment, Anthony and Stanton elsewise acted in racist fashion. In their massive *History of Woman Suffrage*, they largely failed to include Black activists who worked in support of woman suffrage (Lange 2020; Terborg-Penn 1998; Tetrault 2014, 133–135). This might have been due to any number of reasons, none of which could be read as positive. Allison Lange (2020) argued that the exclusion of Blacks from the *History of Woman Suffrage* was part of a larger pattern in which white suffragists tried to paint their movement as one of white feminine respectability. Images of Blacks did not serve their purpose in swaying white audiences. The omissions had long-term injurious effects, as Black women and men who worked in support of woman suffrage were unrecognized and uncredited, and their concerns went unnoticed for too long. Indeed, Anthony and Stanton acknowledged a racist social and political system in the United States, and often chose to ignore it. In an effort to win the support of white men and women, Anthony sometimes spoke to segregated audiences and she asked Frederick Douglass not to address the Equal Suffrage Association in Atlanta, because "I did not want anything to get in the way of bringing the southern white women into our suffrage association" (quoted in Wells 2020, 193).

Finally, and most importantly for this chapter, Anthony and Stanton failed to take an intersectional perspective with respect to woman suffrage. Although the work that they did has been described as feminist, and as leading to winning "votes for women" (across the board), they did not in fact do that. They conceptualized voting rights from the position in which they stood as white women and defined "woman suffrage" accordingly: as accomplished by a constitutional amendment that would forbid governmental interference with voting on the basis of "sex." While at times they took note of the ways in which different groups of women had different concerns with respect to the vote, it seems they did not let such concerns get in the way of their pursuit of a universalist (but ultimately white) woman suffrage. For one, they collaborated much less actively with women of color than with other white women and thereby were unbeholden to their concerns (Terborg-Penn 1998).

In addition, the two women frequently argued for the need for woman suffrage simultaneously with the suffrage of Black men so that Black women would enjoy the same rights as their husbands, but Black women did not always share their vision. In their earlier meetings of the American Equal Rights Association, Stanton and Anthony heard the perspectives of important African-American suffragists, but ultimately disregarded them. For example, in an 1867 meeting of the association, Sojourner Truth wanted to see Black men and all women gain the vote simultaneously because, according to her, Black men were lazy and profligate spenders "and if colored men get their rights, and not colored women theirs, you see the colored men will be masters over the women, and it will be just as bad as it was before" (quoted in Dudden 2011, 96). Stanton and Anthony did not at that time run with this idea because it would have undermined their argument that all people deserved the vote, regardless of race or gender. Ultimately, Truth did not campaign actively for or against the Fifteenth Amendment because of her commitments to assisting newly emancipated people with basic necessities of life (Dudden 2011, 81). Sojourner Truth did not attend that fateful 1869 AERA meeting, but the Black women who did so indicated that they did not want to stand in the way of the Fifteenth Amendment. Frances Ellen Watkins Harper (Figure 3.5) said, "When it was a question of race [I] let the lesser question of sex go. But the white women all go for sex, letting race occupy a minor position" (quoted in Terborg-Penn 1998, 32). The meeting recorders transcribed her conclusion as such: "If the nation could only handle one question, [Harper] would not have Black women put a single straw in the way, if only the men of the race could obtain what they wanted" (33). As Faye Dudden (2011, 81) observed: "none of these black women leaders challenged Phillips's 'Negro's hour' priority,

FIGURE 3.5 Frances Ellen Watkins Harper (1825–1911).
Credit: Internet Archive Book Images.

but none of them endorsed it either." Nonplussed, Stanton and Anthony persisted in fighting the Fifteenth in the name of "universal suffrage," supposedly in support of Black women, as well, but in fact disregarding their expressed wishes. On another occasion, Anthony went so far as to decline an invitation from a group of Black women to help them organize a suffrage organization (Wells 2020, 193), another indication that her campaign for "woman" suffrage was defined in universalist (and therefore racist) terms.

The sets of obstacles to voting that different groups faced varied immensely throughout the late nineteenth and early twentieth centuries, extending far beyond a constitutional amendment. Consequently, when the "Susan B. Anthony Amendment" was adopted, for many people, it was a hollow victory. At the Republican National Convention in August 2020, the president's daughter-in-law, Lara Trump, said that "100 years ago today, the Nineteenth Amendment was ratified granting the right to vote to every American woman" (L. Trump 2020). However, the Nineteenth Amendment (ratified August 18, adopted August 26) secured the right to vote for white women primarily. Millions of women of color faced obstacles to voting that were not addressed by the white-led women's suffrage associations (neither the NWSA, the AWSA, nor the NAWSA, when the two associations were reunited under Stanton and Anthony's leadership). While people often talk about the Nineteenth Amendment "giving," "granting," "securing," or "guaranteeing" women the right to vote, it did none of those. It simply states that the "right of citizens … to vote shall not be denied or abridged … on account of sex." It could still be denied for any number of reasons.

When the Nineteenth Amendment was adopted, women of color were still blocked from voting in several ways. In southern states, poll taxes, literacy tests, prohibitive paperwork requirements, violent intimidation, and other tactics of voter suppression prevented Black men from voting and would do the same to Black women, all the way up until the passage of the Voting Rights Act of 1965 (Jones 2020). Most Indigenous people were ineligible to vote in US elections until they were recognized as citizens in 1924, and for decades, they and Mexican-American residents in the Southwest faced the same types of voter suppression techniques used against Blacks, plus others stemming from doubts about belonging and loyalty. Chinese immigrants were barred from US citizenship on the basis of race until 1943, and Japanese and other Asian immigrants until 1952 (Block 2020). In addition, women in America's colonies (Puerto Rico, the Philippines, Guam, the US Virgin Islands, American Samoa, and the Northern Mariana Islands) gained citizenship and voting rights piecemeal and only in part or not at all (Prieto 2020). The Nineteenth Amendment was, in essence, a white feminist piece of legislation because, designed from the perspective of white women, it secured their voting rights and therefore allowed them to participate in shaping the future of US leadership and legislation for decades, celebrating this supposed achievement "for women," while ignoring the specific obstacles faced by people of color. Because it was an amendment designed in relationship to white women's goals, its first major effect was to increase the power of whites in the country, as white women voted largely with white men. It was an amendment, therefore, that advanced white supremacy.

In fact, Martha Jones (2020) has suggested that we should not celebrate "suffrage" as centered upon the Nineteenth, but take a broader perspective, looking at "voting rights." Doing so, she writes, we see that many of the Black women who worked in support of the Nineteenth did not stop their work in 1920. Rather, they continued to work in support of voting rights for Black women and men in the South, and those who took the torch from them continued this work all the way to the Voting Rights Act of 1965. Furthermore, since the Supreme Court ruled against a key part of the Voting Rights Act in 2013, racist voter suppression tactics have proliferated, including via voter ID laws, voter registration restrictions, voter purges, polling station closings, and partisan gerrymandering (Anderson 2018). The right to vote is not something given on one day through one piece of legislation, but something that must be safeguarded through every election cycle.

Needless to say, the standing exhibits, brochures, and websites of the Women's Rights National Historical Park and the National Susan B. Anthony Museum & House are silent about these racist aspects of the Stanton and Anthony legacy.

The museums celebrate the passage of the Nineteenth, and that is where their story of voting rights ends. Unfortunately, by replicating the universal feminist perspective of Stanton and Anthony, which is ultimately a white feminist perspective, the museums feed into a broader cultural process of erasing women of color, denying their importance, and denying ongoing struggles to vote. By equating victory with the victory of white women, the museums unwittingly reinforce the power and privileges of whites in this country. The standard narrative about women's voting rights is a white feminist history about a white feminist movement: white feminism, squared.

The cultural power of Stanton's and Anthony's legacies extends far beyond these two museums. Throughout the last century, Stanton and Anthony have been given central stage in recounting of the story of women's suffrage in the United States. Both women have been featured on US stamps. Anthony is one of a handful of women ever to be featured on US currency (the silver dollar, issued in 1979). In the Capitol Rotunda in Washington, DC, a statue called the "Portrait Monument" was unveiled in 1921, dedicated to women's voting rights activists, but featuring only Anthony, Stanton, and Lucretia Mott. Seneca Falls remains considered the geographic heart of women's activism in the United States. On January 21, 2017, the day after Trump's inauguration, the Women's March—a protest against his perceived misogyny—was the largest single-day demonstration in US history with the main march in Washington, DC, and sister marches in all 50 states and on all 7 continents. Although Seneca Falls is a quiet, rural town, with a population just shy of 7,000, the population more than doubled on the day of the Women's March, as an estimated 10,000 people turned out, all invited by the organizers to dress in the signature colors of the women's suffrage movement, and many carried signs bearing the visages and words of Anthony and Stanton. Just in time to celebrate the centennial of the Nineteenth, the new National Women's Hall of Fame opened in August 2020 in the former Seneca Knitting Mill, just across the lake from the Women's Rights National Historical Park visitors' center; it includes, of course, Anthony and Stanton.

Donald Trump and Susan B. Anthony

When Donald Trump entered office, he did so in the midst of feminist uproar. At least 17 women had accused him of sexual misconduct and the October surprise of 2016 was the *Access Hollywood* recording of him bragging about sexual assault and "grab[bing] 'em by the pussy" (Kray, Carroll, and Mandell 2018). The Women's March revealed the widespread severe concern about how he had treated and would treat women. The new president had a lot of work to do to prove that he was not misogynistic.

Trump especially needed to prove that he would treat women of color with respect, for he had stumbled badly with respect to Harriet Tubman. In April 2016, Obama's Treasury Department announced that Tubman—the formerly enslaved abolitionist and Underground Railroad conductor—would replace Andrew Jackson on the $20 bill. Jackson's image had long been problematic as he was a slaveholder and he ordered the genocidal removal of Indigenous people westward in the Trail of Tears. Tubman was to be the first person of color and the first woman set to be featured on a US currency bill since the mid-nineteenth century, yet candidate Trump dismissed the selection of Tubman as "pure political correctness." Four days into his presidency, he requested that a portrait of Andrew Jackson be hung in the Oval Office, just behind the resolute desk, and he later postponed issuing the new currency with Tubman's likeness until after the end of his term in office (Rappeport 2019).

The news media therefore attended closely to remarks that he would make in the first Women's History Month of his presidency. During his scheduled remarks before a women's empowerment panel, he said, "We've had leaders like Susan B. Anthony." Then, he said to the audience, "Have you heard of Susan B. Anthony? I'm shocked that you've heard of her." Twitter erupted with criticism as people thought that he had just learned about her (although, watching the clip, it is clear that he was joking) (Cummings 2017). However, the problem is not that he had not heard of her, but that it seems he had heard of no one but her. Susan B. Anthony became Donald Trump's go-to women's rights activist, a person whose name he would invoke frequently—with Elizabeth Cady Stanton running a close second. Throughout his presidency, Anthony and Stanton were useful symbols at commemorative ceremonies when the public would be expecting him to recognize women's rights. Yet in all of these statements, he revived and retrenched the tired, problematic narrative about women's voting rights.

Every year in March the president is expected to issue a proclamation naming that month Women's History Month, and Trump did his duty, although in ways that, once again, made white women the heroes. In his 2017 proclamation, he lauded the achievements of 13 women, only 3 of whom might be characterized as women's rights advocates. He did mention Harriet Tubman, who spent her later years speaking on behalf of women's rights, but he characterized her only as an escaped slave and abolitionist. He referred to Susan B. Anthony, not with reference to voting rights, but rather with "her friend, Dr. Charlotte Lozier ... both of whom advocated for the dignity and equality of women, pregnant mothers, and their children" (Proclamation No. 9576, 82 Fed. Reg. 12711 (Mar. 1, 2017)). Pairing Anthony and Lozier, and referring to their work on behalf of pregnant mothers and children, he thereby characterized Anthony as an antiabortion activist. This characterization is critical for the antiabortion organization called Susan B. Anthony List, even though historians have concluded that it is based on a misreading of the historical record (Carroll, Mandell, and Kray 2018, 342, 347–348). Invoking Anthony as an antiabortion activist was a way for Trump to commemorate historical women while also signaling to evangelical Christian voters his attention to their causes. The Women's History Month proclamations in 2018 and 2019 made no reference to women's rights activists (Proclamation

No. 9702, 83 Fed. Reg. 9409 (Feb. 28, 2018); Proclamation No. 9847, 84 Fed. Reg. 8241 (Mar. 1, 2019)). In his 2020 Women's History Month proclamation, Trump noted the upcoming centennial of the Nineteenth stating,

> This milestone in our country was made possible by the devotion, leadership, and perseverance of pioneers like Elizabeth Cady Stanton and Susan B. Anthony. The ratification of the 19th Amendment enabled women to finally have their voices counted in voting booths.
> *(Proclamation No. 9990, 85 Fed. Reg. 12719 (Feb. 28, 2020))*

In this narrative, once again, 1920 is the end of the story, with victory achieved long ago, for women across the board, and all honor is afforded to two white women.

In July 2020, the president once again turned to Susan B. Anthony. In the weeks following the killings of George Floyd and Breonna Taylor, and other examples of racist and/or police violence, Black Lives Matter protestors in various locations across the country, and even internationally, directed anger toward public buildings and installations viewed as symbols of institutionalized violence, racism, and colonialism. Public buildings and statues were marked with graffiti and protestors toppled or attempted to remove statues of historical figures seen as agents of institutionalized racism, particularly Confederate leaders and generals and participants in colonial and genocidal regimes, such as Christopher Columbus and Juan de Oñate (Mitter 2020). The Trump administration spun the violence against statues as an attempt to destroy American history, values, and freedoms. On July 3, 2020, he delivered a speech at the fireworks celebration at Mount Rushmore in South Dakota. Mount Rushmore is itself a symbol of racism and colonialism, as the sculptor was a white supremacist with ties to the Ku Klux Klan and the Daughters of the Confederacy, and the monument is on Black Hills lands sacred to the Lakota Sioux, forcibly taken from them by the US government in violation of a treaty (Bernard 2020). In his speech, the president misrepresented the attacks on property, characterizing them as attacks against the presidents represented in Mount Rushmore, which was not the case. He characterized the "founders" of the nation as responsible for "the unstoppable march for freedom" and the "advance[ment] of the human condition." He warned that

> there is a growing danger that threatens every blessing our ancestors fought so hard for, struggled, they bled to secure. Our nation is witnessing a merciless campaign to wipe out our history, defame our heroes, erase our values, and indoctrinate our children ... Make no mistake: this left-wing cultural revolution is designed to overthrow the American Revolution.

He announced that he would send federal law enforcement to protect federal monuments (D. Trump 2020). The following day, on July 4, the president issued an "Executive Order on Building and Rebuilding Monuments to American Heroes" (Exec. Order No. 13,934, 85 Fed. Reg. 41165 (2020)). He ordered the creation of a task force to open a National Garden filled with statues "to depict historically significant Americans ... who have contributed positively to America." The order announced that the "National Garden should be composed of statues, including statues of John Adams, Susan B. Anthony, Clara Barton, Daniel Boone" and 27 other named individuals. Susan B. Anthony comes second in the list, but because the types of positive contributions included "the Founding Fathers, those who fought for the abolition of slavery ... heroes of the United States Armed Forces" and other reasons, but not voting rights or women's rights activism, she appears as a token woman. The order reads:

> These monuments express our noblest ideals: respect for our ancestors, love of freedom, and striving for a more perfect union.... In preserving them, we show reverence for the past, we dignify our present, and we inspire those who are to come. To build a monument is to ratify our shared national project.

By singling out nineteenth-century figures such as Susan B. Anthony and abolitionists, the Trump administration could show support for civil rights, while pretending that rights for women and Blacks have long been secured.

The following month, on August 18, 2020, Donald Trump convened an Oval Office signing of a "Proclamation on 100th Anniversary of the Ratification of the Nineteenth Amendment." In attendance were members of the Women's Suffrage Centennial Commission—several wearing white clothing and the white, gold, and purple "Votes for Women" sash—among them some major antiabortion leaders for whom Susan B. Anthony bears special significance. In that speech, he credited the passage of the Nineteenth to the "bold trailblazers like Susan B. Anthony, Elizabeth Cady, Stanton, Harriet Forten Purvis, and Frances Ellen Watkins Harper.... The faith, fortitude, and resolute determination of those committed to this noble cause brought about a victory that continues to inspire today." Once again, Anthony and Stanton get top billing, although the final two women mentioned were African American. He offered no further detail or nuance, and once again, the proclamation implied that the fight ended in 1920. He surprised the assembled crowd, announcing that he would pardon Anthony for her 1872 crime of illegal voting (C-SPAN 2020). The tiniest nod to Black women's voting rights activists was immediately overshadowed by news media attention to Susan B. Anthony for the remainder of the day. Then, as his final official act of suffrage commemoration, for Women's Equality Day, August 26, 2020, the centennial anniversary of the adoption of the Nineteenth, Trump issued a proclamation, stating:

> I was proud to issue a Proclamation honoring the women's suffrage movement and sign a full pardon for one of its greatest leaders, Susan B. Anthony.... On Women's Equality Day, we remember the trailblazers like Anthony who worked tirelessly to achieve a more just and equal United States.
>
> *(Proclamation No. 10063, 85 Fed. Reg. 53643 (Aug. 25, 2020))*

Susan B. Anthony was, for Donald Trump, a useful figure at a time when his words about women were subject to intense scrutiny. As a white woman, a person who primarily supported Republicans, and a person whose name has been claimed for antiabortion activism, her memory served various ends. Through elevating Anthony, Donald Trump could signal support for women's rights, reassure evangelical Christians, and dodge considerations about women of color or post-1920 voting rights struggles. However, by reiterating the overworked, problematic narrative of women's rights centered upon white heroes who demonstrated racism in word and deed, Donald Trump fueled the cultural machinery of racism. Susan B. Anthony's memory profits those who would identify the United States as a white, patriarchal, Christian nation.

Centering Black women

Since 2016, the chorus of voices denouncing racism within the historic women's suffrage movement and calling for an expanded vision of the movement has grown ever louder. In Central Park in New York City in 2014, there were 23 statues, all of men (or fictional women). A group called "The Elizabeth Cady Stanton and Susan B. Anthony Statue Fund" organized to raise money for a statue of these two women in the park. After public outcry criticizing the design "for placing only white women on the pedestal," Sojourner Truth was added (Gupta 2020). The Women's Rights Pioneers Monument was unveiled on August 26, 2020, the centennial of the Nineteenth's adoption. Throughout the summer of 2020, leading up to the centennial, numerous opinion pieces, podcasts, and televised and video-streamed interviews with historians discussed the racism of white suffragists and the need to turn attention to women of color who worked for the voting rights of people for whom the Nineteenth was an insufficient safeguard. Because of COVID-19, talks by historians, webinars, museum exhibits, and commemorative events went online, circulated even further through social media.

As the centennial celebrations rolled out, while the permanent fixtures (standing exhibits, brochures, and website main pages) of the Women's Rights National Historical Park and the Anthony museum remained unchanged and continued to present a white feminist history centered upon Anthony and Stanton, newer, ad hoc programming demonstrated that leadership at those institutions was recognizing a need for a more critical and inclusive history. In October 2019, the Women's Rights National Historical Park (2019) added a webpage about the Nineteenth, which mentioned some women of color suffragists and acknowledged that "the amendment did not give voting rights to all women." In 2020, the park also video-streamed a series of lectures, including Laura Free on "Grappling with Suffragists' Racism," Martha Jones on "Race and Gender in the Struggle for Women's Suffrage," and others about the contributions to women's voting rights activism made by Harriet Tubman, Sojourner Truth, Frederick Douglass, and Ida B. Wells-Barnett (WRNHP n.d.b). When I visited the Anthony museum in March, the tour guide offered that they were featuring Hester

C. Jeffrey in their tour speeches, Jeffrey being an African-American Rochesterian social reformer who labored on behalf of African Americans and women, and who collaborated with Anthony. Finally, when Trump pardoned Anthony, the museum rejected the pardon, the director, Deborah Hughes, explaining "the activist did not think she'd done anything wrong," and that "the best way to honor Anthony would be taking a clear stance against voter suppression and advocating for human rights for all" (Uleby 2020).

California Senator Kamala Harris was the first Black and the first Asian woman to be nominated by a major party (Democratic) for the vice presidency, and in her acceptance speech on August 19, she acknowledged the Black female voting rights activists who had preceded her. She said:

> This week marks the 100th anniversary of the passage of the 19th Amendment. And we celebrate the women who fought for that right. Yet so many of the Black women who helped secure that victory were still prohibited from voting, long after its ratification. But they were undeterred.... These women inspired us to pick up the torch—and fight on. Women like Mary Church Terrell and Mary McCleod Bethune. Fannie Lou Hamer and Diane Nash. Constance Baker Motley and Shirley Chisholm. We're not often taught their stories. But as Americans, we all stand on their shoulders.
>
> *(Stevens 2020)*

This passage is remarkable in two respects. She did not mention Anthony and Stanton, but put Black women at the center. Further, just as Martha Jones (2020) has done, Harris established that rather than two stories—one of women's voting rights and one of civil rights activism—there was one thread that united them: the fight for voting rights across the board, led by Black women.

In his book on *Commemorations*, John Gillis (1994, 5) wrote, "Identities and memories are not things we think *about*, but things we think *with*." He added: "Just as memory and identity support one another, they also sustain certain subjective positions, social boundaries, and of course, power" (4). Our national museums, monuments, commemorative celebrations, and official proclamations about the nation's past all work together to delineate the contours of the nation through a specific imagining of its past. The standard narrative of the women's suffrage movement in the United States, centered upon Elizabeth Cady Stanton and Susan B. Anthony, is white feminism, squared. Those two women defined "woman suffrage" in relationship to their own legislative desires, used racist strategies in pursuit of their goals, and consequently, their primary legislative legacy, the Nineteenth Amendment, left out millions of women. A retelling of the history of women's suffrage that elevates their memory compounds the injustice by erasing the struggles, past and present, of people of color against myriad tactics of voter suppression and other forms of violence and discrimination. The sticky feminist narrative is ready-made for those who would fashion the United States as a white, patriarchal, Christian nation.

References

Anderson, Carol. 2018. *One Person, No Vote: How Voter Suppression Is Destroying Democracy*. New York: Bloomsbury.
Belluck, Pam. 2019. "Trump Administration Blocks Funds for Planned Parenthood and Others Over Abortion Referrals." *New York Times*, February 22, 2019. https://www.nytimes.com/2019/02/22/health/trump-defunds-planned-parenthood.html.
Bernard, Diane. 2020. "The Creator of Mount Rushmore's Forgotten Ties to White Supremacy." *Washington Post*, July 2, 2020. https://www.washingtonpost.com/history/2020/07/03/mount-rushmore-gutzon-borglum-klan-stone-mountain/.
Block, Melissa. 2020. "Yes, Women Could Vote after the 19th Amendment—But Not All Women. Or Men." *NPR*, August 26, 2020. https://www.npr.org/2020/08/26/904730251/yes-women-could-vote-after-the-19th-amendment-but-not-all-women-or-men.
Brown, Michael J. 2018. "Commemoration and Contestation: Susan B. Anthony, Frederick Douglass, Hillary Clinton, and Barack Obama." In *Nasty Women and Bad Hombres: Gender and Race in the 2016 US Presidential Election*, edited by Christine A. Kray, Tamar W. Carroll, and Hinda Mandell, 121–134. Rochester, NY: University of Rochester Press.
Cahill, Cathleen D. 2020. *Recasting the Vote: How Women of Color Transformed the Suffrage Movement*. Chapel Hill: University of North Carolina Press.
Carroll, Tamar W., Hinda Mandell, and Christine A. Kray. 2018. "Epilogue: Public Memory, White Supremacy, and Reproductive Justice in the Trump Era." In *Nasty Women and Bad Hombres: Gender and Race in the 2016 US Presidential Election*, edited by Christine A. Kray, Tamar W. Carroll, and Hinda Mandell, 337–349. Rochester, NY: University of Rochester Press.
Centers for Disease Control (CDC). 2019. "Maternal Mortality." https://www.cdc.gov/nchs/maternal-mortality/index.htm?CDC_AA_refVal=https%3A%2F%2Fwww.cdc.gov%2Fnchs%2Ffastats%2Fmaternal-mortality.htm. Page last reviewed November 20, 2019.
CNN. 2016. "Election 2016: Exit Polls." *CNN.com*. https://www.cnn.com/election/2016/results/exit-polls/national/president.
Collins, Patricia Hill. 2000. *Black Feminist Thought: Knowledge, Consciousness, and the Politics of Empowerment*, 2nd ed. New York: Routledge.
Combahee River Collective, The. (1977) 1982. "A Black Feminist Statement." In *All the Women are White, All the Blacks Are Men, But Some of Us Are Brave: Black Women's Studies*, edited by Gloria T. Hull, Patricia Bell Scott, and Barbara Smith, 13–22. Old Westbury, NY: Feminist Press.
Crenshaw, Kimberlé. 1989. "Demarginalizing the Intersection of Race and Sex: A Black Feminist Critique of Antidiscrimination Doctrine, Feminist Theory and Antiracist Politics." *University of Chicago Legal Forum* 1: 139–168. http://chicagounbound.uchicago.edu/uclf/vol1989/iss1/8.
———. 1991. "Mapping the Margins: Intersectionality, Identity Politics, and Violence against Women of Color." *Stanford Law Review* 43 (6): 1241–1299. https://www.jstor.org/stable/1229039.
C-SPAN. 2020. "President Trump Signs Proclamation on 100th Anniversary of 19th Amendment." August 18, 2020. https://www.c-span.org/video/?474926-1/president-trump-announces-posthumous-pardon-susan-b-anthony.

Cummings, William. 2017. "'Have you heard of Susan B. Anthony?' Trump Quipped. Twitter Was Not Amused." *USA Today*, March 29, 2017. https://www.usatoday.com/story/news/politics/onpolitics/2017/03/29/trump-speech-asks-about-susan-b-anthony/99801030/.

Dionne, Evette. 2017. "Women's Suffrage Leaders Left Out Black Women." *Teen Vogue*, August 18, 2017. https://www.teenvogue.com/story/womens-suffrage-leaders-left-out-black-women.

———. 2020. *Lifting as We Climb: Black Women's Battle for the Ballot Box*. New York: Viking. Kindle.

DuBois, Ellen Carol. 1999. *Feminism and Suffrage: The Emergence of an Independent Women's Movement in America, 1848–1869*, reprint with a new preface. Ithaca, NY: Cornell University Press.

Dudden, Faye E. 2011. *Fighting Chance: The Struggle Over Woman Suffrage and Black Suffrage in Reconstruction America*. New York: Oxford University Press. Kindle.

Foner, Philip S., ed. 1992. *Frederick Douglass on Women's Rights*, reprint ed. Boston, MA: Da Capo Press.

Ford, Sabrina. 2017. "How Racism Split the Suffrage Movement." *Bust Magazine*. https://bust.com/feminism/19147-equal-means-equal.html.

Fought, Leigh. 2017. *Women in the World of Frederick Douglass*. Oxford: Oxford University Press.

Free, Laura E. 2012. "'To Bury the Black Man and the Woman in the Citizen': The American Equal Rights Association and the New York State Constitutional Convention of 1867." In *Susan B. Anthony and the Struggle for Equal Rights*, edited by Christine L. Ridarsky and Mary M. Huth, 59–85. Rochester, NY: University of Rochester Press.

———. 2015. *Suffrage Reconstructed: Gender, Race, and Voting Rights in the Civil War Era*. Ithaca, NY: Cornell University Press.

Gillis, John R. 1994. "Memory and Identity: The History of a Relationship." In *Commemorations: The Politics of National Identity*, edited by John R. Gillis, 3–24. Princeton: Princeton University Press.

Goodnough, Abby. 2020. "Trump Administration Unveils a Major Shift in Medicaid." *New York Times*, January 30, 2020. https://www.nytimes.com/2020/01/30/health/medicaid-block-grant-trump.html.

Gordon, Ann D., ed. 2000. *The Selected Papers of Elizabeth Cady Stanton and Susan B. Anthony. Volume 2: Against an Aristocracy of Sex, 1866 to 1873*. New Brunswick, NJ: Rutgers University Press.

Gupta, Alisha Haridasani. 2020. "For Three Suffragists, a Monument Well Past Due." *New York Times*, August 6, 2020. https://www.nytimes.com/2020/08/06/arts/design/suffragist-19th-amendment-central-park.html.

Hegewish, Ariane, and Heidi Hartmann. 2019. "The Gender Wage Gap: 2018 Earnings Differences by Race and Ethnicity." *Institute for Women's Policy Research*, March 7, 2019. https://iwpr.org/publications/gender-wage-gap-2018/.

Hohman, Maura. 2020. "'Daddy Changed the World': Video of George Floyd's Daughter, 6, Goes Viral." *Today.com*, June 3, 2020. https://www.today.com/news/george-floyd-s-daughter-6-protest-goes-viral-video-t183126.

hooks, bell. 1981. *Ain't I a Woman? Black Women and Feminism*. Boston: South End Press.

———. 1984. *Feminist Theory: From Margin to Center*. Boston: South End Press.

Hull, Gloria T., and Barbara Smith. 1982. "Introduction: The Politics of Black Women's Studies." In *All the Women Are White, All the Blacks Are Men, But Some of Us Are Brave: Black Women's Studies*, edited by Gloria T. Hull, Patricia Bell Scott, and Barbara Smith, xvii–xxxi. Old Westbury, NY: Feminist Press.

Human Rights Watch. 2018. "Trump's 'Mexico City Policy' or 'Global Gag Rule.'" February 8, 2018. https://www.hrw.org/news/2018/02/14/trumps-mexico-city-policy-or-global-gag-rule#.
Jones, Martha S. 2020. *Vanguard: How Black Women Broke Barriers, Won the Vote, and Insisted on Equality for All*. New York: Basic Books. Kindle.
Kray, Christine A. 2018. "A Renaissance of Feminist Ritual: Susan B. Anthony's Gravesite on Election Day." In *Nasty Women and Bad Hombres: Gender and Race in the 2016 US Presidential Election*, edited by Christine A. Kray, Tamar W. Carroll, and Hinda Mandell, 248–263. Rochester, NY: University of Rochester Press.
Kray, Christine A., Tamar W. Carroll, and Hinda Mandell. 2018. "Introduction: The Historical Imagination and Fault Lines in the Electorate." In *Nasty Women and Bad Hombres: Gender and Race in the 2016 US Presidential Election*, edited by Christine A. Kray, Tamar W. Carroll, and Hinda Mandell, 1–22. Rochester, NY: University of Rochester Press.
Kyung-Hoon, Kim. 2018. "Honduran Migrant, Clutching Two Small Children, Flees Tear Gas." *Reuters.com*, November 27, 2018. https://www.reuters.com/article/idUSKCN1NW10I.
Lampen, Claire. 2016. "Before You Put an 'I Voted' Sticker on Susan B. Anthony's Grave, Remember She Was a Racist." *Mic*, November 8, 2016. https://www.mic.com/articles/158856/before-you-put-an-i-voted-sticker-on-susan-b-anthony-s-grave-remember-she-was-a-racist.
Lange, Allison K. 2017. "We Can Do Better Than the Suffragists." *Nursing Clio*, January 5, 2017. https://nursingclio.org/2017/01/05/we-can-do-better-than-the-suffragists/.
———. 2020. *Picturing Political Power: Images in the Women's Suffrage Movement*. Chicago: University of Chicago Press. Kindle.
Lorde, Audre. 1984. *Sister Outsider: Essays and Speeches*. Trumansburg, NY: Crossing Press.
Mitter, Siddhartha. 2020. "All Statues Are Local: The Great Toppling of 2020 and the Rebirth of Civic Imagination." *The Intercept*, July 19, 2020. https://theintercept.com/2020/07/19/confederate-statues-monuments-local/.
NSBAMH (National Susan B. Anthony Museum & House). n.d.a. "Abolitionist." Accessed August 9, 2020. http://susanb.org/abolitionist.
———. n.d.b. *Thank You for Visiting!* Brochure acquired at the museum, March 2020.
National Women's History Museum. 2018. "Timeline: Woman Suffrage." April 18, 2018. https://www.womenshistory.org/exhibits/timeline-woman-suffrage.
NBC News. 2020. "Trump's Election Year Budget Proposal Slashes Medicaid, Other Social Safety Nets." *NBC News*, February 10, 2020. https://www.nbcnews.com/politics/donald-trump/trump-s-election-year-budget-proposal-slashes-medicaid-other-social-n1134081.
Newcomb, Alyssa. 2020. "Nail Salons Will Be Different When They Reopen: Here's What to Expect." *Today.com*. May 13, 2020. https://www.today.com/style/nail-salons-will-be-different-when-they-reopen-here-s-t181483.
Newman, Louise Michelle. 1999. *White Women's Rights: The Racial Origins of Feminism in the United States*. New York: Oxford University Press.
New York Times Editorial Board. 2017. "Even College Doesn't Bridge the Racial Income Gap." *New York Times*, September 20, 2017. https://www.nytimes.com/2017/09/20/opinion/college-racial-income-gap.html.
Parker, Alison M. 2020. *Unceasing Militant: The Life of Mary Church Terrell*. Chapel Hill: University of North Carolina Press.

Prieto, Laura. 2020. "Votes for Colonized Women." *Process: A Blog for American History*, May 28, 2020. https://www.processhistory.org/prieto-votes-colonized/.
Rappeport, Alan. 2019. "Harriet Tubman $20 Bill Is Delayed Until Trump Leaves Office, Mnuchin Says." *New York Times*, May 22, 2019. https://www.nytimes.com/2019/05/22/us/harriet-tubman-bill.html.
Ray, Raka. 2017. *Facebook Post*, January 21, 2017. https://me.me/i/raka-ray-4-hrs-to-my-white-friends-demonstrating-today-7917157.
Reilly, Katie. 2016. "Read Hillary Clinton's Historic Victory Speech as Presumptive Democratic Nominee." *Time*, June 8, 2016. https://time.com/4361099/hillary-clinton-nominee-speech-transcript/.
Shabazz, Sa'iyda. n.d. "U.N.I.T.Y. Why Intersectionality Is Important in This Post-Election World." *ScaryMommy.com*. Accessed May 26, 2019. https://www.scarymommy.com/intersectionality-is-important-this-post-election-world/.
Stevens, Matt. 2020. "Kamala Harris Accepts Vice-Presidential Nomination: Full Transcript." *New York Times*, August 19, 2020. https://www.nytimes.com/2020/08/19/us/politics/kamala-harris-dnc-speech.html.
Stevenson, Ana. 2017. "The 'Great Doctrine of Human Rights': Articulation and Authentication in the Nineteenth-Century U.S. Antislavery and Women's Rights Movements." *Humanity: An International Journal of Human Rights, Humanitarianism, and Development* 8 (3): 413–439. https://doi.org/10.1353/hum.2017.0026.
Stolberg, Sheryl Gay. 2020. "Trump Administration Asks Supreme Court to Strike Down Affordable Care Act." *New York Times*, June 26, 2020. https://www.nytimes.com/2020/06/26/us/politics/obamacare-trump-administration-supreme-court.html.
Terborg-Penn, Rosalyn. 1998. *African American Women in the Struggle for the Vote, 1850–1920*. Bloomington: Indiana University Press.
Tetrault, Lisa. 2014. *The Myth of Seneca Falls: Memory and the Women's Suffrage Movement, 1848–1898*. Chapel Hill: University of North Carolina Press.
Trump, Donald J. 2020. "Remarks by President Trump at South Dakota's 2020 Mount Rushmore Fireworks Celebration, Keystone, South Dakota." *WhiteHouse.gov*, July 4, 2020. https://www.whitehouse.gov/briefings-statements/remarks-president-trump-south-dakotas-2020-mount-rushmore-fireworks-celebration-keystone-south-dakota/.
Trump, Lara. 2020. "Lara Trump 2020 RNC Speech Transcript." *Rev*, August 26, 2020. https://www.rev.com/blog/transcripts/lara-trump-2020-rnc-speech-transcript.
Ulaby, Neda. 2020. "Susan B. Anthony Museum Rejects President Trump's Pardon of the Suffragist." *NPR*, August 20, 2020. https://www.npr.org/2020/08/20/904321406/susan-b-anthony-museum-rejects-president-trumps-pardon-of-the-suffragette.
Viera, Bené. 2016. "Your Fave Is Problematic: White Suffragettes Were Very Fucking Racist." *The Frisky*, November 11, 2016. https://thefrisky.com/your-fave-is-problematic-white-suffragettes-were-very-fucking-racist/.
Weiss, Elayne. 2019. "The Trump Administration's Impact on Public and Assisted Housing." *American Bar Association*, October 2, 2019. https://www.americanbar.org/groups/crsj/publications/human_rights_magazine_home/vol--44--no-2--housing/the-trump-administration-s-impact-on-public-and-assisted-housing/.
Wells, Ida B. 2020. *Crusade for Justice: The Autobiography of Ida B. Wells*, 2nd ed. Edited by Alfreda M. Duster. Chicago: University of Chicago Press. Kindle.
White House, The. 2019. "President Trump Participates in a Signing Ceremony for the Woman's Suffrage Centennial Coin Act." *Youtube.com*, November 25, 2019. https://www.youtube.com/watch?v=UPoD_JFfQ9g.

WRNHP (Women's Rights National Historical Park). 2018. *Women's Rights*. Washington, DC: Government Printing Office. Brochure acquired at the park, March 2020.
———. 2019. "The 19th Amendment: A Crash Course." October 9, 2019. https://www.nps.gov/wori/learn/historyculture/2020-crash-course.htm.
———. n.d.a. *Elizabeth Cady Stanton's Life in Seneca Falls*. National Park Service. Brochure acquired at the park, March 2020.
———. n.d.b. "Videos." *Youtube.com*. Accessed August 24, 2020. https://www.youtube.com/user/WORINHP/videos.

PART II
The cultural policing of borders

4

"YOUR RACIST ASS DID TOO MUCH"

Hypermasculinity, Donald Trump, and rap music

Matthew Oware

This chapter explores the perceptions of Donald Trump among rap artists decades before and then during his presidency. Over this course of time, he expressed forms of heteronormativity that both converged with and diverged from Black male rappers' performative expressions of masculinity. Specifically, in earlier songs, musicians embraced a pre-political Trumpian masculinity personified as misogynistic, status-seeking, and combative. This posture matches a masculinity otherwise performed in rappers' music, identified in this work as a form of protest masculinity (see Connell and Messerschmidt 2005). In the mid-2000s, many rappers had valorized Trump as a symbol of heteronormative success and the epitome of heterosexual manhood. However, during his 2016 presidential run and his time in office, a majority of performers shunned him for his racist language and behaviors. Once President Trump's rhetoric had veered into what Martin (2018) called "hyper Anglo masculinity," which included the promotion of racist and anti-immigrant sentiments as a type of manhood, rappers began to rebuke him. As I argue in the following, versions of Trumpian masculinity share similarities with the artists' enactment of *protest masculinity*, a discursive performance by men of color (see Connell and Messerschmidt 2005; Messerschmidt 2018). Rap artists embraced Trump's hypermasculine performance, which conveyed materialism and gendered dominance. However, by the presidential run in 2015, Trumpian masculinity had devolved into racist demagoguery. Consequently, rappers condemned his politicized white supremacist "keeper of the white nation" stance that frequently terrorized people of color.

This chapter lays out the pre-political construct of Trumpian masculinity. This figuration of manhood incorporated heteronormative and conventional masculine tropes such as wealth attainment, control, and heterosexual prowess. Here, Trump touted his fortune, took aggressive action against his rivals, and engaged in misogynistic behavior towards women. Before the 2016 election,

DOI: 10.4324/9781003034810-4

these gendered aspects of Trump's persona appealed to alt-right male groups (Dignam and Rohlinger 2019). Additionally, this variant of Trumpian masculinity corresponded to rappers' enactment of a type of protest masculinity, which embraced a "cool pose" demeanor among Black males (Majors and Billson 1992). Echoing other scholars' findings, signifiers of a masculine self—based on heteronormative beliefs rooted in dominance, control, and power—appear among high-status (Trump) *and* low-status (Black male) groups (Schrock and Schwalbe 2009). My analysis of past invocations of Trump's identity in rap songs by Black men reveals its strategic use as a metaphor for prestige and preeminence.

However, another version of Trumpian masculinity moved into the foreground as he launched a 2016 presidential run. During this time, candidate Trump expressed white supremacist views, which many rappers rejected. His full-throated endorsement of xenophobic and racist beliefs turned off many emcees. While Trump was once glorified for hypermasculine expressions of power, musicians drew the line at racial epithets and allusions to a white nation. Rappers spurned this version of Trumpian masculinity and chastised him for his descent into discriminatory and intimidating forms of electoral politics. The second half of this chapter analyzes rap artists' rejection of candidate and later-President Trump's racist language and policies.

I conclude with an analysis of the contradictory views of Trump in the rap world. Curiously, while candidate Trump's adoption of racialized masculinity made him repugnant to many artists, this denunciation was not applied to his pre-electoral and persistent performances of gendered hypermasculinity anchored in misogyny and aggression. The billionaire, once glorified for his riches and aggressive behavior, crossed the line when he engaged in racist politics that threatened communities of color. My work reinforces arguments (Pascoe 2012; Schrock and Schwalbe 2009) that both dominant and marginalized forms of masculinity can promote gendered oppression. Moreover, I explore how intersections of race and popular culture should complicate our understanding of masculinity. Rap artists continue to articulate forms of protest masculinity and cool pose rhetoric in their music, which frequently subordinate women.

Pre-political Trumpian masculinity

Scholars find that popular media, economic, social, and political institutions perpetuate and uphold constructs of masculinity that are mainly competitive, aggressive, domineering, heterosexist, and above all, anti-feminine (Dignam and Rohlinger 2019; Myers 2012; Pascoe 2012; Schrock and Schwalbe 2009; Smith 2018). The pre-political business tycoon Trump offers a case in fact. Before the 2015 announcement of his run for commander-in-chief, Donald Trump projected an image of himself as a self-made billionaire alpha male. His brand as a businessman signified a heteronormative, masculinist self, established through wealth attainment, combativeness, and womanizing (Smith 2018).

An example of his financial success—a valued heteronormative attribute—appeared in the opening sentences of his book, *The Art of the Deal*, coauthored with Tony Schwartz (2015). Referring to his deal-making in the corporate sector, he wrote, "I don't do it for the money. I've got enough [money], much more than I'll ever need" (1). Trump suggested that he was *obviously* well off. Previously, during the 1980s, Trump had planted stories about the apparent success of his real estate companies and casinos in tabloid magazines, sometimes under the aliases John Miller and John Barron (Thrush and Grynbaum 2017). When he would later run for president decades later, he argued that his business acumen would help the government and public-at-large. With his masculinity firmly rooted in his financial accomplishments, Trump's bombastic demeanor transformed into belligerence.

Pre-political Trumpian masculinity also included aggression and combativeness. Weaponizing the judicial system against his rivals, he sued companies and individuals over 2,000 times in 30 years. These included lawsuits against long-time business partners, coauthors, the NFL, Scotland, New Jersey, New York City, Palm Beach, his ex-wife, Ivana Trump, the creators of *Jeopardy!* and *Wheel of Fortune*, and his lender, Deutsche Bank. Trump even sued comedian Bill Maher for comically suggesting that he was the offspring of an orangutan-human pairing. Kruse (2019) speculated that the intents of Trump's lawsuits were multiple: "to harass, to deflect and delay, to punish opponents and protect his brand, his money, his image … to intimidate." However, Trump contended that he "hate[d]" suing people, but "the fact is that if you're right, you've got to take a stand, or people will walk all over you" (Trump and Schwartz 2015, 7). Indeed, as Smith (2018, 207) argued: "Trump performs a masculinity that favors force over nuance [and] subordination of the weak to the strong."

Trump framed his litigious nature as defensive—as a form of protection—however, such an approach overlapped with conventional US masculine notions of strength through hostility (see Connell and Messerschmidt 2005; Pascoe 2012). In his case, Trump deployed the legal system to punish and silence his adversaries. Notably, this is a form of power readily available to wealthy individuals, but not typically to those from working-class backgrounds or people of color. Generally speaking, the penal system punishes these groups while protecting the affluent (Alexander 2010; Reimen 2013).

In his pre-political life, Trump sought to dominate in his corporate transactions and harnessed the law for his benefit. A well-known New York socialite, he earned a reputation as a womanizer. With a penchant for dating models, he bragged about his romantic relationships to media outlets (Sinclair 2018; Thrush and Grynbaum 2017). Characterized as a serial adulterer (Wolff 2018), Trump married three times. He allegedly cheated on his first wife, Ivana Trump, with his second wife, Marla Maples. In 2006, still newly wedded to his current wife, Melania, Trump had affairs with adult film star, Stormy Daniels, and *Playboy* model, Karen McDougal (Sinclair 2018). These behaviors made some men view Trump as an even more compelling figure; for example, on the Red Pill website, an online community hosted by an alt-right internet group, one male posted, "Young HOT women LOVE The Donald" (Dignam and Rohlinger 2019, 603). Trump's pre-political demeanor was not only that of a philandering, heterosexual alpha male, but he also purportedly sexually harassed and assaulted women.

As one example among many, Trump allegedly engaged in sexual misconduct with Miss Universe, Miss USA, and Miss Teen USA contestants, entering the dressing rooms unannounced, leering at their bodies, and forcibly kissing a contestant (Stuart 2016). In a 2005 interview, Trump bragged:

> You know, no men are anywhere. And I'm allowed to go in because I'm the owner of the pageant. And therefore I'm inspecting it... 'Is everyone OK?' You know, they're standing there with no clothes ... And so I sort of get away with things like that.
>
> *(Stuart 2016)*

In his view, ownership of the pageant translated into rightful control over the women's bodies, allowing him, admittedly, to "get away" with actions that otherwise would be off-limits. Trump's predatory stance came into sharp focus when the 2005 *Access Hollywood* tape was aired in 2016. Caught on a live mic talking with reporter Billy Bush, Trump said he "moved on" and tried to "fuck" a married woman who rejected his advances. He boasted about sexual harassment and assault, saying: "You know, I'm automatically attracted to beautiful—I just start kissing them. It's like a magnet. Just kiss. I don't even wait." He rationalized this behavior by claiming that "when you're a star, they let you do it. You can do anything ... Grab 'em by the pussy. You can do anything" (Bullock 2016).

Trump was less concerned with whether the women he encountered were attracted to him, but more so that they satiated his carnal desires. Some males explicitly praised this misogynistic and illegal behavior after the revelation of the *Access Hollywood* tape. One follower opined on Red Pill,

> [the media] criticizing him for being a billionaire womanizer is just absurd. I would be shocked and a bit concerned if he didn't use his status in society on women (who, let's be honest, were probably all over him when this 'assault' happened).
>
> *(Dignam and Rohlinger 2019, 605)*

Bonding around their disapproval of women, Red Pill members expressed beliefs similar to Theweleit's (1987) fascist Freikorps militia who viewed "red women"—undeserving and lascivious females—as deplorable and worthy of murder. Although not as extreme in their pathology, members of the Red Pill hate group dehumanized women, viewing women who resisted or questioned men as deserving of harsh treatment. At their best, according to members, women were playthings for playboys. His apparent acts of assault and rape regardless, Trump's persona not only attracted alt-right white males, but also paralleled conceptions of manhood put forth by some Black males in their expression of a type of protest masculinity.

Protest masculinity

Many Black males may feel disenfranchised due to their race, often encountering forms of racism and discrimination no matter their age, social class, or educational background (Alexander 2010; Collins 2005). Lacking advantages more readily available to white males—racial privilege, political power, or wealth—may lead some heterosexual Black males to enact what Connell and Messerschmidt (2005) refer to as a form of *protest masculinity*. Such a masculinity manifests among ethnically marginalized men and "embodies the claim to power typical of regional hegemonic masculinity, but that lacks the economic resources and institutional authority that underpins regional and global patterns" (Messerschmidt 2018, 50). In this case, some straight Black males may perform conventional heteronormative masculine behaviors, such as aggression and expression of male supremacy; however, they do not benefit from the patriarchal dividend (Pascoe 2012) to the same extent as affluent white males such as Donald Trump.

This form of Black male protest masculinity, I argue here, encompasses a "cool pose" demeanor. Majors and Billson (1992) define the cool pose as a "ritualized form of masculinity that entails behaviors, scripts, physical posturing, impression management, and carefully crafted performances that deliver a single, critical message: pride, strength, and control" (4). The authors posit that Black males present an array of "masks, acts, and facades" as a counterbalance to instances in which they feel enfeebled or humiliated, for example, experiencing the loss of employment, blocked educational opportunities, or institutionalized racism. Furthermore, Majors and Billson contend that cool pose behaviors provide a boost to Black males' egos in the same way that white males gain affirmation by working at prestigious jobs that offer high wages. Attributes of the cool pose include "player talk," aloofness, and physical dominance. The ultimate goal is to communicate power when one feels powerless and control when one feels helpless (Majors and Billson 1992).

Undoubtedly, some Black males may project a masculine self (Schrock and Schwalbe 2009) to address the low self-esteem created from living in poverty-stricken environments. Scripts for this type of performance are provided by famous rap musicians—individuals who frequently serve as mouthpieces for the Black community (Kitwana 2002; Rose 2008). Kubrin (2005) writes that Black male rappers' lyrics serve as "interpretative frames" for the alienation and violence that many within their communities experience. As I have noted elsewhere, hypermasculine themes such as misogyny, violence, and wealth acquisition saturate artists' songs. Out of 371 popular rap songs released between 2005 and 2015, 62 percent contained misogynistic or sexist lyrics, and 43 percent conveyed violent imagery (Oware 2018). Such content must be contextualized, though (Weitzer and Kubrin 2009).

Often reacting to concentrated poverty and racism, the protest masculinity and cool pose behaviors enacted by some Black males may be rewarded with respect and honor—the only material "currency" available to them (Anderson 1999). Even artists who have not personally encountered racism or experienced poverty may face pressures from record producers to create "hardcore" and provocative lyrics filled with aggressive and sexist content, as such themes are thought to increase record sales (Rose 2008; Weitzer and Kubrin 2009). Whether emerging out of personal experience or record-label influence, hypermasculine tropes are stock references in popular rappers' lyrics, and listeners may interpret all rap artists as expressing this type of protest masculinity. As we shall see, performances of this type of protest masculinity overlap with pre-political Trumpian masculinity.

For this work, I performed a content analysis of a large sample of rap song lyrics that mentioned Donald Trump, from the late 1990s to 2016. A content analysis is a qualitative interpretative sociological approach that uncovers the symbolic or explicit meanings of texts, for example, speeches, media images, or movies, among other areas of interest (Glaser and Strauss 1967; Schutt 2011). Examining changing lyrics over time, this content analysis provides a window into how emcees' views of him changed. As my analysis reveals, during his pre-political years, performers fully embraced his affluence, combative style, and playboy status, but rejected him years later.

Pre-political Trump in rap music

Wealth attainment and status represent the primary symbols of masculinity among Black males from impoverished areas. Regarding clothes and jewelry in particular, Kubrin (2005) wrote that they "play an important role in establishing self-image and gaining respect … a look that loudly proclaims that the wearer has overcome [the] financial difficulties faced by others" (440). Consequently, Trump's pre-political masculinity would have appealed to rap artists in the 1990s and 2000s, who could invoke his name as a symbol of status. With his prestigious properties in New York and throughout the world, Donald Trump, as the tycoon businessman, signified male economic power and prestige. That high status rubbed off on the occupants of those properties. 50 Cent (2002), in his song "Crazy," therefore, could assert that because he is "rich," one can "catch [him] in the Trump Tower lobby." For 50, wealthy individuals congregate with other affluent people. The song was released early in the artist's career, before his meteoric rise in the genre, and Trump was for him an admirable and aspirational figure.

Bun B (1992) similarly valorized Trump in his "Pocket Full of Stones," as he rhymed, "forget Black Caesar, brothers call me Black Trump." Undoubtedly referring to the 1973 Black exploitation film, *Black Caesar*, about a fictional African-American head of a Harlem crime syndicate, Bun implored his listeners to identify with him instead of with Donald Trump. In the film, the Black character Tommy Gibbs is a gangster who wages war against racist white police officers and the Italian mafia. Gibbs defeats both groups, a triumph of Black will and demonstration of Black power. However, in his song, rapper Bun B shuns this character, instead bragging that he is the "Black Trump." The artist appropriates Trump's actual power and status as opposed to that of a fictional character. While the everyday lives of Black men in the 1990s were characterized by high rates of unemployment and poverty (Anderson 1999), Trump's name provided gravitas and conferred clout upon the artists.

Black male artists were not the only ones who borrowed the cachet of Trump's affluence. Black women also used Trump as a metaphor for grandeur. On her track "Shut Up Bitch," Lil' Kim (2005) says, "I'm in the Trump International, 30 floors up," referring to a more expensive floor at one of Trump's already costly hotels. Nicki Minaj (2013), a millennial Black female rapper, also boasted of wealth and status, by bragging, on the track "I Wanna Be With You," that she was "at Trump [Hotel], and you bitches at the Radisson." She elevated herself as a Trump property resident, while simultaneously putting down her competitors as "bitches," who stayed at an inferior establishment. Both Lil' Kim and Nicki Minaj leveraged Trump's name to establish their credibility in a predominately Black male genre.

Donald Trump and rap artists alike have regularly assumed aggressive stances to intimidate their opponents. Throughout his 2016 campaign, Trump boasted that he would use excessive force to destroy the United States' enemies abroad. For example, in an interview with Bill O'Reilly, he said that his strategy for fighting the terrorist group ISIS was to "bomb the hell out of them" and that he "would hit them so hard your head would spin" (Phillips 2015). Past presidents similarly have adopted a warlike posture, reflecting hypermasculinity, and Smith (2018) writes that presidential candidates have relied on the trope of the "warrior hero" even if they have not demonstrated successful military leadership, as was the case for Trump during his campaign. Notwithstanding his lack of military experience, he signaled that he could dominate enemies and protect the nation.

Trump also regularly made a show of intimidating competitors at home. For example, during the 2016 presidential primary debates, Trump frequently referred to fellow Republican candidate Marco Rubio as "Little Marco." At a rally in Virginia in 2016, Rubio mentioned that Trump had small hands—"if they're small, something else must be small"—insinuating that he possessed small genitalia. At a rally in Detroit, Trump retorted, "I guarantee you, there's no problem," concerning the size of his penis (Rosenthal 2016). Both men thereby engaged in gendered and masculinist rhetoric in order to present themselves as dominant heterosexual males. In another instance, repeating a comment made by a woman at his rally, he called Republican presidential opponent Ted Cruz a "pussy" (Byrnes 2016). Within a hypermasculine framework, this slur is one of the harshest put-downs of another male, characterizing him as weak or feminine (Kitwana 2002; Majors and Billson 1992). We see similar dominance plays in the rap world.

For example, in Nas' (2001) seminal rap song, "Ether," he described his rival Jay-Z as "a phony, a fake, a pussy." The feminization of Jay-Z, in turn, configured Nas as the dominant, masculine figure. Equally disdainfully, Nas insinuated that a "pussy" was also inauthentic or fake. "Authenticity," understood as expressing one's true beliefs and not succumbing to external pressures, remained central within hip hop identity (McLeod 1999). In rap lore, if one's reputation was called into question or disrespected, violent retaliation must follow. 50 Cent (2003) understood this ethic or code of the street (see Anderson 1999). In "Don't Push Me," hinting at a brutal reprisal for individuals who questioned his masculinity, he rhymed, "I got something for your ass, keep thinking I'm pussy." For Trump and some rappers, violence and aggression were proper and necessary performances of dominance.

Critics have decried rap music for its antagonistic tone (Kitwana 2002); however, before his candidacy, Trump's combative persona was largely taken as public entertainment. On the reality show, *The Apprentice*, contestants competed in various tasks as they sought to become the apprentice to the real estate mogul. The climax of each episode was evident when Trump delivered the punch line, "You're fired!" to an outgoing participant. Although choreographed and hackneyed—an overly dramatic Trump raised his arm and aggressively pointed his finger at a contestant—the message was clear. Trump entertained through shaming and humiliating others.

Similarly, in his political life, Trump used gesture to intimidate and demean. At political rallies and press conferences, Trump routinely waved his hands, crossed his arms over his chest, and pantomimed his opponents. He intimidated as well through slurs, taunting journalists at such gatherings as "fake news" and "the enemy of the people" (Perlberg 2018). Such actions are reminiscent of rap artists who, in their music videos and concerts, gesticulate and assume exaggeratedly masculine poses, such as finger-pointing, crouch grabbing, or crossing their arms. Such hypermasculinist behaviors configure Trump and rappers alike as intimidating and dangerous if confronted.

Referencing Trump's imperious posturing on *The Apprentice*, Lil Wayne (2002) rhymed, "I'm a fire my blunt like Donald Trump." In his song, Wayne aggressively lit and inhaled his drug of choice confidently, in a manner similar to the simulated bellicose dismissal of participants on the television series. As other emcees have done, in these lyrics, Wayne aligned himself with an outspoken and prominent media figure, thereby establishing masculine dominance through this song. Just as Trump's swagger appealed to rap artists such as Lil Wayne, so did his misogyny.

Playboy status has been a common hypermasculine trope among rap musicians (Kitwana 2002; Kubrin 2005). Emcees routinely have rhymed about how they sexually conquer, manipulate, and discard women for their benefit. In his song "I Get Around," Tupac (1993) made it clear: "But when will you learn; you can't tie me down/Baby doll, check it, I get around." The rapper implored his paramour to recognize his refusal to remain monogamous. He dated and mated with many women and reveled in his "male whore[ness]," similarly to the high school boys that Pascoe (2012) interviewed. Trump's "Grab 'em by the pussy" comment (Bullock 2016) demonstrated a similar claim to sexual privilege, taking his womanizing one step further. While Trump would later characterize this utterance as "locker-room talk," or exaggerating language that heterosexual males bandy about in private company, it was in fact clearly boasting about sexual assault. Given that, by 2019, he stood accused by 15 women of sexual misconduct (Blau and Vazquez 2019), his dismissal of the comments as exaggeration, at the very least, is suspect. Interestingly, no prominent rap artist criticized Trump for these boasts. His predatory behavior towards women apparently failed to anger emcees. Moreover, before the *Access Hollywood* tape became public, some rappers drew upon Trump's "playboy" reputation to establish their own credibility in the rap world.

For example, in "Money is My Bitch," Nas (1999) used Trump's relationship with model and actress Marla Maples as a metaphor for his intimate connection with money. He said, "The best couple they seen since Trump and Marla Maple." As was true for other artists who referenced Trump's wealth to build their status, Nas' lyric operated on two levels. First, he acknowledged the significance in elite social circles of Trump's association with the actress. But Maples served as a stand-in for wealth in Nas' rhyme. Wealth was a "bitch" for the rapper, something to be possessed and used, and by extension, women were commodities. Trump's player status was a useful trope for Nas as both appeared to elevate themselves through the subjugation of women.

Pre-political Trump reigned supreme in the rap world. For male rap artists, from famous to relatively unknown emcees, Trump's affluence, belligerence, and lothario status exemplified an exalted form of masculinity. Trump was a symbol of respect for a population who found this attribute hard to come by in their daily lives. Mentioning his name in their music meant aligning themselves with American royalty, and building an identity rooted in self-importance and self-worth. However, as he pursued the presidency, other aspects of Trump's personality took center stage, and his masculinist image transformed from that of playboy billionaire to a white supremacist. And he fell from grace in the rap universe.

Political-era Trumpian masculinity

Donald Trump's political campaigning and governance frequently fused masculinity and racism. In his piece on Trump's immigration policy campaigning, Martin (2018) argued that Trump's "use of border imagery and anti-Mexican stereotypes played a critical role" (60). Trump created a racist caricature to address and whip up fear of undocumented immigrants and clandestine crossers of the US-Mexico border. For example, in his campaign announcement speech in June 2015, Trump charged that Mexicans are "bringing drugs, they're bringing crime, [and] they're rapists" (62). Not surprisingly, this description of Mexicans as drug-dealers, criminals, and rapists drew on racist Hispanic stereotypes spanning back to the post-Reconstruction era (Takaki 2008).

Moreover, Trump's hardline immigration policies had a particular masculinist character. Martin (2018) suggested that Trump presented a nativist white masculinity that would presumably protect America from brown intruders. Similarly, in the final 2016 presidential debate, Trump referred to border-crossers as "bad *hombres* [men]." They represented dangerous individuals who threatened the social fabric of real (read: white) America and assaulted white women (Aidan 2018). Martin added that Trump "beseeches *hyper Anglo masculinity* to solve a series of real or imagined problems" (2018, 61; emphasis added). Along those same lines, Gorski (2017) noted that Trump discarded the Reagan-era racist characterizations of the "welfare queen" in favor of old standbys such as "rapists" and "invaders." Thus, Trump positioned himself as not only as a "hardliner"—an essential attribute of conventional presidential masculinity—but also the premier protector of whiteness.

Rap artists challenged and critiqued Trump's explicit racist masculine persona. In response to his proposal to build a wall along the US-Mexico border (his most prominent campaign promise), in the song "FDT" (2016), YG and Nipsey Hussle yelled, "Fuck Donald Trump" in the chorus to their tune. The reason for the vulgarity, according to Hussle, was because "[i]t wouldn't be the USA without Mexicans," alluding to the contributions of this group to US economic growth. As Martin (2018) noted, asymmetrical neoliberal policies with Mexico have benefitted the United States, as, for example, the North American Free Trade Agreement (NAFTA) created a "cyclical demand for cheap, undocumented labor," frequently supplied by Mexican workers (63). Calling for unity between Black and Latinx populations, YG and Nipsey Hussle proclaimed, "Black love, brown pride in the sets again." While likely understanding that each group travels in separate ethnic circles or "sets," they encouraged bonding based upon caring, respect, and pride, which are intangible resources upon which men of color rely (Anderson 1999; Majors and Billson 1992). Such accord rebuked Trump's vitriolic rhetoric and policies that threatened both Black and Latinx communities.

In another verse, YG exclaimed, "your racist ass did too much," reacting to the forced removal of Black teenagers by police officers from a 2016 Trump rally in Georgia (Jacobs 2016). In the introductory section of the song "FDT" (2016), the group included a statement from one of the teenagers: "I think we got kicked out [of the rally] because we're a group of Black people … and they're afraid we gonna say something or do something." YG's response exemplified the changing views rap artists held toward Donald Trump as his racism came into sharper focus during the campaign. Instead of praising his wealth and status, these artists rebuked his race-baiting and race-hating language.

Indeed, in "FDT Pt. 2" (2016), rap artist G-Eazy rhymed, "A Trump rally sounds like Hitler in Berlin or KKK shit, now I'm going in." The artist directly critiqued racist and anti-immigrant messages circulating at Trump gatherings by linking them with the anti-Semitic fascist, Hitler, as well as the homegrown white supremacist group, the Ku Klux Klan. According to this artist, Trump's hateful invective was little different from that of these other historical hatemongers, and that such divisive language required a proportionate response—"going in" to fight it. This tone and tenor resounded among other artists.

Nas, who over a decade earlier had glamorized Trump in his song, "Money is My Bitch" (1999), articulated a different message in 2017. Penning a letter to the online publication *Mass Appeal*, the artist wrote: "We all know a racist is in [the President's] office" (Blistein 2017). Similarly, Nicki Minaj, who previously (2003) bragged about staying at a Trump hotel, sideswiped Trump's hardline immigration policies when she rhymed, "Island Girl, Donald Trump want me go home" ("Black Barbies" 2016). Minaj, born in Trinidad and Tobago, implied that his desire to halt or slow immigration was particularly directed at dark-skinned people. Trump's privately expressed desire to bar immigrants from "shithole" countries in Africa as well as Haiti (Dawsey 2018) lent credence to Minaj's conjecture. Hence, for these artists, Trump's intimidating rhetoric and nationalistic views towards non-whites changed their view of him.

The rap artist Common argued that Trump's beliefs conveyed the feelings of many in the United States, asserting that the president "supports some of the racist ideals that this country does have, and we've got to acknowledge that." In his mind, Trump's election was the outcome of a racist American society, rather than an anomaly or a mistake. Similarly, questioning those who wanted Trump to be removed from office, rap activist David Banner tweeted: "Why do we wish someone else was in office? Is it so the snake can go back in the grass? No, let it show its head so we can deal with it" (Zaru 2017). These artists admonished what they considered his scapegoating of immigrants of color and bigoted fearmongering.

Rapsody echoed this point when responding to Trump's "very fine people … on both sides" remark after the "Unite the Right" protest held in Charlottesville, Virginia, in August 2017. At that rally, white supremacists and Neo-Nazis marched to protest the removal of the statue of Confederate General Robert E. Lee. Trump seemed to suggest a moral equivalency between the white supremacists and the counterprotesters at the rally. The event devolved into a violent confrontation between the two groups, ending with a white supremacist murdering a white woman and injuring others using his vehicle as a weapon. Trump's characterization of the encounter offended Rapsody, who reflected:

> In the beginning of Trump's campaign, I really thought he was playing on the ugly underbelly of racism in America … But seeing what happened at Charlottesville, it made me think like if you can even play on that and support it, then inside you are a racist, without a doubt.
>
> *(Zaru 2017)*

Even one of the most famous contemporary white rappers rejected Trump: Eminem. In his music, Eminem performs the type of protest masculinity that is characteristic of rap music, yet he also challenged Trump's rhetoric. On a track with artist Big Sean ("No Favors" 2017), he yelled, "Trump's a bitch, I'll make his whole brand go under." The sexist slur ("bitch") typically reserved for subordinate men and women now was applied to Trump. Eminem, who has received criticism for homophobic and misogynistic language in his music, effectively deployed Trumpian tactics against the president. In this line, the artist cast Trump as effeminate and went one step further by suggesting that Trump's overall political strategy was part of his "brand"—an image created and sold—which Eminem would personally destroy if the two ever met. Hence, Trump, the inferior man, would suffer his demise at the hands of a supposedly more muscular, hypermasculine, white male figure.

In rap tradition, Eminem initiated "beef" with an imaginary competitor and bested him. On the BET awards show in 2017, Eminem stated that "racism is the only thing [Trump] is fantastic four." In addition to centering race in his critique, Eminem embraced a hypermasculine rap guise, claiming that the president does not "hav[e] the balls to go against [him]" (Eminem 2017). The rapper deployed a masculinist and misogynistic trope to challenge the commander-in-chief, a staple in rap music (McLeod 1999), and relied on the same approach that both pre-political and politicized Trump had deployed against his opponents. Overall, many artists had turned away from Trump, but he still had one famous supporter, Kanye West.

In an October 2018 visit to the White House, Kanye exclaimed:

> I love Hillary. I love everyone, but the campaign [slogan] 'I'm with her' just didn't make me feel—as a guy that didn't get to see my dad all the time, like a guy that could not play catch with his son—it was something about this hat [Trump's signature red "Make America Great Again" hat] that made me feel like Superman. You made [me] a Superman.

Donald Trump represented a positive male figure in Kanye's life, filling a gaping hole of virile masculinity for him that Hillary Clinton could not. For Kanye, Trump served as a surrogate manly figure. At the White House meeting, he lamented, "You know, my dad and my mom separated, so I didn't have a lot of male energy in my home" (Henderson 2018). Some Black males who have strained or fractured relationships with their biological parents may turn to poor-quality role models (Anderson 1999; Kitwana 2002). For Kanye, Trump may have manifested a type of protest masculinity rooted in heteronormative dominance and manhood. Before his White House visit, Kanye tweeted about Trump, "We are both dragon energy. He is my brother," defining "dragon energy" as "natural born leaders [with] very instinctive great foresight" (Tennent 2018). While multiple rap artists shunned the newest manifestation of Trump for his racial demagoguery, Kanye continued siding with the president, refusing to label his behavior as racist. Trump's *hypermasculinity* and status continued to resonate with the rapper, just as they had done for many other rappers in the past.

First gangsta, now racist

Pre-political Trump was as "gangsta"—aggressive and ostentatious—as most rap artists. As he was once the "don" of rap because of his celebrity status, truculence, and wealth, using Trump's name in one's song meant expressing heterosexual domination and intimidation of real and imaginary competitors in the rap world. Trump's hypermasculinity and Black male protest masculinity neatly aligned. For some Black individuals, especially urban Black males, he represented someone who made his mark on the world stage. He was an aspirational character for those who came from impoverished backgrounds. Trump (seemingly) *always* bested opponents through heteronormative posturing and control, and *always* did so with beautiful women on his arms—an elusive, but sought-after fantasy for many rappers. Trump's supposed "self-made" biography might have inspired Black males who felt powerless and invisible. His rise to fame and fortune was their dream as well. And rappers loved him for it. This wealthy billionaire from Park Avenue played into the definition of Black manhood. Moreover, his womanizing only added to his—and by extension, their—fame.

Yet, political Trump's sheen dulled with many in the rap universe. He came to represent someone who trafficked in xenophobia and racism, and this was a bridge too far for many musicians. Trump fell from the mountaintop of Black manhood because of his hateful remarks and targeting of people of color. During his 2016 and 2020 campaigns, crowds packed his rallies to witness his white tough-guy act. The billionaire businessman promised to "Make America Great Again," by which he meant to restore the racial and gender order in white men's favor. And many Black rap artists found this racialized masculinity dangerous.

The critical finding here is that it was not Trump's blatant sexism that undermined him among rappers; it was his xenophobia and racism that crossed the line. Indeed, in the rap culture, misogyny and sexism are staples, seemingly necessary for establishing credibility. For example, Lee (2016) found that record-label producers inform up-and-coming rappers to include more references to "bitches" and "hoes" in their music if they want to become successful. Put crudely, white men who are rich womanizers rank high among emcees, but racists, especially those who tacitly endorse white supremacist and neo-Nazi propaganda, deserve criticism. Misogyny takes a backseat to racist language and sentiments. Trump's support waned among the very group who had depicted him as the epitome of heterosexual masculinity. According to many, he may have been virile, but he was also vile.

This chapter addressed the significance of heteronormative hypermasculinity within the rap community, but also the primacy of race. Those who are closer to the hegemonic ideal of masculinity—white, middle-class, heterosexuals—may signify a masculine self similarly to those further away from the ideal—working-class, Black, or LGBTQ individuals. This work adds to the literature that posits that males in dominant *and* marginalized positions contribute to maintaining conventional constructions of masculinity rooted in gender oppression (Messerschmidt 2018; Schrock and Schwalbe 2009), but adds that racism continues to matter to Black artists in the rap world.

This chapter has pointed to the contours of hypermasculinity in rap music by showing the various engagements with Trumpian masculinity. Though contradictory, rap artists' lyrics can reinforce sexism and glorify violence; they also promote movements such as Black Lives Matter and actively speak out against instances of police brutality against people of color. Hence, continued analysis of the intersections between race, gender, and popular culture is necessary to flesh out our understanding of how, at times, black heteronormative expressions of masculinity—protest and cool pose masculinity—mirror white heteronormative forms, but also differ from white performances of masculinity due to Black male marginalization along racial and economic lines. Trump likely will continue receiving the ire of many in the rap world, but challenges to his sexism are unlikely.

References

Alexander, Michelle. 2010. *The New Jim Crow: Mass Incarceration in the Age of Colorblindness*. New York: The New Press.

Anderson, Elijah. 1999. *Code of the Street: Decency, Violence, and the Moral Life of the Inner-City*. New York: Norton and Company.

Armstrong, Jenice. 2016. "The Case of Trump vs. the Beauty Contestant." *The Philadelphia Inquirer*, June 20, 2016. https://www.inquirer.com/philly/news/20160620_The_case_of_Trump_vs__the_beauty_contestant.html.

Blau, Max, and Maegan Vazquez. 2019. "These Women Have Accused Trump of Sexual Harassment." *CNN*, June 24, 2019. https://www.cnn.com/2016/10/14/politics/trump-women-accusers/index.html.

Blistein, Jon. 2017. "Nas on Trump: 'We All Know a Racist Is in Office'." *Rollingstone*, May 31, 2017. https://www.rollingstone.com/music/music-news/nas-on-trump-we-all-know-a-racist-is-in-office-112314/.

Bullock, Penn. 2016. "Transcript: Donald Trump's Taped Comments about Women." *New York Times*, October 8, 2016. https://www.nytimes.com/2016/10/08/us/donald-trump-tape-transcript.html.

Byrnes, Jesse. 2016. "Trump Calls Cruz a 'Pussy'." *The Hill*, February 8, 2016. https://thehill.com/blogs/blog-briefing-room/news/268714-trump-calls-cruz-a-puy.

Collins, Hill Patricia. 2005. *Black Sexual Politics: African Americans, Gender, and the New Racism*. New York: Routledge.

Connell, Raewyn, and James Messerschmidt. 2005. "Hegemonic Masculinity: Rethinking the Concept." *Gender and Society* 19 (6): 829–859. https://doi.org/10.1177/0891243205278639.

Dawsey, Josh. 2018. "Trump Decries Protections for Immigrants from 'Shithole' Countries." *Washington Post*, January 12, 2018. https://www.washingtonpost.com/politics/trump-attacks-protections-for-immigrants-from-shithole-countries-in-oval-office-meeting/2018/01/11/bfc0725c-f711-11e7-91af-31ac729add94_story.html.

Dignam, Pierce Alexander, and Deana A. Rohlinger. 2019. "Misogynistic Men Online: How the Red Pill Helped Elect Trump." *Signs: Journal of Women in Culture and Society* 44 (3): 590–612. https://doi.org/10.1086/701155.

Glaser, Barney, and Anselm Strauss. 1967. *Discovery of Grounded Theory: Strategies for Qualitative Research*. Chicago, IL: Aldine.

Gorski, Philip. 2017. "Why Evangelicals Voted for Trump: A Critical Cultural Sociology." *Annual Journal of Cultural Sociology* 5 (3): 338–354. https://doi.org/10.1057/s41290-017-0043-9.

Henderson, Cydney. 2018. "Here's Every Word of Kanye West's Bizarre Meeting with President Trump." *USA Today*, October 12, 2018. https://www.usatoday.com/story/life/people/2018/10/12/heres-every-word-kanye-wests-bizarre-meeting-president-trump/1609230002/.

Jacobs, Jennifer. 2016. "Black Students Ejected from Trump Rally in Ga." *USA Today*, March 1, 2016. https://www.usatoday.com/story/news/politics/elections/2016/02/29/donald-trump-georgia-rally-valdosta/81129964/.

Kitwana, Bakari. 2002. *The Hip Hop Generation: Young Blacks and the Crisis in African-American Culture*. New York: Basic Civitas Book.

Kruse, Michael. 2019. "Can Trump Still Sue His Way Out of Trouble?" *Politico Magazine*, June 3, 2019. https://www.politico.com/magazine/story/2019/06/03/donald-trump-lawsuits-white-house-227036.

Kubrin, Charis. 2005. "'I See Death around the Corner': Nihilism in Rap Music." *Sociological Perspectives* 48 (4): 433–459. https://doi.org/10.1525/sop.2005.48.4.433.

Lee, Jooyoung. 2016. *Blowin' Up: Rap Dreams in South Central*. Chicago, IL: University of Chicago Press.

Majors, Richard, and Janet Mancini Billson. 1992. *Cool Pose: The Dilemmas of Black Manhood in America*. New York: Simon and Schuster.

Martin, Joshua D. 2018. "The Border, Bad Hombres, and the Billionaire: Hypermasculinity and Anti-Mexican Stereotypes in Trump's 2016 Presidential Campaign." In *Nasty Women and Bad Hombres: Gender and Race in the 2016 US Presidential Election*, edited by Christine A. Kray, Tamar W. Carroll, and Hinda Mandell, 60–73. Rochester, NY: University of Rochester Press.

McLeod, Kembrew. 1999. "Authenticity Within Hip-hop and Other Cultures Threatened with Assimilation." *Journal of Communication* 49 (4): 134–150. https://doi.org/10.1111/j.1460-2466.1999.tb02821.x.

Messerschmidt, James. 2018. *Hegemonic Masculinity: Formulation, Reformulation, and Amplification*. Lanham, MD: Rowan & Littlefield.

Myers, Kristen. 2012. "'Cowboy Up!' Non-hegemonic Representations of Masculinity in Children's Television Programming." *Journal of Men's Studies* 20 (2): 125–143. https://doi.org/10.3149/jms.2002.125.

Oware, Matthew. 2018. *I Got Something to Say: Gender, Race, and Social Consciousness in Rap Music*. Cham (Switzerland): Palgrave MacMillan.

Paquette, Danielle. 2016. "Why the Most Outrageous Part of Donald Trump's 'Hot Mic' Comments Isn't the Vulgar Language." *Washington Post*, October 7, 2016. https://www.washingtonpost.com/news/wonk/wp/2016/10/07/the-real-issue-with-donald-trump-saying-a-man-can-do-anything-to-a-woman/?utm_term=.df7d62bdfa9a.

Pascoe, C. J. 2012. *Dude, You're a Fag: Masculinity and Sexuality in High School*. Berkeley: University of California Press.

Perlberg, Steven. 2018. "Donald Trump Singled Out a CNN Reporter as an 'Enemy of the People'." *Buzzfeed News*, November 7, 2018. https://www.buzzfeednews.com/article/stevenperlberg/donald-trump-jim-acosta-cnn-enemy-people.

Phillips, Amber. 2015. "Donald Trump's Guide to the World." *Washington Post*, August 26, 2015. https://www.washingtonpost.com/news/the-fix/wp/2015/08/26/donald-trumps-guide-to-the-world/.

———. 2017. "Hillary Clinton Says 'Misogyny Played a Role' in Her Loss. Research Suggests She Might Be Right." *Washington Post*, April 8, 2017. https://www.washingtonpost.com/news/the-fix/wp/2017/04/08/hillary-clinton-says-misogyny-played-a-role-in-her-loss-research-suggests-she-might-be-right/.

Reimen, Jeffrey. 2013. *The Rich Get Richer and the Poor Get Prison: Ideology, Class, and Criminal Justice*. Boston, MA: Pearson.

Rose, Tricia. 2008. *The Hip Hop Wars: What We Talk about When We Talk about Hip Hop—and Why It Matters*. New York: Basic Civitas Books.

Rosenthal, Andrew. 2016. "Donald Trump Defends His Hands." *New York Times*, March 3, 2016. https://takingnote.blogs.nytimes.com/2016/03/03/donald-trump-defends-his-hands/.

Schrock, Douglas, and Michael Schwalbe. 2009. "Men, Masculinity, and Manhood Acts." *Annual Review of Sociology* 35: 277–295. https://doi.org/10.1146/annurev-soc-070308-115933.

Schutt, Russell. 2011. *Investigating the Social World: The Process and Practice of Research*. Thousand Oaks, CA: Pine Forge.

Smith, Aidan. 2018. *Gender, Heteronormativity, and the American Presidency*. New York: Routledge.

Sinclair, Harriet. 2018. "All the Women Trump Has Dated, Married, or Been Linked to Sexually." *Newsweek*, January 17, 2018. https://www.newsweek.com/all-women-trump-has-dated-married-or-been-linked-sexually-783370.

Stuart, Tessa. 2016. "A Timeline of Donald Trump's Creepiness While He Owned Miss Universe." *Rollingstone*, October 12, 2016. https://www.rollingstone.com/politics/politics-features/a-timeline-of-donald-trumps-creepiness-while-he-owned-miss-universe-191860/.

Takaki, Ronald. 2008. *A Different Mirror: A History of Multicultural America*. New York: Bay Back Books.

Tennant, James. 2018. "What Is Dragon Energy? Donald Trump Has It, Kanye West Says." *Newsweek*, April 26, 2018. https://www.newsweek.com/dragon-energy-donald-trump-kanye-west-901759.

Theweleit, Klaus. 1987. *Male Fantasies: Volume 1: Women, Floods, Bodies, History*. Minneapolis: University of Minnesota Press.

Thrush, Glenn, and Michael Grynbaum. 2017. "Trump Ruled the Tabloid Media. Washington Is a Different Story." *New York Times*, February 17, 2017. https://www.nytimes.com/2017/02/25/us/politics/trump-press-conflict.html.

Trump, Donald J., and Tony Schwartz. 2015. *Trump: The Art of the Deal*. Reprint, New York: Ballantine Books.

Twohey, Megan, and Michael Barbaro. 2016. "Two Women Say Donald Trump Touched Them Inappropriately." *New York Times*, October 12, 2016. https://www.nytimes.com/2016/10/13/us/politics/donald-trump-women.html.

Weitzer, Ronald, and Charis Kubrin. 2009. "Misogyny in Rap Music: A Content Analysis of Prevalence and Meanings." *Men and Masculinities* 12 (1): 3–29. https://doi.org/10.1177/1097184X08327696.

Wolff, Michael. 2018. *Fire and Fury: Inside the Trump White House*. New York: Henry Holt and Company.

Zaru, Deena. 2017. "Hip Hop Reacts to Trump: 'I'd Rather an Ugly Truth Than a Beautiful Lie'." *CNN News*, August 16, 2017. http://www.cnn.com/2017/08/16/politics/hip-hop-donald-trump-white-supremacy/index.html.

Discography

50 Cent [Curtis Jackson], vocalist. 2002. "Crazy." MP3 audio. Track 7 on 50 Cent, *God's Plan*. BCD Music Group.

50 Cent [Curtis Jackson], vocalist. 2003. "Don't Push Me." MP3 audio. Track 15 on 50 Cent, *Get Rich or Die Tryin'*. Shady/Aftermath Records.

Big Sean [Sean Anderson], vocalist. 2017. "No Favors." Featuring Eminem. MP3 audio. Track 4 on Big Sean, *I Decided*. Getting Out Our Dreams Inc.

DJ Khaled [Khaled Mohamed Khaled], vocalist. 2013. "I Wanna Be With You." Featuring Nicki Minaj and Rick Ross. MP3 audio. On DJ Khaled, *I Wanna Be With You*. Cash Money Records.

Eminem. 2017. "Eminem Rips Donald Trump in BET Hip Hop Awards Freestyle Cypher." 2017. *BETNetworks*, October 10, 2017. https://www.youtube.com/watch?v=LunHybOKIjU.

Lil' Kim [Kimberly Jones], vocalist. 2005. "Shut Up Bitch." MP3 audio. Track 5 on Lil' Kim, *The Naked Truth*. Atlantic Records.

Nas [Nasir Jones], vocalist. 2003. "Ether." MP3 audio. Track 2 on Nas, *Stillmatic*. Columbia.

Nas [Nasir Jones], vocalist. 1999. "Money is My Bitch." MP3 audio. Track 15 on Nas, *I Am...*. Columbia.

Nicki Minaj [Onika Maraj-Petty], vocalist. 2016. "Black Barbies." MP3 audio. On Nicki Minaj, *Black Barbies*. Eardruma/Interscope Records.

T.I. [Clifford Harris], vocalist. 2012. "Ball." Featuring Lil Wayne. MP3 audio. Track 5 on T.I, *Trouble Man: Heavy is the Head*. Grand Hustle, LLC.

Tupac [Tupac Shakur], vocalist. 1993. "I Get Around," MP3 audio. Track 14 on Tupac, *Strictly for my N.I.G.G.A.Z...*. Interscope Records.

UGK [Chad Butler and Bernard Freeman], vocalists. 1992. "Pocket Full of Stones." MP3 audio. Track 3 on UGK, *Too Hard to Swallow*. Jive Records.

YG [Keenon Jackson], vocalist. 2016. "FDT." Featuring Nipsey Hussle. MP3 audio. Track 15 on YG, *Still Brazy*. Def Jam Recordings.

YG [Keenon Jackson], vocalist. 2016. "FDT Pt. 2." Featuring G-Eazy and Macklemore. MP3 audio. On YG, *FDT Pt. 2*. Def Jam Recordings.

5
COMMONPLACE TERROR
Everyday harassment of Latinx immigrants in Central Florida

Mary Vickers and Nolan Kline

We stood outside Rosa's aging but well-kept mobile home in the intense Central Florida sun, waiting to interview her about her experience as an immigrant and how recent political changes affected her and her family. Rosa opened the door, greeted us with a warm smile, and welcomed us in. Her living room was immaculate, yet sparsely decorated, adorned with wall hangings of Christian iconography. The window-mounted air conditioning unit hummed loudly, providing reprieve from the heat. At that time, Rosa had lived in the Orlando area for 13 years, and had legal work authorization. Like many other immigrants in the United States, Rosa lives in a mixed-status family. Her husband and teenage son are undocumented, but her two younger children are citizens, having been born in the United States. Sitting in her home, Rosa told us that she and her family have faced many hardships, but they encountered new difficulties after the 2016 presidential election. When her eldest son learned of the election results, he even begged her to leave the United States, and she recounted him saying: "Mom, why don't we go back to Mexico? Why do we have to endure this? Why do we have to be here?" Rosa reminded him that for all that they might encounter in the United States, they were better off here than in Mexico, telling him: "In Mexico, they get paid five dollars a day. How is one going to survive if they have kids?" Immigrating to the United States under those circumstances was logical, and she added: "[Trump] as a father himself would do it, if he saw his family in danger, wouldn't he want to leave from there?"

In truth, when real estate investor and reality-television star Donald Trump, despite lacking political experience, announced his 2016 presidential bid, a victory seemed unlikely (Sargent 2016). However, the unorthodoxy of his political campaign did not deter millions of supporters from embracing his message. Central to his run for office and eventual win was a well-worn narrative

DOI: 10.4324/9781003034810-5

of xenophobia focused on immigrants from Mexico, like Rosa. Presaging the anti-immigrant politicking to come, in the opening speech of his campaign, Trump asserted:

> When Mexico sends its people, they're not sending their best.... They're sending people that have lots of problems, and they're bringing those problems with us [*sic*]. They're bringing drugs. They're bringing crime. They're rapists. And some, I assume, are good people.
>
> *(Washington Post Staff 2015)*

Throughout the 2016 presidential contest and once in office, Trump became well-known for sharp anti-immigrant rhetoric and a tendency to characterize Latinx immigrants as violent criminals. Setting the interests of a white American electorate against those of "illegal aliens," he conflated immigrants arriving from the southern border with "an invasion of drugs, invasion of gangs, [and an] invasion of people" that necessitated declaring a national emergency, building a multi-billion-dollar wall along the US-Mexico border, and other anti-immigrant measures (Boston Globe Staff 2019). As we show in this chapter, Trump's xenophobic rhetoric permeated dispersed social settings as his supporters now emboldened, publicly echoed and acted on such racist political discourse, in ways in which they might not have done in the pre-Trump era.

Recent border studies research explores how borders are not merely concrete geopolitical sites, but also are symbolic boundaries of inclusion and exclusion that are flexibly invoked, enacted, performed, and reinforced in myriad locations and social situations (Kaiser 2012). Similarly, our collaborative, activist anthropological research with immigrant-serving community organizations in Central Florida illustrates the proliferation of internal borders far beyond the US-Mexico divide. In the Trump era, commonplace and habitual expressions of racism shaped immigrants' daily lives in ways that call for policy change and activist responses.

Exclusion and fear

US immigration policies have long served to racialize and criminalize Latinx immigrants, particularly those who are undocumented (Dowling and Inda 2013; Horton 2017; Stuesse 2016). Within the context of an ongoing conflation of undocumented immigration and criminality, Latinx immigrants' "illegality" has become not only a juridical category and sociopolitical condition, but a way of "being in the world" (Willen 2007, 11), that is, daily human life defined by experiences of terror, social vulnerability, exploitation, and threat of deportation (De Genova 2002). Further, as Coutin (1991) argues, everyday social relations can emphasize and sustain social difference based on illegality—underscoring what she calls alienation, or how people become defined as "illegal aliens."

Prior to Trump's inauguration, several immigration laws and enforcement techniques contributed to immigrants' vulnerability. For example, beginning in 1994, through a program known as Prevention through Deterrence, the federal government strategically used drones, immigration enforcement personnel, walls, and fencing to funnel immigrants into the harshest areas of the Sonoran Desert where they risked violent attack and death (De León 2015). Furthermore, measures such as Section 287(g) of the Immigration and Nationality Act (which allowed local officials to enforce federal immigration law) and the Secure Communities program (a fingerprint-sharing program that matches arrestees' fingerprints to federal immigration databases) authorized local police to in effect act as auxiliary deportation agents, thereby spreading the border's threats of apprehension and deportation into all US spaces (Coleman 2007). These oppressive mobile enforcement technologies proliferated immigrant policing efforts throughout the polity, multiplying the risks and threats of the border (Coleman 2007; Dowling and Inda 2013; Kline 2017, 2019; Novak et al. 2017). Subsequently, under the Trump administration, existing 'security' measures to protect a white electorate from brown (Latinx) 'invaders' were further amplified. The ubiquitous threat of deportation and the mobile technology of the national border were augmented by an increasingly aggressive social border. As Kaiser (2012) has argued, borders should not be understood exclusively as physical barriers but also as social constructs that are produced throughout the (American) polity by practices that perform and reify social categories of inclusion and exclusion. Borrowing Butler's (2011) notion of performativity, Kaiser suggests that borders can be constituted by performative enactments, which "naturalize and essentialize socio-spatial categories by materializing borders and separating interior from exterior" (2012, 523). The constant drumbeat of Donald Trump's multiple and varied efforts to exclude and expel immigrants can be read, in addition, as a series of bordering performances that invoked, magnified, and reified the border as a social construct.

It might be said that the exclusion and expulsion of immigrants was the highest priority of the Trump administration, as shown in the proliferation of administrative actions and legislative workarounds generated, from the earliest days of his presidency. In his first week in office, Trump issued an executive order that temporarily banned all immigrants and refugees from a number of predominantly Muslim countries (Exec. Order No. 13,780, 82 Fed. Reg. 13209 (2017)). In addition, by the end of 2017, he had enacted an indefinite ban on immigrants and refugees from Iran, Chad, Yemen, Somalia, Libya, and North Korea (Proclamation No. 9645, 82 Fed. Reg. 45161 (Sept. 24, 2017)). The administration justified the second ban by arguing the US government had been unable to attain adequate information from these countries to determine whether potential migrants would pose a threat to national security. While a waiver was technically available to those who could prove they were not a threat, no separate application for this waiver was made available, nor were the requirements to prove suitability publicly stated (Irwin 2019). These bans were widely criticized as thinly veiled Islamophobia that did little to protect national security (Hurley 2018). Such executive orders thereby underscored a key element of the performative bordering processes initiated by the Trump administration: the perpetuation of ethno-racial exclusion.

Additional actions to exclude and expel immigrants rolled out, month after month. For example, while Congress had created a Temporary Protected Status (TPS) program in 1990, which permitted immigrants from specified countries to stay in the United States when conditions in their home countries were unsafe due to civil conflict and natural disaster, President Trump revoked the temporary protected status for immigrants from Haiti, El Salvador, Nicaragua, Sudan, Nepal, and Honduras, rendering them vulnerable to deportation (Cohn, Passel, and Bialik 2019). In addition, the administration drastically reduced the number of refugees accepted in the United States with each successive year, reaching historic lows (Blizzard and Batalova 2019).

While immigrants come to the United States from all over the world, and more enter the country through airports than across the US-Mexico border, the president's fixation on the southern border revealed a particular disquietude about Latinx immigrants. For example, in July of 2019, the administration passed an interim ruling targeting Central and South American asylum seekers. In it, migrants who passed through a third country (not the United States or their country of origin) were required to first apply for asylum in that country before they would become eligible to seek asylum in the United States (Department of Homeland Security, RIN 1615-AC44, 84 Fed. Reg. 33829 (July 16, 2019)). This policy strained Mexico's backlogged system and kept vulnerable asylum seekers in Mexico while awaiting their court appointments. Similarly, the Migrant Protection Protocol (released January 24, 2019), more commonly known as the "Remain in Mexico" policy, worked to keep asylum seekers from entering the United States while their cases were processed, funneling people into Ciudad Juárez (over 8,000 in the first few months alone) (Moore 2019). Overall, these policies, focused on the southern border, broadcasted a hierarchy of immigrant desirability even within an overall strategy of exclusion.

In addition to the focus on the southern border, other instances during his presidency revealed that racism informed Trump's hardline immigration stance. In a 2018 closed-door meeting, in reference to Haiti and some African countries, Trump asked lawmakers why the United States should accept immigrants from "shithole countries"; he added that he wanted to allow in more from countries like Norway (Davis, Stolberg, and Kaplan 2018). In another instance, he told four congresswomen of color to "go back" to where they came from, even though only one of them was an immigrant (Quilantan and Cohen 2019). Such statements revealed a close association in his mind of immigration and race, and that he considered black and brown people, even children or grandchildren of immigrants, as abject outsiders. His racialization was expansive, and when given an opportunity, he would fold in for exclusion all who were non-white.

President Trump's exclusionary strategies also targeted children and those brought to the United States as children. Although ultimately blocked by a federal judge, Trump also set into motion efforts to dismantle Deferred Action for Childhood Arrivals (DACA), an Obama-era program that provided the right to work and temporary protection from deportation to undocumented immigrants brought to the United States as children (Gonzales 2018). While awaiting the Supreme Court's determination about the constitutionality of Trump's termination of DACA, the administration stopped accepting new DACA applications (although the approximately 700,000 beneficiaries of the program could continue to apply for status renewal). This uncertainty created fear and desperation among immigrants at risk of deportation.

In fact, stirring up fear among immigrants in many cases seemed central to Trump administration policies, an extension of the "Prevention through Deterrence" strategy. As another example, in 2019, the Department of Homeland Security altered a nineteenth-century rule that permitted immigration officials to deny entry to those deemed likely to become impoverished and ultimately a "public charge." The "Inadmissibility on Public Charge Grounds" rule permitted immigration officials to bar entry to those who could not prove that they would remain self-sufficient and not rely upon government benefits, and to deny permanent resident status to immigrants who had ever relied on any such programs. Public conversations about this rule immediately sent a chill through immigrant communities, leading parents to avoid using programs such as food stamps, free school lunches, and Medicaid, even on behalf of their US-citizen children, out of fear that later they might be deported or denied the opportunity to adjust their immigrant status (Narea 2020). Similarly, the Census Bureau attempted to add a question to the 2020 census that would have required respondents to disclose whether they were US citizens (ACLU 2019). Critics of the citizenship question saw the proposal as an attempt to undercount immigrants (and thereby reduce political representation and resources for their communities) since it would have made noncitizens, undocumented residents, and citizen members of their households less likely to respond (ACLU 2019). Although census information cannot be publicly linked to a respondent's identity until 72 years after the census form was submitted (92 Stat. 915; Public Law 95–416; October 5, 1978), this provision was widely misunderstood. While federal courts ruled that the citizenship question could not appear on the 2020 census, test forms sent out in 2019 still carried the question, which likely sparked confusion (Wang 2019). Combined, these efforts suggest that the creation of uncertainty and fear was integral to the administration's exclusionary strategy.

Another immigration enforcement measure of the Trump administration again reveals that deterrence through fear was purposeful, and further, that children might be used as pawns to deter parents from entering the country. Under Department of Homeland Security Director John Kelly, immigration enforcement agents were directed to separate children and parents as part of an effort to deter immigrants from crossing into the United States (Davis and Shear 2019). The administration justified this policy through the Clinton-era Flores Settlement Agreement, which forbade the long-term detention of children. Under the Trump administration, children were moved to shelters operated by the Office of Refugee Resettlement, while their parents remained in detention (Chanda 2018). However, separating families, especially those with small children, had not been recommended by the Flores Settlement or any other previous law. The policy gained attention when politicians and journalists reported that children were held in overcrowded cells and within fencing resembling cages (Dickerson 2019) and were denied basic hygienic items such as toothbrushes, soap, beds, blankets, and clean clothing—a position the Trump administration defended in subsequent court challenges (Chapin 2019; Flynn 2019; Montoya-Galvez 2019).

Most emblematic of Donald Trump's politicking regarding immigration was his vision of a US-Mexico border wall. Since the beginning of his 2016 presidential run, Trump insisted a full-length continental border wall (extending 1,954 miles) was essential to protecting national security. His campaign rallies invariably included him leading the crowd in a chant: "Build the wall! Build the wall!" Despite evidence that a full border wall would be ineffective in deterring both migrants and drug trafficking, and almost certainly would create additional problems, such as an increased migrant mortality rate, the administration continued to prioritize the project (American Immigration Council 2019; Felbab-Brown 2017) because the wall was ideologically significant. The wall broadcasted that immigrants and asylum seekers were not welcome in the United States, and that militarized force would be used to keep them out. The symbolic importance of the wall was perhaps best illustrated by Trump's ideas for its design, which included a moat filled with alligators and snakes (which he later denied suggesting), and a wall barrier topped with sharp, "piercing" spikes, which, at various times, he both confirmed and denied (Crowley 2019).

An "invasion"

President Trump's litany of policies did more than express a desire to limit immigration into the United States. These national defense measures were bordering practices that reinforced notions of belonging and exclusion by way of perpetuating narratives that Latinx immigrants are dangerous, criminal, and undesirable. Overall, such efforts were intrinsic to broader biopolitical endeavors to control immigrants and perpetuate white hegemony. Conflating Latinx immigrants and criminality in particular constitutes a biopolitical technique of power. As Foucault (2003) describes, "biopower" is a form of power exercised through population management, and the concept of race is one type of biopolitical control technique, as it can be used to divide and hierarchize subject populations. Such divisions ultimately benefit the dominant racial group, or, in this example, serve to privilege whiteness.

Through relentlessly characterizing Latinx immigrants as dangerous and criminal (Lee 2015; Washington Post Editorial Board 2019), Donald Trump perpetuated the racialization and criminalization of Latinx immigrants. As Inda and Dowling (2013, 2) explain, in the United States, even prior to the Trump presidency, immigration and criminal matters have become increasingly conflated in an effort to "govern undocumented immigrants through crime," which entails "mak[ing] crime and punishment the institutional context in which efforts to guide the conduct of immigrants take place." Immigration enforcement regimes have broadened into multiple enforcement strategies that make use of several types of law enforcement agencies and overall attempt to govern immigrants through a number of criminal contexts (Menjívar 2014). Racial difference, immigration status, and criminality are collapsed and conflated. As criminalized, racialized others, undocumented immigrants are blamed for societal ills like overcrowded education and healthcare systems (Calavita 1996), which further justifies their mistreatment (Valdez 2016). Making Latinx immigrants criminally and racially "other" contributes to heightened forms of social vulnerability while providing a way to justify immigrants' labor exploitation and overall mistreatment (Horton 2017).

The president's dogged fixation on closing off the southern border and excluding brown and black immigrants had predicable consequences. Donald Trump, as presidential candidate, both responded to his crowds and fueled their fervor. While many of his supporters may have been buoyed by his promise to "Build the Wall," his willingness to shrug off his detractors' charges of racism allowed his supporters to feel emboldened in their desires to exclude and expel immigrants. Indeed, social psychological research has demonstrated that the 2016 presidential election resulted in an increased acceptance of prejudice against populations that the Trump campaign targeted, including immigrants, a phenomenon that Crandall, Miller, and White (2018) referred to as the "Trump Effect."

One particular incident in 2019 revealed the depth of anti-Latinx-immigrant hatred in some Trump supporters, but at the same time, to many observers, it was not surprising. During the lead-up to the 2018 midterm elections, the president was fixated on what he called a "caravan" of Central American families walking towards the US-Mexico border to seek asylum in the United States. Several times, he referred to this caravan as an "invasion," and he warned of a crime wave. On October 29, 2018, he tweeted, "Many Gang Members and some very bad people are mixed into the Caravan heading to our Southern Border.... This is an invasion of our Country and our Military is waiting for you!" (Fabian 2018).

The anti-immigrant furor whipped up during the Trump presidency had already erupted into violence, as was seen in a marked increase in anti-Latinx hate crimes (Brooks 2019). In 2019, however, this hatred culminated in one of the worst mass shootings in US history. During his State of the Union address in February 2019, President Trump reiterated his common refrain that a border wall between the United States and Mexico was necessary to protect the country. He used the border city of El Paso, Texas, as an example, saying that it had been one of the "nation's most dangerous cities," until the border wall was built in the city (Trump 2019). The claim was factually inaccurate, since violent crime had been on the decline in El Paso since 1993 (Timm 2019), but Trump was apparently unconcerned with that. Several months later, on August 3, at a Walmart in El Paso, a 21-year-old white man shot and killed 22 people and injured 24 others. Of those killed, eight were from Mexico; others were Mexican-American or had spent their lives in the border area (Allyn et al. 2019; Washington Post Staff 2019). The shooter confessed to specifically having targeted Mexicans, and his animus was shown in the fact that he drove over ten hours to reach the border city (Bogel-Burroughs 2019).

Minutes before the shooting, a manifesto that officials believe was written by the shooter was posted to the alt-right message board, 8chan. The unsigned, 2,300-word manifesto, titled "The Inconvenient Truth," ranged over many topics, including immigration. It drew on the white supremacist "replacement theory," a conspiracy theory in which non-white migrants are entering the country and having children to "replace" white Americans (Schwartzburg 2019). The shooter claimed his attack was a response to the "Hispanic invasion of Texas" and wrote, "if we can get rid of enough people, then our way of life can be more sustainable" (Arango, Bogel-Burroughs, and Benne 2019). The shooter's actions, then, were directly informed by white nationalist ideas that immigrants (specifically non-white immigrants) pose a threat to what he saw as the American way of life. While the El Paso shooter specified that his ideas "predate Trump" and that he did not want the president to be blamed, the president's rhetoric aligned with that of online forum-dwelling white nationalists. His xenophobic fearmongering resulted in overt physical violence, as demonstrated in El Paso, and hostile antagonism, as we found during our fieldwork in Central Florida.

The research setting: Central Florida

Trump's anti-immigrant rhetoric and administrative measures were reproduced on local levels, including in states with large immigrant populations, such as Florida. In the 2018 Florida gubernatorial race, President Trump endorsed Ron DeSantis, who leaned heavily into his connection to the president during his campaign. In one campaign ad, he taught his infant son to "build the wall" with toy blocks, read him story books about President Trump, and dressed him in a "Make America Great Again" onesie (Rohrer 2018). One of his campaign promises was to end "sanctuary city" policies: policies that limit local governmental cooperation with federal immigration authorities. Shortly after entering office, DeSantis signed into law Senate Bill (S.B.) 168, in June 2019, which banned all sanctuary policies in the state. It required local law enforcement officers to cooperate fully with all immigration officials, including detaining people if there is probable cause that they are "removable" (deportable) under existing laws (Koh 2019). In effect, the Florida legislature followed Trump's lead in border performances that invoked and reanimated processes of exclusion.

To better understand the consequences of Trump's immigration measures and campaigning on Latinx immigrants, during the summer of 2018, we conducted fieldwork in Apopka, Florida—an Orlando exurb of about 50,000 residents that is quickly transforming as highways and housing developments replace former orange groves. In Apopka, two community centers directly serve Latinx immigrants: the Hope CommUnity Center and the Farmworkers Association of Florida. The two organizations often work in tandem to combat immigrant vulnerability through a variety of social services, advocacy, and activism. Both organizations garnered trust among the immigrants they serve, which facilitated our data collection activities.

We used activist anthropology as a methodological approach in our research. In this methodology, researchers join participants in working for a common goal. Usually, this goal is eliminating inequality based on a particular identity, such as race, class, or gender (Hale 2008). In our case, we joined immigrant-serving organizations in their fight for legal, health, and labor rights for immigrants. As Speed (2006a, 2006b) and Hale (2001) have argued, activist anthropologists bring their positionality to the forefront of their research, which can often be beneficial to the research effort and the participants. By building rapport and trust through a demonstrated commitment to their participants' struggle, activist anthropologists can also collect richer and more useful data.

In keeping with the expectations of activist anthropology, we worked with organization leaders at Hope CommUnity Center, or Hope, and the Farmworker Association during all stages of the project. They gave their input on the research questions, contributed to data collection methods, and were crucial in recruiting participants. Without the support of people at both organizations, our data collection would have been limited, demonstrating the value of activist anthropology not only as a political stance, but as a methodological choice. Organization leaders assisted with recruiting participants for three focus groups with Latinx women with a total of 14 participants, 28 ethnographic surveys with people (11 male, 17 female) seeking services from the partner organizations, and 4 key-informant interviews with women who work for the two nonprofits.

Commonplace racism

In focus groups, interviews, and surveys, we asked participants if they had experienced racism in their local community following the 2016 election. Given existing literature on immigrant policing and racial profiling, we expected to hear accounts of police officers profiling immigrants and stopping Latinx drivers. While many participants experienced racism when encountering local law enforcement officers, we were surprised to find that nearly everyone we talked to had experienced routine racist harassment from white community members. All of the encounters encoded the immigrants as foreign and undesirable, and were therefore instances of citizen surveillance, or citizen policing of borders. These encounters occurred in mundane, everyday spaces, such as retail outlets and restaurants. They can be understood within Kaiser's (2012) framework of "border performances," or discourses that materialize the geographic border through iteration and citation. Notably, while Kaiser focused on border performances in highly visible events in central locations involving hundreds of people, our work shows that bordering practices can take place in everyday locations, involving just a pair of interlocutors, in fleeting interactions that might never reach anyone else's attention. In addition, these instances of harassment took place in establishments that were commonly frequented, rendering it difficult for immigrants to avoid future such interactions.

Lucia shared one experience she had in a Walmart with her husband and children. They ran into her niece and her niece's family, and they greeted one other in Spanish and began chatting. An agitated woman approached them and yelled, "English! In English!" Lucia and her family were shocked. "How could this happen?" she wondered.

Several other participants also shared stories of harassment in retail stores. Paula's friend stopped shopping at Kohl's because, she said, only "white people" go there and they would give her "ugly looks." She added: "They look at us, they look at us strangely, like 'What are they doing here?' They look at us, and they keep looking at us." The stares made her feel unwelcome, that she did not belong, and thus are an example of a "bordering practice" that instantiates a social barrier.

While many of the stories relayed to us were those in which immigrants were made to feel as unwelcome outsiders, others specifically involved imputations of criminality. These confrontations, therefore, are examples of citizen surveillance or citizen policing, in line with the general policy shift that Inda and Dowling (2013, 2) describe as "govern[ing] … immigrants through crime." For example, Rosa shared one experience she had in a Save-a-Lot with her children. At the entrance, a girl said to her father, "Look, dad, some criminals are going in!" When the girl's father reprimanded her, she excused herself by saying, "The news says it." Although Rosa was thankful the father rebuked his daughter, this interaction was embarrassing for both her and her children and, according to Rosa, it produced *coraje*—a deep sense of rage—in her teenage son.

Similarly, Paula, who immigrated from Mexico three decades prior, told us about a time not long before, in which a Walmart shopper confronted her in the self-checkout line. Paula was proceeding slowly because she had a lot of fruit and vegetables, and the name of each produce item had to be inputted separately. The woman behind her said: "Go back to your country. You are so slow that you don't even know how to do things, and I'm sure that you're undocumented." Paula and her teenage daughters were shocked, but she explained that she was taking longer. Paula responded:

> If I were undocumented, you can be sure that it would not be because I wanted to be, but because of the laws of your country and of mine, which make it so difficult for a person to be granted a visa or a permit to come

> here. It is not our fault, but the fault of both countries' systems, but you don't know, right? And if you don't know, don't say it, don't accuse me of something that you don't know to be true.

The woman fell silent. Paula's daughters worried that the woman's teenage children would learn from their mother's response and repeat this behavior at school. Resignedly, Paula told us: "We don't know if they do it because they think it's funny, because the president does it like a joke sometimes, or because they truly have this anti-immigrant [sentiment] inside them. We don't know."

Valdez (2016) discusses how harassment of immigrants may result in immigrants self-governing. Similarly, our interviews revealed that, as a result of routine racism in public spaces, many reduced their engagement in social spaces where they feared they were unwelcome. For example, Paula's friend (mentioned above) stopped shopping at Kohl's where people stared at her. Public schools, however, are one of those spaces in which racist interactions occur that cannot be avoided. Participants in our research explained that their children often faced anti-immigrant bullying from classmates because of their ethnicity and/or national origin. Julieta's brother was told by his classmates, "I can't wait until Donald Trump deport[s] you." Similarly, Rosa explained that her son was often mockingly told by his classmates, "Today is your last day" and "It was nice knowing you," insinuating that he was going to be deported at any moment. Another parent shared that her teenage daughter often said to her: "Mommy, it is really sad.... They say a lot of sad, ugly things about us [Latinx people] because they don't know us."

Community members drew a direct correlation between Trump's election and an increase in racist confrontations in public, which they accredited to his propensity for openly using anti-immigrant and anti-Latinx rhetoric. One interviewee explained: "From the moment when they said, 'This is the president,' immediately in the community, in the stores, one started to feel that which I had never experienced before: racism." Participants explained that they felt President Trump made it acceptable to openly express racist sentiment and that there was more support for xenophobic and racist ideas. For example, Sofia, a woman who recently came to Florida fleeing organized crime-related violence in Mexico, said she had noticed that people treat her and her family differently because, as she explained, "our skin is darker, our features are different.... We're another race." To explain why people felt they could treat them this way, she said, "people are not afraid now to openly discriminate because there is high-level support [for this behavior], which is the president."

Overall, the kinds of routine racism in mundane spaces we report here demonstrate the consequences of a constant drumbeat of anti-immigrant campaigning and policy-making. The anti-immigrant rhetoric Trump espoused sanctioned racism and emboldened racist harassment among some groups in the United States and inspired bordering practices such as reprimanding immigrants for speaking English in public. In mischaracterizing immigrants as racially other, criminal deviants, President Trump justified the legal mistreatment of immigrants, and indirectly deputized citizens to surveil and police immigrant neighbors in their own communities. Governing immigrants through crime, then, became a multifaceted policy agenda that extended far beyond the contexts of official law enforcement and immigration enforcement. Having embraced normative ideas about immigrant criminality, US citizens became involved in efforts to govern immigrants through crime. Our fieldwork highlights how the Trump Effect, or the normalization of prejudice, can result in instances of harassment in places far from the geopolitical border, in mundane spaces in which immigrants unsuspectingly go about their everyday tasks.

The consequences of routine racism extend far beyond the moment of public shaming and could alter immigrants' participation in public spaces. Open racism obstructs immigrants' integration into the community and heightens isolation. Such public intimidation might stop immigrants from seeking social services or the assistance of police, and stop them from potentially demanding political rights. This, consequently, would enhance their vulnerability, conceal injustices, and abet the continued exploitation of immigrant labor.

Resisting commonplace racism

Participants in this study believed that most of the anti-immigrant sentiment they encountered stemmed from ignorance. They believed that if US-born people were more aware of the realities of the immigrant community, they would be less swayed by political and media narratives. Accordingly, some of them advocated for increased efforts like the service-learning program Hope CommUnity Center offers.

One of the largest service-learning efforts Hope CommUnity Center operates is a homestay program. During the program, high school and college students stay with immigrant families in Apopka for several days to learn about the realities of immigration and the challenges the immigrant community faces. Rosa, one of the organizers of this program, explained its importance:

> The same way that school educates our children, [we need to] educate the community. Because the more we educate, the more we inform, the more power we will have to refute what the news says, what the President says [about who we are].

Beyond interventions that reverse commonplace racism, legislative actions can reverse the trend of governing immigrants through crime. While any such federal legislation seems unlikely in the short-term, local and state governments can take the lead in protecting immigrants from discrimination and isolation. Orlando, for example, passed the Orlando Trust Act in 2018, which "prohibit[s] city employees—including police officers—from asking a law-abiding person's immigration status" (Gillespie 2018). While this local-level policy can be challenged at the state level, and while pro-immigrant policies cannot stamp out routine racism, they publicly decouple images of immigration and crime, and thereby serve as important counterhegemonic performances.

As we argued in this chapter, the Trump administration's routinization of rhetorical and legal hostility toward immigrants had individual and interpersonal consequences. Such consequences included routinized citizen policing of borders in the most mundane of spaces, including retail outlets and public schools. Nationalism and xenophobia increasingly have been informing policy agendas globally (Bieber 2018), suggesting immigrant experiences of isolation and marginalization are more widespread. Legislative fixes are needed, but in addition, educators have a role to play. Our research participants advocated for educational programs on the local level. Such efforts could be advanced through the kinds of collaborations we describe between academic institutions and community-based organizations.

Acknowledgments

Special thanks to the Farmworker Association of Florida, Hope CommUnity Center, Sister Ann Kendrick, Chris Furino, and Jeannie Economos for their assistance with this project. Funding for the research was provided through the Rollins College Student Faculty Collaborative Research Program and a Critchfield Faculty Research Grant.

References

ACLU. 2019. "Census 2020: What You Need to Know." *American Civil Liberties Union*. Accessed December 14, 2019. https://www.aclu.org/issues/voting-rights/census-2020.

Allyn, Bobby, Dani Matias, Richard Gonzales, and Bill Chappell. 2019. "Stories of El Paso Shooting Victims Show Acts of Self-Sacrifice Amid Massacre." *National Public Radio*, August 6, 2019. https://www.npr.org/2019/08/06/748527564/stories-of-el-paso-shooting-victims-show-acts-of-self-sacrifice-amid-massacre.

American Immigration Council. 2019. "Fact Sheet: The High Cost and Diminishing Returns of a Border Wall." *American Immigration Council*, September 6, 2019. https://www.americanimmigrationcouncil.org/research/cost-of-border-wall.

Arango, Tim, Nicholas Bogel-Burroughs, and Katie Benner. 2019. "Minutes Before El Paso Killing, Hate-Filled Manifesto Appears Online." *New York Times*, August 3, 3019. https://www.nytimes.com/2019/08/03/us/patrick-crusius-el-paso-shooter-manifesto.html?module=inline.

Bieber, Florian. 2018. "Is Nationalism on the Rise? Assessing Global Trends." *Ethnopolitics* 17 (5): 519–540. https://doi.org/10.1080/17449057.2018.1532633.

Blizzard, Brittany, and Jeanne Batalova. 2019. "Refugees and Asylees in the United States." *Migration Policy Institute*, June 13, 2019. https://www.migrationpolicy.org/article/refugees-and-asylees-united-states.

Bogel-Burroughs, Nicholas. 2019. "'I'm the Shooter': El Paso Suspect Confessed to Targeting Mexicans, Police Say." *New York Times*, August 9, 2019. https://www.nytimes.com/2019/08/09/us/el-paso-suspect-confession.html.

Boston Globe Staff. 2019. "Read the Transcript of Trump's Rose Garden Speech." *Boston Globe*, February 15, 2019. https://www.bostonglobe.com/news/nation/2019/02/15/read-transcript-trump-rose-garden-speech/Sd5RoKOoHjF2jSzPxGyRaP/story.html.

Brooks, Brad. 2019. "Victims of Anti-Latino Hate Crimes Soar in U.S.: FBI Report." *Reuters*, November 12, 2019. https://www.reuters.com/article/us-hatecrimes-report/victims-of-anti-latino-hate-crimes-soar-in-us-fbi-report-idUSKBN1XM2OQ.

Butler, Judith. 2011. *Bodies That Matter: On the Discursive Limits of Sex*. Reprint, New York: Routledge.

Calavita, Kitty. 1996. "The New Politics of Immigration: 'Balanced-Budget Conservatism' and the Symbolism of Proposition 187." *Social Problems* 43 (3): 284–305. http://doi.org/10.2307/3096979.

Chanda, Ishanee. 2018. "Child Migrants and Family Separation." *National Conference of State Legislatures*, December 11, 2018. http://www.ncsl.org/research/immigration/child-migrants-and-family-separation.aspx.

Chapin, Angelina. 2019. "In Their Own Words, Migrant Children Describe Horrific Conditions at Border Patrol Facilities." *HuffPost*, June 28, 2019. https://www.huffpost.com/entry/migrant-children-describe-detention_n_5d1646ffe4b03d61163af666.

Cohn, D'Vera, Jeffrey S. Passel, and Kristen Bialik. 2019. "Many Immigrants with Temporary Protected Status Face Uncertain Future in U.S." *Pew Research Center*, November 27, 2019. https://www.pewresearch.org/fact-tank/2019/11/27/immigrants-temporary-protected-status-in-us/.

Coleman, Mathew. 2007. "Immigration Geopolitics beyond the Mexico-US Border." *Antipode* 39 (1): 54–76. https://doi.org/10.1111/j.1467-8330.2007.00506.x.

Coutin, Susan Bibler. 1991. *The Culture of Protest: Religious Activism and the US Sanctuary Movement*. Boulder, CO: Westview Press.

Crandall, Christian S., Jason M. Miller, and Mark H. White, II. "Changing Norms Following the 2016 US Presidential Election: The Trump Effect on Prejudice." *Social Psychological and Personality Science* 9 (2): 186–192. https://doi.org/10.1177/1948550617750735.

Crowley, Michael. 2019. "Trump Denies Considering a Border Moat." *New York Times*, October 2, 2019. https://www.nytimes.com/2019/10/02/us/politics/trump-alligator-snakes-moat.html.

Davis, Julie Hirschfeld, and Michael D. Shear. 2018. "How Trump Came to Enforce a Practice of Separating Migrant Families." *New York Times*, June 16, 2018. https://www.nytimes.com/2018/06/16/us/politics/family-separation-trump.html.

Davis, Julie Hirschfeld, Sheryl Gay Stolberg, and Thomas Kaplan. 2018. "Trump Alarms Lawmakers with Disparaging Words for Haiti and Africa." *New York Times*, January 11, 2018. https://www.nytimes.com/2018/01/11/us/politics/trump-shithole-countries.html.

De Genova, Nicholas P. 2002. "Migrant 'Illegality' and Deportability in Everyday Life." *Annual Review of Anthropology* 31 (1): 419–447. https://doi.org/10.1146/annurev.anthro.31.040402.085432.

De León, Jason. 2015. *The Land of Open Graves: Living and Dying on the Migrant Trail*. Berkeley: University of California Press.

Dickerson, Caitlin. 2019. "'There is a Stench': Soiled Clothes and No Baths for Migrant Children at a Texas Center." *New York Times*, June 21, 2019. https://www.nytimes.com/2019/06/21/us/migrant-children-border-soap.html.

Dowling, Julie A., and Jonathan Xavier Inda. 2013. *Governing Immigration through Crime: A Reader*. Stanford: Stanford University Press.

Fabian, Jordan. 2018. "Trump: Migrant Caravan 'Is an Invasion'." *The Hill*, October 29, 2018. https://thehill.com/homenews/administration/413624-trump-calls-migrant-caravan-an-invasion.

Felbab-Brown, Vanda. 2017. "The Wall: The Real Costs of a Barrier between the United States and Mexico." *Brookings Institution*, August 2017. https://www.brookings.edu/essay/the-wall-the-real-costs-of-a-barrier-between-the-united-states-and-mexico/.

Flynn, Meagan. 2019. "Detained Migrant Children Got No Toothbrush, No Soap, No Sleep. It's No Problem, Government Argues." *Washington Post*, June 21, 2019. https://www.washingtonpost.com/nation/2019/06/21/detained-migrant-children-no-toothbrush-soap-sleep/.

Foucault, Michel. 2003. *"Society Must Be Defended": Lectures at the Collège de France, 1975–76*. Edited by Mauro Bertani, Alessando Fontana, and Francois Ewald. New York: Picador.

Gillespie, Ryan. 2018. "Orlando Approves Trust Act Policy to Cheers of Immigration Activists." *Orlando Sentinel*, July 23, 2018. https://www.orlandosentinel.com/news/orange-county/os-orlando-trust-vote-20180723-story.html.

Gonzales, Richard. 2018. "2nd Federal Court Blocks Trump from Rescinding DACA." *National Public Radio*, February 13, 2018. https://www.npr.org/sections/thetwo-way/2018/02/13/585597527/second-federal-court-blocks-trump-from-rescinding-daca.

Hale, Charles R. 2001. "What Is Activist Research?" *Social Science Research Council Items and Issues* 2 (1–2): 13–15. https://issuu.com/ssrcitemsissues/docs/i_i_vol_2_no_1-2_2001?e=24618429/35326062.

———. 2008. "Introduction." In *Engaging Contradictions: Theory, Politics, and Methods of Activist Scholarship*, edited by Charles R. Hale, 1–28. Berkeley: University of California Press.

Horton, Sarah Bronwen. 2017. *They Leave Their Kidneys in the Fields*. Berkeley: University of California Press.

Hurley, Lawrence. 2018. "U.S. Top Court Upholds Trump Travel Ban Targeting Muslim-Majority Nations." *Reuters World News*, June 26, 2018. https://www.reuters.com/article/us-usa-court-immigration/u-s-top-court-backs-trump-on-travel-ban-targeting-muslim-majority-nations-idUSKBN1JM1U9.

Inda, Jonathan Xavier, and Julie A. Dowling. 2013. "Introduction: Governing Migrant Illegality." In *Governing Immigration through Crime: A Reader*, edited by Julie A. Dowling and Jonathan Xavier Inda, 1–36. Stanford: Stanford University Press.

Irwin, Richard, ed. 2019. "One Year after the SCOTUS Ruling: Understanding the Muslim Ban and How We'll Keep Fighting It." *National Immigration Law Center*, June 22, 2019. https://www.nilc.org/wp-content/uploads/2019/06/Impacts-of-the-Muslim-Ban-2019.pdf.

Kaiser, Richard J. 2012. "Performativity and the Eventfulness of Bordering Practices." In *A Companion to Border Studies*, edited by Thomas M. Wilson and Hastings Donnan, 522–537. Malden, MA: Wiley-Blackwell.

Kline, Nolan. 2017. "Pathogenic Policy: Immigrant Policing, Fear, and Parallel Medical Systems in the US South." *Medical Anthropology* 36 (4): 396–410. https://doi.org/10.1080/01459740.2016.1259621.

———. 2019. *Pathogenic Policing: Immigration Enforcement and Health in the US South*. New Brunswick, NJ: Rutgers University Press.

Koh, Elizabeth. 2019. "Gov. DeSantis Signs 'Sanctuary Cities' Ban into Law. There Aren't Any in Florida." *Miami Herald*, June 14, 2019. https://www.miamiherald.com/news/politics-government/state-politics/article231552873.html.

Lee, Michelle Ye Hee. 2015. "Donald Trump's False Comments Connecting Mexican Immigrants and Crime." *Washington Post*, July 8, 2015. https://www.washingtonpost.com/news/fact-checker/wp/2015/07/08/donald-trumps-false-comments-connecting-mexican-immigrants-and-crime/?noredirect=on.

Lopez, William D., Daniel J. Kruger, Jorge Delva, Mikel Llanes, Charo Ledón, Adreanne Waller, Melanie Harner et al. 2017. "Health Implications of an Immigration Raid: Findings from a Latino Community in the Midwestern United States." *Journal of Immigrant and Minority Health* 19 (3): 702–708. https://doi.org/10.1007/s10903-016-0390-6.

Menjívar, Cecilia. 2014. "The 'Poli-Migra' Multilayered Legislation, Enforcement Practices, and What We Can Learn about and from Today's Approaches." *American Behavioral Scientist* 58 (13): 1805–1819. https://doi.org/10.1177/0002764214537268.

Montoya-Galvez, Camilo. 2019. "Here's Why the Trump Administration Says It's Not Required to Give Migrant Children Soap." *CBS News*, June 24, 2019. https://www.cbsnews.com/news/trump-administration-migrant-children-in-u-s-custody-dont-need-to-be-provided-soap-and-toothbrushes/.

Moore, Robert. 2019. "In Juárez, 'Remain in Mexico' Policy Casts Asylum-Seekers Back into Uncertainty." *National Public Radio*, July 10, 2019. https://www.npr.org/2019/07/10/740159720/under-trump-policy-migrants-seeking-asylum-must-wait-in-mexico.

Narea, Nicole. 2020. "Trump's Rule Creating a Wealth Test for Immigrants Is Now in Effect." *Vox*, February 24, 2020. https://www.vox.com/policy-and-politics/2019/10/11/20899253/trump-public-charge-rule-immigrants-welfare-benefits.

Novak, Nicole L., Arline T. Geronimus, and Aresha M. Martinez-Cardoso. 2017. "Change in Birth Outcomes among Infants Born to Latina Mothers after a Major Immigration Raid." *International Journal of Epidemiology* 46 (3): 839–849. https://doi.org/10.1093/ije/dyw346.

Quilantan, Bianca, and David Cohen. 2019. "Trump Tells Dem Congresswomen: Go Back Where You Came from." *Politico*, July 14, 2019. https://www.politico.com/story/2019/07/14/trump-congress-go-back-where-they-came-from-1415692.

Rohrer, Gray. 2018. "Ron DeSantis Teaches Kids about Trump in New Ad." *Orlando Sentinel*, July 30, 2018. https://www.orlandosentinel.com/politics/os-desantis-trump-kids-ad-20180730-story.html.

Sargent, Greg. 2016. "Here's How Donald Trump Might Become President. It's Unlikely." *Washington Post*, March 29, 2016. https://www.washingtonpost.com/blogs/plum-line/wp/2016/03/29/heres-how-donald-trump-might-become-president/.

Schwartzburg, Rosa. 2019. "The 'White Replacement Theory' Motivates Alt-Right Killers the World Over." *The Guardian*, August 5, 2019. https://www.theguardian.com/commentisfree/2019/aug/05/great-replacement-theory-alt-right-killers-el-paso.

Speed, Shannon. 2006a. "At the Crossroads of Human Rights and Anthropology: Toward a Critically Engaged Activist Research." *American Anthropologist* 108 (1): 66–76. https://doi.org/10.1525/aa.2006.108.1.66.

———. 2006b. "Indigenous Women and Gendered Resistance in the Wake of Acteal: A Feminist Activist Research Perspective." In *Engaged Observer: Anthropology, Advocacy, and Activism*, edited by Victoria Sanford and Asale Angel-Anjani, 170–188. New Brunswick, NJ: Rutgers University Press.

Stuesse, Angela. 2016. *Scratching out a Living: Latinos, Race, and Work in the Deep South.* Berkeley: University of California Press.

Timm, Jane C. 2019. "Fact Check: Trump Claims a Wall Made El Paso Safe. Data Shows Otherwise." *NBC News*, February 11, 2019. https://www.nbcnews.com/politics/donald-trump/fact-check-trump-claims-wall-made-el-paso-safe-data-n969506.

Trump, Donald J. 2019. "Remarks by President Trump in State of the Union Address." *The White House*, February 6, 2019. https://www.whitehouse.gov/briefings-statements/remarks-president-trump-state-union-address-2/.

Valdez, Inés. 2016. "Punishment, Race, and the Organization of U.S. Immigration Exclusion." *Political Research Quarterly* 69 (4): 640–654. https://doi.org/10.1177/1065912916670515.

Wang, Hansi Lo. 2019. "Why Is the Census Bureau Still Asking a Citizenship Question on Forms?" *National Public Radio*, August 9, 2019. https://www.npr.org/2019/08/09/743296249/why-is-the-census-bureau-still-asking-a-citizenship-question-on-forms.

Washington Post Editorial Board. 2019. "Unauthorized Immigrants Are Overwhelmingly Law-abiding. But It Won't Stop Trump." *Washington Post*, June 2, 2019. https://beta.washingtonpost.com/opinions/unauthorized-immigrants-are-overwhelmingly-law-abiding-but-it-wont-stop-trump/2019/06/02/5f4f696a-8193-11e9-bce7-40b4105f7ca0_story.html.

Washington Post Staff. 2015. "Full Text: Donald Trump Announces a Presidential Bid." *Washington Post*, June 16, 2015. https://www.washingtonpost.com/news/post-politics/wp/2015/06/16/full-text-donald-trump-announces-a-presidential-bid/.

———. 2019. "The Lives Lost in El Paso." *Washington Post*, August 8, 2019. https://www.washingtonpost.com/nation/2019/08/04/el-paso-shooting-victims/.

Willen, Sarah S. 2007. "Toward a Critical Phenomenology of 'Illegality': State Power, Criminalization, and Abjectivity among Undocumented Migrant Workers in Tel Aviv, Israel." *International Migration* 45 (3): 8–38. https://doi.org/10.1111/j.1468-2435.2007.00409.x.

6
SNAKES ON THE BASEBALL FIELD
Unmasking political images of Latinx criminality

Corinne Kentor

During the 2016 US presidential campaign, Donald Trump tapped into incendiary anti-immigrant discourses that directly targeted Latinx communities. Trump warned voters that migrants from Mexico and Central America posed a distinct physical, economic, and criminal threat to US residents, invoking "invader" imagery to bolster a nativist national campaign (Robertson 2018). In the years that followed, Trump and his associates continued to utilize racially inflected discourses to justify punitive immigration policies, including the separation of migrant parents and children along the US-Mexico border (see Vickers's and Kline's chapter in this volume). On April 20, 2020, as the United States grappled with the human and economic losses of the COVID-19 pandemic, Trump (@realDonaldTrump) tweeted his intention to suspend all immigration to the United States, suggesting that such measures would stem the influx of the virus while "protect[ing] the jobs of our GREAT American Citizens," even though the virus already had spread to all 50 states. The announcement immediately incited backlash from advisors and public policy experts (Chacón and Chemerinsky 2020), who questioned both the economic practicality and the legality of the proposed executive order. Though Trump soon backed away from a sweeping suspension, he held tight to underlying suppositions about the role immigrants play in the American economy, revealing how insidious racial prejudices, masquerading as "America First" policies, could create alternative national imaginaries in which immigrants posed a pervasive threat to the lives and livelihoods of citizens.

Some analysts noted that the new "ban" (the executive order signed on April 22) was in effect a reiteration of Trump's favorite campaign strategy (Rogers, Shear, and Kanno-Youngs 2020). They suggested that the president was using the pandemic, and its "foreign" origins, to galvanize his populist base (Edsall 2020). Others pointed out that the Tweet exemplified Trump's governing strategy, in which "broad" public pronouncements about "sweeping initiatives" helped shape

DOI: 10.4324/9781003034810-6

and inspire more specific legislative agenda items (Rogers, Shear, and Kanno-Youngs 2020). In the case of the immigration ban, these measures included the summary expulsion of asylum seekers (including unaccompanied minors) (Lakhani 2020; Montoya-Galvez 2020; Narea 2020), accelerated construction of the southern "Border Wall" (Coleman 2020), the expansion of existing travel restrictions (Kanno-Youngs 2020), and the revision of the "public charge rule," which barred immigrants likely to utilize public assistance from applying for green cards (Liptak 2020). Many of these initiatives were spearheaded by Trump's senior policy advisor, Stephen Miller, who had a track record of using public health concerns to push for the implementation of tougher immigration policies and more restrictive border enforcement practices (Dickerson and Shear 2020). In each of these instances, Trump and Miller, along with their supporters, used their public platform to set up a dangerous dichotomy between American nationals and immigrant invaders who threatened the US with a variety of ills—violence, poverty, competition, and, in the case of the coronavirus outbreak, disease.

In this chapter, I demonstrate how twenty-first-century political cultures make use of discourses emblematic of earlier eras of conquest and geopolitical boundary-making, tying together different theoretical frames that lend insight into the connections among anti-immigrant and settler-colonial ideologies, histories, and policies. In so doing, I draw attention to early warning signs of political campaigns, like Trump's, that reduce, vilify, and persecute immigrants on geographic, racial, and linguistic grounds. As other researchers have shown, Trump's actions, as political candidate and president, were reflective of a wider history of anti-immigrant sentiment that has shaped US foreign relations over generations, incorporating immigrants into the national economy while excluding them from other forms of social and political life (Gomberg-Muñoz 2016; Ngai 2004). As Charanya Krishnaswami, advocacy director at Amnesty International USA, explained on Twitter, "bans on migration," like those favored by Trump and Miller, reflect the "tired, failed, hateful solution[s]" of last resort for "xenophobes" who based national policy on old-school sectarian "bigotry" (@charanya_k, April 20, 2020). At the same time, the Trump era marked a new and troubling turn in US immigration policy. Understanding the particularities of the literal and political violence wreaked on immigrants of diverse national origins requires a careful investigation of both the linguistic practices that propped up Trump's platform and the historical and sociocultural phenomena that preceded his ascension to the White House. What are the connections among contemporary forms of anti-immigrant border-related human rights violations and policy-making and the long-standing practices of conquest and policing that echo throughout America's political history?

Focusing specifically on the surveillance of multilingual Latinx youth in the United States, this chapter traces the evolution of vitriolic anti-immigrant rhetoric over the last several years, placing ethnographic research conducted in 2015–2016 in conversation with the policies and sound bites central to Trump's 2016 campaign and presidency. I examine how these discourses drew on "invader" imagery particular to the history of the southwestern United States, delving into how linguistic practices are reframed and racialized. I thus show how iconographic stereotyping was used to legitimize scrutiny of immigrant communities, emboldening vigilante action at the edges of American infrastructural spaces. The analysis produced here is based on two data sources: (1) data collected as part of a larger ethnographic study on dual-language programming and curricula conducted in southern New Mexico during the 2015–2016 academic year, and (2) key events and speech acts of Donald Trump's political campaign and presidential administration. This chapter primarily discusses events that took place sometime between 2010 and 2020. However, the implications of the analysis extend far beyond the span of a decade. By combining focused research sited in a singular school district in a singular state with an analysis of speech acts emblematic of the Trump presidency, I demonstrate how local dilemmas over language and schooling can shed light on broader controversies over land, belonging, and national identity whose relevance outlasts the specific era in question. I thus work to open up contemporary conversations about the deployment of hate as a political project, discussing the relevance of big and little bigotries in the context of a wider history of regional change and territorial conquest.

Expanding the settler-colonial framework

Three interrelated theoretical concepts anchor the phenomena under consideration in this chapter: settler-colonialism, scaled or disputed citizenship, and the criminalization of immigrants. While related, these concepts are rarely analyzed in conjunction. When brought together, such ideas can reframe and complicate the relationship between legal citizenship, regional residency, and political legibility, providing important context for our understanding of Trump-era politics. To that end, in this section of the chapter, I bring the intersections among these lineages into focus.

My analysis begins with a discussion of the basic premises of settler-colonial projects. Settler-colonialism is a form of "internal colonialism" that focuses on occupying, controlling, and co-opting the various entities and resources of a given territory (Tuck and Yang 2012, 4). Settler-colonial practices include both the localized exploitation of resources and the development of geopolitical "modes of control" like "prisons, ghettos, minoritizing, schooling, [and] policing" (5). Over time, these modes transform into interlocking infrastructural systems that (re)produce ingrained forms of inequality, manifesting as "segregation, divestment, surveillance, and criminalization," as well as generalized instances of stratified discrimination (5). Through settler-colonialism, the distinctive forms of population control used by occupying imperial entities come to be pervasive (or coequivalent) within both the dominant governing body and the territory it oversees. Over time, the "colony" transforms into a "metropole" or polity, and features associated with the original inhabitants of the land are reclassified not only as subpar, but also as a potential threat to the sovereignty of the prevailing power. In this way, rather than excising or co-opting the art, language, and philosophy of conquered inhabitants, settler-colonial projects reconfigure these same elements as threatening, suspect, or even criminal.

These practices can draw attention to or even be augmented by scaled notions of national belonging, otherwise known as "citizenship." At the most basic level, the concept of citizenship delineates the relationship between individuals and the nation-state. Citizens can be identified by virtue of the fact that they are rights-bearing (i.e. they are entitled to certain services and protections) or based on the obligations they hold in relation to the state. In general terms, therefore, the citizen is identified in relation to an interlocking set of entitlements and responsibilities. Under this definition, citizenship encompasses a list of services and protections one can reasonably (and rightfully) demand of governmental infrastructures, but it also makes these rights contingent on a loose set of criteria. As a consequence, enacting citizenship makes the citizen herself vulnerable, as it creates potential conditions under which she can be removed from the polity and, consequently, stripped of rights.

This exchange-based definition of citizenship is useful for understanding the basic premises that undergird a legalistic approach to the concept of membership. However, such a perspective is unsatisfying in a mobile global context. Diasporic populations, for example, can hold varying relationships with multiple nation-states, effectively severing the connections among residency, emotional affiliation, social responsibility, and legal attachment (see Abu El-Haj 2007; Coutin 2007; Délano Alonso 2018; Riggan 2013). Meanwhile, the focus on unauthorized populations can broaden the concept of citizenship beyond a narrow judicial definition to include all forms of relating to a nation-state (De Genova 2002), so much so that undocumented adolescents, for example, can experience social citizenship even as they are denied the rights and privileges that accompany legal citizenship (Gonzales and Chavez 2012).

When people move or live across national boundaries, they inherently complicate transactional understandings of citizenship that link explicit and implicit rights to facts of residence. As Iskander, Lowe, and Riordan's (2010) work on Mexican construction workers in Philadelphia reminds us, immigrant identity can often shape and overshadow other forms of self-knowledge, including that related to workplace skill. In many cases, "immigrant" becomes a consequential modifier attached to other politically substantiated nouns: mothers are distinguished from *immigrant* mothers (Constable 2014); employees are distinguished from *immigrant* employees (Ribas 2016); students are distinguished from *immigrant* students (Gonzales 2015); and criminals are distinguished from *immigrant* criminals (Hernández 2010). What Roberto Gonzales (2015) terms a "master status" thus extends to include the general overarching conceptualization of immigrants in policy and scholarship, and the fact of immigration itself becomes a justification for a host of intrusive practices that further strip individuals of their right to maintain robust, multifaceted public and private selves, regardless of their technical citizenship status.

Distinctions between citizens and noncitizens are further complicated when we take into account the role settler-colonial policies play in the creation of experiences of stratification. As Paul Silverstein (2005) points out, "although the particular characteristics attributed to migrant populations have changed" over time, scholarly portraits in "each historical moment" have generally responded to the era's dominant "geopolitical realignment" and attendant "shift[s] in the organization of capital" (377, 364). When we focus attention not simply on the fact of immigration, but on the story that has been told about it over time and across political eras, we can begin to situate current policies designed to respond to the "problem" of immigration within a larger juridical framework, building a sense of how law has been used to construct and control subpopulations, moving people in and out of the very categories of suspicion that are central to settler-colonial logic. By controlling not only who is able to become a citizen in the most basic, legally binding sense, but also who can *experience* citizenship in its full, layered form, settler-colonial governments are able to reinstate their own authority as the sociological architects—effectively transforming citizenship from a legal category into a phenotypic one.

In the United States, this has been accomplished largely through the management of the US-Mexico border and the criminalization of south-north migration. As Didier Bigo (2002, 76) explains, "immigration" itself "appears as a catchword, a shibboleth, permitting the convergence of a focal point of institutional statements regarding security norms (at the internal and external level)" that allow for the emergence of especially violent forms of defensive policing. The different actors involved in the defense of the US-Mexico border (e.g., Border Patrol) developed in response to this discourse of securitization (Hernández 2010). Policies like Operation Gatekeeper (1994) and Operation Hold the Line (1993) mobilized a series of "enforcers" whose new employment reflected broader changes in the conceptualization of the United States as a nation in relation to other nations (Nevins 2001). These policies participated in the process by which the border was discursively transformed from a "zone of transition" to "a boundary (or strict line of demarcation)" (12–13). This shift simultaneously involved and responded to a complex network of changes taking place in and outside of border regions themselves, which worked to distinguish the United States as an unambiguous land of wealth and opportunity—the veritable migrant Mecca of the western hemisphere.

Borders' ideological functions are also bound up in the politics of their regulation. Politicians and policy-makers create and deploy regionally specific narratives about the "problem" of transborder migration through the controls they institute, utilizing the practice of border policing as a means of "image crafting" (Andreas 2009) in both local and national terms. In delineating a border and articulating who is able to cross it, state actors transform policies into "transversal political technolog[ies]" (Bigo 2002, 65). They also establish certain territories (e.g. the United States) as "inside" and others (e.g. Mexico and Central America) as "outside," transforming the border itself into a dangerously dynamic zone through which one must pass in order to accrue the benefits of membership. The border thus becomes the "stage" (Andreas 2009, 11) on which international politics play out.

Academic research and popular media reports focusing on northern Mexico and the surrounding territories have in many cases implicitly substantiated racialized perspectives of the "other side," positioning Mexico as a nation defined by homogeneous poverty and violence (Alvarez 1995). These stereotypes have been reproduced by US-based politicians, journalists, and social scientists writing both for and against more open immigration policies. Anti-immigrant writers, drawing on a long-standing nativist tradition alternatively aimed at Germans, Catholics, Chinese, Japanese, and others, have deployed a pervasive "Latino Threat Narrative" that positions im/migrants crossing the southern border as unassimilable invaders who undermine the integrity of the United States as an "imagined community" (Chávez 2013). Meanwhile, immigrant advocates have at times hardened such stereotypes through empathetic accounts of the pervasive suffering that characterizes life south of the border (Gomberg-Muñoz 2016). The US-Mexico border has thus been configured as one that simultaneously protects the United States (a destination) from invasion and Mexico (a place from which one desires to escape) from attrition.

The different people and technologies involved in the "defense" of the US-Mexico border have emerged not simply as institutional responses to criminal acts, but rather in dialogue with racial anxiety, political will, and local concerns about change and social order. By suggesting that the United States needs to shore up its defenses against an incoming tide of Mexican infiltrators fleeing inherently inferior forms of life south of the Río Grande, writers and politicians focused on border relations have generated enduring stereotypes about the nation-states they seek to portray. Understanding the historical construction of the immigrant as a politically suspect type thus not only lends theoretical nuance to the study of immigration, but also allows us to better comprehend and respond to shifting legal, political, and economic realities.

When we apply this understanding to the criminalization of Latinx immigrants, we can begin to understand how the settler-colonial mentalities described earlier intersect with the threat narratives that characterize Trump-era politics. Narratives about the "waves" of immigrants descending on the United States simultaneously encourage racialized policing of phenotypically similar individuals—migrants and non-migrants—and shore up reductive narratives about "sending" and "receiving" countries. First, aesthetic markers like language, accent, or skin tone are associated with a particular criminal image, generating a powerful stereotype that reinforces the sociopolitical symbolism of ingrained practices or attributes. At the same time, the criminal category expands to include anyone vaguely associated with those markers. Thus, "criminality" takes on a certain iconographic form, making the category more imagistically specific even as perceived membership in the category grows. In this way, individual stereotypes—which are harmful enough—are used to generate "folk devils" that are "stylized" through media portrayals and presented as both "a threat to societal values and interests" and a direct source of physical danger (Cohen 2002, 1).

To better understand this process in practice, we need only look at one of Donald Trump's rhetorical gimmicks. Over the course of his 2016 campaign, Trump linked his central stump issues to identifiable speech acts, which took on an almost lyrical or storybook quality in the midst of his raucous rallies (Pinchin 2019). His anti-immigrant tirades, for example, frequently climaxed with a dramatic reading of the fable "The Snake." Trump used this poetic narrative as a parable to compare the United States to a "tender-hearted woman" who took in an evil and naturally self-interested reptile, only to be felled by the creature's poisonous bite. Hearing his pleas, and mystified by his "pretty colored skin all frosted with the dew," she treated him with care, and "wrapped him up all cozy in a curvature of silk/And then laid him by the fireside with some honey and some milk," kissed him, and "clutched him to her bosom." Yet the snake's true nature was revealed:

> "I saved you," cried that woman
> "And you've bit me even, why?
> You know your bite is poisonous and now I'm going to die."
> "Oh shut up, silly woman," said the reptile with a grin
> "You knew damn well I was a snake before you took me in."
>
> *(White 2018)*

The narrative of the snake is based on an Aesop's fable. The text quoted in Trump's speech was adapted from a poem penned by Oscar Brown Jr., an African-American activist and outspoken member of the Communist Party. This irony seemed to be lost on Trump and his public relations team (Rosenberg 2018). Nevertheless, "The Snake" effectively captures the ideologies that undergirded Trump's various attempts at immigration reform. The story, when used as an allegory for transnational migration, simultaneously positions immigrants as subhuman and implies that no immigrant can be trusted as, like the snake, to "bite" is in their nature. In addition, the story emphasizes that the snake *does not belong* inside the house, and that its sole goal is to gain entrance in order to harm the woman the rightful occupant. That the snake attacks a trusting, innocent woman further implies a degree of sexual or gender-based violence, echoing claims Trump made in the speech that launched his presidential campaign, in which he described Mexican immigrants as drug dealers, criminals, and rapists (Phillips 2017; see also Oware's and Martin's chapters in this volume). In case the connection was lost on any audience members, Trump sometimes directly told his listeners to "think of it in terms of immigration" (White 2018), using age-old strategy (Pinchin 2019) to dehumanize and dismiss immigrants as criminals intent on giving naïve hosts a "vicious bite" (Lind 2018).

"The Snake" draws attention to the ways in which regional stereotypes can be employed as a means of transforming individuals into threats against the nation.

Trump often used speeches like this one to (1) associate Latinx heritage with immigration, and (2) link immigration (and, specifically, male immigrants) to a kind of inborn criminality. He thus implicitly tied racialized markers (language, stature, clothing, skin color, etc.) to comprehensive threats that pose individual dangers. In this way, he trapped migrants and non-migrants alike in a socio-political stereotype. The specific brand of racism captured here simultaneously substantiated western European occupation of the American territories and made use of the history of manifest expansionism to reclassify Anglo linguistic and phenotypic attributes as the normative metric of the region. It thus expanded settler-colonial logic in order to configure anyone who looks, speaks, or acts "like" a migrant with criminal behavior.

Where snakes slither

The southwestern United States has long exemplified this particular form of settler-colonialism, in which race, mobility, and invasion are conflated with one another as a means of shoring up Anglo-American power in a contested geographic region. Between 1848 and 1854, the United States acquired 558,670 square miles of Mexican territory. Just under 95 percent of that land was procured via the Treaty of Guadalupe Hidalgo, which marked the conclusion of the Mexican-American War/Intervención estadounidense en México (see Kluger 2008). The Treaty of Guadalupe Hidalgo substantially expanded the reach of the US empire, reorganizing the North American geopolitical landscape and forcing the Mexican nationals who lived in the disputed territory to become US citizens or foreigners with limited rights. It also posed a problem for bureaucrats in charge of governing land that was suddenly situated north of the border. The United States now included a new state (Texas), but there was no easy way for citizens (and, more importantly, capital) to traverse it. Government officials were keen to complete a railway that would connect eastern states to the Pacific Ocean, firmly establishing the United States as a transcontinental power. However, the newly acquired south Texan territory was deemed "too mountainous" for the highly anticipated transit line (Coffey 1933), meaning the invasion of northern Mexico, and the two-year conflict it precipitated, had not provided the United States with enough land to fulfill its expansionist vision. Burgeoning coastal support for the transcontinental railroad thus hit a literal topographical roadblock.

In 1853, James Gadsden, a staunch anti-abolitionist and the acting US ambassador to Mexico, began negotiations with President Antonio López de Santa Anna (Coffey 1933; Schmidt 1961), hoping to acquire an additional stretch of land south of the Río Grande which was currently serving as the (contested) border between the two nations. Ambassador Gadsden employed a grating form of strong-arm diplomacy. In missives sent back to Washington, he described the Santa Anna regime as "a government of plunder and necessity" (Schmidt 1961, 253), intimating that the president was a cash-strapped thug who could be encouraged to give up the desired territory for the right price. After nearly a year of negotiations, the Gadsden Purchase was ratified, in which Mexico ceded 29,670 square miles to the United States in exchange for $15 million. Ironically, most of the funds were allocated to the Mexican defense budget (Greenberg 2009), becoming part of a belated attempt to staunch US expansion.

The Gadsden Purchase incorporated territory that now covers a series of counties in southern Arizona and New Mexico, nestling up against El Paso, TX, to the east and "Mexicali" to the west. Just north of the US-Mexico border, at the easternmost edge of the purchase territory, lies Doña Ana County, home to New Mexico State University, the Doña Ana County Detention Center, and the Gadsden Independent School District (GISD).

The neighboring city of El Paso gained national attention in August 2019, following a horrific mass shooting at a local Walmart (see also Vickers's and Kline's chapter in this volume). The perpetrator, who identified himself as the shooter moments after the massacre, wrote a detailed manifesto in which he explained that the deadly rampage was a "response to the Hispanic invasion of Texas" (Bogel-Burroughs 2019), and that he selected El Paso in accordance with Trump's claim (Moore and Sanchez 2019) that it was a city under siege. The event crystallized for a broader public the direct implications of the "invader imagery" that began with the conquest of the southwestern territory in the nineteenth century and stretched all the way up to the 2016 and 2020 US presidential elections. In the days following the shooting, El Paso's congressional representative, Veronica Escobar, condemned the Trump administration's efforts to "dehumanize" the Latinx community, saying that Trump "has told the country that we are people to be feared, people to be hated" (Wu 2019), people who did not belong.

The El Paso shooting exemplified how extremist groups and individuals can draw on a combination of settler-colonial and "crimmigrant" logics to substantiate acts of aggression against the Latinx community. Areas like El Paso have technically been part of the United States since the middle of the nineteenth century. However, in keeping with the history of the region, many residents continue to "flow" across linguistic and geopolitical borders. These flows run contrary to the kind of colonial logics that link attributes of the occupying culture to citizenship. When exacerbated by nationalist rhetoric, like Trump's, this antagonism can erupt into genocidal violence. The massacre showed how stringent beliefs about who has a right to land (white, Anglophone, documented citizens) and who is seen as a threat to that right (anyone identified, rightly or wrongly, as Hispanic and/or a noncitizen) can instigate brutal acts excused as defense of one's rightful territory.

More than a bad call: profiling Latinx youth in the land of enchantment

The El Paso shooting exacerbated fears within the region's Latinx community and prompted legislators across state borders to take preliminary steps toward forming a hate-crimes unit to investigate acts of domestic terrorism. Fearful of copycat criminals, precincts in New Mexico stationed officers inside of local schools and "other vulnerable public venues" (Lee 2019). This response is by no means surprising. While the shooting was the most obvious and most horrifying example of anti-Latinx sentiment, it marked the climax of a long history of discrimination and regional conflict that had too often escaped notice or masqueraded as "business as usual."

In one notable example, in April of 2013, the Gadsden Panthers, a local baseball team in southern New Mexico, faced off against their rivals, the Tigers, in the nearby town of Alamogordo. At some point during the game, the team's first baseman called out to a fellow player in Spanish. The umpire, a monolingual English speaker named Corey Jones, threatened to eject the player from the game. According to a report filed with the New Mexico Activities Association (excerpts of which were later published by the *Alamogordo Daily News* and the *Las Cruces Sun-News*, and debated heatedly on the latter's Facebook page, @LCSUN-NEWS), Jones was convinced that the GISD player was taunting his opponents. Witnesses alleged that "the player had been encouraging a teammate in Spanish but … Jones said he couldn't tell whether the boy's words were insults and asked everyone to speak English in the interest of monitoring their sportsmanship" (Planas 2013). The assistant coach for the Gadsden team later told reporters that Jones refused to listen to bilingual bystanders or officials, threatening, "Anyone who speaks Spanish – coaches or players – will be ejected" (Romo 2013a).

In the days following the controversy, two community representatives—Bobby Campos, the director of athletics for Las Cruces High School, and David Day, then principal of nearby Oñate High School—spoke out as public advocates for the rights of Spanish speakers on and off the baseball field. In an interview with the *Las Cruces Sun-News*, Campos explained how "the cultures here are so ingrained in the families," pointing to Gadsden's proximity to the Mexican border and alluding to the cultural competency required of "anyone who [lives] in this area" (Feinberg 2013). Striking a similar note, Day categorically condemned Jones' thoughtlessness, saying, "We're in the 21st century, we're on the border, this is the kid's heritage. You don't know the language and you just assume? It was wrong" (Planas 2013).

Less than a week after the incident, Corey Jones resigned, claiming that reports of the incident were "nothing but lies" (Romo 2013b). By the time he submitted his notice of departure, accounts of the controversy had already traveled to national news sites, including *The Huffington Post* (Planas 2013), as well as the conservative platform *Breitbart*, where author "William Bigelow" (who has since been identified as David Shapiro, father of *Breitbart*'s former editor Ben Shapiro [Gold 2016]) alleged that Jones was responding to the use of "foul language" by the Gadsden players (Bigelow 2013).

The Jones incident is emblematic of larger fears over the relationship between language, belonging, and malfeasance central to the reclassification of multilingual adolescents as, to use Trump's own terminology, "bad hombres." By framing the use of Spanish as something suspicious, exclusionary, and inherently unsportsmanlike, Jones created and acted on a new category of surveillance, one which divided the monolingual residents of southern New Mexico from their multilingual neighbors.

First, Jones characterized Spanish as an unintelligible idiom. The Gadsden players, many of their teachers, and most of their supporters were bilingual. Any of these groups could have served as interpreters, clarifying that the players were adhering to generally accepted codes of conduct. In fact, several spectators did exactly that. However, Jones, a monolingual English speaker, insisted that there was no way for him to know precisely what was said on the baseball field, in the heat of the moment, because it was spoken in Spanish, a language he could not trust. In this way, he drew a line not between English speakers and non-English speakers, but between Spanish speakers and everyone else, constructing homogeneous and mutually exclusive linguistic communities that reinforced stereotypes about what it means to "look," "speak," or "act" Hispanic (see also Villenas and Deyhle 1999).

Second, Jones suggested that the Spanish language was itself somehow threatening or improper, largely because it was invoked by youth of a particular "type." He subjected the players to what Hillary Parsons Dick called a "common racializing process" that associates certain "phenotypic [and linguistic] stereotypes" with criminality (2011, E37). Having established Spanish phrases as unintelligible, Jones went on to imply that they were also insulting, inflammatory, and dangerously unsportsmanlike. In this way, he suggested that the use of Spanish is, as Phillip Carter (2014, 209) has described elsewhere, inherently "secretive and dangerous, linking ... tropes about Spanish to national discourses" that configure countries south of the US-Mexico border as homogeneously untrustworthy. Jones used these tacit assumptions to uphold his own moral authority, identifying his primary language (English) as the language of "sportsmanship."

In the span of a single call, Corey Jones invoked a series of assumptions that not only denigrated Spanish and its speakers, but also legitimized the racialization of the surveillance paradigm. Drawing on the power of his position as a uniformed sports official and a hyper-localized representative of law and order, whose domain was admittedly limited to a small spat of dirt and turf, Jones created an environment in which the "rights" of Spanish-speaking players were systematically erased and the actions of those whom Ana Celia Zentella (1995, 13) has elsewhere referred to as "concerned English speakers" were emphatically upheld. Jones thus reinstated a version of the US "imagined community" that elevated speakers of English while denigrating other idioms. All of this was exacerbated by the fact that the controversy involved young Latinx adolescent men, whose gender and ethnicity have in the past been linked in the public imagination to drug use and gang activity (Zatz 1987).

Corey Jones' name disappeared from public records just a few weeks after he first made headlines. However, the incident that began with a bad call on a neglected baseball field ended up drawing attention to deep divisions within the greater southwest, presaging some of the same rhetorical strategies that would become central to Donald Trump's 2016 presidential campaign. In the ensuing months, teachers, administrators, parents, and players in the area continued to worry about whether or not their looks, languages, or cultures would mark them out as "unsportsmanlike," or worse. In this way, Jones's actions, his censure, and his coverage in local media instantly became part of a larger, historically entrenched process of crimmigrant settler-colonialism.

More than a game: tracing links beyond Gadsden

Three years after Corey Jones would have ejected the Gadsden players for their "unsportsmanlike" behavior, Trump weaponized similar regional and racial tensions as part of a broader campaign of hate and fear. Obviously, the stakes of a national presidential campaign are far higher than those of a high school baseball game. However, the fact that the same assumptions and stereotypes underlie these different events points to the pervasive influence of settler-colonial ideologies, which transform citizenship into a disputed status circumscribed by racial and linguistic attributes.

Anti-immigrant rhetoric is simultaneously generic and localized, drawing on aesthetic stereotypes particular to a community or region while producing caricatures stripped of realistic cultural specificity. As Marjorie Zatz (1981, 133) described, in the southwestern United States, as long ago as the 1970s and early 1980s, markers like "gang garb ... pertinent words and expressions in Spanish ... tattoos or scars ... shirts or jackets" have been discursively linked to a monolithic Latin America, substantiating the surveillance and arrest of young people who adopt Chicano symbols or practices. As a juvenile probation officer explained in a 1979 issue of *Phoenix* magazine, "kids in cowboy hats and pickups, drinking beer and cruising Central [Avenue] aren't thought of as a gang," but "Chicano kids driving lowriders, wearing bandannas, and smoking marijuana ... are singled out" and targeted by law enforcement (quoted in Zatz 1981, 136). This example of racial profiling epitomizes a kind of imagistic embedding in which aesthetic makers become inextricably linked to criminal activity perpetrated specifically by (Brown) criminal youth.

Like Jones, Trump expanded regional tropes in order to create absurdist archetypes, reinforcing one stereotype (e.g. the "bad hombre") with another (e.g. the Spanish-speaking adolescent). Each of these cases contributed in their own way to swelling waves of anti-immigrant vitriol that emboldened vigilantes who have since taken it upon themselves to protect the United States from those they perceive as "invaders." One definitive aspect of settler-colonialism in the age of the criminalization of immigration is that it legitimizes the perspective of occupiers, whose loud voices continuously overtake, redirect, and fracture existing public dialogues. At a certain point, the conversation is so completely suffused with settler-colonial logic that it becomes impossible to respond to acts of overt racism without substantiating the underlying idea that linguistic and cultural practices are legitimized through their ties to land and land ownership.

We can see this very phenomenon at work in the Gadsden controversy. Supporters like Day and Campos, who argued (admittedly, rather tepidly) for the rights of the Spanish-speaking players, used a version of Jones's logic to defend their position. While Jones drew on racial and regional stereotypes to demean the use of Spanish, Day and Campos posited that the students' "heritage," as well as Gadsden's proximity to the border, is what made multilingualism "ok." The same questions, fears, and contentions stayed at the heart of the incident, which centered on the rightness or wrongness of using certain languages in certain spaces. Conversations on and off the baseball field thus reinforced the link between language, race, history, place, and nationality, implicitly justifying associations that would later be weaponized by Donald Trump, his proxies, and his most ardent supporters.

Colonial categories of suspicion

While the instances recounted in this chapter differ in degree, they each depend on common assumptions about the rigidity of literal and linguistic borders, the homogeneity of national communities, and the peril posed by people who cross or are thought to cross them. Each time Trump pulled out his folded piece of paper with "The Snake" written on it and smoothed it neatly on the podium, he reinforced the same vague stereotypes—which are at once imagistically specific and categorically expansive—that lurked underneath Corey Jones's concerns that a "foreign" language was inherently "unsportsmanlike." As a writer for *Vox* explained in 2018, "'The Snake' was never a parable about 'illegal immigration. It was always about 'immigration,' full stop" (Lind 2018). Again, Trump himself reminded audiences to "think of [the poem] in terms of immigration." In much the same way, the would-be ejection of the Gadsden players, when viewed in the wider context of Doña Ana County, was never about the "improper" use of Spanish; it was about the *overall* use of Spanish, full stop. Whether or not the students Jones confronted were immigrants, came from immigrant families, or simply spoke a language he associated with a country other than the United States, like many people in the Gadsden area, is ultimately immaterial in the context of this analysis. What is important instead is the way in which various parts of a person's lived identity, including the language(s) they speak, were recast as indicators of non-belonging, exposing individuals to a level of unmerited scrutiny and retribution that, down the line, can prove fatal.

Over the past decade, the North American political sector has played host to violent eruptions of racism and xenophobia, which were brewed over the extended history of US imperialism and heated to a boiling point in the pressure cooker of the Trump presidency. In this context, language became both a weapon and a subject of oppression, lending new weight to long-standing practices of racialization and criminalization. Paying attention to the particular experiences of the people caught up in this process keeps the consequences of regional conflict and conquest at the forefront of the conversation, forcing us to reckon with the lived, as well as the theoretical, repercussions of the racial politics of governance. The would-be ejection of the Spanish-speaking Gadsden players indexed a wider swath of concerns about Brown "youth out of control"

(Poynting, Noble, and Tabar 2001, 71) that only grew in reach and consequence in subsequent years. Meanwhile, immigration from Mexico primarily decreased between 2010 and 2019 (Radforth 2019), despite the Trump administration's warnings that waves of migrants were about to wash over the US' southern border (Pinchin 2019). Understanding the linkages between hyperlocal events and national—or even regional—political change requires an expansive critical mindset that recognizes the easy "slippage" among different forms of discrimination and surveillance.

Exploring the treatment of people living through these times in literal and imaginative "borderlands" allows us to dig into a rhetorical stratagem that, while emblematic of the current political moment, has deep and expansive historical roots. By directing attention to these themes through the experiences of multilingual Latinx adolescents, I hope to have shown how settler-colonialism has manifested new social specters that draw on the intersection of race, status, and gender to discursively transform individuals (particularly, young Spanish-speaking men) into criminals, with significant personal and political implications. In this way, I have worked to unpack and demystify the process by which immigrants are criminalized, showing how seemingly innocuous instances of racial and linguistic profiling can pave the way for more extreme instances of physical and emotional violence.

Paying close attention to the writing done about "vulnerable" populations, like im/migrants, forces one to revisit the political origins of legislative precarity itself, and to recognize the common threads that tie together policies that keep individuals from full membership in the polity. All of the events recounted in this chapter emerge from a wider culture of mistrust that associates Spanish and Spanish-speakers with the borderlands and, by extension, with clashes over legality, nativity, and national belonging. It is only by mapping the threads that connect a grandstanding president telling racist parables, a high school umpire levying decrees against "unsportsmanlike" languages, and a nineteenth-century ambassador bent on acquiring one last strip of land so his country could fulfill its manifest destiny that we can begin to unravel and analyze the intersecting "borders" (literal or linguistic) that constrain life and movement in twenty-first-century North America. Broached in this manner, Donald Trump's anti-immigrant rhetoric and the horrifying actions taken by his administration transformed from political aberrations into contextually situated artifacts that were intrinsically linked to other moments in US history.

Put differently, the phenomena under consideration here preceded and will outlast Donald Trump. Responding to them, therefore, will require that researchers, policy-makers, and citizens of all types and degrees confront the social and bureaucratic origins of institutional vulnerability. By paying attention to the reverberations of criminal discourse that echo across and within sectors, we can expand our understanding of how governance works through both legitimized and fringe actors. In this way, we can begin to *un*settle the colonial ideologies that craft categories of suspicion, rewriting what it means to live, work, and love in the borderlands.

References

Abu El-Haj, Thea. 2007. "'I Was Born Here, but My Home, It's Not Here': Educating for Democratic Citizenship in an Era of Transnational Migration and Global Conflict." *Harvard Educational Review* 77 (3): 285–316. https://doi.org/10.17763/haer.77.3.412l7m737q114h5m.

Alvarez, Robert R., Jr. 1995. "The Mexican-US Border: The Making of an Anthropology of Borderlands." *Annual Review of Anthropology* 24: 447–470. https://doi.org/10.1146/annurev.an.24.100195.002311.

Andreas, Peter. 2009. *Border Games: Policing the U.S.-Mexico Divide*. Ithaca, NY: Cornell University Press.

Bigelow, William. 2013. "Gadsden HS Coaches File Complaint Against Umpire Who Prohibited Player from Speaking Spanish." *Breitbart*, April 16, 2013. https://www.breitbart.com/sports/2013/04/16/high-school-umpire-tries-to-forbid-player-from-speaking-spanish/.

Bigo, Didier. 2002. "Security and Immigration: Toward a Critique of the Governmentality of Unease." *Alternatives* 27 (1): 63–92. https://doi.org/10.1177/03043754020270S105.

Bogel-Burroughs, Nicole. 2019. "'I'm the Shooter': El Paso Suspect Confessed to Targeting Mexicans, Police Say." *New York Times*, August 9, 2019. https://www.nytimes.com/2019/08/09/us/el-paso-suspect-confession.html.

Carter, Phillip M. 2014. "National Narratives, Institutional Ideologies, and Local Talk: The Discursive Production of Spanish in a 'New' US Latino Community." *Language in Society* 43 (2): 209–240. https://doi.org/10.1017/S0047404514000049.

Chacón, Jennifer M., and Erwin Chemerinsky. 2020. "No, Mr. President, Your Immigration Powers Are Not Unlimited." *New York Times*, April 22, 2020. https://www.nytimes.com/2020/04/22/opinion/trump-immigration-executive-order.html?searchResultPosition=3.

Chavez, Leo R. 2013. *The Latino Threat: Constructing Immigrants, Citizens, and the Nation*. Second edition, Stanford: Stanford University Press.

Coffey, Frederic A. 1933. "Some General Aspects of the Gadsden Treaty." *New Mexico Historical Review* 8 (3): 145–164.

Cohen, Stanley. 2002. *Folk Devils and Moral Panics*. Third edition, New York: Routledge.

Coleman, Justine. 2020. "Coronavirus Pandemic Doesn't Stop Arizona Border Wall Construction: Report." *The Hill*, March 31, 2020. https://thehill.com/policy/national-security/department-of-homeland-security/490438-coronavirus-pandemic-doesnt-stop.

Constable, Nicole. 2014. *Born Out of Place: Migrant Mothers and the Politics of International Labor*. Berkeley: University of California Press.

Coutin, Susan Bibler. 2007. *Nations of Emigrants: Shifting Boundaries of Citizenship in El Salvador and the United States*. Ithaca, NY: Cornell University Press.

De Genova, Nicholas P. 2002. "Migrant 'Illegality' and Deportability in Everyday Life." *Annual Review of Anthropology* 31: 419–447. https://doi.org/10.1146/annurev.anthro.31.040402.085432.

Délano Alonso, Alexandra. 2018. *From Here and There: Diaspora Policies, Integration, and Social Rights Beyond Borders*. New York: Oxford University Press.

Dick, Hilary Parsons. 2011. "Making Immigrants Illegal in Small Town USA." *Journal of Linguistic Anthropology* 21 (1): E35–E55. https://doi.org/10.1111/j.1548-1395.2011.01096.x.

Dickerson, Caitlin, and Michael D. Shear. 2020. "Before Covid-19, Trump Aide Sought to Use Disease to Close Borders." *New York Times*, May 3, 2020. https://www.nytimes.com/2020/05/03/us/coronavirus-immigration-stephen-miller-public-health.html?action=click&module=Spotlight&pgtype=Homepage.

Edsall, Thomas B. 2020. "Trump Reaches Back into His Old Bag of Populist Tricks." *New York Times*, April 22, 2020. https://www.nytimes.com/2020/04/22/opinion/coronavirus-trump.html?action=click&module=Opinion&pgtype=Homepage.

Feinberg, Teddy. 2013 "UPDATE: Umpire Resigns after Spanish-speaking Incident with Gadsden High School." *Alamogordo Daily News*, April 17, 2013. https://web.archive.org/web/20130514004448/http://www.lcsun-news.com/las_cruces-news/ci_23043365/nm-ump-quits-over-gadsden-alamogordo-game-no.

Gold, Hadas. 2016. "Breitbart Piece Mocking Editor Who Resigned Was Written Under Father's Pseudonym." *Politico,* March 14, 2016. https://www.politico.com/blogs/on-media/2016/03/breitbart-mocking-ben-shapiro-220712.

Gomberg-Muñoz, Ruth. 2016. *Becoming Legal: Immigration Law and Mixed-Status Families*. New York: Oxford University Press.

Gonzales, Roberto G. 2016. *Lives in Limbo: Undocumented and Coming of Age in America*. Oakland: University of California Press.

Gonzales, Roberto G., and Leo R. Chavez. 2012. "'Awakening to a Nightmare': Abjectivity and Illegality in the Lives of Undocumented 1.5-Generation Latino Immigrants in the United States." *Current Anthropology* 53 (3): 255–281. https://doi.org/10.1086/665414.

Greenberg, Amy S. 2009. "Domesticating the Border: Manifest Destiny and the 'Comforts of Life' in the US-Mexico Boundary Commission and Gadsden Purchase, 1848–1854." In *Land of Necessity: Consumer Culture in the United States-Mexico Borderlands*, edited by Alexis McCrossen, 83–112. Durham, NC: Duke University Press.

Hernández, Kelly Lytle. 2010. *Migra! A History of the U.S. Border Patrol*. Berkeley: University of California Press.

Iskander, Natasha, Nichola Lowe, and Christine Riordan. 2010. "The Rise and Fall of a Micro-learning Region: Mexican Immigrants and Construction in Center-South Philadelphia." *Environment and Planning A: Economy and Space* 42 (7): 1595–1612. https://doi.org/10.1068/a42475.

Kanno-Youngs, Zolan. 2020. "Trump Administration Adds Six Countries to Travel Ban." *New York Times*, February 3, 2020. https://www.nytimes.com/2020/01/31/us/politics/trump-travel-ban.html?action=click&module=Top%20Stories&pgtype=Homepage.

Kluger, Richard. 2008. *Seizing Destiny: How America Grew from Sea to Shining Sea*. New York: Vintage Books.

Lakhani, Nina. 2020. "US Using Coronavirus Pandemic to Unlawfully Expel Asylum Seekers, Says UN." *The Guardian*, April 17, 2020. https://www.theguardian.com/world/2020/apr/17/us-asylum-seekers-coronoavirus-law-un.

Lee, Morgan. 2019. "New Mexico May Form Hate-Crimes Unit after El Paso Walmart Massacre." *Las Cruces Sun News*, November 19, 2019. https://www.lcsun-news.com/story/news/local/new-mexico/2019/11/19/new-mexico-form-special-unit-after-el-paso-walmart-massacre/4244390002/.

Lind, Dara. 2018. "'The Snake': Donald Trump Brings Back His Favorite Anti-immigrant Fable at CPAC." *Vox*, February 23, 2018. https://www.vox.com/policy-and-politics/2018/2/23/17044744/trump-snake-speech-cpac.

Liptak, Adam. 2020. "Supreme Court Allows Trump's Wealth Test for Green Cards." *New York Times*, January 27, 2020. https://www.nytimes.com/2020/01/27/us/supreme-court-trump-green-cards.html.

Montoya-Galvez, Camilo. 2020. "US Suspends Protections for Migrant Kids at the Border, Expelling Hundreds amid Pandemic." *CBS News*, May 7, 2020. https://www.cbsnews.com/news/coronavirus-immigration-migrant-children-protections-border/.

Moore, Robert, and Carlos Sanchez. 2019. "Donald Trump Vows to 'Finish the Wall' in El Paso Political Rally." *Texas Monthly*, February 12, 2019. https://www.texasmonthly.com/politics/donald-trump-vows-to-finish-the-wall-in-el-paso-political-rally/.
Narea, Nicole. 2020. "The US Has Abandoned Asylum Seekers in Mexico during the Pandemic." *Vox*, May 13, 2020. https://www.vox.com/2020/4/27/21232808/asylum-seekers-mexico-coronavirus-trump.
Nevins, Joseph. 2001. *Operation Gatekeeper: The Rise of the "Illegal Alien" and the Making of the US-Mexico Boundary*. New York: Routledge.
Ngai, Mae M. 2014. *Impossible Subjects: Illegal Aliens and the Making of Modern America*. Updated edition, Princeton: Princeton University Press.
Phillips, Amber. 2017. "'They're Rapists.' President Trump's Campaign Launch Speech Two Years Later, Annotated." *Washington Post*, June 16, 2017. https://www.washingtonpost.com/news/the-fix/wp/2017/06/16/theyre-rapists-presidents-trump-campaign-launch-speech-two-years-later-annotated/.
Pinchin, Karen. 2019. "Insects, Floods and 'The Snake': What Trump's Use of Metaphors Reveals." *PBS*, October 22, 2019. https://www.pbs.org/wgbh/frontline/article/insects-floods-and-the-snake-what-trumps-use-of-metaphors-reveals/.
Planas, Roque. 2013. "Corey Jones, New Mexico Umpire Who Allegedly Told Players Not to Speak Spanish, Resigns." *HuffPost*, April 17, 2013. https://www.huffpost.com/entry/new-mexico-spanish-baseball_n_3103782.
Poynting, Scott, Greg Noble, and Paul Tabar. 2001. "Middle Eastern Appearances: 'Ethnic Gangs,' Moral Panic and Media Framing." *Australian & New Zealand Journal of Criminology* 34 (1): 67–90. https://doi.org/10.1177/000486580103400105.
Ribas, Vanessa. 2016. *On the Line: Slaughterhouse Lives and the Making of the New South*. Oakland: University of California Press.
Riggan, Jennifer. 2013. "Imagining Emigration: Debating National Duty in Eritrean Classrooms." *Africa Today* 60 (2): 85–106. https://doi.org/10.2979/africatoday.60.2.85.
Robertson, O. Nicholas. 2018. "The Myth of Immigrant Criminality: Early Twentieth-Century Sociological Theory and Trump's Campaign." In *Nasty Women and Bad Hombres: Gender and Race in the 2016 US Presidential Election*, edited by Christine A. Kray, Tamar W. Carroll, and Hinda Mandell, 83–95. Rochester, NY: University of Rochester Press.
Rogers, Katie, Michael D. Shear, and Zolano Kanno-Youngs. 2020. "Trump Plans to Suspend Immigration to the US." *New York Times*, April 20, 2020. https://www.nytimes.com/2020/04/20/us/politics/trump-immigration.html?searchResultPosition=1.
Romo, Rene. 2013a. "Coaches Cry Foul on Ump's English-only Call." *Albuquerque Journal*, April 12, 2013. https://www.abqjournal.com/187922/coaches-cry-foul-on-umps-englishonly-call.html.
———. 2013b. "Ump Quits After Calling Foul on Spanish." *Albuquerque Journal*, April 17, 2013. https://www.abqjournal.com/189366/ump-quits-after-calling-foul-on-spanish.html.
Rosenberg, Eli. 2018. "'The Snake': How Trump Appropriated a Radical Black Singer's Lyrics for Immigration Fearmongering." *Washington Post*, February 24, 2018. https://www.washingtonpost.com/news/politics/wp/2018/02/24/the-snake-how-trump-appropriated-a-radical-black-singers-lyrics-for-refugee-fearmongering/.
Schmidt, Louis Bernard. 1961. "Manifest Opportunity and the Gadsden Purchase." *Arizona and the West* 3 (3): 245–264. http://www.jstor.org/stable/40167931.
Silverstein, Paul A. 2005. "Immigrant Racialization and the New Savage Slot: Race, Migration, and Immigration in the New Europe." *Annual Review of Anthropology* 34: 363–384. https://doi.org/10.1146/annurev.anthro.34.081804.120338.

Tuck, Eve, and K. Wayne Yang. 2012. "Decolonization is Not a Metaphor." *Decolonization: Indigeneity, Education & Society* 1 (1): 1–40. https://jps.library.utoronto.ca/index.php/des/article/view/18630/15554.

Villenas, Sofia, and Donna Deyhle. 1999. "Critical Race Theory and Ethnographies Challenging the Stereotypes: Latino Families, Schooling, Resilience and Resistance." *Curriculum Inquiry* 29 (4): 413–445. https://doi.org/10.1111/0362-6784.00140.

White, Jeremy B. 2018. "The Snake in Full: Read Donald Trump's Anti-immigration Poem." *Independent*, February 23, 2018. https://www.independent.co.uk/news/world/americas/us-politics/the-snake-read-in-full-trump-poem-cpac-anti-immigration-verses-mexican-border-a8225686.html.

Wu, Nicholas. 2019. "El Paso Congresswoman Says Trump 'Not Welcome' in the City after Mass Shooting." *USA Today*, August 5, 2019. https://www.usatoday.com/story/news/politics/2019/08/05/el-paso-walmart-shooting-veronica-escobar-says-trump-not-welcome/1919915001/.

Zatz, Marjorie S. 1987. "Chicano Youth Gangs and Crime: The Creation of a Moral Panic." *Contemporary Crises* 11 (2): 129–158. https://doi.org/10.1007/BF00728588.

Zentella, Ana Celia. 1995. "The 'Chiquitafication' of US Latinos and Their Languages, OR Why We Need an Anthropolitical Linguistics." SALSA III: Proceedings of a Symposium on Language and Society (Austin, TX, April 5–7, 1995). https://eric.ed.gov/?id=ED416671.

PART III
Re/visions
Crafting social justice

7
ENGENDERING WHITE NATIONALISM

Jeff Maskovsky

When, in September 2018, Dr. Christine Blasey Ford, professor of psychology at Palo Alto University, testified in front of the US Senate Judiciary Committee, she stood as a witness against the Supreme Court justice nominee Brett Kavanaugh, who she remembered had sexually assaulted her in the summer of 1982, when she was 15 years old. As live updates (Lee 2018) on the hearings were posted on the Breitbart.com homepage, comments and responses to the testimony were also recorded on the site. On September 27, Breitbart poster *KYRifles* offered the following remarks:

> Ford lies with ease.
> And why shouldn't she? No one ever calls her on it.
> Remembering is hard!
> She's just a girl! Giggle!!
> In a way, we are seeing before us the pivot point of our civilization, Kavanaugh representing the past, Ford the future.
> Kavanaugh is our past: brilliant, logical, and emphatic. Ford is our (possible) future: ditzy, whiny, and phony.
> God help us.

A like-minded commentator (*just me saying*) replied:

> Yep and for all the women to ponder or think about. If you have brothers male cousins sons fathers uncles they may one day be at the end of these idiots WRATH now as you can see all it takes is I remember so good luck to you all with male family members and to all of those #metool people because if it's your father they can take away your inheritance house and his good name so as they used to say THINK BEFORE YOU LEAP.

DOI: 10.4324/9781003034810-7

In response, *KYRifles* wrote:

> I was just amazed at the comfort she had with the fact that she had of course earlier used the excuse of fear of flying as a reason to delay her testimony while admitting she flew all over the place all the time.
> She just laughed it off, as if the inconsistency was nothing—a joke. Oh sometimes I feel fear, sometimes I don't, but it's OK when I'm doing something fun!
> Who lies like that in a situation of such consequences? What kind of sociopath?
> The answer?
> She, like most women in her social circle, is a practiced liar. She regards lying as a socially approved way for a woman of her class to get what she wants.
> Say she gets pulled over by the cops for speeding. She is not going to make a scene like some ghetto Serena Williams or the black woman who ended up getting arrested and hung herself in her cell. Instead she is going to tell the cop that she just received a phone call that her child has been injured and she is rushing home and she never speeds. Sometimes it works, sometimes the cop calls you on your BS—no harm no foul.
> Or say that you are invited to her house for dinner but she does not feel like cooking. She doesn't tell you that—that would be rude. Instead she says that she is not "feeling well" or that the "stove broke" or something and can we do this some other time. She doesn't expect you to come over and check to see if the stove really works or not.
> It's just that this time the stakes were much higher and she got called on her little white lie. That's why her previously anonymous deceit had to be made public. But it wasn't a disaster for her. She was tossed softball after softball by a female prosecutor who, for some reason, did not use the immunity (from accusations of male chauvinism) her gender offered her to crucify Ford.

These posts on the conservative new media site Breitbart open up a discussion about the gender, race, and class politics of white nationalism in the Trump era. What we see on display in these snide comments are the patriarchal values, end-of-civilization-as-we-know-it misogyny, class- and race-inflected policing of gender norms, and the devaluation of all sorts of unruly women that are commonplace among white nationalist digital posters. These are only 3 of the more than 65,000 comments posted to that site within 72 hours of the September 27 Senate Judiciary Committee hearings. Ninety-nine percent of the content was supportive of Brett Kavanaugh's nomination. Many posters exclaimed the untrustworthiness of Christine Blasey Ford's testimony. Others expressed outrage at the #MeToo Movement (a movement in which women acknowledged that they had been raped or otherwise sexually assaulted), claiming, as Donald Trump did days later, that it was a difficult time for young men in America (Diamond 2018). Some posted expressions of outrage at a vast Democratic Party-led conspiracy against Kavanaugh. California Senator Dianne Feinstein (who is frequently referred to as Difi in the alt-right blogosphere), her husband, investment banker Richard Blum, former US President Bill Clinton, and former Secretary of State Hillary Rodman Clinton were, many posters agreed, agents of the Chinese state. They were attempting to use Blasey Ford to thwart Kavanaugh's Supreme Court appointment on behalf of China, so the story goes. In contrast to the viewpoint of mainstream liberals, many Breitbart posters saw China, not Russia, as the malevolent foreign power attempting to meddle in US politics and elections.

Gun rights also surfaced, unsurprisingly, as a major concern in the Kavanaugh Supreme Court nomination conflagration. Posters staged a sarcastic debate over who was a better shot, conservative men or women. This tongue-in-cheek debate reinforced the widely held view that conservative men and women needed to arm themselves in defense against the threat posed by the "liberal hate mongers and trolls" who supported Blasey Ford. And many cheered in response to Donald Trump's public support of Kavanaugh, which he expressed in this tweet:

> Judge Kavanaugh showed America exactly why I nominated him. His testimony was powerful, honest, and riveting. Democrats' search and destroy strategy is disgraceful and this process has been a total sham and effort to delay, obstruct, and resist. The Senate must vote!
> *(@realdonaldtrump, September 27, 2018)*

My goal in this chapter is to use examples such as these to shed some light on the interpretive processes of white nationalists as they confront political challenges and seek to consolidate and expand the influence of their movement. In particular, I am interested in how gender matters politically to rank-and-file white nationalists. In my main argument, I suggest that for white nationalists, gender equality, nonconformity, and fluidity tend to be viewed as existential threats to the white race, and further that *maintaining sex and gender hierarchies is essential to the white supremacist racial order that they seek to reproduce.* Accordingly, gender is not just a site of difference or inequality that white nationalists use descriptively in their politics. It is also an essential category of difference that informs their worldview, and it is invoked repeatedly to elaborate and refine their political viewpoints. My argument here builds on an important strain of feminist scholarship in anthropology and American Studies that has demonstrated the importance of the coconstitution of race, class, and gender politics, and the maintenance of a racial-gendered order, in the making of the United States as a concrete social formation (see Brodkin 2007; Collins 2017; Davis 2004; Di Leonardo 1998; Morgen 2002; Mullings 2005, 2020). The work of Sarah Haley (2016) has been especially inspiring, as her book, *No Mercy Here: Gender, Punishment, and the Making of Jim Crow Modernity*, tells the history of imprisoned black women's brutalization in convict labor systems and the role that this brutalization played in the making of the late nineteenth- and early twentieth-century US political economy. Haley directs our attention to the historical institutionalization of specific forms of gendered racial terror, organized to devalue and dehumanize Black life more broadly, and enacted in part via the exclusion of racialized subjects from the protected category of "woman" (2). This is precisely what is at stake today in the political ascent of white nationalist movements in the United States and around the world, and understanding the ways these groups innovate politically is part of a broader effort to understand the way that white nationalist gendered racial terror is currently institutionalized and how it can be abolished.

My work on white nationalist political culture is based on a deep ethnographic plunge into the white nationalist digital world. This entailed reading all kinds of online media content including YouTube testimonials, news articles, blogs, opinion pieces, and message board postings on forum websites such as 4chan and 8chan/8kun. The websites I visited most regularly (Breitbart, Reddit, 4chan, Stormfront.org, Gab, and Voat, among others) have maintained digital communities associated with the alt-right, a white nationalist movement that has coalesced in large measure through the use of social media and online platforms (Bjork-James and Maskovsky 2017; Hawley 2017). By the beginning of the Trump presidency, the alt-right constituted the more "mainstream" movement in comparison to other white supremacist groups, about which I will say more below. My ethnographic approach is inspired by scholarship on online political cultures that looks at the proliferation of digital communities and the ways that computer-mediated communication shapes political thought and action (Bjork-James 2015; Coleman 2014; Juris 2008). The rise of new forms of US-based white supremacy online has received a great deal of scholarly attention of late (Bjork-James and Maskovsky 2017; Daniels 2009; Feagan 2013; Hawley 2017). I explore online talk and sentiments about gender to help us to understand political reasoning and improvisation by alt-right proponents and to locate this within the broader US right-wing political culture of the Trump era.

What's new in the new white nationalism?

White nationalism is not a unified movement. It consists of a diverse set of political, social and cultural projects, communities, programs, organizations, and activities. The Southern Poverty Law Center estimated that approximately 100 white nationalist groups were operating in the United States in 2018 (and the number of groups had fluctuated between 95 and 146 since 2003) (SPLC n.d.). Under the banner of white nationalism are what the Southern Poverty Law Center would call "extremist" groups that elaborate explicit racist ideologies rooted in long-standing ideas about white biological or cultural superiority and that seek to transform the United States into a white ethno-state through violent means. Groups that make explicit claims about white superiority remain on the fringe politically, but other groups have moved to the mainstream, mostly through the work of the media-savvy alt-right leaders, who have been careful to emphasize white racial grievances and resentments and the need for white community restoration over overt arguments for racial superiority. With this tactic they have found new audiences for their xenophobic and racist political projects (Bjork-James and Maskovsky 2017).

The alt-right's rising popularity cannot be attributed exclusively to the messaging of its leaders such as Richard Spencer and Steve Bannon, however. Significant shifts in US political culture and political economy have also facilitated its newfound popularity. The freighting of national identity to white ethnic identity has had a long inglorious history in the United States (Saxton 2003). There are, however, several significant developments that make white nationalism in the Trump era different from that of past eras.

A major contributing factor has been the prolonged crisis in political economy in the United States and across the globe and its attendant crisis in political legitimacy. At the economic level, neoliberal capitalism has been prone to crisis since its inception in the late 1970s, and it has failed to guarantee freedom or equality for most people. After the 2007–2008 financial crisis, finance-led neoliberal capitalism has remained in place, but it has taken on an even more dispossessive and hyper-exploitative form. It has become clear that in the eyes of the global financial elites, the solution to the volatility and long-term crisis of the political economy is the severe constraint on popular sovereignty, separating it from capitalist decision-making, and giving almost dictatorial authority to the central banks. But a full-fledged political crisis emerged after 2007–2008, when neoliberals and neoconservatives alike were exposed as corrupt, ineffectual, and beholden exclusively to economic elites. Political elites thus lost legitimacy long before Trump was elected president—and his election is best understood as an effect of this crisis, not its cause. The alt-right rose to prominence and expanded its popular appeal precisely as this legitimacy crisis deepened.

Another factor contributing to the rise of the alt-right is the collapse of the two competing forms of liberal centrist cosmopolitanism, which elaborate different and antagonistic racial projects even as they share a commitment to many classic liberal values and to globalist dreams of one sort or another. The racial projects of neoconservative and neoliberal variety—colorblindness and multiculturalism, respectively—eschew white supremacist ideologies, at least explicitly. On the one hand, neoconservatives have made a political art form out of the selective appropriation of Civil-Rights-era political discourses about enfranchisement and equality to justify the rollback of Civil Rights legislation and policies and to advance color-blind policy and post-racial ideology (Mullings 2005). For their part, neoliberals have countered neoconservatism's post-racialism with a multiculturalist framework that recognizes and celebrates racial and ethnic differences, though the extent to which this recognition is linked substantively to a robust vision of equal proprietorship of public institutions or to redress and eradicate racial inequalities is hotly debated. If there was one similarity between these two positions and one line that was not crossed in the culture wars from the 1980s to the 2000s, however, it was that whiteness was off the table as a project of national unification—or so it seemed. What is now clear in hindsight is the extent to which both neoconservatives and neoliberals failed to address racially inflected grievances expressed across the political spectrum.

The roots of this failure, at least with respect to the rise of a new white racial politics on the right, lies in the extent to which colorblindness was always a stealth political strategy for advancing white nationalist political priorities in the post-Civil Rights era, when explicit claims about white racial superiority became politically unrespectable even as they remained rather popular among the Republican base. Crypto race-baiting has been a hallmark of Republican politics since the 1960s, when, in the context of the Civil Rights movement, Republicans put concerted effort into appealing to white Southerners' racial resentments to gain their support. The politics of white community grievances found new adherents in the 1970s and beyond as white ethnicity became politically legitimate and even fashionable as a white ethnic identity politics formed in direct reaction to Black Power and other militant protest movements of the 1960s and 1970s and as an alternative as well to elite WASP culture (Di Leonardo 1989; Steinberg 1981). During the Reagan era, the racialized and gendered attack on the "welfare queen" was crucial to New Right anti-big-government policy advances, the rise of supply-side economics, the breaking of the Fordist social compact, the rollback on the social wage, the attack on affirmative action, and the rise of nonunionized postindustrialism (Di Leonardo 1989, 79–144; Goode and Maskovsky 2001). The culture wars of the 1980s and 1990s and the neoconservative condemnation of "illiberal" causes such as affirmative action, multiculturalism, "political correctness," and liberal immigration policy helped to further shift white ethnic politics to the right by linking the politics of white ethnic pride to white racial resentments (Steinberg 2001).

The ideological assault against welfare dependency, multiculturalism, affirmative action, and big government widened considerably in the Bush era, especially after 9/11. In this period, the basis for popular compassion and political support for the poor, immigrants, and people of color diminished while new fractions of the middle classes (especially lower- and middle-class white suburbanites) came under fire and financial duress as the libertarian attack against government—any government, not just big government—gained traction. "Welfare queens," already vanquished in the 1990s by the Clinton-era welfare "reform," were joined by teachers and pensioned government employees as the new Republican targets: "government-dependent" profligates living life too large off the government dime (Angelo 2019, 153–176). Finally, during the Obama era, the attack on dependency from the right intensified and was once again elaborated in explicitly racist terms. The Obama administrative was effective in enforcing civil rights laws, reforming immigration, expanding access to healthcare (though on terms set by the right in the 1980s), and reviving the economy after the 2007–2008 financial crisis. But the right was outraged by his soaring rhetoric about the audacity of hope, and his ascent to the presidency itself was viewed by many as an affirmation of neoliberal triumph (Esposito 2011). Importantly, #BlackLivesMatter and the Movement for

Black Lives, with their critique of racialized state violence, also surfaced during the Obama era, posing an overt challenge to some of the institutions where white nationalism had festered and grown in recent decades, such as the criminal justice system (Mullings 2020). Throughout all of this, neoliberal and neoconservative governance struggled to manage "race relations" or to substantively address racial inequalities or white grievances (Steinberg 2007).

A final element fueling the rise of the alt-right has been the rise of the politics of sentiment. In a situation in which the reigning capitalist and racial ideologies are unpopular, and in which neoliberal guarantees of prosperity for all and neoconservative moralizing can no longer persuade people, the politics of sentiment is filling people's hearts (Grossberg 2018; Maskovsky and Bjork-James 2020). This combines with the fragmentation of the public sphere (Di Leonardo 1998) such that facts, authority, expertise, and rationality have been frequently associated with flawed, ineffectual, elitist, and punishing forms of liberal governance such as neoliberalism. Importantly, this critique has been leveled by groups across the political spectrum. The denunciation of the "fake news" of the mainstream media by Trump, his white nationalist supporters, and pundits on Fox News is but one example of popular suspicion of elite forms of expertise and knowledge. Other examples abound, from Black Lives Matter's condemnation of CompStat and other crime statistics as racist (Taylor 2016) to the revolt against vaccinations in some quarters (Kata 2012). Overall, passion has not replaced rationality in politics today, but in the current conjuncture, the politics of resentment, the rise of angry publics, and the crisis over authority and knowledge culminate in a situation in which rage and resentment have been taken to new levels of intensity in liberal democratic politics, bringing these politics to the breaking point. Moral panics around sex and gender were pervasive during this period. Indeed, as we shall see, the restoration of conventional white family "norms" around gender hierarchies, proper gender comportment, public/private dichotomies, and the exercise of authority in work and home have become an urgent set of political preoccupations popularly, and are of central concern in particular to white nationalists in this situation.

Stop fighting nature: "traditional gender roles" as white nationalist common sense

At the core of alt-right thought and action is a visceral, affective sense of masculinity in crisis and in need of restoration, and a celebration of masculine authority. In *White Lies: Race, Class, Gender and Sexuality in White Supremacist Discourse*, Jessie Daniels (2016) documents the existence of a hegemonically white, heterosexual, masculine culture in the online communication associated with the white supremacist group, Stormfront.org. My findings resonate strongly with hers in many ways: the overt use of a white racial frame in nearly every alt-right online post; the commonplace use of the Internet as a tool for harassment and intimidation; frequent comments against the LGBTQ community and in support of efforts to control sexuality in patriarchal and heterosexist ways; a global view on white masculinity's sources; a deep suspicion of democratic rules and norms, which, many alt-right enthusiasts worry, work against the white community; and a coercive, toxic use of irony and jocularity that brings the community together around the ridicule of its political opponents. Humor also works to deflect accountability for the authors of seriously objectionable posts, the content of which can be disavowed as a joke if necessary (Daniels 2009, 61–90).

Yet misogynistic elaborations of white racial identity have proliferated in the decade since Daniels conducted her groundbreaking research. The alt-right community in 2020 seems even more deeply concerned about the demise of "traditional gender roles" and the need for their restoration than it was a decade ago. This position is now frequently justified and legitimated by the use of universalistic claims about a natural order, discoverable by science, of relations between men and women. According to many posts and comments to alt-right.com, the academic and behaviorist flank of the liberal establishment marginalizes daring scientists who are purported to have proof of the existence of universal gender and racial differences, and the liberal establishment, so the story goes, fights against human nature and against the truth of universal gender difference by insisting on universal gender equality. It should come as no surprise that this natural order of things ideology makes women naturally submissive to male authority; prioritizes women's reproductive and child-rearing capacities to which all other behaviors and sensibilities are tied; and views men as naturally more aggressive, more public, and more capable of leadership and effective decision-making than women. These sentiments correspond closely with those expressed by the online men's movement in the lead-up to Donald Trump's election in 2016 (Dignam and Rohlinger 2019).

Central to the alt-right's politics is thus the effort to denigrate, shame, devalue, and pathologize people who violate the norms of the purported natural order. The cast of characters who have waged war on human nature is long, and the rationale for condemning various violators is as nuanced and impressive as they are dangerous and sexist. As such, among the alt-right, a great deal of ire has been directed at feminists, Hillary Clinton, "sluts," "welfare queens," women with too many tattoos, and other wayward woman who are viewed as threats to the white race. I found that transgender people, feminists, and "the liberal establishment" were at the top of the alt-right hate list. Transgender people are often described as violators of a natural order rooted in universal gender differences. Alt-right enthusiasts also describe "the liberal establishment," especially feminists, as suppressors of knowledge of this natural order. Here is how Russell James, a Stormfront.org frequent poster, explained the problem of feminism from a white nationalist perspective, in 2019:

> "Feminism" was never about equality between the sexes. (I use quotes around the word "feminism" because let's face it, there's nothing feminine about it.).... Men and women are not the same, they have very different

musculoskeletal systems, reproductive systems, and brains. Which translates into profoundly different abilities and capabilities. In turn, this means they have profoundly different roles and profoundly different sets of responsibilities. Traditionally the role of women was to have babies, breast feed them (the two things that not only do women do better than men, but men can't do at all), and take care of the home. Men were responsible for provisioning and protecting the family. Modernity abstracts the role of men, making it look as if anyone can do it. But the truth is, men still do those things much better than women. This is borne-out by all the evidence. For example, it is well known that single mother households are far less prosperous than family environments in which the father is present. And that prosperity isn't just financial. Not only do two-parent and single-father households make more money, but the children do better in life in every category. They're more educated, less prone to criminality, less likely to have children out of wedlock, and more likely to feel more "fulfilled" in every way. "Feminism" encourages women to pursue meaningless "careers" in place of doing what comes natural, i.e. have and raise children.... It's clear that men and women can never be "equal." If we were the same, then there would be no point in having two sexes, we would have only one sex.... The funders and organizers of "feminism" understand that the sexes are complementary rather than "equal," so why do they promote the contrived concept of "equality between the sexes." What is their real aim? The answer is clear to anyone who has spent any time pondering the question. They're trying to destroy Western Civilization and "feminism" is one of a handful of Cultural-Marxist "movements" (along with multi-culturalism, queerism, socialism, hyper-consumerism, etc.) they using to do it. "Feminism's" purpose is to weaponize women against men and children.

Posts like this are not atypical. Of equal importance are the time and attention given to shaming emasculated men—men who are too weak to assume the properly aggressive posture needed to defend their race, restore their culture, and honor their heritage. Perhaps the critique of weak men is best exemplified by the condemnation of "cuckservatives," or cuckolded white conservatives, who surrender their honor, masculinity, and their womenfolk by supporting policies such as criminal justice and immigration reform and who exhibit an unhealthy dependency on the liberal establishment.

Underlying these themes is an old story about biology, sex, and gender. Alt-right protagonists seek to use just-so stories about "universal gender difference" and human nature to justify and legitimate a hyper-masculinist authoritarianism counterpoint to liberal multiculturalism and feminist orthodoxy. The alt-right critique of liberalism is rooted in a Romantic view (Löwy and Sayre 2001) that seeks to replace liberal modernity's excesses, especially, so their argument goes, its purported aspiration for racial and gender equality, with an anti-globalist nationalism. Frequent alt-right.com poster Vincent Law wrote a think piece called "Women are Nature's Greatest Nationalists" in 2017 that was later reposted on Stormfront.org. Noting that women are more "hardcore and patriotic" than men in Russia but that this is not the case in the "West," he pondered how race, nationalism, and gender work together in nature. "Women are sub-rationally pursuing their own biological imperative at all times," he wrote, followed by a complicated argument about the way that women respond to "evolutionary pressures" that make them both more tied to their ethnic communities but also more likely to leave them if those communities are threatened by a more powerful outside group. Implicitly, in his view, it is women's reproductive capacity and their essential child-rearing capacities and obligations that have created a situation in which they either demand protection from men of their ethnic group or leave the group to seek the protection of other ethnic nationals. For their part, men can sometimes appear more passive than women in their defense of the tribe/nation, because the threat of violence is more real for men than it is for women because men are inherently active while women are passive. He wrote:

> The men feel a reluctance to go as hardcore as the women because that would necessitate action. I've heard Russian girls say that muds are subhumans with a casual breeziness that blew me away. They say these things though and then go back to being cute and being feminine girls. They aren't going to pick up the AKs anytime soon, no matter how much they hate the hachis. But if a man starts thinking like this … there's a chance he might have to act on his conclusions. And so men are more careful in what they allow themselves to believe, or openly say. Because it has the potential to have actual consequences. Only after women sniff the air and see which way the wind is blowing, and when the situation becomes dire do they start hedging their bets, or engaging in open treachery to their own tribe. This is arguably the state of Scandinavia and much of the Anglo-Sphere as things stand now. But beyond the Hajnal line, there's still some fight left … which is why I lay off the woman hate while I'm there.

Accompanying the idea of women as the handmaidens to their ethnic brothers in arms is thus the heterosexist idea that they are biologically programmed also to be disloyal to the tribe/nation. For Law, this disloyalty has already reached epic proportions in the "Anglo-Sphere," making women-hating a reasonable response there. In contrast, women have not yet reached this stage of treachery in Russia, Law seems to think, presumably because of its more deeply entrenched and less-contested gender hierarchies. I am as interested in teasing out the elegant, if deeply troubling, gendered racial heterosexist nationalistic logic at work in his thinking as I am in invalidating his ethnographic claims. Indeed, this logic, let us call it an alt-right political rationality, prevails across the white nationalist media world. We can see it, for example, in the certainty with which Breitbart posters dismissed the credibility of Christine Blasey Ford, a woman they see as disloyal not just because her testimony threatened Brett Kavanaugh's Supreme Court nomination. She lacked credibility also because she was a white woman whose actions, professional status, and assertiveness challenged the foundations of the white nationalist gendered racial order and as such she posed a threat to white community restoration. Law's piece further gives us some clues about the ideological source of Donald Trump's love of Russia and Vladimir Putin (cf., Ashwin and Utrata 2020). Every pro-Russia, pro-Putin comment that Donald Trump would make worked like a dog whistle for alt-right members whose blog posts are frequently praising strong and masculine Russia in contrast to a weak and feminized West.

This leads me to my final point about the people who make up the alt-right's rank and file. Women in the white nationalist media world are famously invisible and underrepresented (Daniels 2009). There is an obvious reason for this: even cursory attention to alt-right blog posts reveals visceral expressions of misogyny. Women-hating is an alt-right *national* pastime. My perusal of the alt-right mediascape gives me the impression of a space comprised of aging men who are fed up by what they see as a lifetime of disrespect, elaborated mostly in terms of their wounded whiteness and imperiled masculinity, and of young men (some of whom openly identify as Incels [involuntary celibates]), whose embrace of white racial identification and pride is inseparable from their expression of hatred of women. Given the extent of misogyny in the posts, it would seem that hating women is an essential feature of alt-right white identity.

Yet, woman-hating also undermines alt-right movement building. Indeed, many alt-right leaders see women as important to the cause because their presence softens the movement's reputation, helping it to gain mainstream acceptance. Indeed, many alt-right leaders see women as crucial for their ability to help to recruit men. In a comment that resonates with Law's claims about women, race, and nationalism, an alt-right pundit told a writer from *Harper's Magazine* that women are the "lionesses and shield maidens and Valkyries" that inspire men to fight for the future of white civilization. "What really drives men is women," she explained, "and, let's be honest, sex with women" (quoted in Darby 2017). And there are women posters to alt-right websites. Here is one example: Anti-PC pundit and University of Toronto psychologist Jordan Peterson made a series of comments and tweets about "the pathologies of racial pride," as part of his long-term crusade against liberal and left "identity politics" (Bartlett 2018). But this perspective ran afoul of white nationalist sensibilities as well, as one woman on alt-right.com pointed out in a lengthy post from 2018:

> As the daughter of an (M.D.) psychoanalyst, I have witnessed Jew/shabbos goy [sic] pseudo-intellectual fraudulence in the psych field for my entire life…. Red flags are everywhere with this guy. One thing that really stood out to me was the 'recommended reading list' on his website, because it looks like it was created by social workers in the employ of the World Zionist Union. Peterson is now raking in tens of thousands of Patreon shekels

from mislead individuals simply because he didn't toe the Party Line on pronouns. But he's the biggest intellectual fraud of this entire movement. Boycott, divest and sanction from Jordan Peterson—now.

The anti-Semitism expressed here is further confirmation that what is at stake on the alt-right is not just an end to the attack on an imperiled white minority, as its main protagonists frame it for popular consumption. The threat extends as well to nature itself and to a set of racial and gender hierarchies that are closely sutured together by passionate devotion to the just-so stories about science and nature that have circulated popularly and in some academic circles for decades, if not longer (Gutmann 2019; Lancaster 2003).

And there is a class story here as well. The alt-right is generally disdainful of economic and political elites and suspicious of finance and monopoly capital. This disdain is, of course, frequently expressed in explicitly anti-Semitic terms, as it was during the Unite the Right rally in Charlottesville, Virginia, in August 2017 (Green 2017). The alt-right leadership seeks to inspire particular fractions of the white middle and working classes with its rhetoric of pseudoscientific stories about gender, and with its promises of economic prosperity for white men, their womenfolk, and their families, frequently elaborated in precisely these terms. And it is these groups who are contrasted to purportedly uppity feminists whose presumed deceitfulness is rooted in part in their elite class position, as the quotes at the start of this chapter indicate.

To call the racist, misogynistic, heterosexist, and authoritarian logics that inspire belonging in the alt-right digital world politically dangerous would be a gross understatement. But an analytical point also needs to be made about the nature of the alt-right's misogyny. There is a contradiction at the heart of it: women are desirable but inherently distrusted. They are politically necessary for the movement and the white race's survival, because only they have the power to spur wimpy, emasculated men into action, yet they are politically unreliable. Managing this contradiction is a major preoccupation for the movement. Exposing the alt-right's deep-seated misogyny, and its contradictions, is an essential task for those who would seek to undermine its popularity and neutralize its influence.

Towards the abolition of white nationalism

I have argued in this chapter that gender is more than just a marker of difference in alt-right thought. It is a set of essential ideological precepts that sutures together and helps to legitimate a worldview that links condemnation of the liberal establishment with an infinite number of existential threats to the white race, from transgender people, to ineffectual and ideologically compromised conservatives, to immigrants and Black Americans—all groups whose rejection of racial and gender differences has caused the white race to suffer (see also Hochschild 2016). In this formulation, tolerance and the celebration of difference as an intrinsic social good is dangerous, and Donald Trump's xenophobic nativism, racist attack on Black America, and his public misogyny have been music to many a white nationalist's ears. Yet I think Trump was more a follower in the movement than a leader, insofar as he drew upon the interpretive frameworks of the alt-right to make sense of politics and current events. Abolishing white nationalism thus requires more than just the electoral defeat of Donald Trump. What is also needed is an anti-racist political program. There is a long history on the academic left to disregard or underestimate racism's entrenched capacities to shape political, social, and economic life in the United States. As I have written elsewhere (Maskovsky 2020), this was particularly acute during the Trump presidency, when calls could be heard from the social democratic left to use a program of economic populism to overcome Trump-era ethnonationalism. Yet it is my view that only an explicitly anti-racist politics can hope to diminish white nationalism's popular and political influence, as the abolitionist and Civil Rights movements demonstrated against similar foes in past eras and as we saw occurring in June 2020 in the protests against police violence and the reinvigoration of the #BlackLivesMatter movement. I will add here the importance of the fight for gender equality as well, which cannot be deferred while other political battles are waged, particularly since the alt-right has coupled gender and race in its vision of a white nation. The work of building, aligning with, supporting, and acting in solidarity with anti-racist and anti-sexist political projects should continue as a priority that shapes our scholarly agendas.

Coda: an ethnographic refusal

This chapter concludes with a brief discussion of the ethical predicaments that we encounter when studying white nationalism. Such considerations of the ethical dilemmas that emerge in studies of political groups that we see as threats and whose ideologies we ultimately seek to abolish are important. I want to elaborate here, tentatively and without any sort of sanctimony, a brief sketch for what an abolitionist anthropology of white nationalism might look like. For many of these ideas, I am indebted to people of color scholarship, especially that of Black feminists and Indigenous scholars who have written against the plantation system and its afterlife and against settler-colonialism (Haley 2016; Shange 2019; Simpson 2014).

How should we write about the people with whom we are not aligned, people we oppose politically, and groups we seek to defeat, whose ideologies we have an urgent need to abolish? This has been a long-standing issue of concern in feminist and decolonial scholarship (e.g., Abu-Lughod 2002; Mbembe 2015; Simpson 2014), which has pointed out the insufficiencies of using the idea of cultural relativism to justify or legitimate anthropological inquiries into groups we oppose and see as dangerous. In a critique of a recent article by Jon Anderson (2017) that describes the ethical systems of gun enthusiasts in the United States, and the ways they justify gun ownership and use in the aftermath of mass shootings, Hugh Gusterson wrote:

> Anderson bends over backward to see the gun debate from his natives' point of view ... My point [is] that we risk naturalizing the ideology of gun owners if our explication of their worldview is not balanced either by critique or by the juxtaposition of a contrary community's viewpoint.... While it is surely bad ethnographic form, lazily indulging our ideological reflexes, to simply condemn our human subjects, it is also problematic to just recite their worldview without pushing the conversation deeper, probing for friction between belief and reality.
>
> *(2017, 59)*

I could not agree more with Gusterson.

But pushing the conversation deeper also requires the explicit unsettling of the liberal logics that tend to inform ethnographic writing and that establishes the foundational anthropological premise that knowledge of the other is an intrinsic scholarly good. Audra Simpson has written about refusal at some length, to mark a difference in her way of writing about Indigenous peoples in North America (McGranahan 2016; Simpson 2014, 2017). Simpson has refused to represent Indigenous people in her analyses as people who "had all things been equal would have consented to have things taken, things stolen from them" (2017, 12). This requires a refusal to represent Indigenous groups as living in cultural worlds defined by settler-colonial logics, the refusal, in short, to represent Indigenous groups as locked singularly in battles with states that overpower them, and instead to consider the ways that they never accepted the power of those states in the first place.

I want to take Simpson's idea of ethnographic refusal here and see if it can be applied usefully to the study not just of those who themselves refuse the settler-colonial logics that frequently set the terms of their depiction but also of those who are the political proponents of those logics. Let me explain further. As I suggest above, I am leery of applying a conventional "explaining the other" ethnographic approach to the question of gender politics in the alt-right and its allied groups. Take the example of J.D. Vance's memoir, *Hillbilly Elegy* (2016), as a cautionary tale that reveals the limits and limitations of this strategy. This book provides a portrait of multigenerational poverty in Appalachia, and the challenges poor whites face in maintaining middle-class positions in the face of drug addiction, workforce precarity, and their alienation from middle-class standards and values. In popular and some academic circles, it became an inappropriate stand-in for an ethnographically informed account of the white nationalist rank and file (e.g. Senior 2016). One reason for why this is inappropriate is that a vastly different, and more affluent, segment of the white working and middle classes would be the proper ethnographic subjects for such an account. In fact, the author himself, a Yale law school graduate and potential US senate candidate, has more in common with white nationalist supporters of Trump than did the many less affluent relatives he wrote about in his book.

A somewhat more successful attempt to explain the rank and file of the right in the United States has been Arlie Hochschild's *Strangers in Their Own Land* (2016). This book locates the widely held convictions that Black and Brown people are "cutting in line" ahead of more deserving white people, liberals are elitists, and the federal government is to blame for undermining the basis of honor and dignity of the Louisiana residents (Hochschild's ethnographic subjects) in a moral economy that recognizes the harsh realities of capitalism and the sacrificial citizenship that success in the United States now requires. Yet I worry about what kind of political project emerges from Hochschild's ethnographic account. In the book's afterword, she tells us. People on the right felt affirmed by her depictions of people similar to themselves while liberals were outraged that she gave voice to their political opponents. Hochschild understands the difficulties of drawing easy political lessons from her ethnographic material. In the end, she suggests programs that enable young people to cross the partisan divide, to learn about the lives of others, and to gain a sense of the other's alienation. I am sure that this would do some good. But it puts those who are heavily invested in gendered and racialized political violence and those who are targeted by that violence on far too even a playing field. Hochschild imagines some inherent progress from mutual experiences of shared vulnerability. She does not provide a way for us to address the harm that white community grievances routinely cause those who are cast out of the category of the human by them.

What if we refuse to use ethnography to get to know white nationalists on these kinds of intimate ethnographic terms and insist instead on recognizing them as the central protagonists in the project of producing and reproducing hierarchies of human differences (Weheliye 2014)? What if we refuse to use ethnography in the attempt to find the hidden cultural mechanism for convincing white nationalists to "switch sides"? What if we instead put ethnography to use in identifying the political repertoires of white nationalist groups so that they can be defeated? I am not suggesting stripping the humanity of the oppressors. However, they deserve to be taken seriously as political subjects who act of their own volition in ways that are fundamentally invested in the oppression and subjugation of others. We need to understand the political capacities of the groups they form, the extent of the popularity of their ideas, and the dilemmas they face in putting together a coherent political program.

I want to embrace the idea of ethnographic refusal in another sense as well. In addition to refusing to make white nationalists' cultural worlds known so that their secret anguish can be placated, à la Hochschild, I also want to refuse to condone the liberal sanctimony and outrage that might follow from my analysis above. As outrageous and dangerous as their worldview is, liberal outrage is precisely what white nationalists expect from their political opponents. And they use its expression very effectively to score political points about liberal cosmopolitans' elitism and hypocrisy. Indeed, the widespread condemnation of

Trump's racism actually worked politically to reinforce the sense of grievance felt by many who held white nationalist sensibilities, because those who harbored white community resentments frequently felt unfairly characterized as racists by the anti-Trump commentary. Overcoming the long-standing political maneuver of treating the accusation of racism as worse than racism itself is an essential part of the effort to abolish white nationalism.

What we need to think through together is what kind of ethnographic practice can help to abolish white nationalism. What kind of analyses do we need to advance a political victory against illiberal forms of racism that does not settle for reviving the neoliberal governing programs that created the conditions for the white nationalist recent upsurge in the first place? What kind of anthropology do we need that helps us to think of other political possibilities, those that take gender, sex, race, and class seriously and that imagine the new political possibilities that might surface in the defeat of Trump-era white nationalism? In other words, what we need as anthropologists and as people is more than just the defeat of white supremacy in all of its permutations. We also need to develop new forms of political thought and action that go beyond both white nationalism and neoliberal rule to create something that actually looks like justice, freedom, and equality.

Acknowledgments

This chapter has benefited from the insights from those who gave comments when I presented an earlier version at the annual meetings of the American Anthropological Association on a session honoring the work of Sandra Morgen and in an invited talk at the University of Colorado-Bolder. An earlier version of a part of the first subsection of this chapter was published in: Maskovsky, Jeff. 2020. "Other People's Race Problem: Trumpism and the Collapse of the Liberal Racial Consensus in America." In *Beyond Populism: Angry Politics and the Twilight of Neoliberalism*, edited by Jeff Maskovsky and Sophie Bjork-James, 167–176. Morgantown, WV: West Virginia University Press; it is reprinted here with the publisher's permission. For invaluable feedback on the written version, thanks especially to Karen Brodkin, Jessica Cattelino, Louise Lamphere, Leith Mullings, Uli Linke, Christine Kray, and Stephen Steinberg.

References

Abu-Lughod, Lila. 2002. "Do Muslim Women Really Need Saving? Anthropological Reflections on Cultural Relativism and Its Others." *American Anthropologist* 104 (3): 783–790. https://doi.org/10.1525/aa.2002.104.3.783.

Anderson, Joe. 2017. "Gun Owners, Ethics, and the Problem of Evil: A Response to the Las Vegas Shooting." *HAU: Journal of Ethnographic Theory* 7 (3): 39–48. https://doi.org/10.14318/hau7.3.003.

Angelo, Nathan. 2019. *One America? Presidential Appeals to Racial Resentment from LBJ to Trump*. Albany: State University of New York Press.

Ashwin, Sarah, and Jennifer Utrata. 2020. "Masculinity Restored? Putin's Russia and Trump's America." *Contexts* 19 (2): 16–21. https://doi.org/10.1177/1536504220920189.
Bartlett, Tom. 2018. "What's So Dangerous about Jordan Peterson?" *Chronicle of Higher Education*, January 17, 2018. https://www.chronicle.com/article/What-s-So-Dangerous-About/242256.
Bjork-James, Sophie. 2015. "Feminist Ethnography in Cyberspace: Imagining Families in the Cloud." *Sex Roles: A Journal of Research* 73 (3): 113–124. https://doi.org/10.1007/s11199-015-0507-8.
Bjork-James, Sophie, and Jeff Maskovsky. 2017. "When White Nationalism Became Popular." *Anthropology News* 58 (3): e86–e91. https://doi.org/10.1111/AN.455.
Brodkin, Karen. 2007. *Making Democracy Matter: Identity and Activism in Los Angeles*. New Brunswick, NJ: Rutgers University Press.
Coleman, E. Gabriella. 2014. *Hacker, Hoaxer, Whistleblower, Spy: The Many Faces of Anonymous*. London: Verso.
Collins, Jane L. 2017. *The Politics of Value: Three Movements to Change How We Think about the Economy*. Chicago: University of Chicago Press.
Daniels, Jessie. 2009. *Cyber Racism: White Supremacy Online and the New Attack on Civil Rights*. Lanham, MD: Rowman & Littlefield.
Darby, Seyward. 2017. "The Rise of the Valkyries: In the Alt-right, Women Are the Future, and the Problem." *Harpers Magazine*, September 2017. https://harpers.org/archive/2017/09/the-rise-of-the-valkyries/.
Davis, Dána-Ain. 2004. "Manufacturing Mammies: The Burdens of Service Work and Welfare Reform among Battered Black Women." *Anthropologica* 46 (2): 273–288. https://doi.org/10.2307/25606199.
Diamond, Jeremy. 2018. "Trump Says It's 'a Very Scary Time for Young Men in America'." *CNN*, October 2, 2018. https://www.cnn.com/2018/10/02/politics/trump-scary-time-for-young-men-metoo/index.html.
Dignam, Pierce Alexander, and Deana A. Rohlinger. 2019. "Misogynistic Men Online: How the Red Pill Helped Elect Trump." *Signs: Journal of Women in Culture and Society* 44 (3): 589–612. https://doi.org/10.1086/701155.
Di Leonardo, Micaela. 1998. *Exotics at Home: Anthropologies, Others, American Modernity*. Chicago: University of Chicago Press.
Esposito, Luigi. 2011. "White Fear and US Racism in the Era of Obama: The Relevance of Neoliberalism." *Theory in Action* 4 (3): 1–24. https://doi.org/10.3798/tia.1937-0237.11019.
Feagan, Joe. 2013. *The White Racial Frame: Centuries of Racial Framing and Counter-Framing*. Second edition, Hoboken, NJ: Taylor & Francis.
Goode, Judith G., and Jeff Maskovsky. 2001. "Introduction." In *The New Poverty Studies: The Ethnography of Power, Politics, and Impoverished People in the United States*, edited by Judith G. Goode and Jeff Maskovsky, 1–36. New York: New York University Press.
Green, Emma. 2017. "Why the Charlottesville Marchers Were Obsessed with Jews." *The Atlantic*, August 15, 2017. https://www.theatlantic.com/politics/archive/2017/08/nazis-racism-charlottesville/536928/.
Grossberg, Lawrence. 2018. *Under the Cover of Chaos: Trump and the Battle for the American Right*. London: Pluto Press.
Gusterson, Hugh. 2017. "Gun Owners, Ethics, and the Problem of Evil: A Response to the Las Vegas Shooting." *HAU: Journal of Ethnographic Theory* 7 (3): 58–60. https://doi.org/10.14318/hau7.3.003.
Gutmann, Matthew. 2019. *Are Men Animals? How Modern Masculinity Sells Men Short*. New York: Basic Books.

Haley, Sarah. 2016. *No Mercy Here: Gender, Punishment, and the Making of Jim Crow Modernity*. Chapel Hill: The University of North Carolina Press.
Hawley, George. 2017. *Making Sense of the Alt-right*. New York: Columbia University Press.
Hochschild, Arlie Russell. 2016. *Strangers in Their Own Land: Anger and Mourning on the American Right*. New York: New Press.
James, Russell. 2019. "Feminism Is Not about 'Gender' Equality." *Stormfront.org*, March 1, 2019. https://www.stormfront.org/forum/blogs/u151910-e4666/.
Juris, Jeffrey S. 2008. *Networking Futures: The Movements against Corporate Globalization*. Durham, NC: Duke University Press.
Kata, Anna. 2012. "Anti-vaccine Activists, Web 2.0, and the Postmodern Paradigm: An Overview of Tactics and Tropes Used Online by the Anti-vaccination Movement." *Vaccine* 30 (25): 3778–3789. https://doi.org/10.1016/j.vaccine.2011.11.112.
Lancaster, Roger N. 2003. *The Trouble with Nature: Sex in Science and Popular Culture*. Berkeley: University of California Press.
Law, Vincent. 2017. "Women Are Nature's Greatest Nationalist." *Altright.com*, November 17, 2017. https://altright.com/2017/11/17/women-are-natures-greatest-nationalists/.
Lee, Tony. 2018. "***Live Updates***: Brett Kavanaugh, Christine Blasey Ford Testify Before Senate Judiciary Committee." *Breitbart*, September 27, 2018. https://www.breitbart.com/politics/2018/09/27/live-updates-brett-kavanugh-christine-blasey-ford-testify-before-senate-judiciary-committee/.
Löwy, Michael, and Robert Sayre. 2001. *Romanticism against the Tide of Modernity*, translated by Catherine Porter. Durham, NC: Duke University Press.
Maskovsky, Jeff. 2017. "Toward the Anthropology of White Nationalist Postracialism: Comments Inspired by Hall, Goldstein, and Ingram's 'The Hands of Donald Trump'." *HAU: Journal of Ethnographic Theory* 7 (1): 433–440. https://doi.org/10.14318/hau7.1.030.
———. 2020. "Other People's Race Problem: Trumpism and the Collapse of the Liberal Racial Consensus in America." In *Beyond Populism: Angry Politics and the Twilight of Neoliberalism*, edited by Jeff Maskovsky and Sophie Bjork-James, 167–176. Morgantown, WV: West Virginia University Press.
Maskovsky, Jeff, and Sophie Bjork-James. 2020. "Introduction." In *Beyond Populism: Angry Politics and the Twilight of Neoliberalism*, edited by Jeff Maskovsky and Sophie Bjork-James, 1–19. Morgantown, WV: West Virginia University Press.
Mbembe, Achille. 2015. "Decolonizing Knowledge and the Question of the Archive." *Lecture*, May 2, 2015 at the Wits Institute for Social and Economic Research. https://wiser.wits.ac.za/system/files/Achille%20Mbembe%20-%20Decolonizing%20Knowledge%20and%20the%20Question%20of%20the%20Archive.pdf.
McGranahan, Carol. 2016. "Theorizing Refusal: An Introduction." *Cultural Anthropology* 31 (3): 319–332. https://doi.org/10.14506/ca31.3.01.
Morgen, Sandra. 2002. *Into Our Own Hands: The Women's Health Movement in the United States, 1969–1990*. New Brunswick, NJ: Rutgers University Press.
Mullings, Leith. 2005. "Interrogating Racism: Toward an Antiracist Anthropology." *Annual Review of Anthropology* 34 (1): 667–693. https://doi.org/10.1146/annurev.anthro.32.061002.093435.
———. 2020. "Neoliberal Racism and the Movement for Black Lives." In *When Rights Ring Hollow*, edited by Juliet Hooker, 249–294. New York: Lexington Books.
Saxton, Alexander. 2003. *The Rise and Fall of the White Republic: Class Politics and Mass Culture in Nineteenth-century America*. London: Verso.

Senior, Jennifer. 2016. "In 'Hillbilly Elegy,' a Tough Love Analysis of the Poor Who Back Trump." Review of *Hillbilly Elegy*, by J.D. Vance. *New York Times*, August 10, 2016. https://www.nytimes.com/2016/08/11/books/review-in-hillbilly-elegy-a-compassionate-analysis-of-the-poor-who-love-trump.html.

Shange, Savannah. 2019. *Progressive Dystopia: Abolition, Antiblackness, and Schooling in San Francisco*. Durham, NC: Duke University Press.

Simpson, Audra. 2014. *Mohawk Interruptus: Political Life across the Borders of Settler States*. Durham, NC: Duke University Press.

———. 2017. "The Ruse of Consent and the Anatomy of 'Refusal': Cases from Indigenous North America and Australia." *Postcolonial Studies* 20 (1): 18–33. https://doi.org/10.1080/13688790.2017.1334283.

SPLC. n.d. "White Nationalist." *Southern Poverty Law Center*. Accessed August 25, 2018. https://www.splcenter.org/fighting-hate/extremist-files/ideology/white-nationalist.

Steinberg, Stephen. 1981. *The Ethnic Myth: Race, Ethnicity, and Class in America*. New York: Atheneum.

———. 2001. *Turning Back: The Retreat from Racial Justice in American Thought and Policy*. Third edition, Boston: Beacon Press.

———. 2007. *Race Relations: A Critique*. Stanford, CA: Stanford University Press.

Taylor, Keeanga-Yamahtta. 2016. *From #BlackLivesMatter to Black Liberation*. Chicago: Haymarket Books.

Vance, J.D. 2016. *Hillbilly Elegy: A Memoir of a Family and Culture in Crisis*. New York: Harper.

Weheliye, Alexander G. 2014. *Habeas Viscus: Racializing Assemblages, Biopolitics, and Black Feminist Theories of the Human*. Durham, NC: Duke University Press.

8
CRAFT ACTIVISM, VIOLENCE, AND MEMORY-MAKING

Jewish Hearts for Pittsburgh

Hinda Mandell

Why would a group of people turn to yarn as a mechanism for change in the face of bodily violence, terror, and murder? How can a material as pliable, voiceless, domestic, and delicate as yarn be useful as an agent for positivity, caring, and strength? These are questions I continue to ask since the mass shooting at the Tree of Life in Pittsburgh, when a gunman interrupted a prayerful Shabbat-morning service on October 27, 2018; charged into the sanctuary; and murdered 11 congregants. "I'm going in," the accused gunman posted online the morning of the attack. According to his online posts, Jews were "the enemy of white people" (Turkewitz and Roose 2018).

As a Jewish yarn enthusiast, my response was immediate and visceral. I picked up my crochet hook and began casting on stitches to form a plush Jewish Star, and within days of the attack I co-formed Jewish Hearts for Pittsburgh, a Facebook craft campaign with 1,300 members, which ultimately delivered 2,500 'Jewish Hearts' to the neighborhood of the attack in November 2018. We worked fast and furious in the weeks following the Pittsburgh shooting, regarded as the deadliest attack against the American Jewish community in its history (Croft and Ahmed 2018). And two weeks before Chanukah, known as the Festival of Lights, 40 volunteers from Pittsburgh hung these representations of love and peace on tree branches, on fences, around fire hydrants, street signs, and inside businesses within Pittsburgh's Squirrel Hill neighborhood (Figure 8.1).

"On a damp November day with gray skies, the stars came out," wrote Marylynne Pitz, feature writer for the *Pittsburgh Post-Gazette*, in an article profiling these handcrafted and colorful Jewish Stars with hearts at their center (Pitz 2018). By all measures, our craft campaign was a success, and it certainly was time-consuming—comparable to a part-time job (unpaid), where my co-founder Ellen Dominus Broude of New York and I fielded questions online and from the media, posted encouraging comments on Facebook, had our own moments of

DOI: 10.4324/9781003034810-8

FIGURE 8.1 A crochet Jewish Heart that author Hinda Mandell made in 2018 for the Jewish Hearts for Pittsburgh craft campaign.
Credit: Hinda Mandell.

crafting productivity, and—in the case of Ellen—made multiple trips daily to a PO Box rented specifically for this purpose well into November 2018. While my enthusiasm for this project has been unwavering, questions about activism still linger in its wake. Why did a group of women (overwhelmingly) turn to yarn—but also to paper, fabric, and even glass and wood—as the antidote to a heinous act of hate?

★ ★ ★

Before exploring in-depth the Jewish Hearts for Pittsburgh case study as a direct response to violence, and its role in crafting memory among participants, it is necessary to briefly contextualize the role of this "softer" (literally and figuratively) form of activism. "Gentle" is a word that one of the leading voices of contemporary craftivism, Sarah Corbett, applies toward her activist work. Indeed, in her 2018 book, *How to Be a Craftivist: The Art of Gentle Protest*, she explained that she grew up in England as the daughter of activists, but herself became "burnt out" in her 20s from what she came to view as aggressive, activist tactics: shouting slogans, marching, and shouting down opponents across the activist aisle. Her own extended slogan asked, "If we want a world that is beautiful, kind, and fair, shouldn't our activism be beautiful, kind, and fair?" She was quick to point out that this approach can sound like "a novel gimmick" but presses the power of craft-infused activism by arguing that it can be "world-changing" (Corbett 2019, 227). The gendered nature of this form of activism, which Corbett presented, cannot and should not go unnoticed, especially since contemporarily it is practiced mostly by women. And while one could easily imagine conservative bullies or alt-right fanatics belittling the effectiveness of women crocheting doilies, for example, as an antidote to violence and brutality, it is worth noting that craft as a response to violence has a long and serious thread, often in response to war, and throughout history and across geographies. For instance, for the book *Threads of Life: A History of the World Through the Eye of the Needle*, author Clare Hunter visited museum archives to reveal stories of injured (male) soldiers turning to cross-stitch to counter their terror from the trenches in World War I; to Dutch political prisoners in World War II who, upon surviving internment in concentration camps, stitched "liberation skirts" to narrate the circumstances of their survival (Hunter 2019, 80); to the Hmong story cloths, which she described as a form of stitched "war documentary" of their forced and violent cultural displacement in the Vietnam Wars (112). So, even if craft-based activism is "gentle" to borrow from Corbett, because its objects are stand-ins for the crafters' spoken voice, they are hardly meek. They are hardly ineffective. They occupy—quite vibrantly and viscerally—a space in a world that is as much visual as it is auditory, and the results of a craftivist's material journey typically strike a more *personal* chord than more public and vocal forms of activist labor. After all, in her book *A Natural History of the Senses*, the writer Diane Ackerman argued that touch is the first human sense. It is, wrote Hunter, who applied a textile application to Ackerman's text, "the first tool we use to register and remember difference and to record heritage" (Hunter 2019, 85). The tactile objects in a craftivist's tool kit, traditionally including yarn, embroidery floss, and fabrics, offer a sensory language of touch and texture to express a political position. These tools allow its practitioners to respond creatively to violence, and recipients to accept—and even embrace—an interaction that is a tactile intervention to violence, imbued with narrative meaning and rhetorical symbolism.

Crafting as a response to violence

"Textile making is often represented iconically as a stand-in both for tradition and for defiance against the reigning order," wrote contemporary arts scholar Julia Bryan-Wilson in her book *Fray: Art and Textile Politics* (Bryan-Wilson 2017, 10). The "reigning order" during Donald J. Trump's presidency consisted of a barrage of nationalistic vitriol aimed at those who did not share his racial, national, and religious backgrounds. While it is beyond the scope of this chapter to chronicle vitriol and its companionate policies, this chapter must acknowledge the context from which the 2018 Pittsburgh shooter emerged. Yet, the shooter was not a Trump supporter. *The New York Times* reported that the Pittsburgh shooter Robert Bowers wrote online, days before the attack, that "Trump is a globalist [a slur with anti-Semitic connotations], not a nationalist. There is no #MAGA as long as there is an infestation [a slur for Jews]" (Turkewitz and Roose 2018).

Yet even if Trump was not hateful enough for the shooter to offer his support, Bowers shared with the president animosity toward immigrants and refugees. "Refugees are the sort of immigrants for whom Jews feel a special affinity, and about whom Trump has stoked no small amount of fear and revulsion," wrote James Kirchick (2018) in the *Washington Post* following the Tree of Life shooting. In the weeks prior to the Tree of Life shooting, Donald Trump had been railing against a "caravan" of Central American refugees that was heading toward the US border. In alt-right social media circles, commentators placed blame on HIAS (originally, Hebrew Immigrant Aid Society), a Jewish refugee assistance organization, and promoted a conspiracy theory that George Soros, a Jewish Holocaust survivor and philanthropist billionaire, funded the refugee caravan (Achenbach 2018). Donald Trump had previously directed animosity toward Soros, accusing him of funding protesters at his rallies (Satter 2018), and Trump's final 2016 campaign ad accused "global special interests" of teaming up with the Washington establishment; the three people featured in the ad were all Jewish financial figures, including Soros (Haaretz 2016). Just five days before the Tree of Life shooting, George Soros received a pipe bomb in the mail, the first of more than a dozen sent to prominent leftist figures by another man, Cesar Sayoc, and news reports detailing Sayoc's obsession with the Soros/caravan conspiracy theory circled widely (Achenbach 2018). The Pittsburgh shooter had posted on social media, "Open your Eyes! It's the filthy EVIL jews Bringing the Filthy EVIL Muslims into the Country!!," and headed to the Tree of Life synagogue (Turkewitz and Roose 2018). Just after the Pittsburgh shooting, Trump stoked anti-Semitic sentiment by stating that he "wouldn't be surprised" if George Soros funded the caravan (Levin 2018).

While Trump's son-in-law is Jewish, and his daughter Ivanka Trump converted to Judaism and was raising their children as Jews (and the president could use the religious identity of his family members to negate accusations of anti-Semitism), news reports still raised the question of whether Trump's bombastic and nationalistic agenda, and metaphoric winks to an admiring cohort of alt-right and white supremacist supporters, contributed to a climate in which a man felt it was acceptable to murder 11 Jews at worship on Shabbat (BBC 2018). In so doing, news reports were alluding to Trump, although not directly using this phrase, as a "stochastic terrorist." An unnamed blogger in 2011 was the first to coin the term (long before Trump was elected president): "Stochastic terrorism is the use of mass communications to incite random actors to carry out violent or terrorist acts that are *statistically predictable but individually unpredictable*. In short, remote-control murder by lone wolf" ("Stochastic Terrorism" 2011;

italics in the original). While Trump has not been reported to use slurs explicitly against Jews, he was considered the preferred president of white supremacists, and received the endorsement of the former Ku Klux Klan (KKK) grand wizard David Duke—which Trump was slow to disavow (Nelson 2016). Trump was also quoted as saying that there were "some very fine people on both sides" of the "Unite the Right Rally" in Charlottesville, Virginia in 2017, comprised of white supremacists and neo-Nazis who chanted, "Jews will not replace us" (Coaston 2019). CNN also reported that the Tree of Life rabbi, Jeffrey Myers, pointed the finger at hate speech in the United States as the direct cause of the murderous rampage at his synagogue, which he witnessed directly as a survivor—and told Trump so in person, but did not directly blame the president (Burke 2018).

Within this violent morass, we have a group of crafters who see handiwork as a mechanism for solace, and as an opportunity for them to take a stand against this apparent "reigning order" of hate and its violent impacts. While a robust body of scholarly literature has emerged to examine the processes and impacts of craft-based activism (see Bratich and Brush 2011; Bryan-Wilson 2010; Buszek 2011; Chansky 2010; Close 2018; Gökarıksel and Smith 2017; Mandell 2019; Minahan and Wolfram Cox 2007; Parker 2010; Ratto and Boler 2014), less has been written about the contemporary manifestation of craftivism as a direct response to bodily violence and mass shootings. For this reason, it is worth lingering on the *Open Theology* 2016 journal article, "Race and Responses to Violence in Prayer Shawl Ministries" (Bowman 2016). The article offered an analysis of interviews with members of church-associated, African-American and white, prayer-shawl groups, who have made and gifted their work to victims and relatives of those affected by mass shootings. At the heart of such work is understanding a community's response to grief, and the grieving process, after a violent act. The article's author, the theologian Donna Bowman, offered the paradoxical dilemma, and one critical for consideration, to the phenomenon of craft as a response to violence. Craft, in these instances, is at once self-serving and deeply empathic; it is self-involved and thoughtful; it is kind and burdensome. The impetus to craft and gift, the handiwork to those terrorized as a direct response to violence, is an act of sustaining love and also "self-serving," according to Bowman. She wrote:

> acts of sympathy are ways of demonstrating to ourselves that "we are not accomplices to what caused the suffering" … but they also proclaim, perhaps all unawares, our "impotence" in the face of it. We cannot talk ourselves out of the urge, though, paradoxical and self-serving as it may it be, because we cannot escape our kinship to those in mourning; we can only try to deal with it. … In circumstances of disastrous violence and loss of life, this heightened awareness of this condition of being "undone by each other," as Judith Butler puts it, leads many people to seek some sort of self-insertion.
>
> *(Bowman 2016, 927)*

Although sympathetic to the work of prayer-shawl ministries for their potential to understand religious meaning-making, Bowman's word choices of "self-serving" and "self-insertion" are at the same time accurate but limited in scope. It makes intuitive sense that those who were not victims of violence would seek to produce something with their hands as a means of comforting victims. This act serves the "outsiders'" intrinsic needs for doing something as they insert themselves into searing pain in the hopes of relieving it for others and themselves. Yet it is also necessary to state the obvious: acts of kindness that are outward-facing, and that is a positive attribute, even if centered on an individual need to relieve internal anxiety and grief, elevate our humanity. Yet Bowman quoted the philosopher Susan Sontag from *Regarding the Pain of Others*, who argued that people (in this case crafters) seek stability during peaks of unsettling violence through the call to do something (in this case, charitable crafting) as an effort to mend a solution and secure closure although—for the victims' families and survivors of mass shootings—there is no such neat fix (Sontag 2003, 103). Bowman then pulled upon the philosopher Judith Butler, to interrogate, figuratively, what would happen to our humanity if we, as outsider consumers of violence, were to sit with our discomfort and anxiety as opposed to busying our hands (metaphorically) with a solution. Butler posited,

> If we stay with the sense of loss, are we left feeling only passive and powerless, as some might fear? Or are we, rather, returned to a sense of human vulnerability, to our collective responsibility for the physical lives of one another?
>
> *(2004, 30)*

The response to Bowman, Sontag, and Butler's critique of "self-involvement" and "self-insertion" can be found in a comment by the self-proclaimed "godmother" of craftivism, Betsy Greer, who wrote on her website, "Sometimes people ask if craft can save the world. In the short run, maybe not" (Greer n.d.b). It is important, therefore, to match claims with outcomes. Craftivists do not generally claim that craft-based action is *the* solution. An analysis of the 113 letters written by Jewish Hearts for Pittsburgh members reveals that it is not even regarded as *a* solution, a word that Sontag would likely critique for its finality. Rather, if we frame craft-based activism as a response rather than a solution, and frame the response(s) to violence as a continuum with myriad possibilities, we can situate craft-based activism as an action that taps into the human need for kindness and support in the face of catastrophe.

In response to the September 11, 2001, terrorist attacks, Judith Butler wrote the essay collection *Precarious Life: The Powers of Mourning and Violence*, and her reflection on individual versus community responsibility in the wake of mass violence. "Our lives are profoundly implicated in the lives of others," she wrote, a statement that is both obvious but also, potentially, a call to action (2004, 7). If we are bound up in the actions of others, what is our responsibility to respond to cataclysmic events? A perpetrator of mass violence is both responsible for his actions (intentional choice of gendered pronoun) but also emerges from a social environment that has formed his beliefs and motivated his murderous actions. While Butler is clear that assailants are responsible for the destruction they have wrought, she also argued that "we would be making a mistake if we reduced their actions to purely self-generated acts of will or symptoms of individualism" (15). To cast the assailant as a moral failure forecloses on the necessary self-reflection of the collective's role in the formation of individual acts of violence against a group. "How is it that radical violence becomes an option," asked Butler. She continued:

> Our acts are not self-generated, but conditioned. We are at once acted upon and acting, and our 'responsibility' lies in the juncture between the two. What can I do with the conditions that form me? What do they constrain me to do? What can I do to transform them?
>
> *(16)*

For the participants in the Jewish Hearts for Pittsburgh project, as expressed through 113 letters that we received from crafters, and which are analyzed later in this chapter, crafting Jewish Hearts allowed them to craft and share love in a way that was personal and meaningful to them, from the comforts of their home. (The clash of comfort and craft, with murderous chaos, will be explored later in this chapter.) For one Jewish Hearts crafter, who is also a survivor of perhaps one of the most iconic school shootings (the Columbine High School massacre of 1999), the act of crafting her own Jewish Heart was a way to pay forward the kindness she received back in 1999:

> I know, from personal experience, that small and simple acts of kindness can help heal. When I was 17 in 1999, I was a junior at Columbine High School. One April day my life changed forever. I was devastated, but then letters and small tokens of love came pouring in. Each letter or token gave me strength to keep going. I hope I can pass on some of the strength I was given.
>
> *(personal communication, November 6, 2018)*

As Butler wrote:

> Only once we have suffered that violence are we compelled, ethically, to ask how we will respond to violent injury. What role will we assume in the historical relay of violence, who will we become in the response, and will we be furthering or impeding violence by virtue of the response that we make?

Grief, added Butler, lays bare the social relations that hold together human connections and strips away at "the very notion of ourselves as autonomous and in control" (2004, 16). Yet another benefit of crafting as a response to mass shootings is restoring a sense of control through repetition of stitch by stitch, of selecting colors and yarn and patterns. And while the sense of control may indeed be an illusion, it can bring stability as a mechanism of working through fear and anxiety. Craft as a response to high-profile mass shootings does not cure problems but it can restore a sense of humanity through the connections it helps establish with others, by affirming the productive process of making, and bringing the maker into a spiritual alignment of self that is centered on self-reflection. In this way, craft may serve as an antidote to the vulnerability that violence brutally rips bare. It is a response to violence that has restorative and transformative functions throughout the length of a person's engaged participation in the craft-making act: functions that are amplified through a sense of community, typically through an online forum where participants can share their creative output with and receive encouraging responses from other crafters working on the same project.

Background: how the craft campaign Jewish Hearts for Pittsburgh came to be

The day after the Pittsburgh shooting, I turned to my yarn stash, as I have done in the past, as a means to spark my activist self. Not even 18 months prior, in March 2017, I had pulled blue, pink, and red skeins of yarn from this stash to create what would become the "Jewish Hearts" following the desecration of the Waad Hakolel (Jewish) Cemetery in my hometown of Rochester, New York, part of a string of such anti-Semitic acts of vandalism in the early days of the Trump presidential administration. Back then, I crocheted two simple mementoes, a blue Star of David with a red heart at its core, and a pink heart with a Star of David at its center, and I hung these pieces to the scratchy branches of an evergreen at the vandalized cemetery. In October 2018, in the immediate aftermath of the Tree of Life shooting, my mind went to those same skeins of yarn. Did they still live amidst my yarn collection? In an unsettling way, it seemed as if they were waiting for me, since I found them immediately. I wrote a post on my personal Facebook page with a photo of the skeins—the day after the Pittsburgh attack—and I asked for volunteers to join me in creating yarn mementoes to embed love, stitch by stich, in the Jewish Star. "This would be the tiniest of tokens symbolizing love and life," I wrote.

I also posted this "call to action" in the Craftivist Facebook group, and member Ellen Dominus Broude, also of New York, heeded the call with passion and action of the highest order. The two of us were unaware of the other's existence prior to the attack which brought us together. We were joined by outrage, horror, and fear, but also by the driving need to do something that would be positive and community-based, so we could send a message of care to the Squirrel Hill neighborhood that was then besieged by SWAT teams and first responders. We started the Jewish Hearts for Pittsburgh Facebook group only days after the

October 2018 shooting, and within weeks it had nearly 1,300 members from across the United States, but also from Canada, England, Dubai, Costa Rica, and Australia, among other locales.

There was only one restriction that we gave our members: While crafters could create Jewish Hearts of most any color, size, or craft medium (although knit and crochet pieces were the most common, and Ellen's friend Carolyn Bloom created a pattern unique to this group, which one can find on Ravelry [app or website] by searching for "Jewish Hearts for Pittsburgh"), we asked crafters not to create a yellow Jewish Heart. As Jews, we were sensitive to the yellow symbolism of a Star of David that Jews in Nazi-occupied Europe during World War II were forced to wear, as emblematic of their targeted status. When we posted this restriction, some members politely inquired about its origins, which proved a welcome opportunity to talk about persecution, history, symbolism, and craft. What might be notable about this group is that it had members from different political backgrounds, but there was not a single instance of a member posting politically driven content. Our Facebook group became a politically inclusive space that was uplifting, encouraging, and people readily shared their works in progress and completed craft output.

Gendered intervention: compassion, action, community

A number of high-profile or mass shootings occurred in the year following the October 2018 Pittsburgh attack, which affected the Facebook group's craft activities:

- In November 2018, a mass shooting at the Borderline Bar and Grill in Thousand Oaks, California resulted in the murder of 12 people on "college night" at the bar (Jaffee 2018). Indeed, four days after the Thousand Oaks shooting, a crafter and her two daughters wrote a letter to Jewish Hearts of Pittsburgh, enclosing their handiwork. In the letter they explained that they attended a knitting circle the night of the shooting, two highway exits from the Borderline Bar. They learned of their proximity to the mass shooting the following morning, "And we poured our love into the hearts we had started crocheting" (Jewish Hearts for Pittsburgh letter archive, letter 087).
- In March 2019, an Australian white supremacist shot worshippers at two mosques in New Zealand, resulting in 51 deaths (Associated Press 2019). In the immediate aftermath of the mosque massacre overseas, Jewish Hearts for Pittsburgh co-founder Ellen Dominus Broude connected with a yarn-store owner in New Zealand, Jacqui Jewell of Barkers Wool and Haberdashery, and informed her about our activist craft group, which became a model for "Hearts for Christchurch." Members of our US-based group crafted and sent hearts to New Zealand, and in addition to crafters from across the globe, nearly 5,000 hearts were delivered to Christchurch mosques in May 2019.

- In April 2019, a synagogue in Poway, California, was the target of a shooting attack that took the life of one worshipper at the Chabad of Poway on the last day of Passover (Johnson and Stickney 2019). Following that attack, I mobilized our Facebook group to see if we could send Jewish Hearts to Poway. A member of the group, who lives in Dubai, connected me to her friend from Poway, who organized the hanging of 500 Jewish Hearts outside of the California synagogue.
- On the last day of April, in 2019, a gunman killed two students inside a classroom at the University of North Carolina at Charlotte.
- In May 2019, two student shooters attacked their own school, the STEM School Highlands Ranch, killing a student.
- In August 2019, a gunman killed 22 shoppers at an El Paso, Texas, Walmart. The following day a gunman in Dayton, Ohio, killed 9 people in an entertainment district.

Nearly universally in mass shootings in the United States (with the exception of an accused female shooter at the STEM School Highlands Ranch shooting, as mentioned in the above list [Law 2019]), the assailants are male, and overwhelmingly the participants in craft-based interventions in response to the attacks have been women. The violence, vengeance, and bloodlust steal lives and terrorize communities, while the soft, colorful, pliable fibers are adeptly mobilized by caring hands to bring some measure of handcrafted solace. With such yarn interventions, we note the following trend: male hands at the trigger of hard steel bring destruction and chaos, and end lives; while overwhelmingly, female hands create and bring something new into the world. Handcraft borne out of pain tells communities, "I see you and ache for you."

Making and crafting in response to gun violence is a form of "craftivism," which brings craft practice into an activist modality, a phrase attributed to Betsy Greer following the September 11, 2001, terrorist attacks. According to her "craftivism manifesto," "A craftivist is anyone who uses their craft to help the greater good. Your craft is your voice. Craftivism is about raising consciousness, creating a better world stitch by stitch; and things made by hand, by a person" (Greer n.d.a). The need for craftivist activity in the world, asserted Greer, is "because we create to connect beyond ourselves" (Greer n.d.b). According to artist Anthea Black and curator Nicole Burisch:

> The rise of craftivism and other politically engaged crafting practices—which value the radical potential of a particular craft activity rather than its finished end product—shift traditional emphasis away from polished, professionally, made craft objects themselves and toward a political and conceptual focus, positioning, and deployment of the work involved in making them. This emphasis has made room for reconsiderations of craft(wo)manship, performativity, mindfulness, tacit knowledge, skill sharing, DIY, anticapitalism, and activism.
>
> *(Black and Burisch 2011, 205)*

Yet, the motivation for a craftivist to connect their crafting to social change is directly in line with the motivations of nonpolitical (or nonactivist) makers: the allure of craft for its flow-inducing properties; for the opportunity to create something where previously there were only raw materials; for the healing processes of repetition; for the opportunity to make something out of love and to connect with other makers; and for the chance to leave behind creative evidence of their own making in the world, and to have their emotions and beliefs embodied in a material object. Indeed, as creativity scholar David Gauntlett wrote: "These (making) projects are especially valuable if they are not contained at the individual level but involve some form of sharing, co-operation or contribution to other people's well-being" (2011, 126). Gauntlett outlined three ways in which "making is connecting" (the title of his book), which we can apply to the craft process. First, the process of making an object connects pieces together to create an entirely new outcome. Second, crafting often pulls upon social interactions, such as when a crafter asks for help or crafts with friends. And the third reason why "making is connecting" is because it taps into our community through personal engagement when sharing the final piece (18). While the process of crafting may offer a welcome distraction from the stressors of daily responsibilities, and can be a soothing activity, it hardly dulls one's senses and sense of place within the broader environment. Rather, "people often spend time creating things because they want to feel alive in the world, as participants rather than as viewers, and to be active and recognized within a community of interesting people" (182).

Crafters in their own words

In order to probe deeply into the relevancy of yarn as a tool for solidarity and action in the aftermath of a high-profile mass shooting, I have turned to 113 letters that the Jewish Hearts for Pittsburgh organizers received, tucked, as they were, into boxes and envelopes carrying handcraft to their final destination. The 113 letters that we received in November 2018 following the Tree of Life shooting offer a basis for understanding how people used craft as a response to violence. In these letters, two core themes emerge, including: (a) explanations of why crafters chose to engage in the process of making in the shooting aftermath, and (b) personal connections to the shooting/its neighborhood. Letters were read in their entirety multiple times, both as individual units but also as a collective body of work, to allow for shared themes to emerge through these concurrent readings of the texts (as recommended by McKee 2003).

In 48 letters, crafters shared why they chose to create something with their hands following the deadly assault at the Tree of Life synagogue. Their explanations link to intrinsic motivations that guide their process of making. Because the process of making is physical, it is also highly personal as the made objects emerge from the singular hand-mind connection of each contributor, with the multidimensional and cognitive imprint of the maker literally embodied in the finished object.

> I think I do this because I don't always feel that I have the words to express what I feel in my heart. So I let my hands do that for me—I am much better able to express my feelings that way,

wrote one letter writer from Connecticut (Jewish Hearts for Pittsburgh, letter 008). Another crafter, from Kentucky, wrote: "It is empowering to be able to do something in the face of senseless violence" (letter 009). Indeed, many crafters expressed gratitude for the opportunity to engage in the creation process following fatal shootings. A crafter from Florida wrote, "If this project can give even one second of peace to the Tree of Life community, it is worth everything."

Other makers linked the process of crafting as offering the potential to engage in multicultural unity. "I hope you find comfort in this small gesture of support and love," wrote a crafter from Tennessee. "I hope for all Americans to come together and stand united" (letter 027). And a contributor from Illinois wrote:

> Elie Wiesel said 'The opposite of love is not hate, it's indifference.' My wish is that these hearts will show the [J]ewish community we stand with them, regardless of different religious backgrounds, and we will not be silent when love demands action.
>
> *(letter 031)*

A crafter from New York wrote:

> As a teacher I taught 'The Diary of Anne Frank' and The Holocaust. I often wondered how I would react to the hate and persecution of those at that time. I never thought I would find out, but now I know I cannot let hate win. Please accept these stars and hearts as a symbol of my solidarity and resistance.
>
> *(letter 045)*

And a maker from Michigan acknowledged that "Although I am not Jewish, I feel that it is vitally important that we all stand together in times like these" (letter 070).

Lastly, crafters acknowledged that the crafting process offered pathways to personal healing that they found soothing. According to a contributor from Pennsylvania,

> This project of kindness helped me work through some of my feelings of sadness and anger. By taking scissor to paper, glue to poster board, and tape to ribbon to create my own tokens of love, I felt part of a community that cared.
>
> *(letter 041)*

According to a New York crafter:

> It has been so healing for me to use my hands in these small tasks–to have the crochet to look forward to each evening. It is wonderful to know that these small, tangible lists of love are heading off where others who are hurting can see them and know how much more love there is than hate.
>
> *(letter 017)*

And according to another crafter: "Although this group was created for a very sad reason, it has brought the best out in crafters. We are able to use our skills to provide comfort + compassion" (letter 055). And lastly, a maker from Minnesota noted: "Knitting has been very therapeutic for me, so when I learned about this, I knew I had to participate" (letter 043). This theme demonstrates that the core reasons why people chose to participate in Jewish Hearts for Pittsburgh include: the opportunity to do something, to move toward action with a positive outcome, in the wake of fatal violence; to engage in an act of multicultural positivity; and to find solace in the process of making.

In 19 letters, Jewish Hearts crafters expressed their intimate connections to the Pittsburgh neighborhood, Squirrel Hill, which was affected by gun violence at the synagogue shooting, or in some instances, crafters expressed a connection to other sites of violence. For instance, a crafter from Parkland, Florida, which was the site of a high-school shooting where the gunman killed 17 students in February 2018, wrote: "We knew two of the Parkland victims personally. Our hearts are with Parkland and Pittsburgh" (letter 012). Other crafters wrote about family and personal connections to the Squirrel Hill neighborhood and commented on how their own ethnic backgrounds facilitated these connections. For instance, one crafter listed her family members who were born in Squirrel Hill, along with the schools and programs they attended there. She then reflected:

> I feel a close connection to Pittsburgh for these reasons; but these are not the only ones. As one thread in the large tapestry of Judaism, I feel that in spite of our wide variety of observances and viewpoints, we are all one family, 'MISHPACHAH'.
>
> *(letter 015)*

Another crafter said she felt connected to the Jewish Hearts for Pittsburgh group because her sons have paternal Jewish heritage. "Their great-grandfather was a Polish Jew who survived a concentration camp and afterwards moved to Israel," she wrote (letter 048). And yet another crafter said that she used to live a few blocks from the Tree of Life synagogue, and her children attended nearby schools there. She added: "Although we are not Jewish, my children and I had many close Jewish friends and we all respected and enjoyed the Jewish culture of Squirrel Hill" (letter 069). This theme demonstrates that for some participants in the

Jewish Hearts for Pittsburgh project, a connection to gun violence, or the neighborhood affected by a mass shooting, played an important role in their decision to craft for this cause.

Handcraft, the hierarchy of needs, and collective memory

The two themes threaded through the crafters' letters reveal deeply personal and intrinsic motivations for participation, as they ultimately turned to yarn as a tool for meaning-making in the wake of the Tree of Life mass shooting. Since the letters offer a snapshot of craft motivation, it is helpful to situate the reasons why people craft in response to (gun) violence within psychologist Abraham Maslow's "hierarchy of needs." Maslow posited that within this pyramid depicting the wants and needs of human behavior and curiosity, the foundational layers of the pyramid, including physiological and safety needs, must be met before people can express the "higher-level" wants and needs of human experience, including love and belonging, esteem, and self-actualization (Gawel 1996). It is worth noting that a number of the sentiments expressed in this body of letters relate to the midlevel of the pyramid, or "love and belonging." This indicates that the act of crafting in the wake of violence should not be dismissed as an act of leisure far removed from the emotional site of violence. The act of giving, or wrapping, affected individuals in tokens of love and warmth can be central to the human experience. We saw this in the instance of Jewish Hearts for Pittsburgh participants (including a mother and her two teenaged daughters), who were displaced from their family home during the November 2018 California wildfires. While finding safety in a hotel room, according to their letter, they learned that

> 34 homes within our community were burned to the ground. While in the hotel, as we listened to the news and stayed tuned to the Twitter feeds and NextDoor app to gather information about our community, we continued crafting Jewish stars as our way of reaching out to others, showing our care and concern.
>
> *(letter 087)*

This anecdote demonstrates that even when a family was faced with a threat to its most foundational human needs of physiological well-being and safety, they turned to craft to bring them toward the third brick in Maslow's pyramid: love and belonging. Indeed, the mother wrote in her letter, "Among the items we packed were the yarn and hooks to continue creating stars for the Squirrel Hill community" (letter 087). This family, in the midst of a personal tragedy, chose craft as a mechanism to express their concern and love for members of another community dealing with their own grief.

When all letter writers shared their stories and motivations or participation, which often took the form of reflecting on family, friends, neighborhoods, and important life events that they connected to their craft action, they expressed "personal memory claims," which, according to social anthropologist Paul Connerton, is the act of drawing upon their own unique history. Included in the letters may also be instances of "cognitive memory claims," which is remembering a fact or an anecdote (Connerton 1989, 22). Yet Connerton, and his predecessor sociologist Maurice Halbwachs, argued that memory is ultimately a cultural enterprise, which is understood through a relational framework; that is, people acquire their memories through their interactions with family and close associates within tightknit networks, often centering on community groups, educational settings, and religious institutions. According to Connerton: "we all come to know each other by asking for accounts, by giving accounts, by believing or disbelieving stories about each other's past and identities" (21). Halbwachs took the collective framing of memory a step further, by arguing that all memory—even in basic instances of cognitive recall—is relational, since even if people are recalling a private moment involving themselves alone, their thoughts at that memorable moment are derived not from a vacuum but from a specific sociocultural context. Wrote Halbwachs:

> But individual memory is nevertheless a part or an aspect of group memory, since each impression and each fact, even if it apparently concerns a particular person exclusively, leaves a lasting memory only to the extent that one has thought it over—to the extent that it is connected with the thoughts that come to us from the social milieu. One cannot in fact think about the events of one's past without discoursing on them. But to discourse upon something means to connect within a single system of ideas our opinions as well as those of our circle. It means to perceive in what happens to us a particular application of facts concerning which social thought reminds us at every moment of the meaning and impact these facts have for it. In this way, the framework of collective memory confines and binds our most intimate remembrances to each other.
>
> *(1992, 53)*

The Jewish Hearts for Pittsburgh letters offer, then, a testament to the confluence of craft and memory through the body of a collective. The act of making can be both a solitary and a social process and enterprise, but it is critical to situate craft as a collective act that reaches across time into the past, and acts as a bridge to the future. Most obviously the time-craft mechanism is at play through the passage of skills from an older craftsperson to a younger one, or through the gifting of a material good that is worn, kept, displayed, and passed down over a number of years. But in less obvious yet pressing ways, the process of crafting and making is reflective, contemplative, and relational, as these letters indicate. To engage in craft is to reflect on one's relationships; to take trips down memory's lane; to imagine more peaceful, aspirational futures; to engage in self-soothing behavior; to think fondly, and sometimes sadly, of family and friends, present, and passed (or past). Crafting in the wake of violence is reflective and collective, and tied intimately to the memories of the maker; it offers the pathway to intrinsic healing with the hope for extrinsic benefit. To think of craft as a solitary act is akin to thinking of memory as an individual receptacle divorced from social standing. Therefore, while crafting in the aftermath of gun violence may involve "self-insertion," it would be disparaging, too simplistic, and even dehumanizing to degrade the process of crafting as "self-serving" full stop. It is a collective act that is foundational to a genuine, human need for connection, reflection, doing, making, communing, and sharing. The goal, of course, is to do so sensitively and with the well-being of the intended recipients in mind.

A template for craft activism campaigns and mass shootings

The inflow of well-meaning material objects to a site following a mass shooting can be burdensome to the community. It requires personnel to oversee the transportation, storage, and delivery of the goods, which diverts people power from otherwise helping and aiding survivors and the affected community. For instance, in the wake of the December 2012 shooting deaths of 20 students and 6 school teachers at Sandy Hook Elementary School in Newtown, the Connecticut community received, among other things, 65,000 teddy bears, which became the responsibility of one town employee, the town's tax assessor, to manage. Additionally, a local "Congregational church had 20-by-25-feet Sunday School rooms filled from floor-to-ceiling with teddy bears and toys. The post office had to shut down its facility to process the letters it received by the thousands" (Kix 2015). It is clear that a craft campaign, borne out of love and compassion, should not impose a management burden on a town afflicted by gun violence in an acute attack. With that in mind, I would like to put forth a blueprint of suggestions for people who seek to engage in a craft intervention following a shooting. This list is not exhaustive, but can be referenced as a jumping-off point, a barebones manual for crafting after violence:

1. Convene a group of people through social media platforms and "analog" networks by posting about one's craft interventionist intentions.
2. Come up with a name and a handcraft pattern or a theme that can be conveyed through handcraft. Be sensitive to colors or motifs that should be excluded.
3. Select a point-person to receive the handcraft objects and establish a deadline by when people should mail them. Consider renting a PO Box.
4. It is important for members of the stricken community to be and feel involved, so that the craft intervention is not merely being done on their behalf, but so they too can engage in the positive effects of community crafting if they choose.
5. It should be left to the discretion of the on-the-ground organizers (local point people and their discretion) whether to let the targeted institution/site that was a victim of the shooting know about the installation in advance.

6   A note about installation day and private property. It is illegal to hang material on private property without the permission of the property owner. Even hanging objects on what may be considered public property (such as trees, bridges, fire hydrants, railings, and signs) is not legal. Therefore, proceed at your own risk and after doing your own research. We found that with Jewish Hearts for Pittsburgh, business owners welcomed "yarn volunteers" hanging the Jewish Hearts outside and inside their businesses. Often times, well-intentioned acts of community and craft are well received, so do not be shy!
7   Wherever possible, be collaborative and community-facing.

The ethics of a craft response to violence

At its best, craft as a response to violence—and in particular high-profile mass shootings—exists in concert with other concurrent acts of activism occurring during the crisis, but the Pittsburgh case offered a unique opportunity for crafters to connect their own histories, recollections, and experiences with the afflicted space through embodied practice. In such a process, craft as action becomes memory-making and memory-tapping in practice. Memory is understood as a collective experience, as revealed through the letters' themes. Craft becomes a mechanism to connect past with present—and even future as people express hope for peace and change. Therefore, it may be helpful to shift our thinking about craft in response to violence not as a tool for action (which it is) but also as part of a craft-memory continuum at the intersection of collective memory and action.

In Carolyn Nordstrom's book *A Different Kind of War Story*, the author, an anthropologist, offered a useful thesis for the Jewish Hearts for Pittsburgh craft campaign, even though her scholarship focused on creatively rebuilding an utterly devastated society in war-torn Mozambique. With the destruction of nearly all social, health, educational, and governmental systems, and one million killed (most civilians), Nordstrom found people guiding themselves according to "a strong code of ethics." And what she wrote next has direct application to the Jewish Hearts, as expressed in the 113 letters analyzed in this chapter: "It is a profound ethics; it is an ethics intricately linked with the constitution of self and world when both are under attack" (1997, 13). While there may be little comparable between the mass shooting in Pittsburgh and the Mozambican Civil War, Nordstrom's expression of moral principles guiding a person's behavior has strong ties to this craft-activist campaign. People are moved to action in a manner that is comfortable, personal, and resonant with them. In short, they are crafting the world they wish to see: one guided by love, compassion, and support for people of all backgrounds in which a social fabric is whole, even if the seams are visible but mended with care. In Nordstrom's words, "It is not the space of death, but the will to create, that is utmost. And that will to create, not to destroy, is what most people in warzones consider fundamental to the human condition" (15).

Acknowledgments

I would like to thank Rochester Institute of Technology graduate Felicia Swartzenberg for transposing the 113 letters that the *Jewish Hearts for Pittsburgh* received, and the College of Liberal Arts at RIT that funded a Faculty Research Fund award to hire Felicia, who graduated in 2019 with a double major in journalism and museum studies.

References

Achenbach, Joel. 2018. "A Conspiracy Theory about George Soros and a Migrant Caravan Inspired Horror." *Washington Post*, October 28, 2018. https://www.washingtonpost.com/national/a-conspiracy-theory-about-george-soros-and-a-migrant-caravan-inspired-horror/2018/10/28/52df587e-dae6-11e8-b732-3c72cbf131f2_story.html.

Associated Press. 2019. "Death Toll from Christchurch Mosque Grows to 51 After Turkish Man Dies." May 3, 2019. https://www.nbcnews.com/news/world/death-toll-christchurch-mosque-attacks-grows-51-after-turkish-man-n1001476.

BBC. 2018. "Pittsburgh Shooting: White House Denies Trump Rhetoric to Blame." October 30, 2018. https://www.bbc.com/news/world-us-canada-46025867.

Black, Anthea, and Nicole Burisch. 2011. "Craft Hard Die Free: Radical Curatorial Strategies for Craftivism." In *Extra/Ordinary*, edited by Maria Buszek, 204–221. Durham, NC: Duke University Press.

Bowman, Donna. 2016. "Race and Responses to Violence in Prayer Shawl Ministries." *Open Theology* 2 (1): 924–937. https://doi.org/10.1515/opth-2016-0070.

Bratich, Jack Z., and Heidi M. Brush. 2011. "Fabricating Activism: Craft-Work, Popular Culture, Gender." *Utopian Studies* 22 (2): 233–258. https://www.muse.jhu.edu/article/451893.

Bryan-Wilson, Julia. 2010. *The Politics of Craft: A Roundtable*. In *The Craft Reader*, edited by G. Adamson, 620–628. London: Bloomsbury.

———. 2017. *Fray: Art and Textile Politics*. Chicago: University of Chicago Press.

Burke, Daniel. 2018. "Pittsburgh Rabbi Told Trump That Hate Speech Led to Synagogue Shooting." *CNN*, November 4, 2018. https://www.cnn.com/2018/11/03/us/pittsburgh-shooting-first-shabbat/index.html.

Buszek, Maria, ed. 2011. *Extra/Ordinary*. Durham, NC: Duke University Press.

Butler, Judith. 2004. *Precarious Life: The Powers of Mourning and Violence*. London: Verso.

Chansky, Ricia A. 2010. "A Stitch in Time: Third-wave Feminist Reclamation of Needled Imagery." *Journal of Popular Culture* 43 (4): 681–700. https://doi.org/10.1111/j.1540-5931.2010.00765.x.

Close, Samantha. 2018. "Knitting Activism, Knitting Gender, Knitting Race." *International Journal of Communication* 12 (2018): 867–889. https://ijoc.org/index.php/ijoc/article/view/6122/2273.

Coaston, Jane. 2019. "Trump's New Defense of His Charlottesville Comments Is Incredibly False." *Vox*, April 26, 2019. https://www.vox.com/2019/4/26/18517980/trump-unite-the-right-racism-defense-charlottesville.

Connerton, Paul. 1989. *How Societies Remember*. Cambridge: Cambridge University Press.

Corbett, Sarah. 2019. "How to Be a Craftivist: The Art of Gentle Protest and the Case of the 'Living Wage' for One of the Largest Retail Companies in the United Kingdom." In *Crafting Dissent: Handicraft as Protest from the American Revolution to the Pussyhats*, edited by Hinda Mandell, 227–232. New York: Rowman & Littlefield.

Croft, Jay, and Saeed Ahmed. 2018. "The Pittsburgh Synagogue Shooting Is Believed to Be the Deadliest Attack on Jews in American History, ADL Says." *CNN*, October 28, 2018. https://www.cnn.com/2018/10/27/us/jewish-hate-crimes-fbi/index.html.

Gauntlett, David. 2011. *Making Is Connecting: The Social Meaning of Creativity from DIY and Knitting to YouTube and Web 2.0.* London: Polity Press.

Gawel, Joseph E. 1996. "Herzberg's Theory of Motivation and Maslow's Hierarchy of Needs." *Practical Assessment, Research & Evaluation* 5 (11). https://scholarworks.umass.edu/cgi/viewcontent.cgi?article=1066&context=pare.

Gökarıksel, Banu, and Sara Smith. 2017. "Intersectional Feminism beyond U.S. Flag Hijab and Pussy Hats in Trump's America." *Gender, Place & Culture* 24 (5): 628–644. https://doi.org/10.1080/0966369X.2017.1343284.

Greer, Betsy. n.d.a. "Craftivism Manifesto." Accessed June 4, 2019. http://craftivism.com.

———. n.d.b. "What Is Craftivism, Anyway?" Accessed June 4, 2019. http://craftivism.com/what-is-craftivism-anyway.

Haaretz. 2016. "Trump's Last Campaign Ad 'Has Anti-Semitic Overtones.'" November 6, 2016. https://www.haaretz.com/world-news/trump-s-last-campaign-ad-has-anti-semitic-overtones-1.5457546.

Halbwachs, Maurice. 1992. *On Collective Memory.* Chicago: University of Chicago Press.

Hunter, Clare. 2019. *Threads of Life: History of the World through the Eye of the Needle.* New York: Abrams Press.

Jaffe, Ina. 2018. "Authorities Describe 'Confusion and Chaos' at Borderline Bar Shooting in California." *NPR*, November 28, 2018. https://www.npr.org/2018/11/28/671353612/no-motive-yet-found-for-mass-shooting-at-borderline-bar-and-grill.

Jewish Hearts for Pittsburgh letter archive. Rochester, New York, in the possession of the author.

Johnson, Andrew, and R. Stickney. 2019. "1 Dead, 3 Injured at Synagogue Shooting in Poway, Deputies Detain Suspect." *NBC SanDiego.com*, April 27, 2019. https://www.nbcsandiego.com/news/local/poway-synagogue-shooting-chabad-way-san-diego-sherrifs-department-509162631.html.

Kirchick, James. 2018. "How Much Blame Does Trump Truly Bear for the Pittsburgh Synagogue Shooting?" *Washington Post*, November 21, 2018. https://www.washingtonpost.com/opinions/how-much-blame-does-trump-truly-bear-for-the-pittsburgh-synagogue-shooting/2018/11/19/f69ef8f0-e9f2-11e8-bbdb-72fdbf9d4fed_story.html.

Kix, Paul. 2015. "65,000 Teddy Bears for Newtown, and One Man to Sort the World's Grief." *TheTrace.com*, December 13, 2015. https://www.thetrace.org/2015/12/sandy-hook-shooting-donations/.

Law, Tara. 2019. "Here We Are Again. Juvenile Female, Adult Male in Custody after Shooting at K-12 School in Denver Suburb." *Time*, May 8, 2019. http://time.com/5585312/school-shooting-colorado-stem/.

Levin, Bess. 2018. "Trump: 'A Lot of People Say' George Soros Is Funding the Migrant Caravan." *Vanity Fair*, October 31, 2018. https://www.vanityfair.com/news/2018/10/donald-trump-george-soros-caravan.

Mandell, Hinda, ed. 2019. *Crafting Dissent: Handicraft as Protest from the American Revolution to the Pussyhats.* New York: Rowman & Littlefield.

McKee, Alan. 2003. *Textual Analysis: A Beginner's Guide.* London: Sage Publications.

Minahan, Stella, and Julie Wolfram Cox. 2007. "Stitch'nBitch: Cyberfeminism, a Third Place and the New Materiality." *Journal of Material Culture* 12 (1): 5–21. https://doi.org/10.1177/1359183507074559.

Nelson, Louis. 2016. "Trump's Campaign Disavows David Duke's Robocall." *Politico*, August 29, 2016. https://www.politico.com/story/2016/08/david-duke-trump-robocall-227510.

Nordstrom, Carolyn. 1997. *A Different Kind of War Story*. Philadelphia: University of Pennsylvania Press.

Parker, Rozsika. 2010. *The Subversive Stitch: Embroidery and the Making of the Feminine*. London; New York: I.B. Tauris.

Pitz, Marylynne. 2018. "Crafters Create Jewish Hearts for Pittsburgh and More Than 40 Volunteers Hang Them in the City." *Pittsburgh Post-Gazette*, November 17, 2018. https://www.post-gazette.com/news/faith-religion/2018/11/17/Jewish-Stars-of-David-Tree-of-Life-Pittsburgh-volunteers-knit-crochet-twelve-countries-crafts-facebook/stories/201811170055.

Ratto, Matt, and Megan Boler, eds. 2014. *DIY Citizenship: Critical Making and Social Media*. Cambridge, MA: MIT Press.

Satter, Raphael. 2018. "Mail Bomb Suspect Cesar Sayoc Obsessed with George Soros, Conspiracy Theories." *Washington Times*, October 28, 2018. https://www.washingtontimes.com/news/2018/oct/28/cesar-sayoc-obsessed-george-soros-conspiracy-theor/.

Sontag, Susan. 2003. *Regarding the Pain of Others*. New York: Farrar, Straus & Giroux.

"Stochastic Terrorism." 2011. January 26, 2011. http://stochasticterrorism.blogspot.com/.

Turkewitz, Julie, and Kevin Roose. 2018. "Who Is Robert Bowers, the Suspect in the Pittsburgh Synagogue Shooting?" *New York Times*, October 27, 2018. https://www.nytimes.com/2018/10/27/us/robert-bowers-pittsburgh-synagogue-shooter.html.

9
REFRAMING THE US-MEXICO BORDER CRISIS

Prosecutorial and parental rhetoric in the Kamala Harris presidential campaign

Joshua D. Martin

Since the 1980s, the US-Mexico border and immigration matters have loomed large in political discourse, shaping the ways in which politicians framed national security and identity. Such preoccupations also presented presidential hopefuls with a basic litmus test in their bid to occupy the nation's highest elected office. Embarking upon his 2016 presidential campaign, Donald Trump knew this political truism well. He invoked the trope of a perilous southern border for his meditation on the US' allegedly imperiled exceptionalism, harnessing an abrasive rhetoric to extol what he framed as the country's former greatness. Although the border was a perpetual obsession for Trump and his loyalists during his presidency, we might ask how other political actors have represented the area in order to reclaim a pluralistic vision of national belonging. How could they contest a political culture that sought to normalize the abjection of immigrants and non-white communities by defining them as threats to civil society and as an illegitimate presence? Given the prominence of both immigration and the border in US national discourse, the analysis of political rhetoric acquires increased importance. As political theory scholar James Martin asserted, "rhetoric helps to reassemble words and meanings in order for the world to make sense again," especially since "politics itself *is* the ongoing practice of reassembling self and world" (2014, 10; italics in the original).

Inasmuch as the border trope allows political actors to engage with policies on security, it likewise informs a broader vision of the national community, often inviting communality or animus depending upon the rhetorical devices used to frame immigration and border-related phenomena. In her bid to become the 2020 Democratic presidential candidate (prior to her election as vice president), California Senator Kamala Harris employed rhetoric as a creative resource to combat social injustices stemming from the Trump administration and to dignify Latino immigrants, whose abjection had long buttressed Trump's insular vision

DOI: 10.4324/9781003034810-9

of national belonging. Through an intersectional lens, combining scholarship on political rhetoric and political culture, the present project employs a critical discourse analysis concerning representations of the US-Mexico border and Trump's family separation policy in Harris's presidential campaign, which was announced on January 21, 2019, and suspended nearly 11 months later on December 3. Specifically, this chapter analyzes how Harris's use of prosecutorial and parental language inverted a crisis narrative endemic to Trump's political brand, thereby situating the Trump administration itself, rather than border-crossing immigrants, as a threat to the body-politic.

Crises and moral contours: the US-Mexico border in political rhetoric

Drawing largely on journalist Naomi Klein's (2007, 2017) analyses of crisis narratives and cognitive linguist George Lakoff's (2009, 2014, 2016) scholarship on the moral hierarchies that permeate political speech, this project analyzes the slogan, first campaign speech, and select tweets by Senator Harris in the context of her presidential campaign, contrasting those with select examples of Trump's border rhetoric and border-related policies. This chapter argues the following points. Casting the US-Mexico border as a moral metric, Harris enlisted parental and prosecutorial rhetoric within a crisis framework that allowed her to deconstruct a value hierarchy and law-and-order (citizen vs. alien) discourse critical to Trump's political brand. Whereas Trump continued to portray the United States as threatened by Latino immigrants in economic, cultural, and public safety terms, Harris reversed this script and its attendant threats altogether by framing the Trump administration as a crisis writ large. Whereas Trump advanced a racialized nativism, fostered by a sense of aggrieved patriarchy and nostalgia for an ephemeral greatness, Harris characterized the administration's border and immigration policies as a paragon of moral bankruptcy and an inversion of human rights and cultural pluralism, thus imperiling both the US' moral authority and national identity.

This framework operated as a springboard toward a necessary transformation that Harris, by her own account, was uniquely positioned to spearhead not only as a former prosecutor, foremost, but also as a woman of color and the child of two immigrants. Indeed, Harris regularly reminded her audiences, as she did at her first presidential campaign rally, that the United States was "at an inflection point in the history of our nation" (2019). In this context, she invoked an imaginary of the border that was as much temporal as it was cultural, compelling listeners to reach toward a horizon of anticipative change—unmoored by Trump's nativist sympathies and rhetorical predilections for division and doom. Important questions emerge: if our conceptual thinking is "fundamentally metaphorical in nature" (Lakoff and Johnson 1980, 3), why is border language so effective in political rhetoric, and how does it shape competing representations of the body-politic? Moreover, how did Trump configure the border as a political tool, and how might parental and prosecutorial rhetoric, as in the case of the Harris campaign, be used to counter misrepresentations of the border and immigrants as part of a broader strategy to reclaim the trajectory of US political culture?

In the United States, borders have long operated as inveterate staples in political discourse, constituting what cultural studies scholar D. Robert DeChaine identifies as "a public *doxa* [a taken for granted idea] that informs cultural values, shapes public attitudes, and prescribes individual and collective actions" (2012, 2). In political rhetoric, the metaphorical dimensions are especially significant. Understood in both geopolitical and cultural terms, borders often invoke binaries that pigeonhole individuals into easily digestible oppositional groups, each evoking connotations that play into audiences' tacit knowledge and biases regarding policies (diplomacy vs. hawkishness, novelty vs. convention) and persons (alien vs. citizen, liberal vs. conservative, male vs. female). Just as "borders are discursively defined and constructed by ever-changing rhetorics" (Ono 2012, 23), they are likewise imbued with power relations that intersect with questions of civic duty and identity (DeChaine 2012, 1; Lucaites 2012, 229). The geopolitical border in particular provides a symbolic terrain for ruminations on national identity and belonging, while ultimately serving as a potent backdrop for political mobilization.

Popularized by Ronald Reagan, the framework of tying border defense to the nation's livelihood has acquired a type of sacrality. As such, presidential candidates must often navigate discussions of the border and immigration within the framework of national security. In its most antagonistic variants, candidates' rhetoric has tended to blame select actors (immigrants and refugees, for example) instead of structures and historical processes (neoliberalization and asymmetrical trade pacts) that have been among the more likely culprits for widespread anxiety and alienation. Oftentimes, too, the depiction of the border in political rhetoric has been linked to an invitation to "an ethnonationalist form of civic identity" (DeChaine 2012, 8), as in the case of Trump's "wall" and his hostile anti-immigrant agenda. In these instances, the political ends were especially fruitful for Trump, since, for the purposes of identity construction and solidarity, "[b]uilding walls in minds was more important than building it from bricks" (Sonnevend 2018, 89).

The need for (b)order: crisis framing and the abjection of immigrants

Given the tendency of the US-Mexico border to be framed as "the greatest source of *insecurity* in the national imaginary" (Chávez 2012, 49; italics in the original), a crisis narrative proves especially attractive in political rhetoric. In her research on crisis framing in political culture, Klein argued that powerful actors tend to exploit shocking events in order to advance political and socioeconomic agendas, a strategic operation she termed "disaster capitalism," a practice that might otherwise provoke widespread opposition (2007, 6–7). The approach also proves politically expedient for frameworks that create the specter of chaos, including Trump's representation of the border, since "a great many people," according to Klein, "become vulnerable to authority figures telling us to fear one another" (2017, 7). Indeed, Trump exploited the crisis framework well in his campaign and presidency. His comments regarding the border and immigration substituted nativism for nuance, bolstering a vision of the body-politic that was insular and often hostile to non-white nonnationals in light of the impending danger that this group allegedly posed.

On at least one occasion, for example, he located undocumented immigrants outside the realm of "human," homogenizing them as "animals" and as gang criminals (Korte and Gomez 2018). In his January 8, 2019, national address from the Oval Office, Trump, contrary to fact, insisted that immigrants are more prone to crime and that his proposed wall would curb the entry of illegal drugs (Kight 2019). He has also sympathized with the threat of violence against immigrants. At a May 8, 2019, rally in Florida, when an audience member suggested that officials shoot border-crossing immigrants, Trump laughed at the recommendation along with his audience, who also offered applause (Diamond 2019). His policy instincts proved even more heinous, prioritizing human turmoil such that violence against immigrants becomes a type of perverse spectacle. In March 2019, for example, Trump reportedly sought to curtail undocumented immigration by authorizing soldiers to shoot immigrants in the legs, and he privately touted the possibility of constructing an electrified border wall topped with spikes and flanked by an alligator or snake-infested moat (Shear and Davis 2019). In Trump's border rhetoric, crises emerged exclusively south of the border and because of the activities of non-white non-nationals.

Kamala Harris, as we shall see, reversed the script altogether and for good reason. As linguists and critical discourse scholars Isabela and Norman Fairclough argue,

> getting people to accept a particular narrative of the crisis, to see it in a certain way, is generally a political concern precisely because it gives people *a reason* for favouring or accepting certain lines of action and policies rather than others.
>
> *(2012, 4; italics in the original)*

Indeed, Trump's border rhetoric represented the United States as beleaguered by globalization, bureaucratic elitism, and unchecked immigration, all of which threatened not only cultural intelligibility (hence the necessarily vague call to reinstate greatness), but also national sovereignty. Consequently, the border wall was part of his "America First" slogan and strategy, along with reducing the US' international commitments and otherwise advancing nationalism (Oprysko and Kumar 2019). Given the pragmatic and moralistic dimensions that underlie all political rhetoric (Lakoff 2009, 43), language about the border proves advantageous due in part to the moral hierarchies that such language imparts to the voting public (Johnson 2012, 35). Accordingly, invoked crises (legitimate or feigned) buttress the moral contours of candidates' rhetoric since they enjoy a "rationalizing function" (Fairclough and Fairclough 2012, 2–3), informing decisions and necessitating investments (emotional or otherwise) from audience members while providing politicians a rich base from which to construct narratives that demand urgent action.

When Trump asserted the need for a physical wall to abate alleged criminals, he trafficked in rhetoric that "provide[s] symbolic grist for normalizing a view of boundary-making as a necessary and natural function of the state" (DeChaine 2012, 8). When he profiled Mexican immigrants as thieves and murderers, as he did during a 2015 rally in Phoenix, Arizona (Schreckinger 2015), he feigned a crisis that transferred the porosity of the geopolitical border onto audience members' immediate surroundings, thus creating the specter of impending danger and cultural erosion (Aguirre Jr. and Simmer 2008–09, 103–104). Accordingly, the ideal body-politic that emerged from Trump's language and policies was necessarily regressive, hostile to cultural pluralism and to the increasing participation of minorities in the language and look of the republic's present and future. Through parental and prosecutorial rhetoric, Harris framed the Trump administration as a crisis writ large that endangered the nation's value hierarchy, extending that representation to US identity as she criticized, too, the metaphorical borders Trump summoned between select groups. In order to better assess the efficacy of Harris's rhetorical strategies, let us first consider a brief history of Trump's anti-immigrant rhetoric and some of the policies that have ensued.

Violence as a virtue: immigration policies and the crisis framework

In the United States, conservative politicians have typically lauded the heteronormative family unit and its (varyingly patriarchal) conventions as a bedrock from which they develop social and political moral codes (Lakoff 2014, 126–128), including the promotion of "Strict Father morality," self-discipline, and responsibility, among other values (Lakoff 2016, 163). In the final year of Trump's presidency, he presented several contrasts to familial and political norms upheld by most modern Republican presidents and presidential candidates. At various points before his election, Trump boasted about sexually assaulting women, mocked a reporter with a disability, and openly lauded interpersonal violence and war crimes; moreover, as president, he showed hesitance in condemning white supremacists, openly engaged in sexist and racist remarks, and praised foreign authoritarian leaders whose policies have proven hostile to the US' national security interests, among other questionable behaviors. How, then, were these contradictions allowed to persist?

Writer Matthew Schmitz opined that as opposed to red (conservative) or blue (liberal) values, Trump embodied purple values, evoking "a real if imperfect model of family values" whereby his obvious transgressions conferred a more realistic caliber to his populist and paternal bravado. In regard to the power of metaphor and framing, Lakoff and Johnson remind us that "the people who get to impose their metaphors on the culture get to define what we consider to be true" (1980, 160). Accordingly, we should attend to how Trump extended the family metaphor to the nation itself—a collective that he consistently represented in racialized and insular terms within his own crisis framework that demanded a strongman figure. The abjection of immigrants was crucial to this process. For example, Trump began his unlikely 2016 bid for president from within the Trump Tower in Manhattan, prioritizing nativism in his first official campaign speech by stereotyping Mexican immigrants as criminals and rapists. Though Trump's comments provoked ire and outrage across the political spectrum, his popularity increased throughout the Republican nominating process, with many voters commending his unconventional and unapologetic brashness. The promise to construct a physical wall between the United States and Mexico emerged as an effective rallying point for Trump's populist campaign, a plan he often invoked as part-and-parcel of his strategy to "make America great again." Additionally, Trump recycled old, factually inaccurate stereotypes about Latino immigrants, claiming that they steal American jobs, weaken social programs, evade taxes, and are more likely to commit crimes. At the 2016 Republican National Convention, Trump further consolidated his paternal appeal within this crisis framework by configuring himself as a salvific figure, asserting that he alone could remedy the nation's problems.

As president, Trump's executive policies on the border largely mirrored his xenophobic rhetoric. After facing numerous setbacks in his bid to construct his promised wall, Trump officially declared a national emergency in February 2019, misrepresenting the border as a nexus of crime and lawlessness and incorrectly stating that the majority of illegal drugs passed through unsecured areas along the southern border. In fact, John F. Kelly, Trump's former Secretary of Homeland Security, bemoaned the wall as a waste of money that would not deter illicit drugs given their demand in the United States (O'Keefe 2018). Data affirmed that roughly 90 percent of illicit drugs were transferred through private vehicles at legal ports of entry where fencing already existed (Rodgers and Bailey 2019). Nonetheless, the national emergency declaration was tactically advantageous, as the move allowed Trump to reallocate military funding from US-led security projects at home and abroad. But ironically, and as detractors highlighted, it created strong potential for security risks by weakening military commitments in those regions where real crises could emerge (Scholtes, Ferris, and Feldscher 2019). Perhaps the most shocking attempt to curb undocumented immigration came in the form of Trump's unprecedented "zero tolerance" border policy, first secretly tested in 2017 and announced as official policy nearly a year later in the spring of 2018.

Disturbing reporting emerged, highlighting the structural and psychological violence that the measure imposed. Specifically, the policy required authorities to forcibly separate undocumented children from their parents, with the former oftentimes confined to fenced enclosures with poor sanitation. Infants and toddlers were often housed hundreds or even thousands of miles away from their parents, and the Trump administration took additional steps to ensure that any relatives already in the United States would be prohibited from caring for the undocumented youth (Jordan 2019a). No plan for family reunification informed this directive, and attempts at reunification, following a June 2018 federal court order, faced numerous obstacles due in part to inadequate record keeping. Trump officially rescinded the policy on June 20, 2018, but even so, more than 900 additional children were removed from their parents over the course of the following year (Jordan 2019b). By July 2019, it was estimated that at least 3,000 children had been separated from their families, though the exact number remained unknown, and data on family reunification was equally nebulous (Jordan 2019a). By May 2019, at least seven children had died in immigration custody under Trump's policy, whereas the number in the preceding decade was zero (Acevedo 2019).

The family separation policy provoked widespread condemnation among citizens, human rights activists, and medical professionals alike. Both the American Psychiatric Association (APA) and the President of the American Academy of Pediatrics (AAP) strongly opposed the measure, respectively, citing the "lifelong trauma" (Stewart 2018) and "irreparable harm" (Kraft 2018) that the policy would cause for the children in question. While many have considered such actions egregious and appalling, we should recall Trump's own crisis framework in order to understand how he and like-minded voters might justify such actions. Even though the vast majority of border-crossers were political refugees fleeing violence, crucial facts such as these did not figure into the Trump border script. In this mythology, we recall, the United States remains besieged by dangerous nonnationals, thus inviting endeavors that, however harsh and unforgiving, nonetheless work toward an allegedly higher and purer end—the preservation and strengthening of the national family, whose culture, identity, and economic security face possible destruction by criminal foreigners. To contest these representations, Kamala Harris prioritized parental and prosecutorial language in her language about the border, underscoring Trump's actions as transgressions of the nation's moral fabric and as affronts to a pluralistic polity.

From the crucible of California: Kamala Harris for the people

Before she took the stage on January 27, 2019, in Oakland, California, to launch her candidacy for the Democratic nomination for President of the United States, Kamala Harris had long attracted favorable attention in Democratic political circles, possessing what many acknowledged as "a background that operates as a kind of universal passport" (Wallace-Wells 2019). Born to two immigrant graduate students (Donald Harris of Jamaica and Shyamala Gopalan of India) who fell in love in California at the height of the Civil Rights movement, Harris boasted a personal narrative unlike that of any other 2020 presidential contender and one that contrasted perhaps the most remarkably with Trump's anti-immigrant nationalism. Among other important qualifiers, Harris's story emerged from the arc of her parents' respective immigrations, and she prioritized the consciousness that she cultivated from within the cultural interstices of the Indian and African-American communities (Sedensky 2019; Sullivan 2019). That she hails from California likewise provided several advantages in the context of a political narrative relying in part on immigration and border tropes. As of 2019, California was home to 26 percent of all Latinos in the United States, with 39 percent of all California residents claiming Latino heritage (Krogstad and Noe-Bustamente 2019). For her own part, Harris unambiguously highlighted California as a crucible for US identity (if not a harbinger for the country's collective trajectory), lauding her native state as "a microcosm of who we are as America," as she did during her first speech on the Senate floor (2017).

Following numerous appearances on national television, with a rising reputation as a fierce Trump critic, and a recently released memoir, Harris declared her candidacy for president on January 21, 2019, via social media and an appearance on ABC's *Good Morning America*. That the announcement took place on Martin Luther King Jr. Day underscored her African-American heritage and suggested the enduring need for a like-minded fighter for truth and justice. Her campaign color scheme (yellow and red) likewise held significance, paralleling that of congresswoman Shirley Chisholm, the first African American woman elected to Congress and the first woman to seek the presidential nomination of a major US political party (O'Kane 2019). Harris gave her first campaign speech on January 27 in Oakland, California, among an estimated 20,000 attendees—a crowd size that surpassed Barack Obama's at his 2007 announcement (Beckett 2019).

Much like the rhetoric she would employ in the ensuing months, Harris's slogan ("For the People") paid homage to her training as a prosecutor while positioning her as a dogged public servant fighting for higher truths and an ever-threatened justice "for the people." The phrasing proved clever in several other ways. For one, it subsumed her career into a public service narrative with a people-centric tenor befitting of rising populism and weariness with the Washington, DC status quo. Second, rather than frame her candidacy as sympathetic to "tough on crime" policies, a specter that has haunted Democratic candidates since the end of the 1990s (Williams and Kaplan 2019), Harris instead situated herself as a firm and fearless defender of common values that ran the risk of continued erosion: democracy, justice, and truth—all necessarily abstract concepts that framed her candidacy as restorative, necessary, and long overdue in the context of the public good. Harris's framework, juxtaposed alongside the tacit knowledge of Trump's numerous legal troubles, summoned a binary that positioned Harris as an ideal candidate: unquestionably prosecutorial, arguably progressive, and ultimately pragmatic given the threats posed by the Trump administration.

Indeed, for their numerous contrasts, both politically and in regard to their personal backgrounds, the optics of a Harris-Trump confrontation were nothing if not fascinating. The dangers here were not lost on the Trump camp, with

Trump himself offering atypical, however muted, admiration for Harris's campaign rollout and crowd size (Baker and Haberman 2019). Yet, whereas Harris framed her background as advantageous, positioning herself as a pragmatic reformer who bypassed ideological borders, Trump defended his contentious actions as enduring positives, necessary to confront Washington actors, or "the swamp," in his words (Collinson 2019). Trump's rhetoric and use of border tropes, as the past examples demonstrate, antagonized immigrants as unidimensional scapegoats, using vitriol against them to consolidate a nakedly and unapologetically nationalistic political brand. Harris, for whom immigration and cultural pluralism played out as enduring and necessary positives, reversed this rhetorical framework, representing the US collective as threatened by the Trump administration's cronyism and moral vacuity—a value system both sinister and toxic that generated an ultimately existential crisis to both the US' collective moral fabric and its national identity. Just as the US-Mexico border proved critical to Trump's political branding, so too did it inform Harris's message, albeit in markedly different ways.

Speaking from the Frank Ogawa Plaza, named after the Oakland City Council member and Civil Rights leader, Harris delivered her first campaign speech on January 27, 2019. Employing language both ameliorative and tactically combative, she presented a narrative that juxtaposed her training as a prosecutor alongside a personal background that buttressed a heterogeneous vision of the United States in sharp contrast to Trump's regressive nativism. She first referenced her parents' immigrations, their "pursuit of a dream … for themselves, for me and for my sister Maya," and a community-forged worldview in which "public service is a noble cause and the fight for justice is everyone's responsibility" (2019). She employed anaphora (the repetition of certain words at the beginning of neighboring clauses) in the first-person plural, synthesizing a series of threats into an overarching crisis in regard to US identity, thus demanding bold action and emphasizing a fearless leadership that she was equipped to offer:

> We are here because we have another battle ahead. We are here knowing that we are at an inflection point in the history of our world. We are at an inflection point in in the history of our nation. We are here because the American Dream and our American democracy are under attack and on the line like never before. We are here at this moment in time because we must answer a fundamental question. Who are we? Who are we as Americans? So, let's answer that question. To the world. And each other. Right here. And right now. America, we are better than this.
>
> *(2019)*

The series of dangers and antagonists enumerated implicitly underscored the Trump administration's dubious moral and patriotic standing ("leaders who lie and bully and attack a free press and undermine our democratic institutions"), as well as economic precarity ("bankers who crashed our economy") and long-standing racial divisions ("white supremacists [who] march and murder in Charlottesville or massacre innocent worshipers at a Pittsburgh synagogue") (2019). The partitioning of threats along political, economic, and social axes allowed Harris to subsume these dangers into a narrative arc that ended in a rumination on US identity ("Who are we as Americans?") and culminated in a focus on her preparedness to lead.

Shortly thereafter, Harris appealed directly to pathos, criticizing the Trump administration's family separation policy at the border. She asserted, "When we have children in cages crying for their mothers and fathers, don't you dare call it border security, that's a human rights abuse and that's not our America" (2019). The inclusion proves important for several reasons. Trump, however indirectly, long positioned himself as a tough and effective father figure, whose instincts and initiative, in this view, were long overdue in a political climate dominated by ineffective Washington elites. Indeed, as political scientist Kelly Dittmar affirmed, "familial roles can serve to reflect the masculine power of male candidates in ways that do not easily translate to women seeking political office" (2018, 71). Here, Harris flipped the script, framing Trump's policy as a marker of moral vacuity and unimaginable cruelty—abusive in nature, rather than effective or salutary.

Regarding the physical border, too, Harris highlighted the incompetence of the incumbent. First, she invoked her prosecutorial acumen, reminding listeners that her prior public service "meant fighting transnational gangs who traffic in drugs and guns and human beings," and then contrasted her experience with the political theater of Trump's proposed border wall: "let's be clear: the President's medieval vanity project is not going to stop them" (2019). Collectively, these representations complemented a long-standing trope in Harris's career: rather than approach problems through a "tough on crime" lens, she opted for one that was smart on crime. Thus, in addition to allowing Harris to highlight the Trump administration itself as a crisis, the border also took on the quality of a moral testing ground, whereby listeners were compelled to affirm the dignity of immigrants and, therefore, the sacrality of a broader and more inclusive national family.

Immigration thus operated as a fulcrum for Harris's crisis framework. Complementing the first-person plural anaphora cited previously, Harris enlisted epistrophe (the repetition of select words in consecutive phrases) with "truth," providing a broad base from which she constructed a value hierarchy through the lens of cultural pluralism and no-nonsense leadership:

> And their response is to blame immigrants as the source of all our problems. And guys, let's understand what is happening here: People in power are trying to convince us that the villain in our American story is each other. But that is not our story. That is not who we are. That's not our America. Our United States of America is not about us versus them. It's about we the people! And in this moment, we must all speak truth about what's happening. Seek truth, speak truth, and fight for the truth.
>
> *(2019)*

One should note that Harris did not mention Trump by name at any point throughout her speech, relying instead on connotations and audience members' tacit knowledge of the historical moment, so as to underscore her vision for the future. She did, however, mention immigrants specifically, identifying their scapegoat status as a lynchpin for the Trump administration's dichotomous "us versus them" national vision. Their inclusion served another function, too. That is, she located immigrants explicitly within the national community, affirming their belonging and drawing contrasts between her audience, on the one hand, and "people in power," on the other. The resulting mix of grit and optimism positioned Harris as a candidate equipped to respond to visceral cultural schisms while offering a no-nonsense candidacy that was both curative and restorative. Rhetoric incorporating the border proved essential, both for its metaphorical implication (underscoring Harris's ability to navigate political divides and champion reform) and for the immediacy of material struggles along the geopolitical border, which likewise shaped reflections on the national family, an attendant value hierarchy, and US identity.

Similar to the examples studied previously, the conclusion of her speech stressed, again through anaphora, the need for social amelioration, doing so in the context of health, posterity, and morality. Harris (2019) asserted:

> We can achieve the dreams of our parents and grandparents. We can heal our nation. We can give our children the future they deserve. We can reclaim the American Dream for every single person in our country. We can restore America's moral leadership on this planet.

Both optimistic and tactically adversarial, Harris's speech received widespread praise, with media attention identifying her as a contender whose candidacy would likely prove formidable to her competitors. Rhetoric about the border and immigration proved essential in the ensuing months, allowing Harris to capitalize on her background and to maximize her message from the outlook of a prosecutor and self-proclaimed progressive. A similar dynamic played out in Harris's Twitter feed in the months leading up to her campaign launch. There, Harris criticized the aforementioned family separation policy in parental and prosecutorial language, framing the Trump administration, rather than border-crossers, as threats to the nation's moral standing.

Kamala Harris's border tweets

Because of its utility in immediately connecting politicians with supporters, Twitter has acquired significant power in political communication and has altered how voters access and interpret information. Given its tendency to operate as a "me-centred medium that lives through the accumulation of followers, likes and retweets" (Fuchs 2018, 211), Twitter maximized Trump's nativism and belligerence, such that his Twitter feed alternated "between self-congratulatory announcements of his achievements and bombastic attacks on those he sees as enemies" (Turner 2018, 147). In his analysis of Trump's tweets from July 18, 2016, to January 21, 2017, communication and social media scholar Christian Fuchs observed that "[i]mmigrants and refugees are among the groups that Trump most frequently mentioned negatively in the dataset" (2018, 222). Accordingly, Twitter both facilitated Trump's abjection of immigrants and endowed his mischaracterizations with an authority emblematic of presidential rhetoric. In her representations of the US-Mexico border and Trump's family separation policy, Harris sought to delegitimize his words and actions through a rhetoric that was prosecutorial and parental, dignifying Latino immigrants and casting Trump as a catalyst of chaos and cruelty.

The following section analyzes Harris's tweets beginning with her ascension to the US Senate (January 2017) until the formal suspension of her presidential campaign (December 3, 2019). The aggregation was enabled by Twitter's advanced search function with the term "border" chosen as the exclusive filter criteria. The terms selected for this analysis were chosen based on their saliency and relevancy after an extensive reading of Harris's tweets, and the subsequent findings were organized into two categories: language construed as (a) prosecutorial (see Table 9.1) and (b) parental (see Table 9.2) in nature. In the period in question, a total of 104 tweets mentioned the US-Mexico border: 19 in 2017, 56 in 2018, and 29 in 2019 (through October 29). Of those total 104 tweets, 78 were tweeted out before she announced her candidacy for the presidency (January 21, 2019) and 26 thereafter. I have characterized as "prosecutorial language," those which drew attention to human rights abuses, a humanitarian crisis, or used the words "accountable" or "lawless." I have characterized as "parental language" those tweets that referred to children, babies, infants, mothers, fathers, and (immigrant) families, or variations thereof.

Harris's tweets throughout 2017 (Trump's first year in office) underscored the dubious feasibility of his proposed wall. As such, she framed Trump's project in the context of both waste and ignorance, using terms such as expensive, stupid, terrible, unrealistic, and wasteful to highlight both the nonviability of the wall and the inefficacy of the project in terms of curbing undocumented immigration. Her initial representations called readers' attention to the damning logistics of a

TABLE 9.1 Prosecutorial Language in @KamalaHarris Border Tweets, 2017–2019

Terminology	Frequency of Mentions in 2017	Frequency of Mentions 2018	Frequency of Mentions in 2019 (through Oct. 29)
Human rights	0	16	9
Humanitarian crisis	0	0	1
Accountable	0	1	1
Lawless	0	0	1
Total per year	0	17	12

TABLE 9.2 Parental Language in @KamalaHarris Border Tweets, 2017–2019

Terminology	Frequency of Mentions in 2017	Frequency of Mentions in 2018	Frequency of Mentions in 2019 (through Oct. 29)
Child/children	3	23 (in 21 tweets)	8
Baby/babies	0	1	3
Infant	0	0	1
Mother(s)	2	2	0
Father(s)	0	5 (in 2 tweets)	5 (in 2 tweets)
Family/families	1	26 (in 19 tweets)	7 (in 8 tweets)
Total per year	6	57	24

project that worked well in political theater but would face several obstacles in funding, implementation, and efficacy. In 2018, however, her representations took on a marked shift following the revelation of Trump's family separation policy, a tone that continued throughout 2019. Consider the following examples:

> Ripping babies from their mothers' arms is not border security. And when more than 400 of those children go to sleep tonight without their parents, that's called a human rights abuse.
>
> *(August 5, 2018)*

> Our American values are under attack. Babies have been ripped from their parents at the border. A tax bill passed that benefits corporations and the top 1%, while millions of middle-class families struggle to pay the bills. We're better than this.
>
> *(February 12, 2019)*

> Trump's anti-immigrant agenda couldn't be more clear. He has separated families. Locked children in cages. Sought to spend billions on his border wall, which is nothing more than a vanity project. That is not reflective of our values and it has to end.
>
> *(June 27, 2019)*

Here, Harris's tweets reflected a moral outrage, and she used language with prosecutorial and parental tenors in ways that responded to pathos and a value hierarchy prioritizing the family unit and immigration, much as we saw in her first campaign speech. Accordingly, Harris most frequently mentioned children, families, and human rights in her 2018 and 2019 tweets, focusing attention on the brutality of the Trump administration's policy and using its impunity as a reflection of the US' imperiled moral standing under Trump.

Interestingly, while Harris's own mother was, by her own admission, the most significant driving force in her life, she mentioned the terms "father(s)" in her border tweets more frequently than she mentioned "mother(s)." On Father's Day

2018 and 2019, for example, she issued tweets that underscored the ill effects that the policy in question created for immigrant families, citing "potentially thousands of fathers who won't be spending Father's Day with their children because of the human rights abuses that are happening at our southern border" (June 17, 2018) and, one year later, calling readers' attention to "the fathers who can't be with their children because they were ripped from their sons and daughters at the border" (June 16, 2019). She made no similar tweet in the context of the border on or in regard to Mother's Day. Her decision to do so may have been strategic given that Trump often profiled Latino immigrants, usually men, as dangerous assailants who imperil the country at large, thereby summoning a moral hierarchy conducive to a commanding father presence (as Lakoff [2016, 427–430] might have suggested) and, in doing so, "supply[ing] authoritative metaphors with which audiences can easily identity" (Martin 2014, 154). In Harris's tweets, though, she delegitimized these representations, first highlighting Trump's policies as abusive and corrosive to the immigrant family unit, and then affirming the dignity of Latino men disenfranchised by cruel executive directives. Rather than appear as threatening, then, Latino immigrant men in Harris's tweets emerged primarily as virtuous and tenacious father figures and secondarily as victims of a policy that jeopardized the US' moral authority by advancing human rights abuses.

Harris's language in her border tweets evoked her professional training, highlighting her prosecutorial dexterity as a safeguard against policies that endangered immigrants and, by extension, US identity. Whereas Trump invoked crises explicitly, highlighting the nation-state as jeopardized by a porous border and pernicious nonnationals, Harris's language inverted the hierarchy of threats altogether and pinpointed entirely different crises under the arc of human rights violations, thus beseeching immediate action. If, for Trump, the United States was a violated figure in need of a strongman executive, for Harris, it was the executive himself who posed the most significant threat. Importantly, she used the term "crisis" only once (March 27, 2019), doing so alongside the important qualifier "humanitarian." By doing so, she framed immigrants as victims and avoided representations that, as critical discourse scholar Otto Santa Ana would argue, have historically tied immigrants to destructive forces (2002, 32–33). In sum, Harris's border tweets throughout her campaign largely underscored the plight of immigrant families, framing Trump's directives as transgressions of US values and undercutting the representation of Trump himself as a paternal safeguard, with prosecutorial and parental language suggesting a necessary change in leadership: from incompetency and cruelty to efficacy and inclusivity.

Crafting social justice through border rhetoric

The benefits of such rhetoric in the scope of progressive resistance and crafting social justice are several. Most notably, it reclaims the crisis narrative and the family framework, locating immigrants within the latter as opposed to the toxic centerpiece of the former. Moreover, it creates the potential for solidarity within the folds of a broader, more demographically authentic, framework of US identity, and it retains a narrative arc that is explicitly moralistic—a component critical for broad public support (Lakoff 2009, 53). What is more, rhetoric of this nature works to delegitimize a patriarchal framework of law-and-order moral rectitude, configuring anti-immigrant policies (such as Trump's) as abusive, negligent, and illicit. Even so, several risks emerge.

For her part, Klein advocates examining "clear political and economic ends" that crisis narratives serve (2007, 118), while Lakoff suggests using consensus-building frameworks that foster empathy and systemic thinking (2014, 160). The task would likely remain arduous, though. As communication scholar Daniel Kreiss reminds us, politics remains "an identity-based phenomenon" whereby voters typically prioritize affective attachments (2018, 95), many of which have acquired greater power in a "culture-war conservatism," to use columnist David Brooks's term (2020), that Trump's divisive and xenophobic rhetoric inspired and sustained. Going forward, scholars, students, and political actors alike should consider the power of rhetoric that, even with parental and prosecutorial tenors, better tackles the root causes driving undocumented immigration. As such, we should contemplate the efficacy of rhetoric that, for example, assesses the far-reaching effects of neoliberalism (policies that favor free-market capitalism), which, in addition to spurring US-bound immigration (Ackleson 2005, 167), has tended to create broad socioeconomic inequality, resulting in "an atomized society of disengaged individuals who feel demoralized and socially powerless" (McChesney 2008, 11). Rhetoric of this nature would shed light on an unpopular hierarchy of winners (corporatists) and losers (the working class, immigrant laborers, etc.) while cultivating a consciousness regarding powerful structures that maintain unjust asymmetries from within and beyond the nation's borders.

In spite of the unpredictability of US politics in the Trump era, language about the US-Mexico border endures and is likely to persist beyond Trump's tenure. The reasons are numerous, but we should keep in mind the strong symbolic dimensions that such language promotes, as well as its significance in a late capitalist society such as that of the United States. Here, the physical border and language about the border reinforce the perceived sanctity of the nation's contours (and, thus, the "national family") in an era of free trade, cyclical migration, and an ensuing cultural heterogeneity. Often erroneous and xenophobic, Trump's own crisis framework and border language proved effective, perhaps because, as Klein has observed, "in moments of crisis, people are willing to hand over a great deal of power to anyone who claims to have a magic cure" (2007, 168). Harris sought to harness rhetoric in order to help reverse this dynamic entirely given that public discourse, as scholar Josue David Cisneros reminds us, "creates, contests, and moves the borders of belonging, both metaphorically and materially" (2013, 2). In her campaign launch speech and on Twitter, Harris employed a different crisis framework through prosecutorial and parental language to capitalize on her personal and professional background, where immigration and cultural pluralism operated as foundational concepts for her vision of US identity and, in the end, how to remedy a fractured polity. Rather than profile the border as a moral vacuum of lawless nonnationals, she cast it as a moral testing ground emblematic of the nation's higher values, while framing the Trump administration, rather than border-crossing immigrants, as a national crisis par excellence.

References

Acevedo, Nicole. 2019. "Why Are Migrant Children Dying in U.S. Custody?" *NBC News*, May 29, 2019. https://www.nbcnews.com/news/latino/why-are-migrant-children-dying-u-s-custody-n1010316.

Ackleson, Jason. 2005. "Constructing Security on the U.S.-Mexico Border." *Political Geography* 24 (2): 165–184. https://doi.org/10.1016/j.polgeo.2004.09.017.

Aguirre, Adalberto, Jr., and Jennifer K. Simmers. 2008–09. "Mexican Border Crossers: The Mexican Body in Immigration Discourse." *Social Justice* 35 (4): 99–106. https://www.jstor.org/stable/29768517.

Baker, Peter, and Maggie Haberman. 2019. "Trump, in Interview, Calls Wall Talks 'Waste of Time' and Dismisses Investigations." *New York Times*, January 31, 2019. https://www.nytimes.com/2019/01/31/us/politics/trump-wall-investigations-interview.html.

Beckett, Lois. 2019. "Kamala Harris Kicks Off 2020 Campaign with Hometown Oakland Rally." *The Guardian*, January 27, 2019. https://www.theguardian.com/us-news/2019/jan/27/kamala-harris-2020-campaign-oakland-rally-democrats.

Brooks, David. 2020. "The Bernie Sanders Fallacy." *New York Times*, January 16, 2020. https://www.nytimes.com/2020/01/16/opinion/the-bernie-sanders-fallacy.html.

Chávez, Karma R. 2012. "Border Interventions: The Need to Shift from a Rhetoric of Security to a Rhetoric of Militarization." In *Border Rhetorics: Citizenship and Identity on the US-Mexico Frontier*, edited by D. Robert DeChaine, 48–62. Tuscaloosa: University of Alabama Press.

Cisneros, Josue David. 2013. *The Border Crossed Us: Rhetorics of Borders, Citizenship, and Latina/o Identity*. Tuscaloosa: University of Alabama Press.

Collinson, Stephen. 2019. "Trump's Audacious, Reelection-focused Impeachment Defense." *CNN*, November 1, 2019. https://www.cnn.com/2019/11/01/politics/donald-trump-impeachment-reelection-2020/index.html.

DeChaine, D. Robert. 2012. "Introduction: For Rhetorical Border Studies." In *Border Rhetorics: Citizenship and Identity on the US-Mexico Frontier*, edited by D. Robert DeChaine, 1–15. Tuscaloosa: University of Alabama Press.

Diamond, Jeremy. 2019. "Trump Jokes after Rally Attendee's Suggestion to 'Shoot' Migrants at the Border." *CNN*, May 9, 2019. https://www.cnn.com/2019/05/09/politics/donald-trump-rally-shoot-migrants/index.html.

Dittmar, Kelly. 2018. "Disrupting Masculine Dominance? Women as Presidential and Vice-Presidential Contenders." In *Gender and Elections: Shaping the Future of American Politics*, edited by Susan J. Carroll and Richard L. Fox, 48–77. Fourth edition, New York: Cambridge University Press.

Fairclough, Isabela, and Norman Fairclough. 2012. *Political Discourse Analysis: A Method for Advanced Students*. New York: Routledge.

Fuchs, Christian. 2018. *Digital Demagogue: Authoritarian Capitalism in the Age of Trump and Twitter*. London: Pluto Press.
Harris, Kamala. 2017. "User Clip: Senator Kamala Harris Delivers Maiden Senate Speech." Speech, Senate Session, Washington, DC, February 16, 2017. C-SPAN. https://www.c-span.org/video/?c4657632/user-clip-senator-kamala-harris-delivers-maiden-speech.
———. 2019. "Democratic Presidential Candidate Senator Kamala Harris (D-CA) Campaign Speech." Speech, Oakland, CA, January 27, 2019. C-SPAN. https://www.c-span.org/video/?c4776819/democratic-presidential-candidate-senator-kamala-harris-campaign-speech.
Johnson, Julia R. 2012. "Bordering as Social Practice: Intersectional Identifications and Coalitional Possibilities." In *Border Rhetorics: Citizenship and Identity on the US-Mexico Frontier*, edited by D. Robert DeChaine, 33–47. Tuscaloosa: University of Alabama Press.
Jordan, Miriam. 2019a. "Family Separation May Have Hit Thousands More Migrant Children Than Reported." *New York Times*, January 17, 2019. https://www.nytimes.com/2019/01/17/us/family-separation-trump-administration-migrants.html.
———. 2019b. "No More Family Separations, Except These 900." *New York Times*, July 30, 2019. https://www.nytimes.com/2019/07/30/us/migrant-family-separations.html.
Kight, Stef W. 2019. "Reality Check: Trump's Claims on Immigrants and Crime." *Axios*, January 9, 2019. https://www.axios.com/immigration-crime-border-trump-national-address-facts-6d752931-1a2b-40b2-a9e8-a912853b81ca.html.
Klein, Naomi. 2007. *The Shock Doctrine: The Rise of Disaster Capitalism*. New York: Metropolitan Books.
———. 2017. *No Is Not Enough: Resisting Trump's Shock Politics and Winning the World We Need*. Chicago: Haymarket Books.
Korte, Gregory, and Alan Gomez. 2018. "Trump Ramps Up Rhetoric on Undocumented Immigrants: 'These Aren't People. These Are Animals.'" *USA Today*, May 16, 2018. https://www.usatoday.com/story/news/politics/2018/05/16/trump-immigrants-animals-mexico-democrats-sanctuary-cities/617252002/.
Kraft, Colleen. 2018. "AAP Statement Opposing Separation of Children and Parents at the Border." *American Academy of Pediatrics*, June 15, 2018. https://bettercarenetwork.org/news-updates/news/aap-statement-opposing-the-border-security-and-immigration-reform-act.
Kreiss, Daniel. 2018. "The Media Are about Identity, Not Information." In *Trump and the Media*, edited by Pablo J. Boczkowski and Zizi Papacharissi, 93–99. Cambridge: The MIT Press.
Krogstad, Jens Manuel, and Luis Neo-Bustamante. 2019. "7 Facts for National Hispanic Heritage Month." *Pew Research Center*, October 14, 2019. https://policycommons.net/artifacts/616600/7-facts-for-national-hispanic-heritage-month/.
Lakoff, George. 2009. *The Political Mind: A Cognitive Scientist's Guide to Your Brain and Its Politics*. New York: Penguin Books.
———. 2014. *The All New Don't Think of an Elephant! Know Your Values and Frame the Debate*. White River Junction: Chelsea Green Publishing.
———. 2016. *Moral Politics: How Liberals and Conservatives Think*. Third edition, Chicago: University of Chicago Press.
Lakoff, George, and Mark Johnson. 1980. *Metaphors We Live By*. Chicago: University of Chicago Press.

Lucaites, John Louis. 2012. "Afterward: Border Optics." In *Border Rhetorics: Citizenship and Identity on the US-Mexico Frontier*, edited by D. Robert DeChaine, 227–230. Tuscaloosa: University of Alabama Press.

Martin, James. 2014. *Politics and Rhetoric: A Critical Introduction*. New York: Routledge.

McChesney, Robert W. 1998. "Introduction." In *Profit Over People: Neoliberalism and Global Order*, edited by Noam Chomsky, 7–16. New York: Seven Stories Press.

O'Kane, Caitlin. 2019. "Kamala Harris' Campaign Launch Pays Tribute to Shirley Chisholm's 1972 Run." *CBS News*, January 21, 2019. https://www.cbsnews.com/news/kamala-harris-2020-presidential-campaign-logo-pays-tribute-to-shirley-chisholm/.

O'Keefe, Ed. 2018. "Trump Pushes Back on Chief of Staff Claims That Border Wall Pledges 'Uninformed.'" *Washington Post*, January 18, 2018. https://www.washingtonpost.com/politics/trump-pushes-back-on-chief-of-staff-claims-that-border-wall-pledges-uninformed/2018/01/18/78960980-fc68-11e7-8f66-2df0b94bb98a_story.html.

Ono, Kent A. 2012. "Borders That Travel: Matters of the Figural Border." In *Border Rhetorics: Citizenship and Identity on the US-Mexico Frontier*, edited by D. Robert DeChaine, 19–32. Tuscaloosa: University of Alabama Press.

Oprysko, Caitlin, and Anita Kumar. 2019. "Trump Pushes Aggressive 'America First' Message to World Leaders." *Politico*, September 24, 2019. https://www.politico.com/story/2019/09/24/trump-america-first-unga-1509356.

Rodgers, Lucy, and Dominic Bailey. 2019. "Trump Wall—All You Need to Know about US Border in Seven Charts." *BBC News*, September 27, 2019. https://unitedwestay.org/trump-wall-all-you-need-to-know-about-us-border-in-seven-charts/.

Santa Ana, Otto. 2002. *Brown Tide Rising: Metaphors of Latinos in Contemporary American Public Discourse*. Austin: University of Texas Press.

Schmitz, Matthew. 2018. "Trump's 'Purple' Family Values." *New York Times*, July 1, 2018. https://www.nytimes.com/2018/07/01/opinion/trumps-purple-family-values.html.

Scholtes, Jennifer, Sarah Ferris, and Jacqueline Feldscher. 2019. "Trump Administration Raids Military Construction Projects for Border Wall." *Politico*, September 3, 2019. https://www.politico.com/story/2019/09/03/trump-administration-prepares-to-raid-military-projects-for-border-wall-1479981.

Schreckinger, Ben. 2015. "Donald Trump Storms Phoenix." *Politico*, July 11, 2015. https://www.politico.com/story/2015/07/donald-trump-storms-phoenix-119989.

Sedensky, Matt. 2019. "For Harris, Memories of a Warrior Mother Guide Her Campaign." *Associated Press*, May 11, 2019. https://apnews.com/0b55116cc42c4a80b3a34b5080e98e40.

Shear, Michael D., and Julie Hirschfeld Davis. 2019. "Shoot Migrants' Legs, Build Alligator Moat: Behind Trump's Ideas for Border." *New York Times*, October 1, 2019. https://www.nytimes.com/2019/10/01/us/politics/trump-border-wars.html.

Sonnevend, Julia. 2018. "Facts (Almost) Never Win Over Myths." In *Trump and the Media*, edited by Pablo J. Boczkowski and Zizi Papacharissi, 87–92. Cambridge: The MIT Press.

Stewart, Altha. 2018. "APA Statement Opposing Separation of Children from Parents at the Border." *American Psychiatric Association*, May 30, 2018. https://www.psychiatry.org/newsroom/news-releases/apa-statement-opposing-separation-of-children-from-parents-at-the-border.

Sullivan, Kevin. 2019. "'I Am Who I Am': Kamala Harris, Daughter of Indian and Jamaican Immigrants, Defines Herself Simply as 'American.'" *Washington Post*, February 2, 2019. https://www.washingtonpost.com/politics/i-am-who-i-am-kamala-harris-daughter-of-indian-and-jamaican-immigrants-defines-herself-simply-as-american/2019/02/02/0b278536-24b7-11e9-ad53-824486280311_story.html.

Turner, Fred. 2018. "Trump on Twitter: How a Medium Designed for Democracy Became an Authoritarian's Mouthpiece." In *Trump and the Media*, edited by Pablo J. Boczkowski and Zizi Papacharissi, 143–149. Cambridge: The MIT Press.

Wallace-Wells, Benjamin. 2019. "Kamala Harris's Choices." *The New Yorker*, January 29, 2019. https://www.newyorker.com/news/the-political-scene/kamala-harriss-choices.

Williams, Timothy, and Thomas Kaplan. 2019. "The Criminal Justice Debate Has Changed Drastically. Here's Why." *New York Times*, August 20, 2019. https://www.nytimes.com/2019/08/20/us/politics/criminal-justice-reform-sanders-warren.html.

10

THIS IS HOW WE WIN

On unruly hope, autocracy, and transgender children

Sally Campbell Galman

> Today, millions around the world live in circumstances where it might seem that nothing will ever change. But they must remember that the rebellions that took place all across Eastern Europe in 1989 were the result of a series of individual actions by ordinary people which together made change inevitable … [I]n my lifetime, I have repeatedly seen that small acts of resistance have had incomparably greater impact than anybody could have predicted at the time.
>
> —*Václav Havel*

Crystal and her mother spent the afternoon in their backyard with a pair of old kitchen scissors, cutting down the raw, early spring rushes and reeds from the swampy area at the bottom of the hill. Cutting the reeds themselves took a lot of effort, and sawing through the thick stems hurt Crystal's hands. She was strong, yet only nine years old, and she kept going because she was excited about their project. Her mother had explained that here, in late January, the holiday of Imbolc was approaching, an ancient Celtic festival that celebrated the return of light and warmth after a long, dark winter. Two of her mother's friends from their transgender family group had decided that they would make traditional Imbolc crosses to send to some elected representatives with a record of anti-trans legislative efforts—typical for their red state. The three women planned to use these small crosses, historically made of reeds (known as St. Brigid's crosses), to accompany a message about how the light—the human arc of the final Obama years—was returning, regardless of their actions. Crystal was having fun twisting the reeds into shape, but her mother was the one with a sparkle in her eyes. "We've called and written and marched and it hasn't done much. So now we are going to make ourselves a different kind of nuisance."

DOI: 10.4324/9781003034810-10

The three women, together with two others from their online parent group, made over 100 of these Imbolc crosses and mailed them to Washington DC along with notes that said: "Imbolc greetings. We know what you have done to transgender children and their families. But the light is coming back and nothing you can do will stop it. Get ready." Crystal's mother said: "We think it's just ominous enough, even if a staffer just throws it in the trash. It will get their attention." Crystal took a break to draw transgender flags with her pink and blue crayons. "I'll cut one of these out and put it in every one. So they will know that we are still here." By then end of the afternoon they had an impressive pile of reed crosses. Crystal hung one on the front door. "Then people know this is a safe place to be transgender."

Even if every staffer threw the notes and crosses in the trash, the act of making and sending the crosses still would be impactful because in addition to being a "different kind of nuisance," it was also a kind of sustenance for the oppressed. In action there lies hope. As Stephan and Snyder (2017) proposed, "successful movements need to be able to inspire hope and optimism in order to sustain popular participation in the resistance." Even making little reed crosses to show that "we are still here" represented an empowering hope within what seemed an unchecked and mean-spirited Trump autocracy.

As I have noted elsewhere, during the Trump era, the pace of life for transgender children and their families was nothing short of exhausting (Galman 2018). In addition to endless letter-writing, protest attendance, election work, grassroots campaigning, and phone calls, parents and families of transgender children also had to do the everyday work of parenting, reassuring, and fighting the small battles from the playground to the classroom to the school district to the Thanksgiving dinner table. To say that they were tired is an understatement. They often have been full of grinding despair, but kept up a cheerful visage for their children. One parent asked me, her hands full of postcards protesting the latest proposed anti-trans legislation in her state, "I don't know if these are actually making a difference." She paused and looked me in the eye. "What do we do when nobody cares?"

What follows is an exploration of that question, and the answers provided by parents and family members in my ongoing study of young transgender children in the United States. Providing sustenance for the present and for a future after Trump, these families and communities have engaged strategies of hope, following Adam Michnik (1986), using creativity, persistence, and what Khanna (2012, 162) called "unruly political action." This chapter overviews legislative and executive measures of the Trump administration and Republican officials at federal and state levels that rolled back transgender rights from the 2017 presidential inauguration through March 2020. I then discuss the tactics of "unruly" politics enacted by family members of transgender children. Vignettes from the study data contextualize "unruliness" in the contemporary United States, and this chapter concludes with a vision of possible futures. In the words of the Imbolc Crossmakers, "the light is coming back."

For the record

Establishing a pattern of targeted attacks on transgender people by the Trump regime is not difficult. Keeping track of them is a different matter altogether. As West (2017) writes, "human consciousness has been reduced to a panicked blur, a zoetrope of galloping despair. There are simply too many emergencies to hold all of them in your mind at once." This is certainly by design, as Stephan and Snyder (2020, 154) remind us: "Authoritarians thrive on popular fear, apathy, resignation, and a feeling of disorientation."

From his less-than-convincing show of LGBTQ advocacy while on campaign through his time in office, Trump's anti-trans track record was indisputable and overwhelming (Guilford 2016; National Center for Transgender Equality n.d.). What follows is a sample of actions taken at the federal level by the Trump administration and also state-level efforts by Republican allies. The actions, diffused throughout areas of government, employing tactics of erasure, refusal, exposure, and occlusion, worked in tandem to circumscribe the rights of trans people.

The first tactic was erasure. Working quietly, the Trump administration took steps to eliminate transgender people from discussions of policy. On Inauguration Day 2017, all references to LGBTQ people were removed from the White House website. In March of 2017, the Department of Health and Human Services excised questions about the sexuality and transgender identity of residents in its assessment reports for centers for independent living and from its national survey of older adults. That same month, the Census Bureau scuttled Obama-era plans to collect such information in the 2020 Census (Human Rights Campaign n.d.). In December of that year, Centers for Disease Control and Prevention staff were counseled not to use the word "transgender" in official documents (Cohen 2018). In October 2018, US representatives at the United Nations tried to edit out explicit and implicit references to transgender people in UN general assembly policy statements on human rights (Borger 2018). If transgender people were written out of existence and not counted, they could be ignored.

The second tactic was refusal. On July 26, 2017, President Trump (@realdonaldtrump) announced, via Twitter, that "the United States Government will not accept or allow Transgender individuals to serve in any capacity in the U.S. Military." Despite legal challenges and the objection even of high-ranking military officers, in 2019, the ban on transgender service members went into effect. Accordingly,

> anyone ... who is taking [gender-affirming] hormones or has already undergone a gender transition will not be allowed to enlist. Further, any currently serving troops diagnosed with gender dysphoria after [that] date will have to serve in their sex as assigned at birth and will be barred from taking hormones or getting gender-affirming surgery.
>
> *(Jackson and Kube 2019)*

The third tactic was exposure: to remove various protections for transgender people, and further, to shield others from legal retaliation should they discriminate against transgender people. This tactic was spread across a wide variety of government agencies, including education, healthcare, housing, and prisons. First, as regards schools, in only the first month of Trump's presidency, the Departments of Justice and Education withdrew 2016 Obama administration guidance related to federal Title IX law detailing how schools should protect transgender students (Human Rights Campaign n.d.). In 2018, the Department of Education went a step further to indicate that it would no longer hear complaints by transgender students about discrimination on the basis of gender identity. In November 2019, the Department of Education issued regulations that would permit religious schools to disregard LGBTQ nondiscrimination standards set by educational accrediting agencies. Similarly, in 2018, the Bureau of Prisons removed protections for transgender prisoners, requiring that they be housed in prisons on the basis of "sex at birth," rather than gender identity (National Center for Transgender Equality, n.d.).

Similarly, protections for LGBT people were rolled back by the Department of Housing and Urban Development (HUD). In March 2017, HUD withdrew two Obama-era policies designed to protect homeless LGBT people. Days later, it also excised from its website links to documents providing recommendations to homeless shelters about how to best protect the safety of transgender people (Human Rights Campaign n.d.). In July 2019, HUD dismantled requirements that homeless shelters that received HUD funds needed to have anti-discrimination policies that would protect LGBTQ people (National Center for Transgender Equality n.d.).

Regarding the workplace, since the beginning of Trump's term, his administration took various steps to permit workplace discrimination on the basis of transgender identity. As one such measure, in August 2018, according to the National Center for Transgender Equality (n.d.): "the Department of Labor released a new directive for Office of Federal Contract Compliance Programs (OFCCP) staff encouraging them to grant broad religious exemptions to federal contractors with religious-based objections to complying with nondiscrimination laws." Ultimately, in August 2019, the Justice Department filed a legal brief with the US Supreme Court, arguing that businesses have a constitutional right to discriminate on the basis of transgender identity (Law 2019).

A key feature of the Trump administration was the privileging of religious liberty in relation to other civil rights. In effect, the religious identity of one person could become the basis for denying rights to others. Precedent had been set in Burwell v. Hobby Lobby Stores (2014), in which the Supreme Court ruled that an employer would not be required to contribute to employees' health insurance coverage that included birth control, on the basis of religious faith. Similarly, in Masterpiece Cakeshop v. Colorado Civil Rights Commission (2018), the Supreme Court ruled that a baker could refuse to bake a wedding cake for a same-sex couple on the basis of the baker's religious faith. In its consideration of civil rights issues, the Trump administration continued to privilege religious liberties over the rights of people of gender and sexual minorities. The importance of religious liberty within the Trump administration's notions of civil rights was revealed most clearly when Trump announced his opposition to the Equality Act, a bill proposed by House and Senate Democrats in March 2019, which would explicitly "add sexual orientation and gender identity to federal civil rights law to prevent discrimination" against LGBTQ people. A Trump administration statement expressed opposition to the bill, stating that it "undermine[d] parental and conscience rights" (Fitzsimmons 2019).

This contest over the relative priority of civil rights played out most drastically in the realm of healthcare. In 2018, the Department of Health and Human Services' Office of Civil Rights opened a "Conscience and Religious Freedom Division" that provided legal protection for medical providers to use religious grounds to deny treatment to transgender people, among others, on the basis of religious belief (US Department of Health and Human Services 2018). This principle was supported by changes in administrative procedure. For example, Section 1557 of the Affordable Care Act (ACA) had included a provision prohibiting "discrimination based on race, color, national origin, sex, age, and disability." However, in June 2019, the Department of Health and Human Services proposed revisions which would "eliminat[e] the general prohibition on discrimination based on gender identity, as well as specific health insurance coverage protections for transgender individuals." With discrimination on the basis of gender no longer prohibited under ACA regulations, medical providers were given that much more latitude to deny healthcare to transgender people (Musumeci et al. 2019). This exposure of transgender people to greater health risks fell in line with other Trump administration measures, such as when, in December 2017, the president dismantled the White House Presidential Advisory Council on HIV/AIDS. Ultimately, in November 2019, Health and Human Services (HHS) announced that it would no longer require agencies that received HHS funding to maintain nondiscriminatory practices on the basis of gender identity or sexual orientation (National Center for Transgender Equality, n.d.).

Finally, through processes of occlusion, beginning in 2017, the president nominated for judgeships several men with a record of anti-LGBTQ decisions or campaigning who could be counted upon to block any legal challenges to Trump-era anti-LGBTQ measures down the line (those whom Millhiser [2020] called "ideologically reliable" appointees). These included Neil Gorsuch, who was appointed to the Supreme Court (Lambda Legal 2017), and Mark Norris, who was appointed to the United States District Court for the Western District of Tennessee following a record of judgments against transgender children and their families. Trump's nominee for United States District Judge for the Eastern District of Texas, Jeff Mateer, had called transgender children part of "Satan's plan" and advocated for conversion therapy (Michaelson 2017). Finally, his nominee to serve as Judge for the US Court of Appeals for the Fifth Circuit, Stuart Kyle Duncan, had invested years arguing cases to undermine LGBTQ rights regarding marriage and parenting; in several cases he also worked to deny transgender people, whom he called "delusional," access to public restrooms on the basis of their gender (Greenblatt 2018).

Federal actions to curb the rights of LGBTQ people worked in tandem with efforts at the state level. For example, just in the closing months of 2019 and the first two months of 2020, the states of Idaho, South Dakota, New Hampshire, Illinois, Oklahoma, Colorado, and South Carolina proposed legislation that would jail or fine doctors who provided transgender people with gender-affirming care. The South Dakota bill was directed at doctors who would treat transgender minors, and seemed fueled by intentional misinformation (Bauer 2020). The South Dakota bill was defeated, but only narrowly and due to the exhaustive efforts of parents, youth, medical professionals, and others. A similar situation occurred in Idaho (a state often seen as a testing ground for anti-trans legislation) where HB 465—which proposed to make it a felony for doctors to provide gender-affirming care to transgender children—was scuttled after hours of testimony and the mustering of hundreds of advocates for transgender youth.

While advocacy groups have been victorious in many of these cases, working with parents, businesses, clergy, and medical professionals to kill the bills before they can be put into action, several have gotten close to being enacted. Over 200 anti-trans bills had been introduced in various state legislatures just in 2019 and the first month of 2020 (Moreau 2020). One cannot help but imagine that the destabilizing and dispiriting effects are intentional.

But what does this mean? This kind of relentless legislative drive might be less about winning court cases and nominations, and more about fostering hopelessness and confusion among adults and children alike (Taylor 2019) under a tyrannical leader for whom hopelessness was a strategy (see Snyder 2017). But the stakes are high in other ways. As Zein Murib (2020) of the *Washington Post* found, the effects of such bills on transgender children and youth is particularly dangerous; these groups are already more likely to be harassed, to be the victims of violence at the hands of peers or others, and more likely to attempt suicide. Wrote Murib: "Pediatricians who care for gender-nonconforming or transgender-identified children and adolescents regularly describe transition-related care as lifesaving." Legislative efforts to block transition-related medical care therefore represent a type of violence enacted upon these children. That all of this is against a backdrop of widespread anti-trans violence and the routine murders of transwomen—mostly African American (Kaur and Kopp 2019)—makes this pattern of targeting transgender children—especially under the discursive guise of protecting them—chilling.

The research background

The study from which these descriptive accounts come was a qualitative, ethnographically informed research project focusing on young transgender and gender-nonconforming children, their families, friends, and schools. Data were collected before, during, and after the 2016 US presidential election, beginning in mid-2015. The study was open-ended and discovery-oriented, and while enrollment was fluid, it involved over 70 children aged 3 to 12 and their families in diverse political and socioeconomic contexts across the United States. Data collection involved multiple, semi-structured ethnographic interviews with parents and teachers, artifact collection, and a range of task- and arts-based methods with children, in addition to participant observation across contexts, initially for an 18-month period, but continuing on a longitudinal basis from 2019 onward. Most of the parents, but not all, belonged to private Facebook and other social media support and advocacy groups, and communicated with me via email, telephone, or in person at playgroups and social gatherings. Even online, the parents formed tight bonds with one another, and those living in geographic proximity came to know other families very well. Most of the parents and families had engaged to some degree politically, whether that meant phone calls or emails to legislators, public marches, or protest gatherings. Several participants lived in states that had been subject to conservative anti-trans legislation tests, and while most worked to find community and sustain their children even in the most conservative contexts, at least two families moved out of one state in particular because the situation became unsafe and untenable for their transgender children.

As I have described elsewhere (Galman 2018), I developed close relationships with the children and their families, in part because when I began this work in 2015, very few social science researchers were working on this topic, or recognizing gender diversity in young children outside of the medical or psychological pathology literature. This was also a function of my own position as the parent of a transgender child searching for information. As "in-group," I was trusted, and privy to families' private moments and struggles, all of which they shared with me as a researcher, in the hopes that by telling their stories I might be able to generate empathy in a research and reading public, and generate positive change for their families. In keeping with their trust in me, I did not then, nor do I now, pretend at agnosticism. As I argued in 2018, it "would have been unethical to assume a neutral and uninvolved stance in light of what participants endured" (278). I approached my own researcher role and subjectivity with a critical and reflexive eye, and my analyses were conducted according to accepted standards for maintaining study rigor and trustworthiness (Bhattacharya 2017). To that end, this work is intended to frame and document a moment in history such that others might read and know what has transpired here among what has been, until recently, a largely hidden population on its way to greater equality and safety.

Details such as geographical location, names, ages, and other potentially identifying descriptors have been changed to protect participant confidentiality and safety. The transgender and gender diverse community is very small, and families and children are often identifiable, even with pseudonyms and other standard changes commonly used by qualitative researchers, because they are the "only ones" in their towns, schools, or neighborhoods. Therefore, I have taken steps beyond simply using pseudonyms and made more significant alterations, none of which affect the analyses presented here, or change the larger comparable study demographics. In particular, I have employed the ethnographic strategy of the composite narrative, in which stories are presented as composites rather than faithful concretely reported data. The thrust of the presented story is essentially the same, but the composite nature of the narrative "is valuable for anonymizing sensitive or commercially confidential accounts where exact reporting may make a specific actor identifiable" (Jarzabkowski, Bednarik, and Lê 2014, 281).

Unruly politics

All participant families participated in some form of resistance to national and local anti-trans legislation and posturing. These actions were sometimes the everyday acts of maintaining normalcy, and sometimes things much bigger in scope (Galman 2020). Families persevered in following both traditional channels of political resistance, including emotional appeals to conservative politicians, although such efforts typically went unrewarded. Similarly, more direct avenues of legal action were often costly, slow, and ineffective, though some legislative successes were had, in places like South Dakota. It is of no surprise that, in the face of the zoetrope and limited effectiveness, many parents, families, and communities began to consider other forms of resistance. While no participants engaged in illegal activities, I would frame these new mechanisms of resistance as what Khanna (2012) called "unruly politics" or what Otpor! founder Srdja Popovic might call nonviolent but extralegal mischief. As Popovic (2015, ix) wrote, "even though the suits, the bullies and the brutes—the whole cadre of grim men who usually run things—may look invincible, often all it takes to topple them is a good bit of fun." While perhaps not exactly "fun," the spirit of unruliness has been the next best thing. As Popovic said: "I'm full of humor and irony and you're beating me, arresting me. That's a game you always lose" (quoted in Crawshaw and Jackson 2010, 53).

In this context, I frame resistance—big or small—that takes on the qualities of extralegal transgressive action as "unruly politics." These are means of political resistance that go beyond what Popovic's "cadres of grim men who usually run things" might expect. They might expect (and dismiss) letters and phone calls, emails, or protests on the steps of city halls. Yet, as Khanna and their colleagues wrote in a manifesto on unruly politics, such tactics are

> political actions which escape, exceed or transgress 'civil' forms of civic and democratic engagement in that they characteristically take forms that are juridically illegible, extra-legal, disruptive of the social order, strident or rude, whether this be in the form of riots or revolts, or through the use of humor, disruptive aesthetics or eroticism in engagements with power.
>
> *(Shankland et al. 2011, quoted in Khanna 2012, 166)*

They added that unruly politics are transgressive, disruptive actions that "force official attention to the specific concern being voiced" (quoted in Khanna 2012, 166). Further, Khanna affirmed that unruly politics are not simply a fancy term to describe yet another loud, rude, disruptive mob:

> Unruly politics, as we define it, is political action by people who have been denied voice by the rules of the political game. … [I]t draws power from transgressing these rules—while at the same time upholding others, which may not be legally sanctioned but which have legitimacy, deeply rooted in people's own understandings of what is right and just. This preoccupation with social justice distinguishes these forms of political action from the banditry or gang violence with which threatened autocrats willfully try to associate them.
>
> *(quoted in Khanna 2012, 166)*

Khanna wrote, further, that rather than simply trying to get a government to do something or change their position, unruly politics present a challenge that is "simultaneously far more fundamental and far more nuanced—it is a challenge to the very logics of capitalism and representative democracy" (164). Indeed, it is what we do when things do not work and is radical in its admission that the government is neither representative nor responsive. It is about changing the game by speaking a political language that is both foreign to and unexpected by the ruling power. Even if nothing changes in a material way, the oppressor is destabilized. One particularly evocative example of this destabilizing effect is as follows:

> As has now become regular policing practice in UK protests, a large group of people were 'kettled in', or trapped by the riot police. Among these protestors were a group of clowns from CIRCA (the Clandestine Insurgent Rebel Clown Army)—an innovative activist group of clowns (not people pretending to be clowns) that 'aims to make clowning dangerous again, to bring it back to the street, restore its disobedience and give it back the social function it once had: its ability to disrupt, critique and heal society'. The Clown Army, a regular feature in protests in the United Kingdom and other parts of Europe, play a significant role in the dynamics and flavour of the protest, very often at the boundaries of the protest, placing themselves strategically between protestors and the riot police. Clowning with the riot police, kissing their intimidating shields, mocking and turning the military establishment on its head, they diffuse mounting tensions between the aggressive face of the state and the protestors. At one such interface, says Heckert, a senior member of the police force approached the clown who seemed to be in charge of the Army, perhaps with the intention of negotiating the dispersal of the march. Taking him aside, he said, 'Can I have a serious word?' The Clown thought deeply for a moment and said in return, '"Encyclopaedia"—is that a serious word?'
>
> *(Khanna 2012, 165)*

The clowning is funny, but, more importantly, it destabilizes the oppressor—catching him off guard with something so bizarre. According to unruly politics, when one is locked out of the political process, and targeted by an autocratic regime, one should send in the literal and metaphorical clowns. Finally, and most importantly, even if the effects of unruly action are transient, they do force official attention to be paid (Shankland 2011).

During the Trump presidency, as the normal governmental channels for securing civil rights for transgender people appeared completely obstructed, the channels that remained were those best traveled by kissing clowns and other agents of unruly politics. This is what we do when we are out of options, and this is how we win.

Open the window

Study participants engaged in the quotidian revolution. They kept on with keeping on, holding smiles on their faces for their children, going through the everyday paces of making lunch and reading bedtime stories, and doing soccer pickup—and making sure that their kids got to be kids to the greatest degree possible. All the while, they did the standard work of political protest: postcard mailings and organizing meetings, phone calls, letters to the principal, and supporting other parents on social media. Both the everyday work and the standard political work became, as described above, more difficult in the midst of what seemed an onslaught of legal and social persecution.

However, other participants opted to also engage in unruliness as a strategy for creating productive chaos and attention getting. As one father who became a member of the Bathroom Brigade (described below) said,

> You know that whole thing about how when God closes a door he opens a window? Well, this is the window. We're not breaking laws but we are getting attention. I'm fine with confusing people if it brings them to our way of thinking. It's like throwing a parade—it doesn't hurt anyone but it damn sure stops traffic.

Like the Imbolc Crossmakers, several groups engaged in small actions that could be called unruly politics. Below I tell two such stories.

The Bathroom Brigade

During the Trump 2016 campaign and the first year of his administration, states began proposing "bathroom bills" (Kralik 2019). These bills required all people to use public bathrooms aligned with their "biological" gender or the gender reported on their birth certificate, with foreseeable humiliating consequences. LGBTQ community advocates pressured legislators to not pass such bills, and were largely successful, except in the case of North Carolina. That state managed to pass such a bill in 2016, and the Obama administration had planned to challenge the state to rescind the law, but these complaints were withdrawn following Trump's January 2017 inauguration (Simmons-Duffin 2020). In the case of North Carolina, HB2 was only enforceable in public restrooms in state facilities, but the practice of enforcement was also adopted by some private businesses eager to jump on the bandwagon. Then there were the schools.

One group of parents, along with allies from several different communities including but not limited to the LGBTQ community, organized an elaborate guerrilla bathroom protest: The Bathroom Brigade (name changed for privacy). The proposed bathroom bills depended somewhat on citizen reporting, but it was never quite clear who was supposed to report, nor was it clear how the "reward" structure worked—some proposed legislation suggested up to $2500 in "damages" to students and others affected by finding someone in the "wrong" restroom—and who could collect, and which state was proposing them. Further, the mechanism of enforcement was never clear; indeed, few people knew what would happen if a person was "caught" or who was supposed to be called, and even what was to be done. The legislation was shoddy and, therefore, ripe for the picking.

The Bathroom Brigade turned this confusion to their advantage. It worked like this: a protest volunteer would report a person using the wrong restroom. This usually resulted in confusion. However, on occasions when the police arrived, and the alleged bathroom interloper was confronted, the police or business owners were forced to engage in an awkward and haphazard interrogation which resulted, always, in the realization that the person was in fact the "correct" gender for that restroom. The second person was, of course, another Brigadier, but having many different volunteers and plausible deniability on their side, made this protest effective and virtually untouchable. Then, the caller would begin to ask for a monetary reward. This made the enforcers confused and frustrated and certainly with better things to do than explain—in this case—that there was no "reward" and that they had made a mistake. The volunteers looked on in mock amazement, claiming ignorance. As one elderly Brigadier and grandmother said, "Nobody would ever believe that a nice little old lady was hopping around town creating a disturbance!" As soon as that encounter was wrapped up, with apologies all around, another call would come in from across town. And so on. Over and over again.

It is no surprise that the North Carolina bathroom bill was repealed and that so many others failed. While ultimately the legislative push for bathroom bills ended for lots of reasons—including massive business losses for North Carolina (Simmons-Duffin 2019)—I would like to believe that groups like the Bathroom Brigade did their part.

We've got your number

While young children were intentionally insulated from much political action such as rallies or protests—and certainly from direct action—there were some children who participated in unruly actions: teenagers. Siblings were usually powerful advocates for their transgender family members, and teenagers, often discounted as political actors because they are not voters, were formidable and creative. Mattie, the 17-year-old sister of Cory, a transgender third grader, began with stickers. She said:

> It started because I like to make stickers. I learned how to do it first with this nasty wheat paste and then with my printer. My friends and I made them as jokes and stuck them on stuff at school at first. But then I realized that I could put them everywhere with any message. *Any* message. Then I thought about Cory.

Mattie had watched her out-and-proud little brother become a bit shyer, even afraid, over the prior year. She and her friends were members of her high school's tiny LGBTQ group, and had tried, with limited success, to write letters to legislators, the school board, and others. "I know my parents are doing what they can, and they don't listen to a bunch of teenagers, or really think we can do anything to them. We're mostly girls too so there's that."

Stickers are easy, fast forms of anonymous guerrilla protest art. Mattie's stickers had numbers on them and the phrase "We've Got Your Number" in blue and pink tones (blue and pink being the colors of transgender rights activism). At first glance the numbers did not seem to have rhyme or reason—a few said 25, others said 16, 18, 36—followed by phrases like "for hate crimes" or "for felony child abuse" and "for crimes against humanity." Mattie explained that the numbers represented years in prison. She said she and her friends had been following what Trump and her own state representatives had been doing to transgender people's rights locally, nationally, and internationally. They then looked up which federal, state, and international laws had been broken and the minimum recommended sentences they carried:

> It took serious time, but we went through all this stuff and found lots of things they've done in the hate crime category. I loved finding out that crimes against humanity can pretty much get you life in prison, but for Trump we figure that's going to be a short sentence. So we sent him a few sheets of stickers that said 20. The best was when I stuck probably 50 of them to the front of magazines with his picture on them and a lady standing next to me in the bookstore said, 'Oh, what is that for?' and I explained that he would serve 20 years in prison for crimes against humanity. And I had her attention. I gave her a sheet to take with her. We also made a bunch of "20s" for my congressman because our state says that hate crimes require no less than 20 years. There was this big poster billboard thing for [a legislator's] reelection and we covered it in stickers—all the numbers of years he would serve for his crimes against transgender people. It made me feel like I was doing something.

Mattie and her friends sent stickers and sticker-making instructions to friends in 20 states. Cory knew what she was doing and was proud of his sister for being an ally. Mattie's parents were a bit more cautious and worried that she would be charged with vandalism, but told her to be careful and otherwise "have at it." Mattie said she was fine playing dumb. "After all, I'm just a dumb teenage girl they wouldn't listen to when I was writing letters," she said with a shrug. At this writing, she was working on a batch of 10s for Trump's "inciting violence" via Twitter. She did not know if the sticker campaign would make a legislative impact, but she was conscious that while legislators and certainly the federal government "don't give a shit," ordinary people might. "And they don't know who the 'we' is. They don't know it's just a bunch of teenagers putting them up all over the place. We could be thousands."

This is how we win

As I write, in March 2020, the morning news featured expressly LGBTQ-allied Senator Elizabeth Warren's withdrawal from the race for the Democratic presidential nomination, and the novel coronavirus was causing wholesale chaos nearly everywhere. Photographs of Vice President Pence and his virus task force bent in prayer highlighted both the administration's ineffectiveness and its disregard for the principle of separation of church and state. Evangelical Christians' firm support for the president certainly influenced the Trump administration's dogged efforts to undermine the rights of LGBTQ people, and within that group, transgender people specifically. The administration's disproportionate investment of resources and energy on erasing what is actually a very small group of people seemed obsessive, and may have represented continued pandering to the evangelical Christian vote.

While the Trump administration faintly backpedaled and framed its persecution of transgender people—and most recently, transgender youth—as addressing the previous administration's "executive overreach," the consensus is clear. As Fadulu (2019) wrote,

> while socially conservative policies have been mainstays of the Trump White House, what distinguishes the transgender initiative is its sweep ... to the people who identify as transgender, less than one percent of the population, the comprehensive nature of the policies feels mystifying.

Well, perhaps not *that* mystifying. As Fadulu and others have noted, it may be simply tried-and-true, politically advantageous strategies for pandering to a conservative, transphobic constituency.

Activists say that despite the flurry of anti-trans legislation and the Trump administration's fixation on transgender people, we have been winning. Much state-level test legislation has been defeated, most bathroom bills were similarly killed. Even though the effects of the zoetrope are difficult to ignore, the truth is this: the anti-LGBTQ measures of the Trump administration may be the actions of a party losing the culture war. Even at the beginning of the Trump presidency, the majority of Americans polled supported rights for transgender people (Chapman 2017). As Mattie says, even if the test legislation in red states continues, and even if legislators stop responding to letters and phone calls, ordinary people will, as she says, "give a shit."

Consequently, unruly politics work in three ways: they destabilize the oppressor, they mobilize ordinary onlookers, and they sustain the protestor herself.

First, they destabilize the oppressor by not following the rules. In Khanna's (2012) example, the riot police certainly did not know how to handle clowns. The municipal infrastructure had no way of handling the Bathroom Brigade. And while a congressional staffer reads and responds (or simply disposes of) hundreds of letters every day, what do they do with ominous straw crosses? These tactics are just unsettling enough to make people stop and see the writing—or in this case, the stickers—on the wall and realize that activists are no longer doing business as usual but are bypassing them to take their message to the public. Officials' power is undermined and their ineffectiveness is exposed.

In this way, unruly politics are aimed not as supplications to unsympathetic officials but rather as performance for ordinary people, who might, in fact, be swayed. Mattie did mail her stickers to elected officials, but she did not expect any change in their behavior. Instead, like the Imbolc Crossmakers, she sent the stickers to show them her creative campaign, as if to say, "this is going on and nothing you can do can stop it." Similarly, the sticker protest suggests a much larger "we" that is actually behind the creative campaign—that larger "we" being something that often appeals to bystanders and frightens oppressors. When officials cannot be reached, activists will appeal to those who might abandon complacence and join in. And that should be terrifying.

The third audience for these unruly politics is the resisters themselves. While Khanna and others acknowledge that unruly politics do not always have a permanent political effect—in other words, it is unlikely that they would effect permanent change—their process of disruption is still valuable for both the disruption and the sense of community. And in the economy of valuing process over product, we must acknowledge that the act of engaging in unruly politics is affirming for the person who makes the stickers, or the crosses, or participates in the Bathroom Brigade. The pace and size of such unruly protests may be universally accessible and manageable in the face of what might otherwise feel unsurmountable and hopeless. As one Polish protestor documented by Crawshaw and Jackson (2010, 5) said, "if you see your neighbors [engaging in protest] it makes you feel part of something. The aim of dictatorship is to make you feel isolated. [The pro-democracy movement] broke the isolation and built confidence." While many parents and families of transgender children found community in online and other groups, doing something together enhanced that feeling of community.

The small hope

That last quality of unruly politics—hope and sustenance for its agents even in the face of the zoetrope—is perhaps the most important. As Elizabeth Warren suspended her presidential campaign, she issued a statement to her campaign staff. Within that statement, she added:

> One last story: When I voted yesterday at the elementary school down the street, a mom came up to me. And she said she has two small children, and they have a nightly ritual. After the kids have brushed teeth and read books and gotten that last sip of water and done all the other bedtime routines, they do one last thing before the two little ones go to sleep.
>
> Mama leans over them and whispers, "Dream big." And the children together reply, "Fight hard."
>
> *(Team Warren 2020)*

This mother certainly knew that even as she said these words to her young children in the hope of bigger dreams and eventual victories, the dizzying images of the zoetrope would keep on spinning. But no one would accuse her of wasting her time or breath. Hope is itself political, for when that is gone, so is all else. This may be the greatest gift of unruly politics, and the thing most terrifying to conservative politicians. Unruly politics affirms the value of the small hope, whispered at bedtime, or printed on a sticker, or shouted in the street.

There is a proverb, the origin of which I cannot exactly remember. It goes something like this: "Never despair at being small in the face of big things. For a very small flea can make a very big dog very uncomfortable for a very long time." Even though as an American I am prone to root for the underdog, I have always taken great comfort in the victories of the small against the wicked and powerful, from David against Goliath, to the unknown man in Tiananmen Square to Ruby Bridges or Greta Thunberg. I was 16 years old when I saw individual people—people made small by years of oppression—tear down the Berlin Wall with their bare hands. Small can be powerful.

As I have described elsewhere (Galman 2016), my own father voted for Donald Trump in the 2016 election. On Thanksgiving in 2019, my partner asked my father if he would consider voting for Trump again in 2020, and if so why. My father gave a measured and thoughtful answer that did not address Trump's social policies, religious extremism, or hate speech, but instead focused on foreign policy. It was a reasoned response, but at the end of the day it was clear that he was planning on voting for Trump again, even though he admitted he did not like the man. My 11-year-old daughter, who is transgender and very much aware of the administration's record on transgender rights, was silent. She sat next to her grandfather, who had turned on the TV and started watching something. Then, without missing a beat, my daughter stood up, took the remote control out of her grandfather's hand, changed the channel and said, in an emotionless deadpan,

"Well, Grandpa, we can't watch that show because the person who produces it is a Trump supporter and we don't give hate a pass." She then flipped through channels wordlessly while we all sat in silence.

This is how we win.

Acknowledgments

In this text, all names and identifying details have been changed to protect the participants' privacy.

References

Bauer, Sydney. 2020. "New Anti-Trans Culture War Hiding in Plain Sight." *New Republic*, February 11, 2020. https://newrepublic.com/article/156539/new-anti-trans-culture-war-hiding-plain-sight.

Bhattacharya, Kakali. 2017. *Fundamentals of Qualitative Research*. New York: Routledge.

Borger, Julian. 2018. "Trump Administration Wants to Remove 'Gender' from UN Human Rights Documents." *The Guardian*, October 25, 2018. https://www.theguardian.com/world/2018/oct/24/trump-administration-gender-transgender-united-nations.

Chapman, Steve. 2017. "Trump's Transgender Policy Is on the Losing Side of the Culture War." *Chicago Tribune*, July 28, 2017. https://www.chicagotribune.com/columns/steve-chapman/ct-trump-transgender-culture-war-perspec-20170728-column.html.

Cohen, Elizabeth. 2018. "The Truth about Those 7 Words 'Banned' at the CDC." *CNN*, January 31, 2018. https://www.cnn.com/2018/01/11/health/cdc-word-ban-hhs-document/index.html.

Crawshaw, Steve, and John Jackson. 2010. *Small Acts of Resistance: How Courage, Tenacity, and Ingenuity Can Change the World*. New York: Union Square Press.

Fadulu, Lola. 2019. "Trump's Rollback of Transgender Rights Extends through Entire Government." *New York Times*, December 6, 2019. https://www.nytimes.com/2019/12/06/us/politics/trump-transgender-rights.html.

Fitzsimmons, Tim. 2019. "Trump Opposes Federal LGBTQ Nondiscrimination Bill, Citing 'Poison Pills'." *NBC News*, May 14, 2019. https://www.nbcnews.com/feature/nbc-out/trump-opposes-federal-lgbtq-nondiscrimination-bill-citing-poison-pills-n1005551.

Galman, Sally Campbell. 2016. "We Ain't Whupped Yet: Memo from America 11/10." *Gender and Education Association Newsletter*, November 10, 2016. http://www.genderandeducation.com/issues/donald-trump-wins-us-election-gea-members-respond-3/.

———. 2018. "This Is Vienna: Parents of Transgender Children from Pride to Survival in the Aftermath of the 2016 Election." In *Nasty Women and Bad Hombres: Gender and Race in the 2016 Presidential Election*, edited by Christine A. Kray, Tamar W. Carroll, and Hinda Mandell, 276–290. Rochester, NY: University of Rochester Press.

———. 2020. "Parenting Far from the Tree: Supportive Parents of Young Transgender and Gender Nonconforming Children in the United States." In *Parents and Caregivers across Cultures*, edited by Brien N. Ashdown and Amanda N. Faherty, 141–155. Berlin: Springer.

Greenblatt, Jonathan A. 2018. "Final ADL Letter of Opposition to Stuart Kyle Duncan Fifth Circuit Court of Appeals." *Anti-Defamation League*, April 24, 2018. https://www.adl.org/news/letters/final-adl-letter-of-opposition-to-stuart-kyle-duncan-fifth-circuit-court-of-appeals.

Guilford, Gwynn. 2016. "Donald Trump's 'Support' of LGBT Communities in One Image." *Quartz*, October 31, 2016. https://qz.com/823649/donald-trump-unfurled-a-rainbow-flag-with-lgbt-written-on-it-at-a-rally-in-greeley-colorado-to-express-his-so-called-support/.

Havel, Václav. 2010. "Foreword." In *Small Acts of Resistance*, edited by Steve Crawshaw and John Jackson, x–ix. New York: Union Square Press.

Human Rights Campaign. n.d. "Trump's Timeline of Hate." Accessed May 28, 2020. https://www.hrc.org/timelines/trump.

Jackson, Hallie, and Courtney Kube. 2019. "Trump's Controversial Transgender Military Policy Goes into Effect." *NBC News*, April 12, 2019. https://www.nbcnews.com/feature/nbc-out/trump-s-controversial-transgender-military-policy-goes-effect-n993826.

Jarzabkowski, Paula, Rebecca Bednarek, and Jane K. Lê. 2014. "Producing Persuasive Findings: Demystifying Ethnographic Textwork in Strategy and Organization Research." *Strategic Organization* 12 (4): 274–287. https://doi.org/10.1177/1476127014554575.

Kaur, Harmeet, and Jeffrey Kopp. 2019. "At Least 22 Transgender People Have Been Killed This Year. But Numbers Don't Tell the Full Story." *CNN*, November 18, 2019. https://www.cnn.com/2019/11/18/us/transgender-killings-hrc-report-trnd/index.html.

Khanna, Akshay. 2012. "Seeing Citizen Action through an Unruly Lens." *Development* 55 (2): 162–172. https://doi.org/10.1057/dev.2012.21.

Kralik, Joellen. 2019. "'Bathroom Bill' Legislative Tracking." *National Conference of State Legislatures*, October 24, 2019. https://www.ncsl.org/research/education/-bathroom-bill-legislative-tracking635951130.aspx.

Lambda Legal. 2017. "We Reviewed All of Judge Gorsuch's Record. And Here Is What We Found." January 31, 2017. https://www.lambdalegal.org/blog/20170131_gorsuch-record.

Law, Tara. 2019. "Trump Administration Asks Supreme Court to Permit Employment Discrimination against Transgender Workers." *Time*, August 17, 2019. https://time.com/5654844/title-vii-trump-transgender-department-of-justice-supreme-court/.

Michaelson, Jay. 2017. "Trump's Judicial Picks Call Trans Children 'Satan's Plan,' Says Gays Are 'Brainwashing' Kids, and More." *The Daily Beast*, November 16, 2017. https://www.thedailybeast.com/trumps-judicial-picks-call-trans-children-satans-plan-says-gays-are-brainwashing-kids-and-more.

Michnik, Adam. 1986. *Letters from Prison and Other Essays*, translated by Maya Latynski. Berkeley: University of California Press.

Millhiser, Ian. 2020. "What Trump Has Done to the Courts, Explained." *Vox*, February 4, 2020. https://www.vox.com/policy-and-politics/2019/12/9/20962980/trump-supreme-court-federal-judges.

Moreau, Julie. 2020. "Advocates Tracking Over 200 Active State Bills Targeting LGBTQ Americans." *NBC News*, February 4, 2020. https://www.nbcnews.com/feature/nbc-out/advocates-tracking-over-200-active-state-bills-targeting-lgbtq-americans-n1129711.

Murib, Zein. 2020. "A New Kind of Anti-Trans Legislation Is Hitting the Red States." *Washington Post*, February 25, 2020. https://www.washingtonpost.com/politics/2020/02/25/new-kind-anti-trans-legislation-is-hitting-red-states/.

Musumeci, MaryBeth, Jennifer Kates, Lindsey Dawson, Alina Salganicoff, Laurie Sobel, and Samantha Artiga. 2019. "HHS's Proposed Changes to Non-Discrimination Regulations under ACA Section 1557." *KFF [Kaiser Family Foundation]*, July 1, 2019. https://www.kff.org/disparities-policy/issue-brief/hhss-proposed-changes-to-non-discrimination-regulations-under-aca-section-1557/.

National Center for Transgender Equality. n.d. "The Discrimination Administration: Trump's Record of Action against Transgender People." Accessed May 28, 2020. https://transequality.org/the-discrimination-administration.

Popovic, Srdja, with Matthew Miller. 2015. *Blueprint for Revolution: How to Use Rice Pudding, Lego Men, and Other Nonviolent Techniques to Galvanize Communities, Overthrow Dictators, or Simply Change the World.* New York: Spiegel and Grau.

Shankland, Alex. 2011. "Occupy LSX, Unruly Politics, and Subversive Ruliness." *Institute of Development Studies*, December 27, 2011. http://participationpower.wordpress.com/2011/12/27/occupy-lsx-unruly-politics-and-subversive-ruliness/.

Shankland, Alex, Danny Burns, Naomi Hossain, Akshay Khanna, Patta Scott-Villiers, and Mariz Tadros. 2011. "Unruly Politics: A Manifesto." Photocopy, Institute of Development Studies, University of Sussex, Brighton, Great Britain.

Simmons-Duffin, Selena. 2020. "'Whiplash' of LGBTQ Protections and Rights, from Obama to Trump." *NPR*, March 2, 2020. https://www.npr.org/sections/health-shots/2020/03/02/804873211/whiplash-of-lgbtq-protections-and-rights-from-obama-to-trump.

Snyder, Timothy. 2017. *On Tyranny: Twenty Lessons from the Twentieth Century.* New York: Tim Duggan Books.

Stephan, Maria J., and Timothy Snyder. 2017. "Authoritarianism Is Making a Comeback." *The Guardian*, June 20, 2017. https://www.theguardian.com/commentisfree/2017/jun/20/authoritarianism-trump-resistance-defeat.

———. 2020. "The Time-Tested Way to Defeat Authoritarianism." In *The Rise of Authoritarianism*, edited by Gary Wiener, 151–156. New York: Greenhaven Publishing.

Taylor, Josh. 2019. "How Children Became the Target in a Rightwing Culture War over Gender." *The Guardian*, August 24, 2019. https://www.theguardian.com/society/2019/aug/24/how-children-became-the-target-in-a-rightwing-culture-war-over-gender.

Team Warren. 2020. "The Fight Goes On." *Medium*, March 5, 2020. https://medium.com/@teamwarren/the-fight-goes-on-8f5ca2b4b557.

US Department of Health and Human Services. 2018. "HHS Announces New Conscience and Religious Freedom Division." January 18, 2018. https://www.hhs.gov/about/news/2018/01/18/hhs-ocr-announces-new-conscience-and-religious-freedom-division.html.

West, Lindy. 2017. "The First 25 Days of Trump Have Been a Zoetrope of Galloping Despair." *The Guardian*, February 14, 2017. https://www.theguardian.com/commentisfree/2017/feb/14/first-25-days-trump-despair-united-states.

INDEX

abortion *see* anti-abortion activism and policies
ACA *see* Affordable Care Act (ACA)
Access Hollywood tape recording 88, 104, 109
activist anthropology 126
Adorno, Theodor W. 12, 39
AERA *see* American Equal Rights Association (AERA)
affective life of the state 38–40
affectivity/political affect/love politics 25–40
Affordable Care Act (ACA) 72, 217
aggression 102, 103, 105, 108, 143
AIPAC *see* American Israel Public Affairs Committee (AIPAC)
alt-right 16, 102, 104, 105, 125, 158, 159, 161–168, 176, 177
America First slogan 75, 135, 197
American Equal Rights Association (AERA) 82–85
American Woman Suffrage Association (AWSA) 79, 84, 86
Anderson, Benedict 8, 10, 26, 33
Anderson, Jon 167–168
Anthony, Susan B. 68, 69, 71, 75, 77–79, 81–88, 93; Trump and 88–92
anti-abortion activism and policies 72, 89, 91
anti-Asian violence *see* immigrants, terror, violence
anti-Semitism 59, 111, 166, 177, 181
Apprentice, The 5, 52, 108
Arendt, Hannah 1, 9, 37

Art of the Deal, The (Schwartz) 103
authoritarianism 3, 4, 8, 9–15, 17–18, 37, 49, 64, 163, 166, 198, 215
AWSA *see* American Woman Suffrage Association (AWSA)

"banality of evil" (Arendt) 37
Bannon, Steve 159
Barber, Alan 53–54
Baudrillard, Jean 32
beauty/glamour 3, 14, 15, 47–64, 71
Bee, Samantha 56
Benjamin, Walter 11, 38
Bhabha, Homi 34, 39
Biden, Jill 36–37
Biden, Joseph 12, 17, 25, 36
biologism/biological theories of gender and sexuality 112, 158, 163, 164, 222
biopower 123
Black Americans/African Americans 79, 80, 85, 91, 93, 106, 141, 166, 178, 201, 218; *see also* voting rights
Black Caesar 106–107
Black Lives Matter (BLM) 1, 5, 6, 12, 14, 29, 38, 90, 114, 160, 161, 167
Black women, 71, 73, 74, 76, 84–86, 87, 91, 107, 157; centering 92–93
Blee, Kathleen 57
BLM *see* Black Lives Matter (BLM)
Bowman, Donna 178–179
Breitbart 144, 155–158
Broude, Ellen Dominus 182
Butler, Judith 57–58, 120, 179–181

capitalism: disaster 196–197; free market 208; global 26, 29, 38; neoliberal 28, 29, 40, 159
Celebrity Apprentice, The 5
Census Bureau (US) 122, 215
ceremony *see* performance
Chakrabarty, Dipesh 32
Charlottesville, Virginia ("Unite the Right" march in 2017) 60, 111, 166, 178, 203
Chisholm, Shirley 93, 201
Christianity/evangelical Christians 3, 12, 13, 16, 59, 89, 92, 93, 118, 225
civil rights 8, 79, 91, 93, 202, 216, 217, 222; legislation 87, 159, 217; movement 160, 167, 200; Office of Civil Rights 53, 217
Civil War 81
Clinton, Bill 157
Clinton, Hillary 6, 47, 61, 62, 68, 75–76, 112, 157, 162
CNN 6, 76, 178
collective memory 187–189
Collins, Patricia Hill 74
commemoration and nationalism 68, 72, 74–77, 93
commemoration and racism 69, 75, 77
commemoration/monuments 14, 15, 29, 74–77, 88, 90–92, 93
community (national/social/imagined) 4, 8, 10, 16, 26, 33, 34, 36, 39, 40, 59, 102, 104, 105, 110, 113, 119, 120, 122, 126, 128, 129, 135, 137, 140, 143–147, 158–162, 164, 165, 169, 170, 174, 178, 179, 181–185, 187–190, 194, 201, 202, 204, 214, 219, 220, 222, 223, 226
compassion 18, 34, 35, 56, 160, 182–184, 186, 189, 190
Connell, Raewyn 101, 103, 105
Connerton, Paul 30, 187, 188
Corbett, Sarah 175–176
craft activism campaigns and mass shootings 189–190
crafting, as a response to violence 176–181, 190
creativity/craft 16, 55, 77, 105, 139, 148, 174–190, 207–209, 214
Crenshaw, Kimberlé 73

DACA *see* Deferred Action for Childhood Arrivals (DACA)
Daniels, Jessie 161–162
Daniels, Stormy 103
DeChaine, D. Robert 196, 198
Deferred Action for Childhood Arrivals (DACA) 27, 122

Democratic party/Democrats 12, 17, 27, 50, 63, 83, 93, 157, 200, 201, 217, 225
Department of Education (US) 216
Department of Health and Human Services (US) 215, 217
Department of Homeland Security (US) 121, 122
Department of Housing and Urban Development (HUD) 216
Department of Justice (US) 61, 216
DeSantis, Ron 125
Deutsche Bank 103
dictator *see* authoritarianism
disaster capitalism *see* capitalism
Discourses (Machiavelli) 32
Dittmar, Kelly 63, 203
domination/aggression 3, 7, 11, 12, 17, 27, 37, 74, 102, 103, 105, 108, 113, 143, 148
Douglass, Frederick 81, 85, 92
Dowling, Julie A. 119, 120, 124, 127

Economy and Society (Weber) 7
Eco, Umberto 10, 12
EEOC *see* Equal Employment Opportunity Commission (EEOC)
Eley, Geoff 31, 33
Elizabeth Cady Stanton and Susan B. Anthony Statue Fund, The 92
El Paso, Texas (2019 mass shooting) 14, 16, 124–125, 143, 183
embodiment/sensory/sensual 12, 26, 30, 31, 33, 38–40, 51, 57, 105, 176, 184, 185, 190, 198
Eminem 112
emotional violence *see* domination or violence
Equal Employment Opportunity Commission (EEOC) 54
equality 8, 18, 27, 47, 50, 55, 59, 79, 157, 159, 170, 208, 219; gender equality 51, 59, 89, 91, 157, 162, 163, 167, 215–217, 222–223; racial in/equality 15, 30, 37, 126, 127, 137, 157
Equality Act 215–217
Equal Suffrage Association 85
ethnographic refusal 167–170
Executive Order(s) 7, 17, 51, 56, 68, 90, 120–121, 135
Executive Order on Building and Rebuilding Monuments to American Heroes 90
Executive Order on Combating Race and Sex Stereotyping 17

Executive Order on Protecting the Nation from Foreign Terrorist Entry into the United States 51
extremist groups 143, 158; Oath Keepers 17; Proud Boys 15, 17

"fake news" 29, 50, 60, 161; *see also* journalists, attacks on
Falwell, Jerry, Jr. 13
Farmworkers Association of Florida 126
fascism 4–5, 7, 9, 11, 12, 14, 26, 37; definition of 3, 10
fascist allure 4, 10–12, 26, 27, 40
fascist (autocratic) leader 3, 4, 8, 10, 11, 12, 13, 14, 26, 35, 36, 52, 58, 62, 162, 165, 198, 202, 218
fascist politics 3, 4, 10–12, 14, 15, 17
femininity 15, 48, 49, 51, 52, 56, 58, 60
feminism 48, 50, 53, 55, 59, 63, 64, 162–163; marketplace 52, 53; white 68–93
Fifteenth Amendment to the US Constitution 79, 81–85
50 Cent 106, 108
Fiorina, Carly 63
Flores Settlement Agreement 123
Floyd, George 1–3, 40, 70, 90
Ford, Christine Blasey 155–157, 164–165
Foucault, Michel 7, 8, 31, 123
Fourteenth Amendment to the US Constitution 79, 82
Fox News 37, 61, 107, 161
free-market capitalism *see* capitalism
Freud, Sigmund 11–12

Gadsden Panthers 143–147
Gadsden Purchase 142–143
Gage, Matilda Joslyn 78
Gauntlett, David 184
gender 11, 13, 62, 73, 74, 83, 85, 92, 113, 126, 145, 148, 158, 218, 223; -based violence 141; bias 63; biological 222; diversity 219; equality 51, 59, 63, 89, 91, 157, 162, 163, 167, 215–217; identity 216, 217; inequality 26, 72; minorities 50; normative performance 52, 53; norms 58, 156; oppression 52, 114; politics 157, 168; traditional roles 161–166; wage gap 54, 71
genocide 1, 29, 30, 143
Gessen, Masha 3, 5, 13, 37
Gillis, John 68, 74, 93
Gilroy, Paul 30
Giuliani, Rudy 36
glamour *see* beauty

global capitalism *see* capitalism
Gonzales, Roberto 138
Gramsci, Antonio 15, 50
Greer, Betsy 179, 183
grievance *see* victimhood
gun violence 14–15, 183, 186, 187, 189; rights 157
Gusterson, Hugh 13, 168

Halbwachs, Maurice 188
Haley, Sarah 157–158, 167
handcraft 187–189
Harper, Frances Ellen Watkins 81, 85, 86, 91
Harris, Kamala 16, 93, 194–209; border tweets 204–207; "For the People" slogan 200–204; social justice through border rhetoric, crafting 207–209
hegemonic masculinity *see* masculinity
heteronormative masculinity *see* masculinity
heterosexual masculinity *see* masculinity
HIAS (Hebrew Immigrant Aid Society) 177
Hillbilly Elegy (Vance) 168
Hispanic *see* Latinx
History of Woman Suffrage 78, 84
Hochschild, Arlie 169
Hope CommUnity Center 126, 129
HUD *see* Department of Housing and Urban Development (HUD)
Hunter, Clare 176
hypermasculinity *see* masculinity

Imbolc Crossmakers 214, 222, 226
immigrants/immigration 138–140, 148, 160, 194, 196, 197, 201–206, 208, 209; abrogation of rights of 34; criminalization of 16, 123–125, 135–148; Latinx immigrants in Central Florida, everyday harassment of 118–130; status 124, 129; undocumented 5, 109, 110, 118–119, 122, 124, 127, 138, 147, 197, 199, 200, 205, 208
Immigration and Nationality Act, Section 287(g) 120
immigration policy 27–28, 51, 56, 109–111, 119, 120, 129, 135, 136, 140, 160, 195, 198–200; ban 51, 120, 136; child separation 26, 51, 123, 125, 199, 200, 203, 206; enforcement of 120, 122, 124, 129; reform 72, 141, 163
Inda, Jonathan Xavier 119, 120, 124, 127
institutionalized racism 90, 105
institutionalized violence 90
Insurrection Act of 1807 2

interpersonal violence *see* violence
intersectionality 72–75

Jewish Hearts for Pittsburgh 16, 174–190
Jews 16, 58–60, 64, 174, 177
Jim Crow policies 56
Jones, Corey 145–147
Jones, Martha 87, 92
journalists, attacks on 6, 13, 37
judicial nominations, conservative 17, 156–157, 217–218

Kaiser, Richard J. 120, 127
Kavanaugh, Brett 155–157, 165
Kelly, John F. 122, 199
Khanna, Akshay 214, 220, 221, 226
Kim Jung Un 35, 36
KKK *see* Ku Klux Klan (KKK)
Klein, Naomi 195–197
Ku Klux Klan (KKK) 57, 90, 111, 178
Kushner, Jared 47, 49, 52, 59, 61
Kushner, Yael Esther 49

Lakoff, George 195, 208
Latinx 14, 16, 26, 76, 110; criminalization of 135–148; harassment of 119–123; immigrants in Central Florida 118–130; invasion narrative 14, 16, 119, 123–125, 140–143; profiling of youth 143–146; resisting racism 129–130; and settler-colonialism 137–142; suspicion of 147–148
Law, Vincent 164
Lee, Robert E. *see* Charlottesville, Virginia
Lewis, John 40
linguistic profiling 16, 143–148
Lorde, Audre 73
love *see* affectivity

Machiavelli, Niccolò 9, 32
#MAGA *see* Make America Great Again slogan
Make America Great Again slogan 55, 75, 112, 113, 125, 199
Maples, Marla 103, 109
marketplace feminism 52, 53
masculinity 15, 161, 163, 165; "cool pose" 102, 105, 106, 114; fascist 26; hegemonic 17, 105; heteronormative 35, 113; heterosexual 113; hypermasculinity 63, 101–114; paternalistic 33; protest 101, 102, 105–106, 112, 113; racialized 102, 113; toxic 40; Trumpian 101–113; white 110, 162

mass shootings 14, 16, 168, 182–183: craft responses to 174–190; in El Paso, Texas (Walmart) 14, 16, 124–125, 143, 183; in Pittsburgh, Pennsylvania (Tree of Life Synagogue) 14, 16, 59–60, 174, 177–178, 203
May, Theresa 58
McDougal, Karen 103
media, television 4–6, 17, 26, 29, 35, 38, 39, 49, 52, 76, 89, 102–104, 108, 129, 140, 141, 146, 156, 158, 161, 164, 165, 174, 201, 204, 227
Medicaid 72, 122
Medicare 72
Merkel, Angela 58
Messerschmidt, James 105
#MeToo Movement 156; *see also* sexual violence
Mexican people/Mexican Americans/ Mexican immigrants 87, 110, 125, 138, 140–144, 198, 199
Migrant Protection Protocol ("Remain in Mexico" policy) 121
military/militancy 2, 3, 10, 14, 15, 17, 29, 31, 107, 199, 215, 221
militias *see* extremist groups
Miller, Stephen 136
Minaj, Nicki 107, 111
misogyny 17, 49, 51, 68, 88, 101, 102, 104, 105, 108, 112, 113, 156, 162, 165–167
Modi, Narendra 58
monuments *see* commemoration
motherhood/maternity/maternal 49, 56–58, 62, 63
Mount Rushmore 15, 28, 29, 90, 97
Mott, Lucretia 78, 88
Movement for Black Lives 161
museums and commemoration 4, 72, 74, 78–81, 87–88, 92–93
Muslims/Islamophobia 5, 12, 37, 51, 120, 121, 177; bans on immigration from Muslim-majority countries 51, 120–121

NAFTA *see* North American Free Trade Agreement (NAFTA)
Nas 108, 109, 111
National American Woman Suffrage Association (NAWSA) 80, 86
National Center for Transgender Equality 216
nationalism/nation-building/citizenship 4, 10, 12, 13, 14, 17, 26, 27–28, 30–34, 39–40, 74, 75, 82, 87, 90, 93, 122, 130, 137–139, 143, 146, 169; anti-immigrant

nativism 199–201; racist 3, 10; white 155–170
National Susan B. Anthony Museum & House (NSBAMH) 78, 79, 87
National Woman Suffrage Association (NWSA) 79, 84, 86
National Women's History Museum 78, 80
NAWSA *see* National American Woman Suffrage Association (NAWSA)
neoliberal capitalism *see* capitalism
Netanyahu, Benjamin 59
Nineteenth Amendment to the US Constitution 68, 69, 75, 76, 80, 86–88, 90, 91, 92
North American Free Trade Agreement (NAFTA) 110
North Korean–American conflict 35; *see* Kim Jung Un
NSBAMH *see* National Susan B. Anthony Museum & House (NSBAMH)
NWSA *see* National Woman Suffrage Association (NWSA)

Oath Keepers 17
Obama, Barack 54, 88, 122, 160, 161, 201, 213, 215, 216, 222
O'Donnell, Lawrence 25, 34–35
OFCCP *see* Office of Federal Contract Compliance Programs (OFCCP)
Office of Civil Rights (US) 53
Office of Federal Contract Compliance Programs (OFCCP) 216
Office of Management and Budget (US) 54
Office of Refugee Resettlement (US) 123
Operation Gatekeeper 139
Operation Hold the Line 139
overt racism 146

Pascoe, C. J. 109
passion 30–34; *see also* affectivity
paternalistic masculinity *see* masculinity
patriarchy 3, 11, 15, 33, 52, 62, 92, 156, 162, 195, 198
Paxton, Robert O. 1, 4–5, 10, 12
performance/spectacle/theatrics/showmanship/ceremony 3–8, 11, 14, 26, 30, 31, 34–38, 47, 52, 53, 58, 69, 70, 101, 102, 105, 106, 108, 114, 120, 125, 127, 130, 197, 226
performativity 120
Peterson, Jordan 165
physical violence 125, 148, 174, 178
Pittsburgh, Pennsylvania (2018 Tree of Life Synagogue mass shooting) 14, 16, 59–60, 174, 177–178, 203

police violence 29, 37, 71, 90, 167
political correctness 50, 160
political culture 4, 7, 30, 35, 38, 136, 158, 159, 194–196; in Trump era 12–15
political violence 136, 169
Popovic, Srdja 220
power 6–8, 10, 17, 33, 35, 37, 48, 57, 58, 62, 63, 74, 82, 83, 87, 102, 103, 138, 142, 145, 157, 166, 168, 176, 189, 196, 199, 203, 204, 208, 221, 226; autocratic 4; biopower 123; cultural 88; economic 106; male 27; political 26, 28, 31, 36, 38, 50, 105; sensualization of 31; state 30, 32, 39; symbolic 3; white 15
pre-political Trumpian masculinity 102–106; in rap music 106–109
presidential election of 2016 5, 13, 25–26, 38, 50, 63, 101, 118, 124, 126, 141, 143, 162, 219, 227; suffragist commemoration and 75–77
presidential election of 2020 16–17, 143, 200
"Prevention through Deterrence" strategy 120, 122
Prince, The (Machiavelli) 9, 32
protest *see* resistance
protest masculinity 101, 102, 105–106, 112, 113
Proud Boys 15, 17
Putin, Vladimir 36, 165

race/racialization 12, 16, 26, 27, 30, 40, 119, 121, 124, 137, 140, 142, 145, 147, 158, 160, 161, 169, 199; racialized masculinity 102, 113; racialized nativism 195; racial violence 26, 34
racism 28, 49, 58, 60, 68, 69, 71, 72, 74, 75, 77, 92, 106, 109, 110, 112–114, 119, 121, 124, 142, 147, 167, 170; anti-racism 16; commonplace 126–130; institutionalized 90, 105; overt 146; systemic 37; violent 37
racist nationalism 3, 10
racist violence 1, 15, 60
rap music, pre-political Trump in 106–109
Reagan, Ronald 160, 196
reality television 4, 5, 35–36, 52, 118
Red Pill website 103–104
religious liberty 216–217
representational intersectionality 73–74
Republican party/Republicans 13, 15, 17, 27, 51, 56, 63, 69, 79, 82, 92, 107, 160, 198, 199, 214, 215
resistance/protest 1, 3, 6, 14–16, 29, 36, 37, 40, 50, 51, 70, 88, 101, 102, 105–106, 111–114, 160, 167, 175, 207, 214, 220–224, 226

Rubio, Marco 53, 107
Russia/Russian 36, 37, 157, 164, 165

sadopopulism 13–14
Salman, Mohammed bin 36
Sanders, Sarah Huckabee 60
Sayoc, Cesar 177
Schwartz, Tony 103
Seneca Falls, New York 75, 77, 78, 88
sensation 30–34; *see also* affectivity
settler-colonialism 137–142, 167–168
"1776 Commission" 17
sexuality 162, 215
sexual violence/sexual domination/sexual harassment 104, 113, 141, 156
showmanship 4, 36, 38
Simpson, Audra 167–168
Snyder, Timothy 9, 13–14, 214, 215, 218
social media 6–7, 29, 35, 49, 57, 76, 92, 144, 158, 174, 177, 181, 189, 222; Facebook 14, 76, 144, 174, 181–183, 219; Instagram 51, 56, 57, 58, 59; Internet forums and message boards 125, 156, 158, 161–165; Twitter 2, 3, 6–7, 13, 15, 17, 28, 29, 35, 36, 51, 56, 60, 63, 89, 124, 135, 157, 165, 187, 204–207, 215, 225
Social Security (US) 53, 54, 72
Sojourner Truth 80, 81, 85, 92
Sontag, Susan 179
Soros, George 177
Southern Poverty Law Center (SPLC) 158
Spanish language *see* linguistic profiling
spectacle *see* performance
Spencer, Richard 159
SPLC *see* Southern Poverty Law Center (SPLC)
Stanley, Jason 3, 9–11
Stanton, Elizabeth Cady 69, 71, 75, 77–79, 81, 83–86, 88, 89, 91, 93
state terror 7, 15, 26, 27
state violence 2–3, 5–9, 29, 40, 161
Stephan, Maria J. 214, 215
stochastic terrorism 14, 177
Stormfront.org 158, 161, 164
structural intersectionality 73
structural violence 72, 199
Suny, Ronald Grigor 30, 31, 33
suffrage *see* voting rights
systemic racism 37

Taussig, Michael 26, 30, 31, 33, 40
Taylor, Breonna 90
Temporary Protected Status (TPS) program 121

terror/terrorism 9, 14, 51, 107, 143, 174, 177, 179; commonplace terror 118–130; *see also* gun violence, mass shootings, state terror, stochastic terrorism
theatrics *see* performance
Theweleit, Klaus 104
threats of violence/intimidation 3–4, 5–13, 15, 16, 26, 27, 29, 87, 102, 103, 107, 108, 111, 113, 118–130, 158, 161, 164, 167, 176, 221; *see also* terror, state terror
Tree of Life Synagogue *see* Pittsburgh, Pennsylvania
Title IX 53, 216
toxic masculinity *see* masculinity
TPS *see* Temporary Protected Status (TPS) program
transgender 16, 48, 162, 166, 213–228; "bathroom bills" 222–223; identity 215, 216; laws and policies regarding 214–218, 222–223; rights 48, 214, 224, 227
transphobia 16, 17, 225
Trump, Donald: administrative policies affecting women 47–64, 71–72; aliases 103; as businessman 5, 26, 50, 52, 53, 103, 106–107; criminality, suspicions of 61; era, political culture in 12–15; as gangsta 113–114; and hypermasculinity 101–114; impeachment 17, 36, 55, 56; and Kim Jung Un 35; norm breaking 5, 26, 35, 38, 50–51, 198–199; playboy reputation 103–104; sexual harassment and assault 38, 88, 104, 198; "Snake, The" 141–143, 147; and Susan B. Anthony 88–92; UK visit 36; *see also individual entries, including immigration policy, racism, white supremacy, and US-Mexico border*
Trump, Donald Jr. 52, 61
Trump Effect 124, 129
Trump, Eric 52, 61
Trump Foundation 61
Trump, Melania 103
Trumpian masculinity 101–114; political-era 109–113; pre-political 102–109
Trump, Ivana 9, 103
Trump, Ivanka (Ivana Marie) 2, 15, 47–64, 177; criminality, suspicions of 60–61; normative gender roles 50–51; as daughter 51–52, 58–60; and Judaism 58–60; political ambitions 61–64; work in the White House 53–58
Trump Organization 5, 50, 51, 52, 53
truth/lies/misinformation 4, 5, 8, 9, 29, 47, 48, 60, 118, 144, 160, 161, 162, 163, 199, 201, 203, 214, 218, 225; *see also* "fake news," journalists, attacks on

Tubman, Harriet 80, 88–89, 92
Twitter *see* social media

"Unite the Right" march *see* Charlottesville, Virginia
unruly politics 220–222
US–Mexico border 5–6, 14, 15–16, 25, 26, 27, 28, 30, 38, 51, 53, 56, 58, 70–71, 109–110, 119–125, 135, 139–148, 177, 194–209; abjection of immigrants 196–198; "border performances" 120, 127–128; political rhetoric about 5–6, 16, 25, 27–28, 109–111, 119, 123–125, 135–136, 139–143, 177, 194–209; *see also* immigration policy
US–Mexico border wall 5–6, 27, 110, 119, 120, 123, 124–125, 136, 196–199, 203, 205–206

Vance, J.D. 168
victimhood/grievances 3, 10, 28, 159, 160, 161, 169, 170
violence 5–7, 9, 12, 13, 17, 27, 59, 80, 93, 105, 108, 114, 124, 128, 140, 164, 175, 184, 185, 197, 225; aestheticization of 6, 11–13; anti-transgender 218; crafting as response to 176–181, 190; emotional 148; gender-based 141; genocidal 143; gun 183, 186, 187, 189; institutionalized 90; interpersonal 198; physical 125, 148, 174, 178; police 29, 37, 71, 90, 167; political 136, 169; psychological 199; racial 26, 34; racist 1, 15, 60; sexual 140; state 2–3, 5–9, 29, 40, 161; street 26; structural 72, 199; threat of 3–4, 5–13, 29, 164, 167; as virtue 198–200; *see also* threats of violence/intimidation
violent racism 37
voter suppression 87, 93
voting rights and voting rights activism (US) 15, 159; Women's Suffrage Centennial commemorative activities 69–70, 88–93; for Black men 79, 81, 82–87; for women 75, 77–88; white feminist history of the women's suffrage movement 77–88; *see also individual entries*
Voting Rights Act of 1965 87; *see also* civil rights

Walmart *see* El Paso, Texas
"war of maneuver" (Gramsci) 50
Weber, Max 7–8, 36, 39
Wells-Barnett, Ida B. 81, 92
West, Kanye 122–123
white feminism: definition 72–73; and representational intersectionality 73–75; suffragist commemoration and 2016 election 75–77; white feminist history of the women's suffrage movement 77–88
white masculinity 110, 162
white nationalism 155–170; abolition of 166–167; new forms of 158–161; and traditional gender roles 161–166
whiteness 15, 26–30, 51, 57, 58, 110, 123, 159, 165
white supremacy 15, 26, 27, 29, 47–64, 72, 76, 87, 158, 170
Wolff, Michael 62, 103
women's suffrage *see* voting rights
women's equality *see* equality
Women's History Month 89–90
Women's Rights National Historical Park (WRNHP) 78, 80, 87, 88, 92
Women's Rights Pioneers Monument 92
Women's Suffrage Centennial commemorative activities 69–70, 88–93
WRNHP *see* Women's Rights National Historical Park (WRNHP)

xenophobia 58, 102, 113, 119, 125, 128, 130, 147, 159, 167, 199, 208
Xi Jinping 36, 58

"zero-tolerance" border policy 51, 199